THE CALEDONIAN
SCOTLAND'S IMPERIAL RAILWAY
A HISTORY

David Ross

CR Dunalastair III No. 892 at the main Up platform, Perth.

Stenlake Publishing Ltd

© 2013 David Ross
First Published in the United Kingdom, 2013
Stenlake Publishing Limited
54-58 Mill Square, Catrine, KA5 6RD
01290 551122
www.stenlake.co.uk

ISBN 9781840335842

Also by David Ross
The Highland Railway
George & Robert Stephenson: A Passion for Success

The geographical situation of Scotland marks out, in a general way, the direction of the main trunks, and railways which can readily form portions of these will have advantages over those which depend entirely on local traffic.

Charles MacLaren, *The Scotsman*, 1825

The True Line
True Convenience,
True Comfort,
True Delight
To the Tune of True Economy
And to the Rhythm of True-to-Time,
True-to-Time,
True-to-Time

– from a poster of *c*.1906, said to refer to the triple beat made on the rail joints by the Caledonian's new six-wheel bogie carriages.

**The Dunalastair I and II locomotives used in the St Rollox excursion of
7 September 1899 stand in the CR yard at Kingmoor, Carlisle.**

Front cover: The station staff of Juniper Green, c.1900.
Back cover: A CR 6-ton dumb-buffer wagon, laden with coal.

Demolition in progress at Bridge Street Station, Glasgow, 1904, to give access to the second Clyde Bridge and the enlarged Central Station. (Caledonian Railway Association).

A 4-6-0 of the Passenger/Goods 179-class (1913-14) with a trainload of horse-carts.

CONTENTS

MAPS

ACKNOWLEDGEMENTS

Research for this book was done at numerous places, and the author would like to record his gratitude to all of them.
Glasgow University Archive Service (Caledonian Railway Association Archive)
Hamilton Public Library
Institution of Civil Engineers
Institution of Mechanical Engineers
London Library
Mitchell Library, Glasgow
National Archives of Scotland
National Library of Scotland
National Railway Museum Library, York
St Andrews University Library (Special Collections)
Science Museum Library & Archive, Swindon
Stephenson Locomotive Society Library

The text was read by Jim MacIntosh, Chairman of the Caledonian Railway Association (see page 221), and I am most grateful to him for supplying numerous corrections and making valuable suggestions for improvement; and also for his help in providing illustrations and captions. Any errors and all expressed judgements and opinions are exclusively those of the author.

Thanks are also due for picture reproduction, to the Caledonian Railway Association, the John Alsop Collection, Richard Stenlake, and the Stephenson Locomotive Society.

FOREWORD

The Caledonian was the only one of the 'big five' Scottish railway companies which tried – or was wooed – to merge at one time or another with all the others: Glasgow & South Western, Great North of Scotland, Highland, and North British. None of these mating attempts was successful, although the Caledonian in its final form was itself the product of numerous amalgamations, preceded by stormy courtships and jiltings. Central to the Scottish railway system in every way, it was the elephant in everyone else's room.

Railways were the monster businesses of the nineteenth and early twentieth centuries. In Scotland, railway investment and financing had a huge impact on economic life. The spread of railways, and their hunger for investment capital, laid the essential foundation for the growth of a commercial and industrial economy. Inevitably, they also had a profound impact on social life. Epitomising mechanical and industrial progress, their plumes of smoke and steam were the banners of armies on the move – of commuters, factory workers, holidaymakers, football supporters, as well as real soldiers. In the heyday of Empire it was their iron wheels which rolled out the frontiers of power.

No previous history of the Caledonian Railway Company has been published. George Graham, for long the company's chief civil engineer, wrote *The Caledonian Railway: Its Origin*, for private distribution, but omitted a great deal. O.S. Nock's *Caledonian Railway* (1961) has some historical background, not all of it accurate. Since 1983 the Caledonian Railway Association's journal *The True Line* has published many articles on aspects of the company's history and development, and in recent years some excellent books have appeared on some of the railway companies which were later subsumed into the Caledonian, and on various aspects of the Caledonian itself. All of these publications are listed in the bibliography and frequently credited in the notes and references, which also offer much supplementary information.

The story is told, as far as possible, in chronological order. Sometimes, in the interest of continuity, the progress of a single venture is followed over a few years. But it seems best to tell the history of the company as it happened, and to keep events in their context as much as possible. In the case of some projects and activities, this means the account is divided, and readers who want to trace the development of particular topics should refer to the index. Chapter 15 is an attempt to sum up some of the qualities and aspects that gave the Caledonian its particular character, and the final chapter gives a summary history of its locomotives.

The Caledonian was a big company, with many ramifications. To give a comprehensive account of its growth, activities, organisation, operations and systems would require a book more than twice as long as this one. This book sets out to give a general picture, with much detail at key points of interest, and touches on most aspects of the company's activities. It tells how the Caledonian began, and grew, and ended; and traces the part it played in the evolution of Scottish railways and industry. Ample scope remains for further work on many aspects, including the Caledonian's operating systems, financial structure and property dealings.

Anyone who explores the various accounts, in books, journals and websites, of Scottish railway development in the 19th century will soon discover discrepancies in dates. This book provides a detailed timeline for the Caledonian Railway. Sketch-maps of some key areas also give dates of significant lines. It should be borne in mind that many stations and even more junctions underwent name changes. Since correct dating is essential to provide a reliable text, great care has been taken in this respect, but perfect accuracy is rare, and the author will be grateful for corrections to these or indeed any other details.

The Caledonian Railway dealt in the old currency of pounds, shillings, pence, halfpence and farthings, which was replaced by decimal coinage in 1974. Through most of its corporate life, the value of money remained relatively stable. The purchasing power of a pound sterling was very much greater then than it is now, though there was a more limited range of consumer goods for it to be spent on. A stationmaster could keep a wife and family on £150 a year, and the majority of the Company's staff earned around £1 a week. Readers interested in comparisons can check the relative amounts on www.measuringworth.com, and may find some of the revelations quite startling. Similarly, the Caledonian measured its distances in miles, furlongs, chains, yards, feet and inches. Eight furlongs made one mile, and 10 chains one furlong, making a chain 22 yards.

8

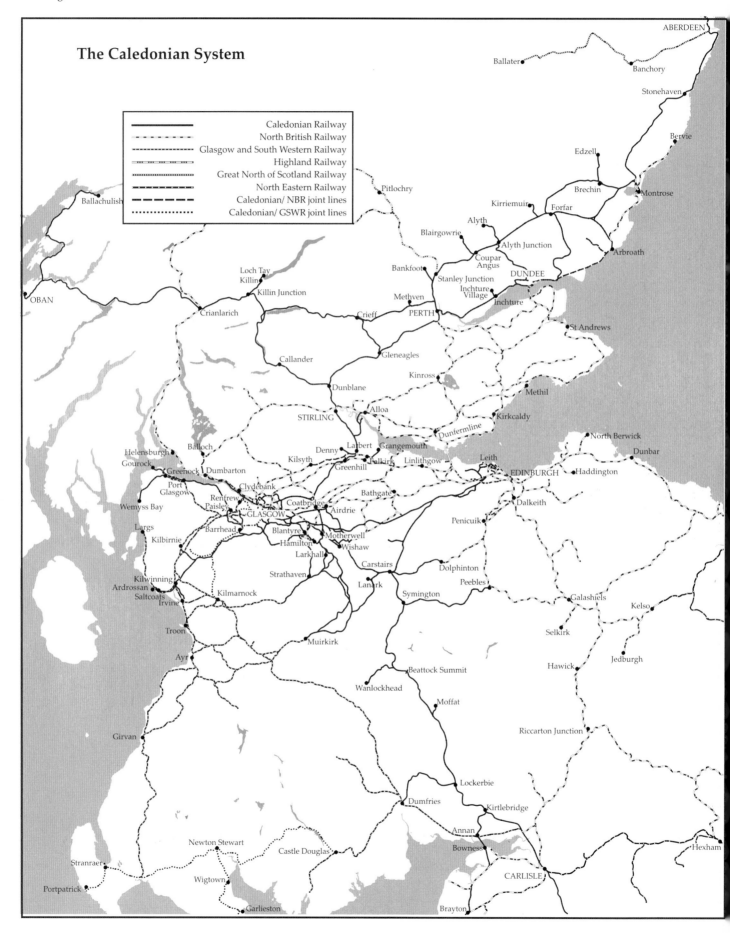

The Caledonian System

Caledonian Railway
North British Railway
Glasgow and South Western Railway
Highland Railway
Great North of Scotland Railway
North Eastern Railway
Caledonian/ NBR joint lines
Caledonian/ GSWR joint lines

ABERDEEN
Ballater
Banchory
Stonehaven
Bervie
Edzell
Brechin
Montrose
Kirriemuir
Forfar
Arbroath
Alyth
Blairgowrie
Alyth Junction
Pitlochry
Coupar Angus
Bankfoot
DUNDEE
Stanley Junction
Inchture Village
Inchture
Methven
St Andrews
PERTH
Crieff
Loch Tay
Killin
Killin Junction
Gleneagles
Kinross
Crianlarich
Methil
Callander
Dunblane
Kirkcaldy
OBAN
Alloa
STIRLING
Dunfermline
North Berwick
Balloch
Larbert
Grangemouth
Dunbar
Helensburgh
Denny
Leith
Gourock
Kilsyth
Falkirk
Linlithgow
EDINBURGH
Haddington
Greenock
Dumbarton
Greenhill
Port Glasgow
Clydebank
Bathgate
Dalkeith
Renfrew
Paisley
Coatbridge
Wemyss Bay
GLASGOW
Airdrie
Penicuik
Barrhead
Motherwell
Largs
Blantyre
Kilbirnie
Hamilton
Wishaw
Dolphinton
Strathaven
Larkhall
Carstairs
Peebles
Galashiels
Kilwinning
Lanark
Kelso
Ardrossan
Kilmarnock
Symington
Saltcoats
Irvine
Selkirk
Troon
Hawick
Jedburgh
Muirkirk
Ayr
Beattock Summit
Wanlockhead
Moffat
Girvan
Riccarton Junction
Lockerbie
Dumfries
Kirtlebridge
Newton Stewart
Castle Douglas
Annan
Stranraer
Bowness
Hexham
Wigtown
Portpatrick
CARLISLE
Garlieston
Brayton

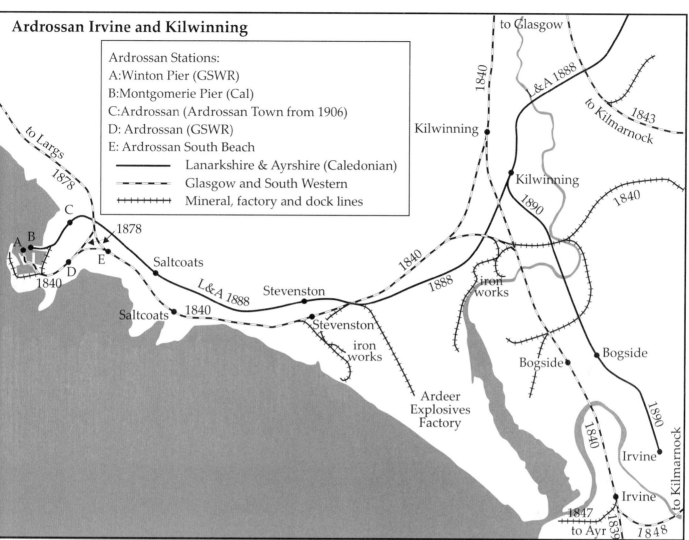

Ardrossan Irvine and Kilwinning

Ardrossan Stations:
A: Winton Pier (GSWR)
B: Montgomerie Pier (Cal)
C: Ardrossan (Ardrossan Town from 1906)
D: Ardrossan (GSWR)
E: Ardrossan South Beach

— Lanarkshire & Ayrshire (Caledonian)
--- Glasgow and South Western
+++ Mineral, factory and dock lines

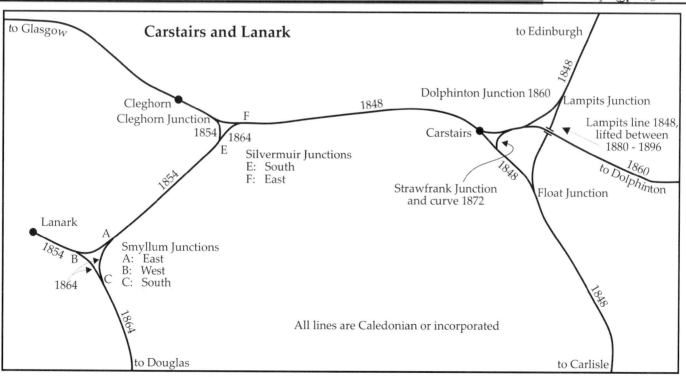

Carstairs and Lanark

Silvermuir Junctions
E: South
F: East

Smyllum Junctions
A: East
B: West
C: South

Strawfrank Junction and curve 1872

Lampits line 1848, lifted between 1880 - 1896

All lines are Caledonian or incorporated

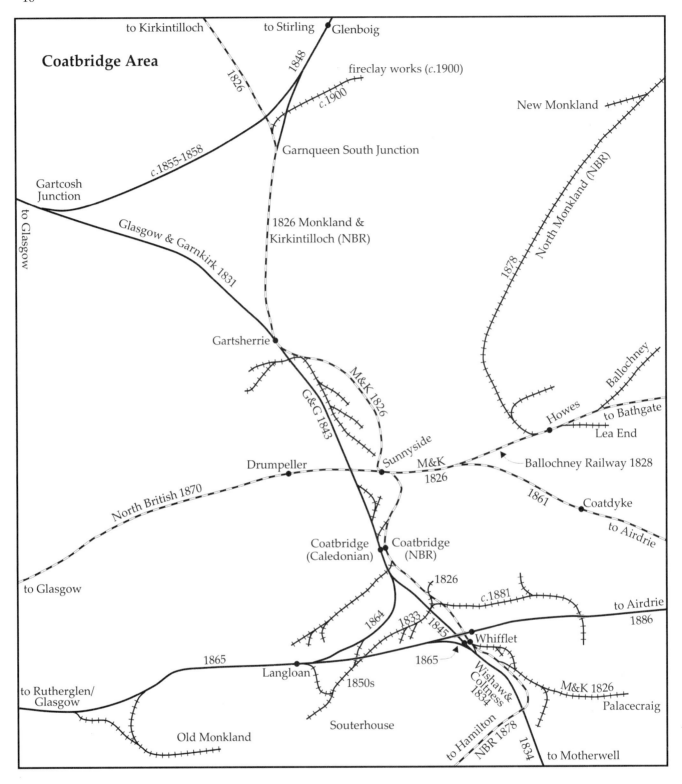

Coatbridge Area

to Kirkintilloch

to Stirling

Glenboig

1848

1826

fireclay works (*c*.1900)

c.1900

New Monkland

Garnqueen South Junction

c.1855-1858

Gartcosh Junction

to Glasgow

Glasgow & Garnkirk 1831

1826 Monkland & Kirkintilloch (NBR)

1878 North Monkland (NBR)

Gartsherrie

M&K 1826

Ballochney

G&G 1843

Howes

to Bathgate

Lea End

Sunnyside

M&K 1826

Ballochney Railway 1828

Drumpeller

North British 1870

1861

Coatdyke

to Airdrie

to Glasgow

Coatbridge (Caledonian)

Coatbridge (NBR)

1826

c.1881

to Airdrie 1886

1864

1833

1845

Whifflet

1865

1865

Langloan

1850s

Wishaw & Coltness 1834

M&K 1826

Palacecraig

to Rutherglen/ Glasgow

Souterhouse

Old Monkland

to Hamilton

NBR 1878

1834

to Motherwell

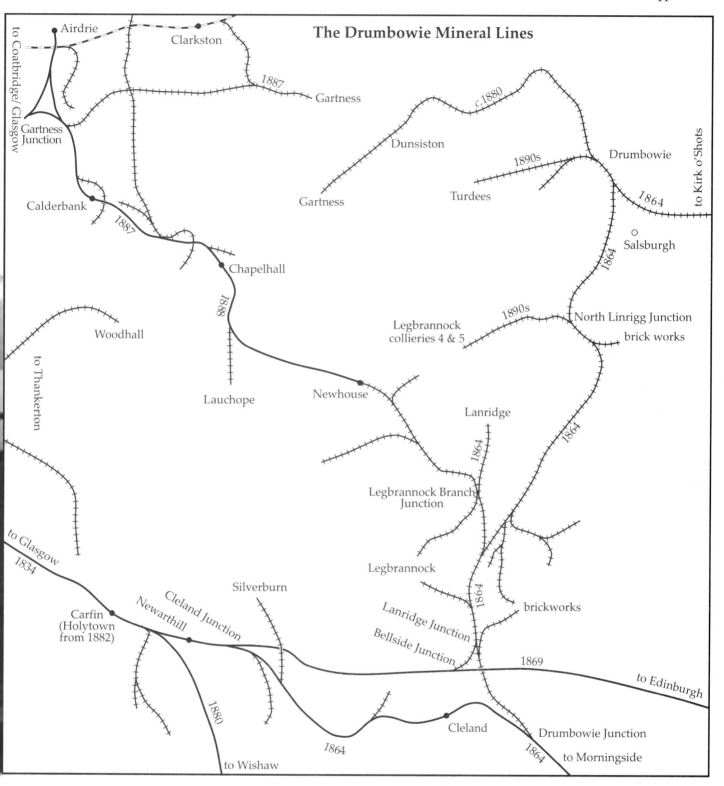

The Drumbowie Mineral Lines

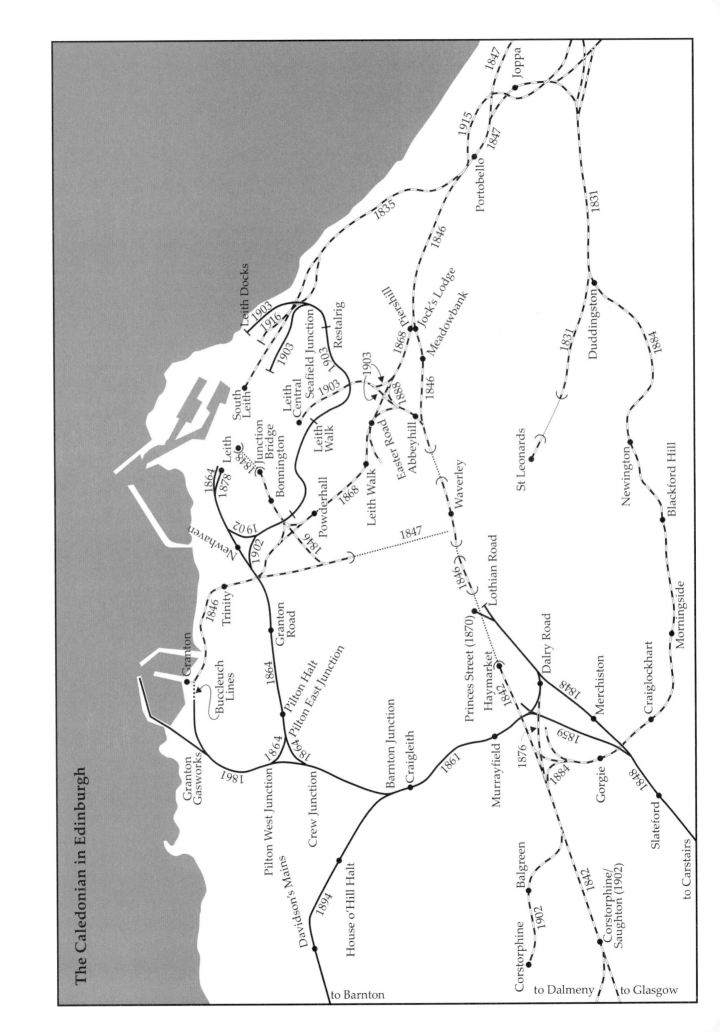

The Caledonian in Edinburgh

to Barnton

House o'Hill Halt

Davidson's Mains

1894

Corstorphine

1902

Balgreen

1842

to Dalmeny

Corstorphine/
Saughton (1902)

to Glasgow

Pilton West Junction

Crew Junction

1864

Barnton Junction

1861

Craigleith

Murrayfield

1876

1884

Gorgie

1859

1848

Slateford

to Carstairs

Granton Gasworks

1861

Buccleuch Lines

Granton

1846

Trinity

Granton Road

1864

Pilton Halt

Pilton East Junction

1894

Haymarket

1842

Princes Street (1870)

Dalry Road

1848

Merchiston

Craiglockhart

Morningside

Blackford Hill

Newington

Newhaven

1864

1878

Leith

1848

Bonnington

1902

1902

Powderhall

1846

1868

Leith Walk

Lothian Road

1846

Waverley

1847

St Leonards

1831

1884

Leith Docks

1903

1916

1903

South Leith

Junction Bridge

Leith Central

Seafield Junction

1903

Leith Walk

1903

Restalrig

1903

Easter Road

1888

Abbeyhill

1846

1835

1868 Piershill

Jock's Lodge

Meadowbank

1846

1831

Duddingston

Portobello

1915

1847

1847

Joppa

13

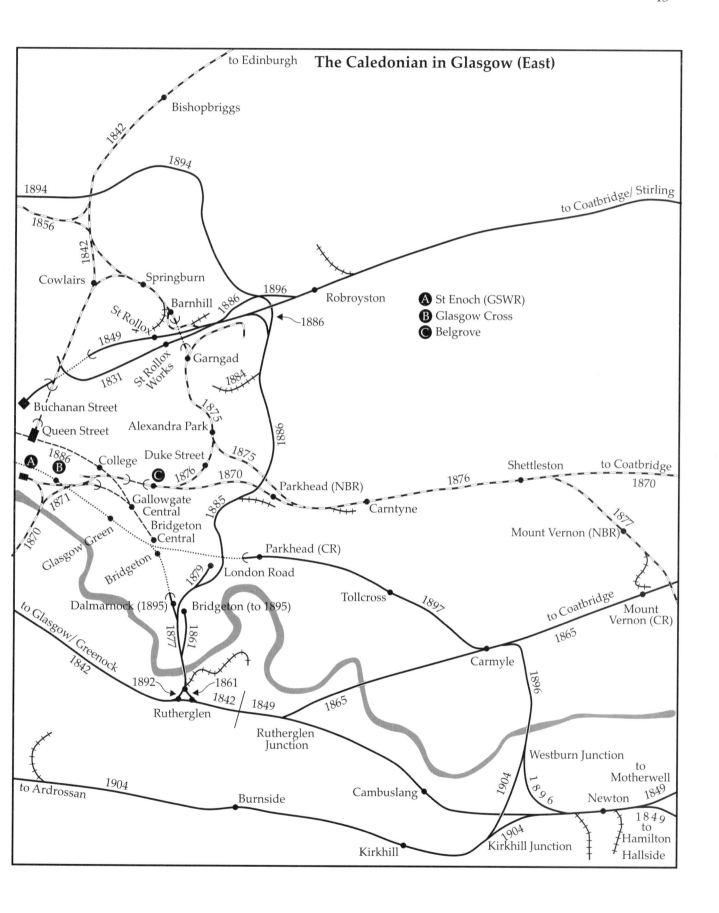

The Caledonian in Glasgow (East)

A St Enoch (GSWR)
B Glasgow Cross
C Belgrove

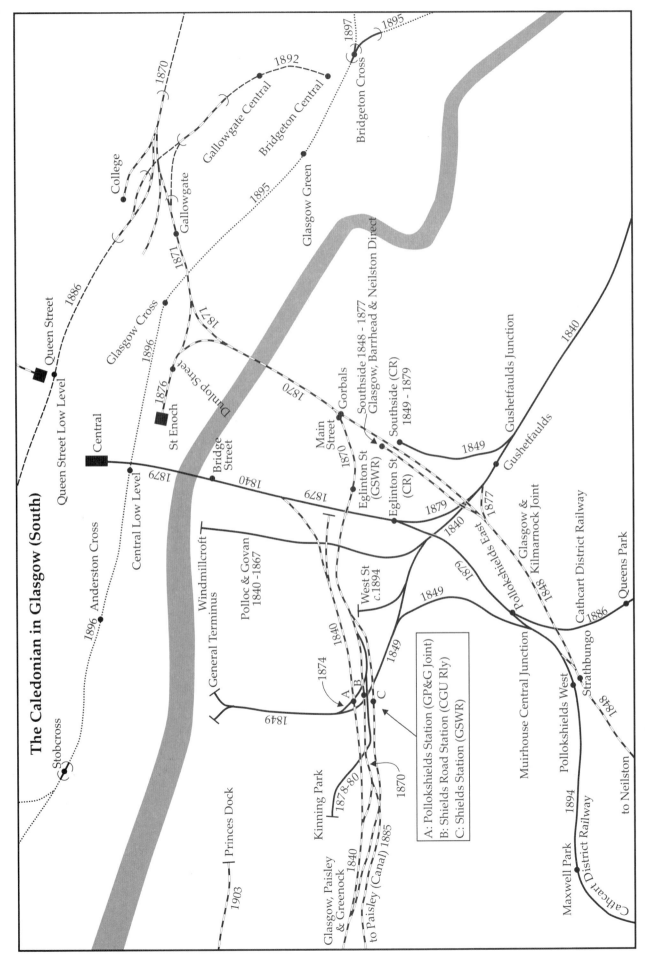

The Caledonian in Glasgow (South)

14

A: Pollokshields Station (GP&G Joint)
B: Shields Road Station (CGU Rly)
C: Shields Station (GSWR)

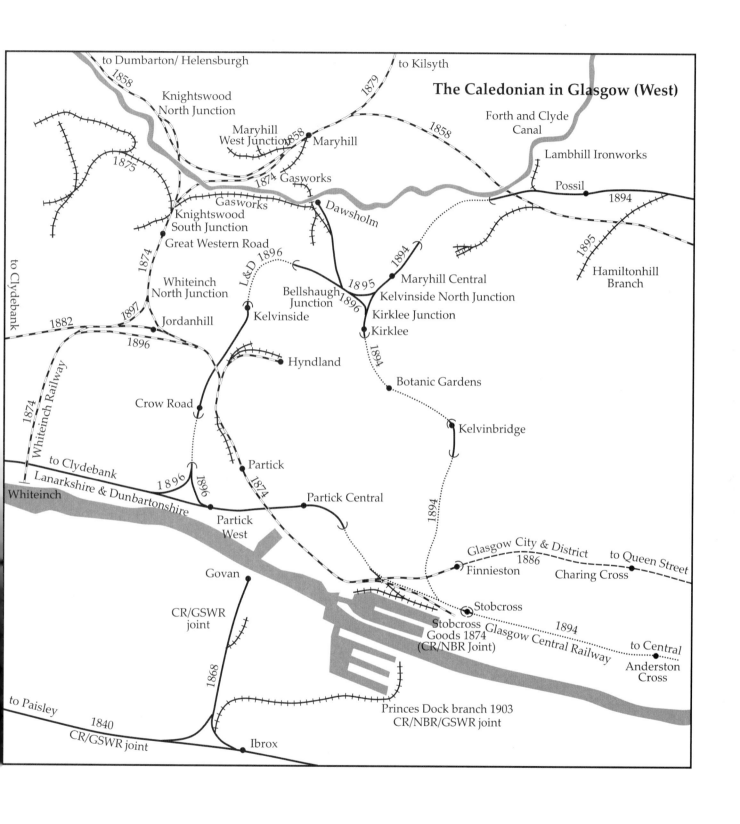

The Caledonian in Glasgow (West)

to Dumbarton/ Helensburgh
1858
to Kilsyth
1879
1858

Forth and Clyde Canal

Knightswood North Junction

Lambhill Ironworks

Maryhill West Junction
1858
Maryhill

Possil
1894

1875

1874 Gasworks

Gasworks
Dawsholm

Knightswood South Junction

Great Western Road

1874

1894

Hamiltonhill Branch

1895

to Clydebank

Whiteinch North Junction

L&D 1896

Bellshaugh Junction

1896

1895

Maryhill Central

Kelvinside North Junction

Kirklee Junction

1897

Jordanhill

Kelvinside

Kirklee

1882

1896

1894

1874

Whiteinch Railway

Hyndland

Crow Road

Botanic Gardens

Kelvinbridge

1894

to Clydebank

Lanarkshire & Dunbartonshire

1896

1896

1874

Partick

Whiteinch

Partick West

Partick Central

1894

Glasgow City & District
1886
to Queen Street

Govan

Finnieston

Charing Cross

CR/GSWR joint

Stobcross

1894

1868

Stobcross Goods 1874
(CR/NBR Joint)

Glasgow Central Railway

to Central

Anderston Cross

to Paisley

1840
CR/GSWR joint

Ibrox

Princes Dock branch 1903
CR/NBR/GSWR joint

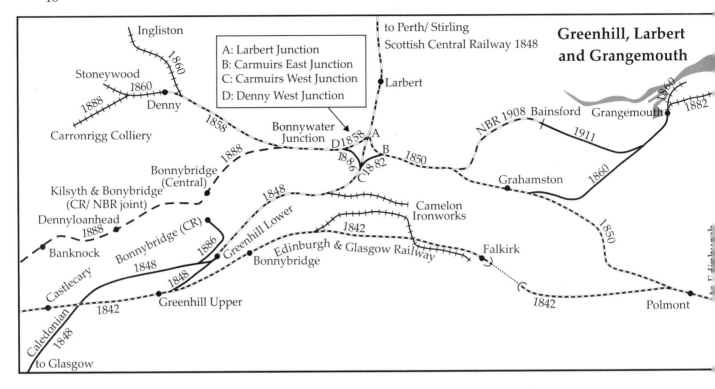

Greenhill, Larbert and Grangemouth

A: Larbert Junction
B: Carmuirs East Junction
C: Carmuirs West Junction
D: Denny West Junction

Ingliston
Stoneywood
1860
1860
1888
Denny
Carronrigg Colliery
1858
1888
Bonnywater Junction
Bonnybridge (Central)
Kilsyth & Bonybridge (CR/ NBR joint)
Dennyloanhead
1888
Banknock
Castlecary
Bonnybridge (CR)
1848
1886
1848
1848
Greenhill Lower
Greenhill Upper
Bonnybridge
Caledonian
1842
1848
to Glasgow

to Perth/ Stirling
Scottish Central Railway 1848
Larbert
D1858 A
1886 B
C1882 1850
NBR 1908 Bainsford Grangemouth
1860
1882
1911
Grahamston
1860
1850
Camelon Ironworks
1842
Edinburgh & Glasgow Railway
Falkirk
1842
Polmont
to Edinburgh

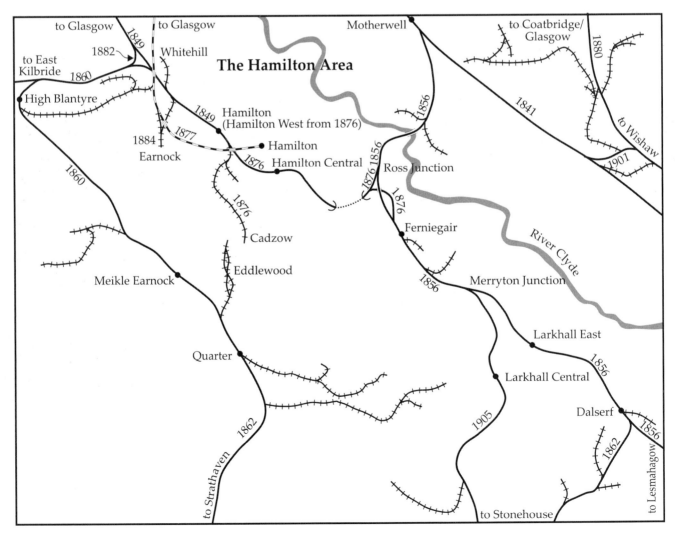

The Hamilton Area

to Glasgow
1849
to Glasgow
1882
Whitehill
to East Kilbride
1860
High Blantyre
1849
Hamilton (Hamilton West from 1876)
1877
1884
Earnock
1876
Hamilton
Hamilton Central
1860
1876
Cadzow
Meikle Earnock
Eddlewood
Quarter
1862
to Strathaven

Motherwell
1856
1856 1856
Ross Junction
1876
Ferniegair
1856
Merryton Junction
1905
Larkhall East
Larkhall Central
1856
Dalserf
1862
1856
to Lesmahagow
to Stonehouse

to Coatbridge/ Glasgow
1880
1841
to Wishaw
1901

River Clyde

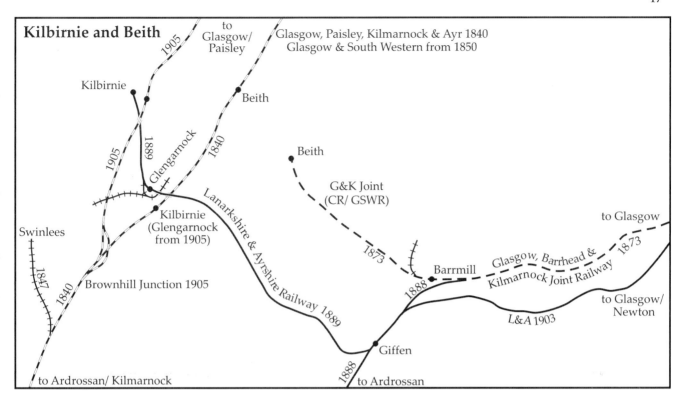

Kilbirnie and Beith

to Glasgow/ Paisley

1905

Glasgow, Paisley, Kilmarnock & Ayr 1840
Glasgow & South Western from 1850

Kilbirnie

Beith

1889

1905

Glengarnock

1840

Beith

G&K Joint
(CR/ GSWR)

to Glasgow

Swinlees

Kilbirnie
(Glengarnock
from 1905)

Lanarkshire & Ayrshire Railway 1889

1873

1873

Glasgow, Barrhead &

Kilmarnock Joint Railway

1847

1840

Brownhill Junction 1905

Barrmill

1888

to Glasgow/
Newton

L&A 1903

Giffen

1888

to Ardrossan/ Kilmarnock

to Ardrossan

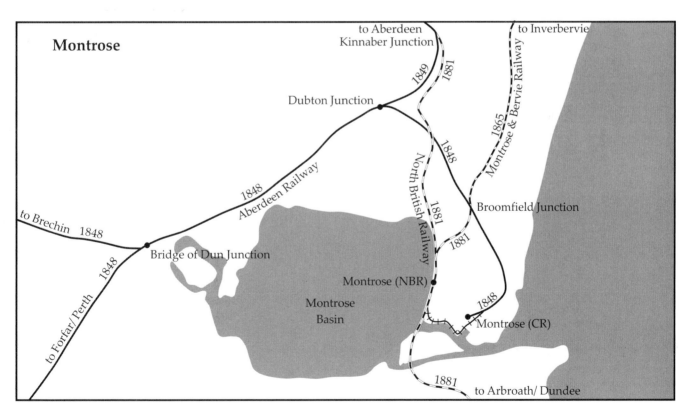

Montrose

to Aberdeen
Kinnaber Junction

to Inverbervie

1849

1881

Montrose & Bervie Railway

Dubton Junction

1865

1848

North British Railway

1881

Broomfield Junction

to Brechin 1848

1848

Aberdeen Railway

Bridge of Dun Junction

1881

1881

1848

to Forfar/ Perth 1848

Montrose (NBR)

Montrose
Basin

Montrose (CR)

1881

to Arbroath/ Dundee

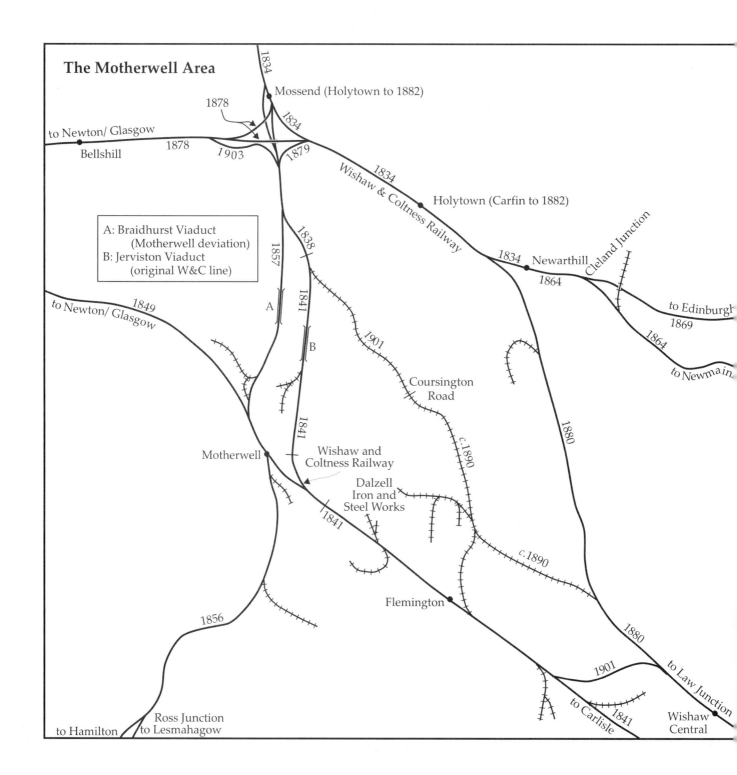

The Motherwell Area

A: Braidhurst Viaduct
   (Motherwell deviation)
B: Jerviston Viaduct
   (original W&C line)

1834

Mossend (Holytown to 1882)

1878

to Newton/ Glasgow

Bellshill

1878

1834

1903

1879

Wishaw & Coltness Railway

1834

Holytown (Carfin to 1882)

1857

1838

1841

A

B

1834

Newarthill

1864

Cleland Junction

to Edinburgh
1869

1864

to Newmain

1901

Coursington
Road

c.1890

1880

to Newton/ Glasgow

1849

1841

Motherwell

Wishaw and
Coltness Railway

Dalzell
Iron and
Steel Works

c.1890

Flemington

1841

1856

1880

to Law Junction

1901

to Carlisle

1841

Wishaw
Central

to Hamilton

Ross Junction
to Lesmahagow

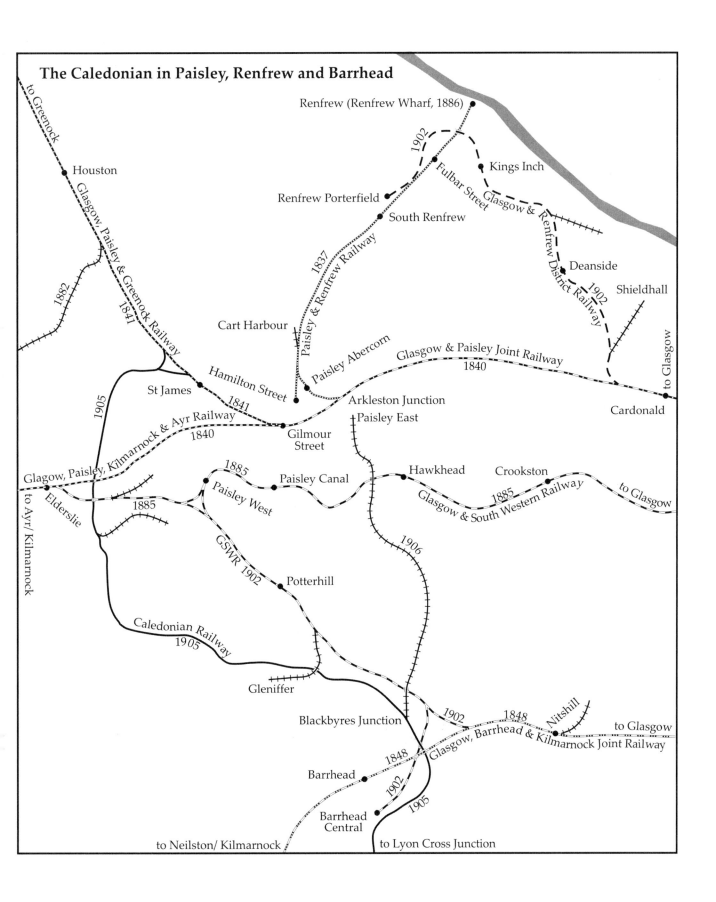

The Caledonian in Paisley, Renfrew and Barrhead

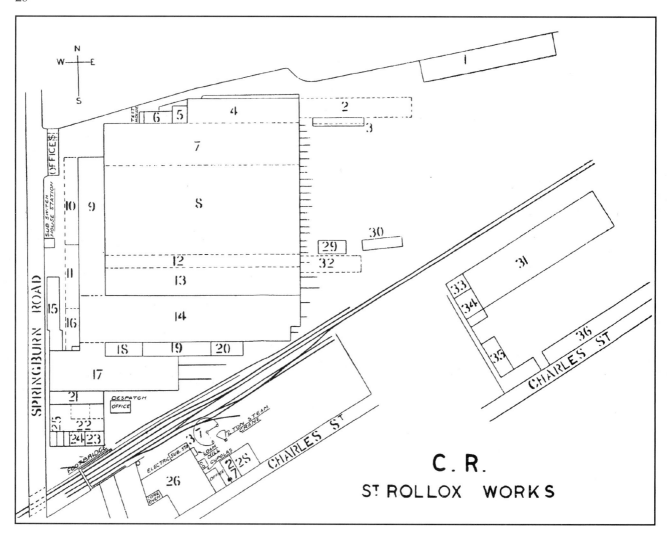

1. Timber drying shed
2. Travelling crane
3. Electricians' shop 1
4. Saw mill
5. Cabinet makers
6. Wagon shop store
7. Carriage shop
8. Wagon shop
9. Smithy
10. Forge
11. Wheel bossing and bolt machine
12. Finishing and wheel-turning shop
13. Iron turning and machine shop
14. Erecting shop
15. Dining hall and iron store
16. Boiler flanging shop
17. Boiler shop
18. Coppersmiths
19. Tinsmiths

20. Erecting shop store
21. Brass foundry
22. Heavy brass machines
23. Millwrights' shop
24. Electricians' shop 2
25. Brass finishing shop
26. Iron foundry
27. Pattern shop
28. Pattern store
29. Tyre heating shed
30. Chain shop
31. Paint shop
32. Travelling crane
33. Paint store
34. Trimming shop
35. Stores office
36. Stores
37. 7-ton electric crane

The 2 p.m. 'Corridor' leaves Glasgow Central, behind 4-6-0 No. 49, built in 1902. The signal gantry and signal box would be swept away as part of the redevelopment of the station, completed in 1906.

4-6-0 No. 180 of the 179-class (built 1913) pulls out of Carlisle with a long merchandise train.

CHAPTER 1. Prehistory – to 1845

Gestation

Although the Caledonian Railway was to be a thoroughly Scottish institution, it was conceived in another country. In the early decades of British main line railways the prime centre of investment and planning was the city of Liverpool, whose merchants and traders were ahead of their time in seeing both the usefulness and the potential profitability of trunk lines. They backed the construction of the Liverpool & Manchester Railway from 1828 to 1831 and were major investors in the London & Birmingham Railway. To link these two pioneering main lines, they planned the Grand Junction Railway, which would complete a railway all the way from London to Lancashire. The vision was clear, an iron road that would be the backbone of national commerce and industry; and it did not stop at Liverpool. The Grand Junction's directors were keen to sponsor the extension of their line, through Preston, Lancaster, Carlisle, and onwards to the expanding city of Glasgow.

Their method was that of the godfather rather than the parent. Local companies were encouraged, generating local support and, to a degree, raising local capital, to construct each new section of line. In this way the shrewd Liverpudlians obtained backing and on-the-spot enthusiasm for each project as well as bringing in useful investment, whilst ensuring that the local companies remained very much aware of their place in a greater scheme. So, in the 1830s the railway extended northwards, the Grand Junction meeting the North Union Railway to Preston, to be followed by the Preston & Lancaster and the Lancaster & Carlisle companies.

By this time, several railways had been constructed and were successfully operating in Scotland. In 1824 Charles MacLaren, editor of an Edinburgh paper, *The Scotsman*, had published a series of articles on railways which aroused great interest and were published as a pamphlet even before the final piece appeared in the newspaper[1]. MacLaren was an early advocate of steam traction and proposed a network of railway routes linking the major towns of Scotland. His pamphlet was widely read and undoubtedly stimulated interest in railway construction and investment, though a mini-boom in railway promotion was just foundering. MacLaren's proposal for a Scottish railway system foresaw a line coming in "from Carlisle to Dumfries; thence along the valley of the Nith, into Ayrshire" and onwards to Glasgow via Ayr, Irvine and Paisley. Another line from England would come via Berwick to Edinburgh, with a northern extension to Stirling, Perth and through Strathmore towards Aberdeen[2]. MacLaren's vision was more important as an indication of what might be, than as a basis for planning. Though all his suggested lines were ultimately built, the map of Scotland's first trunk railways was to take a different form to his scheme.

Despite MacLaren's advocacy of a planned network, the early development of Scottish railways was a piecemeal process. The country's first railways were built to carry minerals, with no thought of a trunk route or even of passenger service. Among the railways which form the pre-history of what became the 'Caledonian System', the first was the ten-mile Monkland & Kirkintilloch, whose authorising Act was obtained on 17 May 1824. Like earlier colliery lines, it was envisaged as a feeder to water-borne transport, in this case bearing coal from the pits in East and West Monklands parishes, near Airdrie, to the Forth & Clyde Canal at Kirkintilloch. This gave a route via the Monkland Canal to Glasgow, whose developing industries and proliferating streets provided a steadily-growing demand for cheap fuel. Edinburgh too could be supplied, by way of the Union Canal, which had opened in 1822 to link the capital with the Forth & Clyde Canal. The Monkland & Kirkintilloch was the first railway whose Act specified the use of locomotives, though it did not make immediate use of them, preferring to employ horses on its lightweight track. The gauge was set at 4ft 6in.

Among the investors were James Merry, a wealthy colliery operator, and Charles Tennant, founder of the large and highly pollutant chemical works at Townhead, on the north-eastern edge of Glasgow. To survey and build their line, the Monkland & Kirkintilloch board employed Thomas Grainger, an Edinburgh graduate who had trained as a surveyor and who with his younger associate John Miller set up the engineering practice of Grainger & Miller in 1825. By May 1826 the Monkland & Kirkintilloch was partly opened, and was completed by October of that year, with a short eastward branch to a colliery at Kipps. On the 26th of the same month, another new railway received parliamentary approval, with a further Act on 14 June 1827 for a revised route. This was the Garnkirk & Glasgow Railway, set up to carry coal on a line through the village of Garnkirk to a terminus close by the Monkland Canal's basin and Tennant's works, at Townhead. Thus it was not a feeder but a rival to the canal system. Branching from the Monkland & Kirkintilloch at the Gartsherrie Inn, the Garnkirk & Glasgow Railway was an independent company, though Charles Tennant was its chairman and James Merry was also a major investor. While the Garnkirk line was building, other colliery railways were also being linked to what would become the Monklands Group, acting as feeders to the canals, including the Ballochney Railway of 1825, extending from the Monkland & Kirkintilloch at Kipps to the Ballochney colliery. In 1828 the Wishaw and Coltness Railway was authorised by Parliament. This line extended southwards from Whifflet (then Whifflat) on the Monkland & Kirkintilloch Railway and the Monkland Canal, through the small country towns of Motherwell and Wishaw to the ironworks and coal pits around Coltness and Morningside. Its construction was slow, with the full line not opened until 1841[3]. Coal haulage was the prime purpose of all these railways, though the iron industry was also expanding in the same districts.

The Tennant Chemical Works at Townhead, Glasgow, in the 1840s, showing the Monkland Canal wharves.

The Coltness Ironworks *c*.1890, with CR mineral wagons behind and iron wagons awaiting loading.

The Garnkirk & Glasgow line opened for goods service in May 1831 and had a formal opening ceremony on 27 September. From 30 May, a passenger service was run between Lea End, north of Airdrie, on a short spur from the Ballochney Railway, and the Townhead terminus in Glasgow, over the Ballochney, Monkland & Kirkintilloch, and Garnkirk & Glasgow lines. Though Grainger and Miller engineered most of the early Scottish railways, they "clearly had as yet no concept even of a Scottish national network", building lines to various gauges between 4ft 6in and 5ft 6in[4]. The Monkland lines, built to the narrower gauge, were also competing for potential customers and haggling over shared use of tracks. Grainger was an active campaigner for the construction of local railways[5], but something more than a local coal line was envisaged when in 1830 he and Miller were commissioned to survey the Slamannan Railway, authorised on 3 July 1835, to link the Monkland collieries from Arbuckle on the Ballochney Railway with the Union Canal at Causewayend, near Linlithgow, and so forming a cheaper way of sending coal to Edinburgh[6]. In July 1840 this line was completed, providing the nearest thing yet to a Glasgow-Edinburgh train route, with a passenger service, jointly-managed with the Garnkirk & Glasgow, between Glasgow and Causewayend, from where a canal-boat completed the trip to the capital. Its service survived the opening of the Edinburgh & Glasgow Railway Company's city-to-city line in February 1842, though it exchanged the canal barges for horse-drawn transport[7].

Outside the original Townhead terminus, sometimes referred to as Glebe Street or St. Rollox, there was a toll-gate through which passengers and carts had to pass on their way to and from the centre of the town[8] or take a long detour. That was not the only inconvenience: to reach the station from the centre of town was a stiff walk uphill through crowded streets. And for passengers and goods there was no rail connection to the quays on the Clyde. Clearly it could only be a temporary terminus, but a tangle of topographical and financial difficulties, and conflicts of vested interests, lay ahead for Glasgow's railway entrepreneurs.

In green countryside a long way from the pit-heads and ironstone mines of Lanarkshire, another early line opened on 16 December 1831. Running from Dundee up and over the Sidlaw Hills for nearly 11 miles, it ended at the locality of Newtyle, scarcely even a village, but centrally placed in the great Vale of Strathmore. One of its backers was Lord Wharncliffe, a member of the 'Grand Alliance' of coal barons and a man keenly interested in railway development (he had been a patron of George Stephenson), who owned land in the area. Wharncliffe might have been expected to take a strategic view but it would seem that he saw the Newtyle railway as a purely local line. Its gauge was 4ft 6in. Short as it was, its gradients required three forms of traction, using both horses and locomotives, and fixed haulage engines on the steepest sections, whose gradients varied from 1 in 10 to 1 in 25, more than a locomotive could cope with. There were no mines or mineral traffic, but a substantial amount of flax and raw cloth was carried between Strathmore and Dundee[9]. Despite only modest financial returns, further capital was raised in 1835 to promote extensions a few miles east and west from Newtyle, to the village of Glamis and the small town of Coupar Angus respectively. The Newtyle & Coupar Angus Railway , 5$^3/_4$ miles, opened in February 1837 and the Newtyle & Glammiss (sic), 7 miles, opened for goods traffic in June 1838. Established as separate companies, both employed only horse traction initially, though wind-power, using a mast-mounted tarpaulin, was also said to be used on the Coupar Angus line on suitable occasions.

In the same region, backed by another local grandee, Lord Panmure, the Dundee & Arbroath Railway gained its Act in 1836. Built along easy coastwise country, it opened on 6 October 1838. Another provisional committee was formed in 1837 under the landowner William Lindsay Carnegie to promote a railway between Arbroath and Forfar, which opened fully on 3 January 1839. Each line had its own terminus in Arbroath, though both were engineered by Grainger & Miller, to a 5ft 6in gauge, which does not suggest they foresaw any link with the lines they built in Lanarkshire. West of Dundee, backers led by Lord Kinnaird had striven since 1835 to establish a railway between Dundee and Perth, but they wound up their efforts in 1838, frustrated primarily by the greed or indifference of landowners. For a decade, the Angus lines operated as an isolated group.

Enter Joseph Locke

**Joseph Locke (1805-60).
(Institution of Mechanical Engineers)**

The strategically-minded entrepreneurs of Lancashire could not fail to notice that some of these local lines ran across, or along, parts of the envisioned London-Glasgow trunk route. In 1835 they began to take action, sending their engineer Joseph Locke to survey and report on the practicability of, and best route for, a railway line to run from Preston to Glasgow. Locke submitted a report in February 1836. If the Grand Junction directors, mostly Liverpool businessmen, were interested in seeing a rail link between Glasgow and London, he was very keen on being its engineer. Trained by George Stephenson, he had emerged from that great man's aegis as an independently-minded and ambitious engineer. As a pupil, he acquired the Stephensonian vision of a national railway system, its trunk as a line from London to the north, with branches to the fast-growing manufacturing cities[10]. Locke was engineer of the Grand Junction and of the Wigan and Preston lines that formed the North Union. He was not the first to prospect a line southwards from Glasgow: Frank Giles, engineer of the Newcastle & Carlisle Railway, had made some investigation of a Carlisle-Glasgow line on behalf of a group of Glasgow businessmen in 1834[11], and Grainger & Miller had also surveyed a possible line via Kilmarnock[12], but Locke's report had more impact. From a point just over the Scottish border, he noted two possible routes. The more direct followed the valley of the Annan Water, but it involved ten miles of gradient, reckoned by Locke as 1 in 75, to reach a summit point near Elvanfoot. Locke considered this too steep to be recommended, and proposed the alternative route, following the valley of the Nith, bending westwards and around

20 miles longer, but with more moderate gradients and a lower summit. It would also pass through the important towns of Dumfries and Kilmarnock, while the Annandale route passed only the small town of Lockerbie.

Strategic political as well as commercial thinking lay behind this initiative. It was generally assumed that "Two great lines from Scotland to England cannot pay"[13] and the Liverpool entrepreneurs wanted to ensure that the single route should be controlled by themselves. Others had the same idea. George Stephenson, by now established as 'The Hengist of Railways' and an immensely influential figure to railway investors, with his associate George Hudson, Lord Mayor of York and railway promoter extraordinaire, were vigorously planning a line to follow the eastern side of the country from York to Newcastle and on to Edinburgh. The 'West Coast' and 'East Coast' routes were in competition before either existed, though 'East' and 'West 'were somewhat approximate terms. Edinburgh's location, at 3° 11' west of Greenwich, is further west than Carlisle's, which is at 2° 56' west of the meridian.

Railway surveys did not go unnoticed by landowners, and among the readers of Locke's report was John James Hope Johnstone, owner of extensive tracts of land in and around Annandale. The Johnstones had been a prominent family in the region for generations. Hope Johnstone was M.P. for Dumfries-shire, in the Tory interest, but was no reactionary, and perceived the value to his estates of having a railway which would bring coal and lime at reduced cost. His factor or man of business, Charles Stewart, lived at Hillside, close to Lockerbie, and Stewart took on the promotion of the Annandale route with vigour. He got in touch with Joseph Locke. By instinct an 'up and over' engineer who preferred direct routes, Locke was happy, when he met Stewart in Liverpool on 5 June 1836, to agree that the Annandale route was possible, perhaps with the use of stationary hauling engines on the steepest sections.

Oddly, the first mention of a "Caledonian Railway" seems to have been as the name for a completely different project, a proposed "Caledonian Railway Company from York to Edinburgh", also mooted in 1836[14]. On 14 September Hope Johnstone convened and chaired a meeting of local proprietors at Dumfries, at which it was agreed to form a provisional committee for the establishment of a railway from Lancashire by Carlisle, Beattock and Lanark to Glasgow and Edinburgh, and £148 14s. 6d. was subscribed towards the cost of a new preliminary survey. This was undertaken by Locke, who helpfully revised his Annandale gradient down to 1 in 93. The Edinburgh and Glasgow lines were to diverge near Biggar, with the Edinburgh line following the eastern edge of the Pentland Hills. Locke went beyond engineering in his encouragement, writing to Stewart from Liverpool on 27 July: "You may certainly calculate on the co-operation of the Grand Junction Railway Company with which I will be in communication at the first opportunity"[15]. Hopes of getting the project quickly under way proved premature, however. Hope Johnstone wrote on 13 April 1837 to John Moss, chairman of the Grand Junction, to inform him that the promoters are now prepared to have a survey done and "… it would obviously be very important in directing Public attention to the results of the survey, were the Directors of the Grand Junction Coy. to add their names, and also to let it appear that the survey was carried on under their Auspices". Moss replied promptly on 19 April to say that, "The Committee are unanimous in recommending that no steps be taken until an alteration takes place in the money market … I question very much whether any new line will go down with the public just now"[16]. Locke remained sanguine, sending encouraging letters to Stewart, but no action was taken. Despite the difficulty of raising funds, certain merchants and industrialists of Glasgow were embarking on schemes of their own, the Glasgow, Paisley, Kilmarnock & Ayr Railway and the Glasgow Paisley & Greenock (both authorised by Parliament in 1837, and intended to share a line from Glasgow as far as Paisley), and the Edinburgh & Glasgow Railway, authorised in July 1838. The Glasgow, Paisley, Kilmarnock & Ayr in particular caused anxiety to Johnstone and Stewart, since it would clearly offer a link to a railway coming up from the south through Nithsdale. But the real problem for them was that important elements of a Scottish railway network were getting under way while their line, envisaged as the essential trunk, existed only on paper.

The rival routes from Carlisle became a subject of public debate, and at a meeting in Glasgow on 8 March 1839, with Lord Provost Dunlop in the chair, it was agreed to form a committee to sponsor reports from two engineers, one Scottish, one English, on the respective merits of the two lines. The committee was speedily approached by the proponents of the Annandale line but waited until the engineers' reports, from Joseph Locke and John Miller, were completed, in March 1840. Miller, by now a railway engineer of considerable experience, put the case for Nithsdale; Locke for Annandale. However, at this juncture the British government chose to make a foray into the arena of railway planning, by appointing two eminent men, Professor Peter Barlow and Sir Frederick Smith, R.E., to make recommendations on the most effective means of railway communication from London to Edinburgh, Glasgow and Dublin. Railway promoters on both sides of the country concentrated their energy and funds on producing plans and evidence for the Commissioners. The Annandale backers had to reach into their pockets for further survey work by Locke's assistant engineer Duncan McCallum, including the Edinburgh arm of their line, which was now to follow the western edge of the Pentlands instead of the original proposed route via Biggar and Broughton. The change of route took the line over or close to known coal deposits. McCallum wrote cheerfully to Stewart on New Year's Day 1840 that, "I have just completed my section … it has already revolutionised the opinion of many in this quarter who have hitherto looked upon Annandale as an impracticable route for a Railway"[17].

While the Caledonian project hung fire, railway construction was going on south of the Clyde, on two lines which the Caledonian would later swallow up. From Rutherglen to Port Eglinton (terminus of the partially-completed

**South Glasgow, *c*.1850: Dixon's Blazes, ironworks in a still-rural landscape.
Painting by William Simpson (1823-99).**

Glasgow, Paisley & Ardrossan Canal) a goods line was built to serve the Dixon's Blazes ironworks and other industrial sites. At Port Eglinton it met the Govan Tramway, an older Dixon venture, to form the Polloc & Govan Railway, opened on 22 August 1840. A branch was laid through the streets from West Street to the small dock on the Clyde at Windmillcroft, opposite the Broomielaw. The joint line to Paisley, of the Glasgow, Paisley & Greenock and Glasgow, Paisley, Kilmarnock & Ayr companies opened from a temporary terminus at Bridge Street, a short distance south of the river, on 13 July 1840.

Barlow and Smith took a year to make conscientious and thorough investigations, publishing a voluminous report on 15 March 1841. The Annandale backers' financial sacrifice was rewarded when they recommended the Lockerbie route, with a branch to Edinburgh. By this time the Edinburgh & Glasgow Railway was under construction. But the commissioners clearly had doubts about the willingness of investors, and stipulated that if "any parties should be ready to undertake the execution of this proposed Clydesdale Railway, they would certainly be entitled to every facility the Government could afford, provided security were given of a *bona fide* intention of completing the whole line from Lancaster"[18]. Without this, and a definite time frame, preference should be given to the East Coast line.

More Delays and Diversions

With the West Coast route via Annandale thus given official sanction, a meeting was held at Liverpool on 21 July, attended by representatives of the railway companies and the landowners, followed by another at Carlisle on 7 August. A powerful supporter was Captain Mark Huish, who had been manager of the Glasgow, Paisley & Greenock company since 1837, and was newly appointed as manager of the Grand Junction, with large ambitions. He wrote to Stewart on 5 October 1841, "I shall not allow the project to sleep"[19]. The line between Paisley and Greenock had opened on 30 March 1841, engineered by Locke and his partner John Errington[20], with a handsome, classical-style terminus at Cathcart Street, Greenock. Further meetings for the Annandale line were held in Glasgow and Lanark, but by the end of 1841, despite much bruiting of it as "the officially preferred line", it was clear that insufficient investment was forthcoming. Many people had supposed that there would be government money to back the scheme, but this was a false hope[21]. Any thoughts of making a start were dashed, and though the railway had reached Lancaster by 1840, it stopped there. C.J.A. Robertson remarks that the delay seems surprising[22], but the backers of Nithsdale did not surrender tamely and the competing claims of Nithsdale and Annandale still exercised a paralysing effect, while money was tight because of a new economic downturn, exacerbated by the American tariff hike of 1842. Moss was again recommending delay to his Scottish associates. A hint of impatience from the north might seem to appear with the observation that in February 1842 the "Caledonian Railway" company intended to apply to Parliament for an Act enabling it to make a railway from Lancaster via Kendal to Carlisle[23]. This seems to be the earliest reference to the Caledonian by that name, but it referred to the Liverpool-centred scheme, and in November it was announced that "the great Caledonian Railway shall proceed from Lancaster by way of Kendal to Carlisle" while "The second part of the great project, from Carlisle to Glasgow and Edinburgh, will also, it is understood, be prosecuted as early as possible"[24]. But a lack of drive in the Annandale project was also perceived. At the end of 1842 John Learmonth of the North British Railway's promotional committee was claiming that the line "might almost be said to be abandoned"[25]. In fact its promoters were waiting for a green light from England – without the Lancaster and Carlisle, their line would be a tail without a dog. Finally, on 24 May 1844, a Bill for the Lancaster and Carlisle was approved by Parliament. Renewed survey work to the north had already begun in January, with a team of surveyors sending figures to McCallum's colleague Dundas in Edinburgh for collation. A third leading promoter had joined Johnstone and Stewart, Colonel Graham of Mossknowe in Lanarkshire, to whom McCallum wrote on 28 January about the new plans, affirming that Locke was "the means of stamping them with value in the eyes of the English Capitalists"[26]. Stewart was busy writing to local landowners for support and subscriptions. With conditions easing in the money market, the activists began to move into high gear.

Advice and assistance, as well as finance, from England remained important. "It was the Grand Junction … which guided the Caledonian promoters through many of the technicalities of establishing their company, and which encouraged English confidence to such an extent that almost four-fifths of Caledonian subscriptions came from south of the border"[27]. Many Scottish investors clearly remained unconvinced of the Annandale line's likely profitability. By 1844 the groups of projectors associated with the East Coast, Annandale and Nithsdale lines had been organised into respectively the North British, Caledonian and Glasgow & Dumfries committees. In its first meeting, in London, on 19 February 1844, the Caledonian 'Preliminary Committee' set up a sub-committee to prepare a prospectus, and appointed Locke & Errington as engineers. Lt-Col John Hambly Humfry was appointed interim secretary[28]. Colonel Graham wrote a letter on 22 February 1844, announcing that "A General Meeting of the County of Lanark, attended by a deputation from Dumfriesshire, unanimously resolved to adopt immediate steps for the promotion of a Railway from Carlisle to Edinburgh and Glasgow, in the line recommended by the Government Commissioners." A provisional committee had been inaugurated, which, meeting in London, "has associated itself with Gentlemen interested in the great leading Railways from London to Lancaster and in the proposed Railway to Carlisle, in order to organise a Company to be called The Caledonian Railway Company"[29]. Who actually suggested the evocative and all-encompassing name is not certain, though the distinction was claimed by McCallum: "If it be an honour to have given it the name by which it is so extensively known, I may justly claim that honour"[30]. Graham's letter was sent to selected gentlemen, with a returnable part accepting a place on the provisional committee. Huish also wrote a letter confirming that the Grand Junction Company was in full support[31]. In March, rooms were taken in Parliament Street for a London office, at 100 guineas a year, and with solid Lancastrian backing the Caledonian prospectus was issued that month. In this document, the line's northern termini were identified as Edinburgh and Glasgow, with the important proviso: "for the time being", and a note that "By a continuation of eight miles … this line may be brought into connection with the projected Railway to Stirling, Perth and Dundee, thus forming one unbroken chain of Railway communication from London to the North of Scotland"[32]. The first committee minutes book records a meeting in London in that month, attended by nine men, of whom five were M.P.s. They drew up a list of 124 people who might give support to their scheme, including five dukes and 29 M.P.s. Seventy persons accepted places on the provisional committee, including John Moss (the Grand Junction was to subscribe £200,000); Mark Sprot, chairman of the Garnkirk & Glasgow, and the entire Wishaw & Coltness and Monkland & Kirkintilloch boards. Others included Tennant, Dixon, and Campbell of Blythswood. The chairman was Lord Belhaven (also the Wishaw & Coltness chairman) and his deputy was Col. Graham. Efforts continued to stave off rival routes. The West Coast interests sent a petition to Parliament asking it to again order a commission to report on the best route between England and Scotland: "I think this may possibly stop the Berwick Line for one year which is all that we require"[33] wrote Hope Johnstone on 6 March.

The involvement of Graham, Belhaven, and Lanarkshire industrialists shows that, somewhat belatedly, the movers and shakers of that county's industrial districts were getting behind the Caledonian project. Even before its Bill was approved by Parliament, the provisional committee had completed the diplomatic process of securing entry to Glasgow. Through 1844 intensive negotiation went on between the Caledonian promoters and the proprietors of the existing Lanarkshire lines. Rather than construct their own line all the way into Glasgow, the Caledonian committee wanted to gain running powers from Garriongill, south of Wishaw, over the existing tracks of the Wishaw and Coltness and the Garnkirk & Glasgow (which had built an extension from Gartsherrie through Coatbridge to Whifflat to meet the Wishaw & Coltness line in 1843 and was renamed as the Glasgow, Garnkirk and Coatbridge Railway in 1844). An agreement was finalised with the Wishaw & Coltness whereby the CR would pay 36% of gross receipts from any of its traffic which travelled for less than 5 miles on the Wishaw line, and 30% of gross receipts from its other traffic, in return for which the single track line would be doubled and re-gauged. Robertson says "it was inevitable that, if the Caledonian offered remotely reasonable terms, they would have to agree"[34], and also no doubt the Wishaw & Coltness directors could see the value of a physical link with the main line to the south. Relations were distinctly cooler with the Edinburgh & Glasgow Railway, which had so inconveniently established itself in the years when the Caledonian project was languishing, and whose shorter route by Falkirk rather blighted the Caledonian project's aim of providing a Glasgow-Edinburgh railway via Carstairs. Over the next two decades the Caledonian would spend much time and money in attempts to get control of it. Initially, though, a combative move saw Joseph Locke authorised to survey a 'Caledonian Extension Railway' from Ayr right across the country to Peebles, Galashiels and Kelso, at which place it would meet a branch of the Newcastle & Berwick Railway. It would intersect the CR main line near Lanark. This plan, hatched with George Hudson's participation, would establish a link from Glasgow to the East Coast main line without involving the Edinburgh & Glasgow or the North British companies. A prospectus was published on 12 April 1845 and capital of £1,500,000 was sought.

Locke & Errington were closely associated with another significant figure, Thomas Brassey, who was well on the way to becoming the greatest and wealthiest engineering contractor of the mid-century. He had worked with Locke on the construction of the Glasgow, Paisley & Greenock line, and (along with another engineer, John Mackenzie) the Paris-Rouen line in France, and they shared an admiration of the strategic planning of the French railway system, compared with the haphazard British approach[35]. Locke and Brassey had been engaged as engineer and contractor on the Clydesdale Junction Railway[36]. There can be no doubt that Locke, Brassey and Mackenzie had given thought as to how the complete London-Carlisle-Aberdeen route could best be achieved. To any group of railway promoters, they offered a compelling package of expertise, confidence and success, embracing survey, construction, locomotives and rolling stock, and maintenance after opening.

Railway Diplomacy

At a promotional meeting held in Edinburgh on 12 March 1844, for the Scottish Central Railway, intended to run from the Edinburgh & Glasgow line, near Falkirk, to Perth, "the immediate prospect of the opening of an unbroken chain of railway communication from Scotland to the south" was a prime consideration[37]. A few days later, one of its leading promoters, William Murray of Polmaise, wrote to the Caledonian Committee to inform them of the SCR's desire "to have the Railway from Perth and Stirling made under the direction of Mr. Locke and Mr. Errington"[38]. On 9 April, the SCR Provisional Committee noted a letter advising them of a proposal to build a railway north-eastwards from Perth through the Vale of Strathmore to meet the Dundee & Newtyle line. This plan was soon extended, as the Scottish Midland Junction Railway, to reach as far as Forfar. The Aberdeen Railway, as originally planned, was to build a line onwards from Forfar through Brechin to Aberdeen[39].

The Edinburgh & Glasgow Railway's view of the Caledonian's ambition for a line to the north was simple. A circular to its shareholders urged them to do "everything in your power to discourage the Scottish or Central Union, and the Caledonian Railways, the latter of which wil be highly injurious to our interests"[40] – a declaration which set the tone of relations between the E&G and the Caledonian for the next twenty years. Officially, however, the Caledonian Railway was still proposed as a two-pronged fork, aimed at the plum destinations of Glasgow and Edinburgh. In describing the infighting between the Scottish Midland Junction and the Arbroath & Forfar companies in 1844, Niall Ferguson observes that the Caledonian "even then intended eventually to operate the [Scottish Midland Junction] line"[41]. A significant letter was considered by the provisional committee on 6 April, from William Murray, intimating his, and the Marquis of Breadalbane's (chairman of the SCR Provisional Committee), desire for "the Railway from Perth and Stirling" to meet the Caledonian Railway by Castlecary, a site on the one-time Roman wall, about half-way between Glasgow and Stirling[42]. Whether Murray's letter was unexpected is not clear. The historian of the Scottish Central says that the initiative was taken by the Caledonian[43], but this letter appears to be the first formal mention of the link, though it is very probable that informal conversations had preceded it. The original SCR proposal had not included a direct link with the Caledonian. It was a somewhat disingenuous letter, however, not framed as coming from the SCR Committee, and making no mention of that body's simultaneous and official negotiations with the Edinburgh & Glasgow company. Locke & Errington were appointed as the Central's engineers on 9 May, ousting the Mitchell brothers of Inverness who had surveyed the line. Joseph Mitchell gives an account of this affair[44], although his memoirs are not wholly reliable. James Walker, the Falkirk-born President of the Institution of Civil Engineers, had agreed to act as the

SCR 2-2-2 No. 7, built by the Vulcan Foundry in 1847, became CR No. 330 in 1865. Rebuilt in 1860, it ran until 1872. The gentleman on the footplate is said to be Alexander Allan.

SCR's consulting engineer, but was abruptly required to accept Locke as a colleague. The incensed Walker preserved and published his increasingly acrimonious correspondence with Breadalbane and Locke[45]. Locke's appointment was said to have been insisted on by the "proprietors of Stirlingshire", of whom Murray was one. In the context of the Caledonian Railway's early history, the affair gives some insight into the ways in which Locke & Errington, stressing their connections with prestigious and wealthy southern powers like the Grand Junction Railway and the Brassey contracting business, as well as their own all-round engineering skills, could convince local railway promoters that their services were indispensable to success in what was still a new field of commerce, with huge sums of money involved[46]. The Caledonian Committee went ahead with plans for its 'branch' to meet the Scottish Central at Castlecary, and a draft of the prospectus was sent to William Murray.

The Caledonian, with its English allies, was staking its claim on traffic to and from the north, but by 1844, eight years after Locke's first report, the Scottish railway scene was looking very different. As well as the early lines, the Edinburgh & Glasgow Railway was now operating between these cities. The Glasgow, Paisley & Greenock, and Glasgow, Paisley Kilmarnock & Ayr Railways were running, very profitably. Though as yet many people had never seen a train, the concept of the railway was already familiar; for those with spare cash, the notion of the railway company as a safe and profitable investment was strengthening every day. Traffic prospects for the Caledonian had improved dramatically: in the decade between 1835 and 1845 Scottish iron production rose by a factor of seven to 475,000 tons and was still increasing. J.B.Neilson's patented hot blast smelting system, applied to the 'black band' combined coal and ironstone of Lanarkshire and Ayrshire, was largely responsible for the boom[47]. The as-yet unformed Caledonian was a new beast on the landscape, primed and eager to swallow up others, and the Scottish Central, with its line from Stirling to Perth, and the Scottish Midland Junction, from Perth to Forfar, were both obvious prey, as were the Garnkirk and Wishaw & Coltness companies. They were willing enough, if the price was right. But now there were other potential buyers. The committee's May meeting was attended by delegates from the Monkland & Kirkintilloch, Wishaw & Coltness, and Glasgow, Garnkirk & Coatbridge Railways. A finance committee was set up. Deposits on 36,000 shares came to £180,000, of which £140,000 was invested in Exchequer bills and the rest banked. To steer the Bill through, a survey and Act committee was also formed, with strong representation from the allied English companies.

Attempts by the Caledonian project's backers at opposing the proposed North British Railway, from Edinburgh to Berwick, had been half-hearted, and the second reading of its Bill was not opposed at all. Once the NBR got its Act on 4 July 1844, the completion of an east-coast London-Edinburgh railway was just a matter of time. For the Scottish Central and the Scottish Midland Junction committees, this was a highly significant development. A junction of the Scottish Central with the Edinburgh & Glasgow line would lead via Edinburgh into England. During August, David Rankine, Manager of the Edinburgh & Dalkeith Railway, was appointed interim secretary of the Caledonian following Humfry's resignation, and that month the provisional committee held a meeting in Liverpool, appointing a sub-committee to deal with the Glasgow, Garnkirk & Coatbridge and the Monkland & Kirkintilloch Railways[48]. In September 1844 the North British, having bought the Edinburgh & Dalkeith Railway, determined to extend it further south to Hawick and, ultimately, to Carlisle. Notice was served that that the Caledonian had an ambitious rival. Rankine was busy ensuring that scrip-holders who had expressed an intention to buy shares now confirmed their subscriptions, at lawyer's offices in Edinburgh, Glasgow, Lockerbie, Carlisle and Liverpool[49].

Discussions on 4 and 7 October led to agreement for working the Garnkirk & Glasgow Railway, which would be paid 36% of gross receipts for traffic up to four miles, and 30% for traffic over a greater distance. In constructing the line to Castlecary, the Caledonian proposed to make use of a short section of the Monkland & Kirkintilloch Railway, from a junction at Gargill, close to Gartsherrie, to a point from which the Caledonian's own northward line would diverge. The required section of track was about 1,170 yards between Gargill and Garnqueen. Agreement was reached with the Monkland & Kirkintilloch in October 1844, including a requirement for that company to convert its gauge to the Caledonian's Stephenson standard of 4ft 8½ins. It would receive 36% of gross passenger receipts for the section (goods and minerals were not noted in the agreement)[50]. In September a provisional agreement was signed with the Wishaw & Coltness. But now the Caledonian was to discover that the small companies could be slippery. The Wishaw & Coltness reneged and agreed on a merger with the Edinburgh & Glasgow Railway. However, the E&G backed out, apparently because Belhaven demanded excessive compensation for coal reserves under the railway line, which could not be mined because of likely subsidence[51]. On 5-6 November, the Caledonian took on the agreement, committing 9,600 £25 shares of Preferential stock at 10.5% interest, against the Wishaw & Coltness capital of £240,000[52]. By the time the Caledonian Committee met in Edinburgh on 19 November 1844, its agreements with the Lanarkshire railways were in place. A deputation from the Scottish Central Railway, headed by Lord Breadalbane, was admitted to the meeting, and Castlecary was agreed on as the end-on junction of the two lines (in fact the junction was made at Greenhill). An investment of £25,000 by the Caledonian (when established) in the Scottish Midland Junction Railway was approved, so long as the SCR did likewise and local subscriptions came to at least £50,000[53]. The Provisional Committee was acting as if Parliamentary authorisation was an accomplished fact, accepting a tender from William Routh of £11 17s. 6d. per ton for 10,000 tons of steel rails[54]. An even vaster sum was committed to in the acceptance of Messrs. Mackenzie, Stephenson & Brassey's tender for construction of the line: £1,275,000, exclusive of land purchase, including a branch to Dumfries, so long as total excavation did not exceed 9,000,000 cubic yards. The contract was brought forward by Joseph Locke, and no competing tender was asked for or provided. Locke told the Committee he thought the bid too high by £25,000, but "they were very eligible contractors"[55]. Mackenzie, Stephenson & Brassey were also recommended by Locke for the SCR and Scottish Midland Junction Railway construction. There is no inference of corruption about this. The Liverpool investors, mostly Quakers, had a very sharp eye for that sort of thing, and Brassey and Locke were men of financial probity in an era when graft and dishonesty were far from unknown in railway affairs. Locke, Brassey and their colleagues and associates had developed a comprehensive 'package' offer, designed to appeal to an inexperienced set of directors who had neither the time nor the specialised knowledge to deal with a detailed breakdown of estimated costs. But the package built in a substantial profit margin, and clauses which gave the engineers considerable freedom in spending the company's money.

At the end of 1844 the Edinburgh & Glasgow Railway agreed to invest £100,000 in the proposed Glasgow, Dumfries & Carlisle company[56]. The North British, the Glasgow, Dumfries & Carlisle, Glasgow, Paisley, Kilmarnock & Ayr, and Edinburgh & Glasgow Railways were all in alliance against the proposed Caledonian Railway, having agreed to create a joint purse of £30,000 to oppose its Bill[57]. If a railway ran from Edinburgh via Hawick to Carlisle, and another from Glasgow via Kilmarnock and Dumfries to Carlisle, what need was there for a line through the thinly-populated Annandale and the barren lands above? The Caledonian's potential existence was threatened by this pincer-type strategy. But it fought back with vigour. In January 1845 it obtained the backing of Edinburgh Town Council, partly by promising to lay a water supply pipe along its Edinburgh line for the Edinburgh Water Company, and partly by promising to reduce the price of high-grade 'parrot' or gas coal in the capital by over half, 8s. 6d. a ton as compared to 20s. It won an influential ally in the Duke of Buccleuch, who had never liked the Nithsdale route and felt sure that the Caledonian line would win approval by Parliament. Nithsdale was also opposed by Sir James Graham of Netherby, who owned much of the territory between Carlisle and the border. Like Buccleuch, he was a Cabinet Minister. Provisional arrangements to lease the Polloc & Govan and Clydesdale Junction Railways were made on 29 January and 13 February.

Lord Dalhousie's Railway Board of 1844-45, a short-lived Government attempt to impose greater control on railway development, published a *Report on the Schemes for Extending Railway Communication in Scotland* on 24 March 1845. Reiterating the view that only one railway between Scotland and England was economically feasible, it backed the proposed Caledonian Annandale line and recommended that the Nithsdale line should stop at Cumnock and the North British should not go beyond Hawick. This endorsement seemed to make parliamentary approval almost a formality. The Railway Board appears to have been the first to identify by name a 'Caledonian System' – a set of railways under construction or proposed, including the Clydesdale Junction, Caledonian & Dumbartonshire Junction, Scottish Central, Scottish Midland Junction, and the Aberdeen Railway, all of which were being actively promoted in their own districts in 1844. "These, although clearly of great value to Caledonian planning, were independent promotions, and asked nothing of the Caledonian company but general support"[58]. It does not seem, though, that they asked anything at all of the Caledonian promoters, but they were being helpfully advised by Brassey and Locke. Clearly, however, the promoters and the Railway Board saw the usefulness of a joined-up system, of uniform gauge.

On the eastern side the North British Company, with an equally national name, was similarly keen to extend and enlarge itself as much by acquisition as by new building. Rivalry was always more likely than co-operation. The insistence that only one line into Scotland could be viable resulted in these grandiose titles of 'North British' and 'Caledonian', both managing to imply that they were *the* line to Scotland. The Caledonian coolly appropriated the ancient Scottish royal arms to underline its national ambitions. After the uncertain years, an unprecedented surge in financial activity generated by railway development was transforming the economic life of the country. In 1844 the Glasgow Stock Exchange was founded, primarily to deal with railway share transactions. Established banks, though willing to lend to railway companies, did not buy railway shares, but during the 1840s nine exchange banks were formed in Scotland, including four launched in Glasgow in 1845 (in that year the Caledonian borrowed £151,436). Exchange banks gave loans based on railway shares as security. To finance this they borrowed funds at above the banking rates, but as long as they could make loans at interest rates varying from 5.5`% to 8.5%, there was a comfortable profit margin of 2.5% or more. The bankers may have thought this happy state of affairs would go on indefinitely, but it was to come to a sticky end quite soon.

Through May and June 1845 the plans and mutual criticisms of the rival Annandale and Nithsdale schemes were argued out before Parliamentary Committee DD, one of numerous committees set up to thrash out the many new railway proposals of the period. Much time was spent in assessing the extent and quality of the coal deposits under each line. The Caledonian found a gas engineer, J.Headley, to confirm that the Wilsontown coalfield, near the Carstairs-Edinburgh line, could supply 100,000-200,000 tons of coal a year to London[59]; their opponents found another expert to denigrate the quality of the Wilsontown coal. Joseph Locke and John Miller as the respective engineers criticised each other's plans. A red herring was raised when it was suggested that the Dalveen Pass, between Thornhill and Elvanfoot, would be a preferable route to those already proposed. Both sides sent out surveyors to report on it. Miller proposed a 2-mile curving tunnel at the head of the pass, and Locke successfully rubbished the scheme. Challenged in turn on his Beattock grades, he said that "assistant engines" would be used, as was already done on other lines[60]. By now the power of locomotives had been increased to such a point that stationary engines and cable hauling were out of the picture for main line railways. The parliamentary committees were not blandly rubber-stamping proposals in a random way but seriously trying to identify schemes with proper planning and solid backing. Committee DD spent six weeks in deliberations and heard upwards of 250 witnesses[61], before approving the Annandale route, and the 'Act for making a Railway from Carlisle to Edinburgh and Glasgow and the North of Scotland, to be called The Caledonian Railway' was given the royal assent on 31 July 1845.

CHAPTER 2. The Years of Preparation, 1845-47

The Caledonian – At Last

A limited company was duly formed, with capital of £1,800,000, divided into 36,000 shares at £50 each. For Hope Johnstone and Stewart the Act marked the end of nine years' effort. During 1841-45, however, it was William Lockhart, M.P. for Lanarkshire, who headed the provisional committee, with John Moss and Colonel Graham as his deputies. Dumfries-shire proprietors had sustained the campaign all the way (though the branch to Dumfries did not gain parliamentary approval) but the later arousal of Lanarkshire interest undoubtedly helped in the final success. Hope Johnstone purchased £44,000 of shares, Lt.Col Graham took £40,000, Robert Johnstone Douglas, of Lockerbie House, £38,000 – in all the Annandale gentry invested £135,500 while the far more populous and richer Lanarkshire invested only £22,000[1]. Nor did the wealthy men of the rapidly-growing cities of Edinburgh and Glasgow, termini of the line, show much interest in this railway link to the south. There had been much more Glaswegian interest in the Nithsdale line (over 70% of the Glasgow, Paisley, Kilmarnock & Ayr Railway's capital was locally raised), and Edinburgh also had the East Coast route. Examination of the original subscription lists showed that though residents of Scotland were the most numerous group (just), they did not have the largest holding[2].

Area	Number	% of total	Amount	% of total	Average shareholding
Scotland	231	40.5	£353,000	21.3	£1,528.9
London area	229	40.2	£889,900	55.3	£3,886
NW England	77	13.5	£260,850	16.2	£3,244.8
Midlands and West	11	2	£ 55,600	3.4	£5,045.4
Yorkshire and East	22	4	£ 49,250	3	£2,386.6

England thus provided 79% of the original subscription. While some investors may have been expatriate Scots, for the majority it must have simply appeared as a good speculation. At the first meeting of the board, on 6 August 1845, Hope Johnstone was elected chairman, and there were fourteen other directors. Rankine was confirmed as secretary. Locke & Errington had been named as engineers to the line in the prospectus, which they had helped to draw up, and their prime task now was to monitor the contractors and report back to the board.

Construction was divided into sections, Carlisle to Garriongill (84 3/4 miles), Carstairs-Edinburgh (27 1/2 miles), and Garnqueen-Greenhill (10 miles). The line ran from Carlisle to Carstairs[3], where it divided, the Glasgow line running to Garriongill, twelve miles north of Carstairs, where it met the already existing Wishaw & Coltness Railway. The Wishaw & Coltness track was followed as far as Whifflat (now Whifflet), and from there the Glasgow, Garnkirk & Coatbridge Railway was to be used. A new agreement had been made with the latter company on 10 September, giving its stockholders a guaranteed dividend of 8% on stock of £156,355 4s. 2d.[4]. At this time the shares of the Glasgow, Garnkirk & Coatbridge were not fully paid up, so the Caledonian had £42,000 of its capital to call on. At Carstairs the junction was laid for direct running between Glasgow and Edinburgh, and Glasgow and Carlisle; Carlisle-Edinburgh trains had to reverse direction. With so much preliminary work already done, construction could begin immediately. A large crowd assembled at Lampitsholm, near Carstairs, on 4 September, to cheer as Ladies Belhaven and Macdonald Lockhart turned the first sod on the line to Carlisle, and Mrs. Cochrane Baillie and Mrs. Monteith did the same for the lines to Edinburgh and Glasgow[5]. At another ceremony near Lockerbie House on 11 October, Lady Jane Johnstone Douglas cut another 'first sod' on the Carlisle line. The Edinburgh line was new all the way, crossing the southern outliers of the Pentland Hills and running on the west side of the range, through the Calder district and terminating at Lothian Road on the west of the city centre. The central spike of the CR's trident diverged at Gartsherrie for the short section on the Monkland & Kirkintilloch Railway to a junction at Garnqueen, from where new Caledonian metals were laid, past Cumbernauld into the Scottish midlands as far as Greenhill, six miles south of Stirling. Agreement about building the new joint Citadel Station in Carlisle had been reached with the Lancaster & Carlisle and Newcastle & Carlisle Railways; only the Maryport & Carlisle stayed aloof[6].

The Railways of 1845

The year of 1845 was a portentous one for Scottish railways. At the first statutory meeting of the Caledonian, on 6 August, Hope Johnstone, commenting on the Acts already passed, remarked that "Companies with ample subscribed capitals and 10 per cent deposited had been formed for extending the Caledonian system into every part of Scotland"[7]. The Caledonian Board's first report on 27 August noted that "The last session of Parliament presents an uninterrupted series of successes in favour of what the Board of Trade aptly designated the 'Caledonian System' of railway communication in Scotland". Even if it was not to be the only railway linking Scotland and England, it intended to be the premier line north of the border. Parliamentary approval was also given to several other lines. From the end-on junction with the Caledonian at Greenhill, the Scottish Central Railway was to run via Stirling to Perth. There it would meet two other newly-approved railways, the Dundee & Perth (now revived), along the Firth of Tay, and the Scottish Midland Junction, to be built through Strathmore to Forfar. The Scottish Midland Junction's Act empowered it to buy up the Newtyle & Coupar Angus and Newtyle & Glammiss Railways, both of which were struggling financially, and these purchases were completed by January 1846. Between Forfar and Arbroath, and Dundee and Arbroath, railways already existed, though of incompatible gauge with the new lines. The Aberdeen Railway Act

J.J. Hope Johnstone, first chairman of the Caledonian Company.

provided for a standard gauge line from Guthrie, between Forfar and Arbroath, to run via Montrose, Laurencekirk and Stonehaven to Aberdeen. This was an alteration of the Aberdeen Railway's first proposal to make its line via Brechin, and caused anger in the Scottish Midland Junction boardroom[8]. Here was a string of local companies, but the effect was to complete a spine of railway all the way from London to Aberdeen. In a single great package, the entire route of the 'Caledonian System' was granted, though the Caledonian appeared only as a segment, albeit a major one, of the Carlisle-Aberdeen railway. If anyone thought that operating it would be a straightforward business, the next few months would disabuse them.

Gushetfaulds in 1848, with the embankment works of the Glasgow, Barrhead & Neilston Direct Railway. Painting by William Simpson (1823-99).

Simultaneously with the Caledonian's Act, Parliament also authorised the Clydesdale Junction Railway, a 14 $\frac{1}{2}$ mile line intended to carry traffic on the south side of Glasgow, from Motherwell to join the already existing Polloc & Govan Railway at Rutherglen, and so completing a link between the Glasgow-Paisley railway and the Wishaw & Coltness at Motherwell. Parliament approved the Caledonian's purchase of these lines on 18 August. Another projected line with whose committee the Caledonian was on friendly and co-operative terms was the Glasgow, Barrhead & Neilston Direct, authorised on 4th August 1845. But with the Scottish Central, a honeymoon spirit was brief. For the management of the SCR, there was an attractive third party in the successful Edinburgh & Glasgow Railway. From the E&G point of view, a link with the line to the north was essential to develop its prosperity. The Caledonian-Scottish Central joint committee for the Castlecary branch agreed unanimously that the Caledonian "should carry the traffic of both Railways on equal terms"; and a sub-committee of three directors from each company was "to see the Garnkirk Railway directors next day and buy that line for the Caledonian and Scottish Central Railway Companies," each paying half[9]. But the SCR board declined the opportunity, and the Caledonian was left to its own negotiations with the Glasgow, Garnkirk & Coatbridge. It was becoming plain that the SCR was more interested in a deal with the Edinburgh & Glasgow, even though the Caledonian made another offer which included the possibility of joint ownership of the Castlecary branch as well as of the Glasgow, Garnkirk & Coatbridge. On 25 September, the Scottish Central informed the CR that it was entering into merger negotiations with the Edinburgh & Glasgow. The West Coast route seemed in danger of falling apart even as its construction was beginning, especially when the Scottish Central, on 25 November, also expressed its intention to either merge with or lease the Scottish Midland Junction Railway[10].

The 'Mania', and its Aftermath

By this time, the so-called 'Railway Mania' was in full swing. Two considerations drove it along. The first was a concern for local welfare – every town and large village was convinced that not to have a railway was to be left behind by progress and prosperity. The second was human greed. Railway shares seemed to be on an ever-upwards price curve. It was possible to put down a deposit on shares with borrowed money, resell them at a higher price, pay back the loan and pocket the profit. Newspapers whipped the atmosphere of speculation into fever. Of course it could not last. The number of schemes proposed could never have been supported by the capital available, even if they had all been perfectly sound and sensible. Many were duplications of one another. By the end of the year, prices were already dropping and in the spring of 1846 fell even further. Thousands of people lost a lot of money and many had got considerably richer. The mania was less apparent in Scotland than it was in England. By the end of that year, 879 projected railway companies had failed to produce their plans. Only seven of these were in Scotland, "and none was carried the length of an issue of scrip"[11]. But the effect was to make the public at large distrustful of railway schemes, and railway shares became hard to sell. Among the projects of 1845 was a railway through Galloway to Portpatrick, harbour for traffic to the north of Ireland; Mark Huish of the Grand Junction Railway encouraged the Caledonian to lease this line or take it over[12]; another was the Peebles & Moffat Direct & Caledonian Junction, to run from Peebles via Tweedsmuir to meet the CR line at Beattock. But these and many other projects did not materialise, and the Caledonian directors had much else to think about. Negotiations were going on with the Glasgow, Barrhead & Neilston Direct company, with a lease agreed on 27 January for 8% on its ordinary stock and 6% on its Debenture stock. Such 'guaranteed dividend' purchases were intended to bypass the cost and hazard of obtaining formal Acts of Parliament, and also to make undertakings not provided for in the Caledonian Company's founding Act[13]. On the face of it there was no obvious reason for the Caledonian to involve itself with the Neilston line, but subsequent events would reveal it as a strategic move, with an eye on the North Ayrshire traffic. The Caledonian Extension Railway was also still a serious proposition. Other proposed lines cited by Hope Johnston as relating to the 'Caledonian System' were the Caledonian & Dumbarton Junction, and the Inverness & Perth Junction Railways. It could be said that in its chairman's view, the 'Caledonian System' was a virtual monopoly of Scottish railways. Further capital of £1,275,000 was to be raised by the issue of 51,000 £25 shares, approved by an extraordinary general meeting on 5 November; a board meeting on the same day approved a proposal for amalgamation with the Glasgow, Paisley & Greenock, and (on 4 December) the purchase of the Airdrie & Coatbridge Railway for £11 a share. A short but strategic line, the General Terminus & Glasgow Harbour Railway, was being projected to provide a link to the southern quays of the Clyde from the Polloc & Govan Railway, and the Caledonian was extremely keen to make a formal agreement with it[14].

A provisional working agreement with the Glasgow, Paisley & Greenock was signed on 27 January 1846, guaranteeing a 4% dividend, or 1% less than the Caledonian Ordinary dividend, whichever was higher, on the Glasgow, Paisley & Greenock original stock of £500,000. Locke & Errington's engineers were well-paid by the Caledonian, but were also involved with other companies, and Rankine complained to Locke that Dundas (salary £500) and Collister (£800) also appeared to be working for the Morningside & Wilsontown Railway. Locke replied that three directors of the CR had sanctioned this, and "it behoves them individually to abstain from soliciting

Engraving of a Caledonian locomotive from the early years of the Company. Other versions represent it as CR No. 15, built by the Vulcan Foundry in 1847. The CR had some 64 engines of this type.

any Agent of the Company to undertake other work"[15]. Engineers were of course in great demand and such lucrative multiple employments were common. Rankine himself left the company, and on 10 June James Butler Williams was appointed manager and secretary. Confirmations of mergers and leases were being pursued through 1846. The Glasgow, Garnkirk & Coatbridge was drawn into the Caledonian, at first by a leasing agreement from 1 January 1846, at 8% a year on a capital of £156,355. While construction went on, in August the Caledonian took over the uncompleted Clydesdale Junction, assuring itself of a southern approach to Glasgow in addition to the line to Glebe Street. Just prior to its amalgamation with the Caledonian, the Clydesdale Junction had acquired the Polloc & Govan Railway. William Dixon got 2,400 Caledonian shares for the Polloc & Govan, and the Clydesdale Junction Railway stockholders were guaranteed an annual 6% on its capital of £450,000[16]. The Caledonian also undertook to work the Wishaw & Coltness Railway from 1 January 1847, taking a lease at 10.5% per annum on a capital of £240,000[17]. The Wishaw & Coltness had already obtained an Act for an extension eastwards to Cleland. Acquisition of this line, in particular, was something of a *coup*, as the company, like the Monklands lines, had been very much within the sphere of influence of the Edinburgh & Glasgow Railway. But the price was steep, committing the CR to pay £25,000 a year.

Other companies were also merging or combining, in what was a tough year for managements, with money again very tight and yet an urgent need to spend, both on construction and on acquisition. Land purchase for the Caledonian, originally estimated at £173,000, had come to £389,000[18]. Landowners had come to see railways as cash cows, and the Caledonian paid heavily for the years of delay. But the road interests were comparatively amenable, and in July 1846 the Caledonian agreed to purchase the public debt of the Glasgow-Carlisle Turnpike Trust (£23,803) for £15,000. The Dundee & Perth company obtained powers to buy the debt-cumbered Dundee & Newtyle, in the Dundee & Perth (Amendment) Act of 1846, but in the end it preferred to take a 999-year lease of the line, at £1,400 per annum, from 1 November 1846[19]. From mid-1846, the position of the Caledonian had been greatly strengthened when the several railway companies operating between Lancaster and London merged to form the London & North Western Railway, making Britain's largest joint-stock company. The ambitious Caledonian Extension Railway plan was modified in an agreement with the North British in March, accepting Peebles as a 'frontier' point between the companies, thus truncating its eastern arm[20], but strong objections were raised by landowners and other railway companies during the committee stage, and it was rejected by Parliament on 29 June. A rival scheme was more successful: the Glasgow, Dumfries & Carlisle Railway was authorised by Parliament in August, despite strong opposition mounted by the Caledonian, and granted running powers over the Caledonian between a junction at Gretna and Carlisle. In triumphal celebrations at Dumfries, Hope Johnstone was burned in effigy[21]. But the Lancaster & Carlisle Railway was firmly allied to the LNWR and the Caledonian, and the Nithsdale company found itself frozen out of discussions on Anglo-Scottish traffic. Its Act provided for the Caledonian to lease the line between Annan and Gretna Junction, but this element was repealed by a further Act of 9 July 1847[22]. Another decision with important implications for the Caledonian was made on 16 July, with the Act for the Stirlingshire and Midland Junction Railway, a subsidiary of the Edinburgh & Glasgow, to run from the Scottish Central line just south of Larbert through the district of Grahamston to Polmont on the E&G, thus giving the Scottish Central a direct Edinburgh connection. Much more helpfully to the Caledonian, on 29 July Parliament refused to sanction the amalgamation of the Scottish Central and the Edinburgh & Glasgow companies. Objections from the Caledonian were crucial to the rejection, though there had also been deep reservations among English shareholders of the E&G, and the CR board meeting of 16 August 1846 expressed its great satisfaction at the outcome. The directors had already launched an initiative to secure the northern lines. A document was prepared setting out a basis of agreement for the Scottish Central Railway to be leased in perpetuity by the Caledonian, Lancaster & Carlisle, and LNWR companies acting jointly. An annual rental of £75,000 was proposed, and the SCR would receive half the profits obtained above a certain level. A joint management board would be established. In October the board created a sub-committee to handle negotiations with the SCR and it was now agreed that the Scottish Central should be leased at £71,400 a year, equivalent to 7% of its capital value of £1,020,000. A 12-man board would have six SCR directors and six from the other companies, with Locke or Errington (doubtless relieved that the West Coast 'Plan A' was back on track) to act as arbiters if necessary[23]. A special meeting of SCR shareholders on Tuesday 10 November 1846 unanimously endorsed the agreement. At this time Errington had already warned the SCR directors that opening of their line from Greenhill to Stirling would be delayed to 1 October 1847, rather than the originally-anticipated April[24]. At the same time, the Edinburgh & Glasgow Railway declared itself willing to transfer its line to the Caledonian. Payment would be 8% per annum on a capital of £2,000,000 from March 1847 to March 1849, and then 9%, until the Caledonian Railway itself should reach a dividend of 6% on its own Ordinary shares, at which point the dividends of both companies should be increased at the same rate until the E&G dividend reached 10%. All profits after that would go to the Caledonian. The Caledonian Board was quite prepared to take on this huge obligation if the LNWR and

Lancaster and Carlisle would share the liability[25], but they refused. From the beginning the Caledonian was setting an expansive style, creating a sort of Caley mystique, as if it had bottomless coffers.

Pressure for Completion

The development of railways within Glasgow was becoming an increasingly complex and disputed issue. Much of the central area was already slums, and new residential districts were spreading on both sides of the river. Acquisition of land was increasingly difficult, and expensive. Vested interests included the Town Council, the Clyde Trustees and the Admiralty, all jealous of their rights. At the beginning of 1846 there was no railway access to the quays on either bank, and no railway bridge over the Clyde. Its north bank was primarily used for landing imports, and two-thirds of the export trade went from the south bank[26]. In the course of 1846 four Parliamentary select committees and one Royal Commission considered a variety of schemes for new terminals for both goods and passengers. Each proposal was energetically opposed by rival interests. Aware that Glebe Street was a badly-placed terminus, the Caledonian Board participated with the Glasgow, Barrhead & Neilston Railway in planning a joint line, the Glasgow Southern Terminal Railway, from a point close to Titwood Place, Pollokshields, to cross the river to a terminus at Dunlop Street (the present St. Enoch Square). An Act was obtained on 16 July, and the ground of the Glasgow Towns Hospital was acquired for £17,275 10s.[27]. William Tite was commissioned to design the terminus, but the Clyde crossing was abandoned, partly through the obstructive attitude of the Admiralty, which demanded a swing bridge over the river[28], and partly through opposition from promoters of rival schemes. The Glasgow Southern Terminal Railway was not to get further than a station named South Side, in the angle of Pollokshaws Road and Cathcart Street in the Gorbals district, and the company was absorbed into the Glasgow, Barrhead & Neilston Direct on 2 July 1847.

Various lines of railway between Dumfries and Canonbie were promoted by the Caledonian during 1847, with the intention of blocking the Glasgow, Dumfries & Carlisle, and the North British company's intentions for a Hawick-Carlisle line, but these spoiling efforts did not succeed. Hope Johnstone's board, while its own project had yet to earn a penny, also remained ready to swallow up anything that came along. The Caledonian & Dumbartonshire Junction Railway, originally intended to run from the Edinburgh & Glasgow line near Cowlairs in a great curve round the built-up area to reach the north bank of the Clyde at Dumbarton, from where it would send one line up the coast to Helensburgh, and another up the Leven valley to Balloch on the south shore of Loch Lomond, had made a leasing agreement with the Glasgow, Garnkirk & Coatbridge company, now folded into the

'Garnkirk & Glasgow Railway, View of the Depot Looking South', by D. O. Hill, S.A., published on
2 January 1832, one of a set of four plates celebrating the opening of the G&GR.
The locomotive 'St Rollox' is about to depart with a train of empty wagons.

Caledonian. The Caledonian, with dreams of extending its system into the western Highlands, was willing to lease it at 5% on its £600,000 capital[29], but in the end the Dumbarton company decided to go it alone. Other schemes for railway development in the western Highlands had emerged in 1845-46, encouraged partly by the 'mania' and partly by hopeful expectations of lead and even silver mining. The Scottish Grand Junction Railway was to run between Callander and Oban, with a northern link to the proposed Inverness & Perth line at Dalwhinnie and a southern arm to Invernan at the head of Loch Lomond. The Caledonian & Great Northern Direct Railway was proposed to run from Milngavie to Crianlarich, and a provisional arrangement was made for it to be worked by the Caledonian. But in the harsh economic climate of 1846 the scheme was dropped. The Scottish Grand Junction obtained an Act, but though it kept up a shadowy existence until 1852, it was never able to assemble enough financial backing to make a start. Its leading promoter was the Marquis of Breadalbane, who would play a prominent part in the Scottish Central Railway's affairs.

The final section of the Lancaster & Carlisle Railway was opened between Kendal and Carlisle on 15 December 1846, and this, together with anxiety about the competing railway schemes, intensified the sense of urgency to get the whole London-Glasgow and Edinburgh line complete. The LNWR and Lancaster & Carlisle joined with the Caledonian in offering a premium to the contractors for the work to be speeded up. If the Carlisle-Beattock section could be completed by 1 August 1847, £20,000 would be paid, or £17,000 if it was completed by the end of that month. And if the entire line were finished by November 1, £50,000 extra would be paid. After negotiation with John Stephenson, this sum was increased to £60,000[30].

In December 1846, shareholders' meetings of both the Scottish Central and the London & North Western had ratified the agreement for lease of the SCR. Still keen to ensure its control of the northern route, the CR board set up a sub-committee in January 1847, consisting of Hope Johnstone, Col. William MacDonald of Powderhall, and John Anderson, to work out the terms of an agreement with the Scottish Midland Junction, on similar lines to that effected (though not yet submitted for Parliamentary approval) with the Scottish Central. SCR members as well as representatives of the Lancaster and Carlisle and LNWR joined this committee. Colonel MacDonald and John Anderson were received as members of the SCR board. But what may have looked like plain sailing soon turned out otherwise. Negotiations with the Edinburgh & Glasgow Railway failed to reach an agreement, and though a letter from Peter Blackburn, the E&G chairman, to Hope Johnstone on 30 January expressed a hope for friendly relations nevertheless, with each company confining itself to its own district, he declared stark opposition to the CR's plan for leasing the Scottish Central: "we can never agree to a Caledonian monopoly of the Central"[31]. February 1847 was a month of intense activity in railway affairs. A new suitor for the SCR had appeared in the form of the Edinburgh & Perth Railway, a North British-backed concern which had risen on the ashes of a previous failed venture, proposing to build a direct Edinburgh-Perth line from the ferry pier at North Queensferry, via Kinross and Glenfarg. Yet another player was the Edinburgh & Northern Railway, which was actually building a line across Fife between the other Forth ferry at Burntisland and the Tay ferry at Tayport, and had authorisation to build a branch from Ladybank to Perth. It also had wider ambitions for lines in Perthshire, and naturally had no wish to see the direct Queensferry-Perth line succeed. Anyone with an interest in the Caledonian now had to realise that instead of a single trunk line from the south to Perth, there would be at least one alternative route via the Edinburgh & Northern – albeit including a ferry crossing – and the threat of another. For investors in the Scottish Central this was not good news, and with vociferous disagreement among its shareholders, the SCR board was in disarray. Meanwhile, the Scottish Midland Junction company was keen to secure its own position, whether by a lease or merger agreement, with another company. With four Caledonian directors, including Hope Johnstone, on the Scottish Midland Junction board, the Caley was in prime position, but negotiations were not easy. On 6 February, representatives of the Caledonian and its English allies, and the Scottish Central, met George Buchanan of the Scottish Midland Junction, in London. Two weeks of haggling ensued. The Scottish Midland Junction's negotiating position was weakened by the fact that it too was now challenged by alternative routes. Traffic coming from the north could be sent by way of Arbroath and Dundee and onwards by the Tay ferry and the Edinburgh & Northern: it had no monopoly other than on traffic originating in Strathmore, and even that could go by the Dundee & Newtyle (on which the Dundee & Perth had its 999-year lease) to Dundee harbour. On the 18th, a lease of the Scottish Midland Junction by the SCR at 6% per annum on its capital of £600,000 was agreed. Any pofits above the £60,000 level would be divided in proportion with the two companies' capital. The Caledonian, the Lancaster and Carlisle and LNWR gave their assent, but this did not end disagreement within the SCR board, and on 29 April 1847, it was informed of Lord Breadalbane's resignation as its chairman and a director. Despite his involvement in the initial overtures, he had never been in favour of the Caledonian link.

Meanwhile, on 19 February the Caledonian set up a committee to negotiate a leasing agreement with the Dundee & Perth company, whose line was almost complete – opening on 24 May 1847 to Barnhill on the east bank of the

Tay at Perth. The board minutes of that date also note the purchase of additional shares in the Scottish Midland, and – conjointly with the Dundee & Perth – of shares in the Dundee & Arbroath Railway "in order to counteract the movements of the Edinburgh & Northern Company". Though noted in the minutes, this misuse of the Caledonian's capital was never made public to the shareholders. In February Mr. Butler Williams, the secretary, died suddenly. The top management team was always very small, and its pressure of work intense. The loss of such a key figure must have made things very difficult at this time of multiple negotiations. On 26 February Archibald Gibson, 28 years old, Edinburgh-born but who had been assistant secretary of the Manchester, Sheffield & Lincolnshire Railway, was confirmed as assistant secretary, at £300 a year. On the same day it was resolved to borrow £100,000 on top of the CR's existing loan debt of £261,000, of which £197,000 was at 5% interest and the rest at 4.5%.

An early amalgamation between the Caledonian and the Glasgow, Paisley & Greenock Railway was considered so certain that the Caledonian joined with it in setting up a new locomotive works by the Greenock terminus. It seems that the works, begun in the autumn of 1846, were financed by the Caledonian: the Greenock company's half-yearly meeting in September 1846 was informed that "Preparations were in progress at the Greenock Station for building a large portion of the engines and carriages required for working the Caledonian line". By the next meeting in March 1847 they were in operation, referred to as "the extensive and valuable works which have been erected by the Caledonian Railway." Managed by Robert Sinclair, the works were described as large and airy. Locomotives had been designed with standardised parts with "little flummery or gewgaw", to haul passenger trains at 40 mph "up the steepest inclines", and goods trains of 600 tons at 20 mph. First class carriages under construction were double-floored with horsehair insulation, second class were mahogany-lined, and even thirds had windows and inside lamps[32].

1846: East Quay Lane, Greenock, leading from Cathcart Street Station to the steamer quay. (*Views and Reminiscences of Old Greenock*)

CHAPTER 3. The First Years, 1847-1850

Open to Beattock

In its determination to assure the Company's position in the Scottish railway scene as a strong and preferably dominant element, the Caledonian board pressed ahead with dynamic zeal, even though the general economic situation was sluggish. The foundation stone of the Edinburgh station at Lothian Road was ceremoniously laid on 9 April 1847, and at the April half-yearly shareholders' meeting, held in Edinburgh, with William Lockhart in the chair, approval was given to a slew of measures, including an increase of borrowing powers by £150,000 on top of the £700,000 of the 1845 Act, and the preparation of 11 bills for Parliament. Among agreements approved were the lease of the Dundee & Perth Railway at 8% per annum on a capital of £450,000, and of the Dundee & Arbroath at 8% on £266,666. With the Dundee & Perth came the lease of the Newtyle Railway, and the undertaking of its £15,000 debts; and the purchase of the Dundee harbour branch for £5,750. Seven Acts were obtained in July, requiring an aggregate capital of £1,700,000 plus borrowing facilities of £665,300. Branches to Granton, Fauldhouse and Rigside, Wilsontown, Biggar and Broughton, and Douglas, Lesmahagow and Strathaven, were all approved, along with a new terminal station in Glasgow, enlargement of the Edinburgh station, the purchase of the Wishaw & Coltness Railway, amalgamation with the Glasgow Paisley & Greenock, and lease of the Glasgow, Barrhead & Neilston Direct Railway. Glasgow's new terminus was to be at Buchanan Street. The Glasgow, Garnkirk & Coatbridge had already obtained an Act for a high-level station here, and had built "numerous and lofty arches" in preparation but the Caledonian's engineers disapproved, and the arches were demolished: "Thus were the elevated pretensions of the Garnkirk … put an end to."[1] The board meeting of 7 July 1847 approved the appointment of Captain Joshua Coddington, R.E., as secretary and general manager. He had been a government inspector of railways, and his contract was for ten years, at a salary of £1,800 for three years and £2,000 thereafter[2]. His expertise was in the engineering side of operations rather than in management and administration. Company uniforms were to be modelled on those of the LNWR, but the CR buttons featured a thistle design, with the company name. On 10 August, Robert Sinclair, locomotive superintendent of the Glasgow, Paisley & Greenock, was confirmed in the same post on the Caledonian, at a total salary of £700 a year, of which the CR contributed £500. By this time, with the Act of amalgamation passed, the Glasgow, Paisley & Greenock considered itself "virtually incorporated with the Caledonian"[3], though stocks had not been merged.

Scottish, English and Irish navvies worked on the line, and apart from one serious riot at Lockerbie in the winter of 1845-46, they were relatively peaceful. On piece-work, a man could earn up to 3s. 6d. a day. The contractors operated the iniquitous 'tommy shop' system, paying the men monthly and letting them run up debts for goods that could only be got from the contractors' own shop. But the Caledonian was praised for employing clergymen of various denominations to minister to the men; and it also hired the Dryfesdale parish teacher to give evening classes at Lockerbie[4]. In the summer of 1847 fever was rife among the navvies on the Ecclefechan-Beattock section, identified as "black-spotted typhus", and there were many deaths. Medical men blamed the men's poor "hard and dry" diet, with no vegetables, the huts of wet turf in which they slept, and their "irregular habits"[5]. Thomas Carlyle, revisiting his home ground, thought "I have not in my travels seen anything uglier than that disorganic mass of labourers, sunk three-fold deeper in brutality by the three-fold wages they are getting"[6]. Builders and joiners were also working on the stations, whose architect was William Tite (appointed by Locke), and who chose the 'Early English' Gothic style. Salaries for station staff were approved on 27 May, including £1 10s. a week for the 'Station Keeper' at Gretna, plus free house and coal; £2 a week for the same post at Lockerbie, £3 at Motherwell and £300 a year at the Glasgow station. Porters were to receive £1 a week. Work on converting the Lanarkshire lines and equipment to standard gauge was also being carried out in the summer of 1847. By now, upwards of 20,000 men were engaged on the works, with four locomotives and 3,500 horses. Much of the track ballast was slag from the Shotts Iron company, to which an access line was built[7].

CALEDONIAN RAILWAY TIME TABLE,

ON AND AFTER 10TH SEPTEMBER, 1847.

(Until further Notice.)

CARLISLE AND BEATTOCK.

NOTICE.—*The Doors of the Booking Offices will be Closed punctually at the Hours fixed for the Departure of the Trains, after which no Person can be admitted.—Passengers, to ensure being Booked, should arrive at the Stations and obtain their Tickets Ten Minutes earlier than the Times mentioned in the following Table.*

Distance.	Edinburgh and Glasgow to Carlisle, &c.	CLASS 1 2 & 3	CLASS 1 & 2	CLASS 1 & 2	Distance.	Carlisle, &c. to Edinburgh and Glasgow.	CLASS 1 & 2	CLASS 1 2 & 3	CLASS 1 & 2
			A.M.	P.M.		Trains leave	P.M.	A.M.	A.M.
	EDINBURGH by Coach	...	7 0	4 30		LONDON	8 45	......	10 0
	GLASGOW do.	...	5 15	2 30		LIVERPOOL.....................	... ..	7 30	3 50
Miles.	Trains leave	A.M.	P.M.			MANCHESTER........................	......	7 40	4 0
5	BEATTOCK	6 30	1 0	10 30		PRESTON...........................	5 35	9 35	5 35
10¾	WAMPHRAY	6 45	1 15	......	Miles.		A.M.	P.M.	P.M.
13¾	NETHERCLEUGH	7 5	1 33	......	4	CARLISLE......	10 0	2 30	10 10
19½	LOCKERBIE..............................	7 15	1 45	11 15	8½	ROCKCLIFF..............................	10 12	2 42	......
26½	ECCLEFECHAN...........................	7 30	2 0	11 30	13	GRETNA	10 25	2 55	10 45
31	KIRKPATRICK	7 50	2 20	... ..	20	KIRKPATRICK	10 40	3 10	......
35½	GRETNA	8 5	2 35	......	25¾	ECCLEFECHAN..................	11 0	3 30	11 10
39½	ROCKCLIFF	8 18	2 48	......	28½	LOCKERBIE.....................	11 15	3 45	11 25
	Arrive at CARLISLE	8 30	3 0	12 30	34½	NETHERCLEUGH..................	11 25	3 55	......
		P.M.	A.M.		39½	WAMPHRAY	11 47	4 15	......
	PRESTON	1 25	7 53	5 10		Arrive at BEATTOCK	12 0	4 30	12 0
	MANCHESTER..............	3 5	......	6 35					
	LIVERPOOL...........................	3 15	9 45	6 45		EDINBURGH by Coach..............	6 P.M.		6 A.M.
			A.M.	P.M.		GLASGOW by Coach......	7 43		7 33
	LONDON..	... ...	5 32	1 0					

FARES.

	First Class and Inside Coach.	Second Class and Outside Coach.
Between GLASGOW AND CARLISLE.....................30/6	...	... 20/
... EDINBURGH AND CARLISLE...........................29/6	...	... 19/6
..., CARLISLE AND BEATTOCK.................. ....8/6 First Class.	5/6 Second Class.	3/4 Third Class.

✱ The Company will not be answerable for any Luggage, unless Booked and Paid for; and, for better security, Passengers are recommended to take Carpet Bags and small Packages inside the Carriages, and to have their address written on all their Luggage in full.—Children under Ten Years of Age, Half Price; Children in arms, unable to walk; pass Free.

HORSES.—Grooms in charge of Horses to pay Second Class Fares.—The Company will not be liable in any case for loss or damage to any Horse or other Animal above the value of £40, unless a declaration of its value, signed by the Owner or his Agent at the time of booking, shall have been given to them, and by such declaration the Owner shall be bound; the Company not being in any event liable to any greater amount than the value so declared. The Company will in no case be liable for injury to any Horse or other Animal, of whatever value, where such injury arises wholly or partially from fear of restiveness.—If the declared value of any Horse or other animal exceed £40, the price of conveying will, in addition to the regular fare, be after the rate of 2½ per cent., or 6d. per pound upon the declared value above £40, whatever may be the amount of such value, and for whatever distance the Horse or other Animal is to be carried.

CARRIAGES.—Passengers travelling by the Railway with Private Carriages are charged First Class, and their Servants, Second Class Fares; and corresponding Tickets are issued for each Class, which are also available for the Company's Carriages. To prevent mistakes, Passengers are requested to declare in each case the number of Servants to whom Second Class Tickets are to be issued.

N.B.—The Servants of the Company are prohibited from demanding or receiving any Gratuity from Passengers, who, it is hoped, will assist the Directors in enforcing this Regulation. Immediate dismissal follows the discovery of any Servant of the Company receiving any Gratuity.

✱ *Smoking in the Carriages and at the Stations is forbidden, under a Penalty, by Act of Parliament.*

Trains marked thus (✱) do not run on Sundays.

Booking Office in EDINBURGH, Nos. 2 & 10, Prince's Street.
... ... GLASGOW, Walker & Co., Tontine Hotel, and A. Mein and Co., Trongate.

By Order,

J. W. CODDINGTON,

Secretary.

George Graham, engineer of the CR from 1847 to 1899.

It was September 1847 before the full £50 on the original shares was collected, after nine calls on the subscribers[8]. On 1 September Captain Symons of the Board of Trade made an official inspection of the line and reported favourably, though he had to return the following week when the embankment at Mossband, just north of the River Esk, partially subsided and was speedily restored. On the 9th, the directors had an inaugural trip in pouring rain, and on the 10th, the first public passenger train from Beattock to Carlisle was driven by a 25-year old engineer, George Graham, who would soon transfer from Locke's employment to the Caledonian's. The engine was Caledonian No. 1, built at Greenock, formerly Glasgow, Paisley & Greenock No. 17; the carriages were built by Dunns of Lancaster[9]. For a few months from 10 September, Beattock was the terminus of trains from London, the 10 a.m. express from Euston reaching it at 11.16 p.m., with stage coaches waiting to complete the journeys to Glasgow and Edinburgh (Croall's Edinburgh coach was named 'The Engineer', in homage to the new technocrats). Arrival time may have been 'local time', as the LNWR, the Lancaster and Carlisle Railway and CR did not formally adopt working to Greenwich standard time until 1 December 1847. The company paid the contractors the premium of £17,000[10].

The board had much else to attend to. Once again, cordiality between the Scottish Central and the Caledonian was short-lived. The SCR, seeing itself not incorrectly as a section of infrastructure rather than a train operator, shamelessly hawked itself about; Lord Duncan, its new chairman said, "… the more anxious parties are to possess us, the more coy we shall be in yielding to the addresses of our admirers"[11]. On 11 June, the Edinburgh & Perth Railway proposal was rejected again by Parliament, and one opponent to the Scottish Central disappeared. In July Peter Blackburn, chairman of the Edinburgh & Glasgow, informed the Caledonian board that the SCR was not proceeding with the leasing agreement approved by its shareholders back in November 1846, and instead would make a contract with the Edinburgh & Glasgow Railway, "their natural ally", at 9% – unless the Caledonian would care to lease the SCR at an annual rental of £91,800. The Caledonian and its allies declined[12] and the Caley obtained a Court of Session interdict against any SCR-E&G agreement being put into effect. Inter-company and legal argument went on through the year. At this time, following the 'mania' period, it was difficult to raise large capital sums on the money market. Then in August, Blackburn proposed that the E&G and the Caledonian, with or without its English allies, should jointly lease the Scottish Central. The Central was not unwilling, if the 9% offer was still on the table[13]. But these proposals came to nothing. By January 1848, with the court interdict against its link with the Edinburgh & Glasgow confirmed, the SCR, with Breadalbane back as chairman, had backed down and was hoping for an "amicable settlement" with the Caledonian[14]. Given the state of enmity now existing between the Caledonian and the Edinburgh & Glasgow companies, it was hardly surprising that efforts at this time, started by Captain Huish of the LNWR, to arrange for a sharing of cross-border traffic between West and East Coast routes, failed to reach any agreement. More auspiciously for the CR, its Amalgamation Bill with the Glasgow Paisley & Greenock received the royal assent in the summer of 1847. Though at the Glasgow, Paisley & Greenock half-yearly meeting on 6 September, the chairman said his line "may be regarded as virtually incorporated with the Caledonian", actual incorporation did not immediately follow.

Open to Glasgow and Edinburgh

In shiny new first class carriages painted "lake colour", the directors made a successful trial trip from Glasgow to Beattock on 14 February 1848. Eighty carriages and 35 engines were ready for service[15]. Writing many years later, an observer claimed that the Company had to press open trucks with plank seating into service, through shortage of carriages[16]. Through carriages began to run between London and Glasgow from 15 February, though work was still going on at various places, including the Beattock Summit cutting, where only a single line was as yet open.

Although the opening was only 13 days before the set date, the Caledonian paid the contractors a premium of £50,000[17]. Completion of the new main line had repercussions for users of the Wishaw & Coltness and Glasgow, Garnkirk & Coatbridge Railways, whose services were absorbed into those of the Caledonian. Morningside, the Wishaw & Coltness terminus, lost its passenger service to Carluke on the new main line. At Edinburgh a locomotive depot had been set up at Dalry Road, and passenger trains between Edinburgh and Glasgow, via Carstairs, began running on 1 April. By this time the Edinburgh & Glasgow Railway was carrying more than a million passengers each year between the two cities, and the Caledonian, despite its longer route, was avid to gain a share of this traffic. At Glasgow, the Townhead Station handled all the English trains until 1 June 1849. Meeting on April 1st, the board was very conscious of the fact that extremely large sums had been paid, more were due, and the earning of real revenue had just begun. Joseph Locke, who enjoyed being known for providing reliable estimates for his engineering work, was perhaps embarrassed. He reported to the board that £1,374,128 had been paid by the company, but the contractors' total bill was now £1,465,315. He recommended that the company should accept the outstanding £91,187, and pay it in instalments, so that "Mr. Brassey would be able to fulfil his part of the contract and likewise engage personally to superintend the execution of the works"[18].

At the half-yearly meeting on 25 February, Hope Johnstone had referred to the very slow response being made by shareholders to cash calls. The directors had requested an extension of the time limit for completion of the line, and were not proposing to enter into any new contracts[19]. This phase of self-denial was short-lived, despite the current economic recession. The Clydesdale Junction project was also struggling for cash; since November 1847 the board had been considering postponement but the "liberal attitude" of the contractors, Brassey, Mackenzie & Stephenson, helped: no further call on shareholders would need be made until the spring of 1849.

In the spring of 1848, the Caledonian's agents were putting together a new Bill for the lease which the Scottish Central had agreed and then disowned, and over which the SCR Board and shareholders remained thoroughly disunited; and it was obvious the E&G would do its utmost to stop it. In June, the Bill was rejected. The House of Commons, having only three years before virtually created the blueprint of the 'Caledonian system', was now unwilling to chart a clear way forward. The 'mania' had left a hostility and sense of doubt about railway business, especially amalgamations, and 'monopoly' was a dirty word. Nevertheless, the Central needed a working agreement, since it lacked locomotives to work more than its own local services, and from 7 August, the two railways would be physically joined at Greenhill. To avoid further trouble from the E&G, an agreement was secured that it would join with the Caledonian, Lancaster and Carlisle and LNWR in equal quarter-shares of a leasing agreement with the Scottish Central. Of seven main heads, the prime ones were the equal shares, the

provision that the E&G should take a quarter share in the Scottish Midland Junction and its associate the Dundee & Perth Railway, and a division of traffic coming off the SCR that gave half the passenger traffic between Glasgow and Greenhill each to the Caledonian and the E&G, while all goods traffic went to the Caledonian. All southern traffic also went to the Caledonian, while all the East Coast traffic went by the Edinburgh & Glasgow. The agreement was to be effective from 1 September 1848. Still the Scottish Central Board, manipulated by Lord Breadalbane (an extremely grand person even for a 19th-century Marquis; he was Lord Chamberlain from 1848 to 1858), hoped for more than it was being offered, and on 26 September it declined the lease arrangement. Once again the house of cards collapsed. A week later, a goods traffic agreement was made between the Caledonian, the Central and the Edinburgh & Glasgow, relating to goods service between Edinburgh and Perth, and primarily intended to cut out the Edinburgh & Northern. Meanwhile,

Thankerton Station, opened on 15 February 1848, seen here with promotional banner for the Central Station Hotel in 1883.

as efforts to bring about a wider agreement continued, the Caledonian's own position was becoming dangerously insecure. Shareholders' anxieties centred on a proposed new issue of £745,180 worth of 7% Preference shares when already it was evident that traffic returns were inadequate to meet the aggregate of working expenses, loans and guarantees. Caledonian £50 shares had slumped to £27 5s.[20] and were still falling, while 'Guaranteed company' stocks were riding high, with Wishaw & Coltness £25 shares at £43.

Heralding what was to be a regular sub-theme of the Caledonian's business activity, various presbyteries along the line wrote to the board hoping there would be no Sunday trains. Sabbatarianism was strong among the middle class, and at successive shareholders' half-yearly meetings a motion would be proposed deploring, or seeking to ban, the running of trains on Sundays. Occasionally a director or two might support the motion, but it was always defeated. Nevertheless, Sunday services would always be extremely limited. Deference to the Sabbatarians played a part in this, though it was also accepted that the working week was from Monday to Saturday, for railwaymen as for other industrial employees. Would-be Sunday travellers were less vocal, though a 'Memorial from the Working Classes of Glasgow' asked for morning and evening Sunday trains to be provided on the Greenock Railway[21]. Anyone concerned with traffic management could not fail to know that on Sundays, the only non-working day, the number of of coaches and carts carrying passengers between adjacent towns like Glasgow, Paisley and Greenock was very large.

A Tayside route to meet the Aberdeen Railway seemed set when in January 1848 the Dundee & Perth company agreed to work the Dundee & Arbroath line, from 30 April. The lease guaranteed an 8% dividend on capital of £66,666 to be created by the Dundee & Arbroath for construction of a linking line, with a joint station in the city centre. An Act for the link line was passed on 14 August and a further Act on the 31st authorised the leasing arrangement and the renaming of the Dundee & Perth as the Dundee & Perth & Aberdeen Junction Railway (the agreement survived only until 1850). In the Spring of 1848 the Caledonian was negotiating with the Scottish Midland Junction Railway, and it was agreed on 5 May that the Caledonian should lease it, at a guaranteed dividend of 6% per annum on a capital of £500,000, and that the Edinburgh & Glasgow company should be "admitted with the Caledonian, for profit or loss on the transaction, to the extent of one fourth part"[22]. That May, the CR's engineer, Robert Sinclair, and John Collister, one of Locke & Errington's engineers, were examining the state of the plant of the Dundee & Perth, Dundee & Newtyle, and Dundee & Arbroath Railways[23], presumably with a view to possible lease or purchase. Nothing came of it, though in June the Board agreed to lend three locomotives to assist with traffic on the Dundee & Perth. At the same time the Caledonian was also seriously considering a takeover of the Newcastle & Carlisle Railway, a wholly English line, until it found that that company had failed to disclose debts in excess of £100,000[24].

English Shareholders and Scottish Directors

Behind all this, a shareholders' revolt was brewing. Many shareholders, including those with big investments, were concerned about the Caledonian's expansionist strategy and its costs. A group met at the London Tavern on 14 July, to protest and to demand that a new board be appointed. From the company's own accounts, published in December 1847, it appeared that annual costs would be £233,313, and revenue only £208,000. Yet the company wanted to raise another £745,180 with the Preference shares, whose dividends would take priority over those of original shareholders. One of the leading protestors, Mr. Abbott, opened a line of criticism that would become increasingly strident. Apart from deploring the profligacy of the expansionist policy, the leasing of other railways, etc., he complained that while 90% of Caledonian shares were held in England, all the directors, with one or two exceptions, "were natives of Edinburgh and Glasgow". English investors, having bought shares in the expectation of a respectable return, were seeing Scots managers dissipate their dividends and reduce the value of their stock. A delegate, Mr. Jacobs, was sent by the protestors to a special shareholders' meeting in Edinburgh on 20 July, but allowed himself to be persuaded that all was well, and the board's proposals were passed by a large majority, helped by proxy votes held by the directors. Divisions opened among the dissentients. A meeting of £50 shareholders in Liverpool protested angrily at the terms of the 7% Preference share sale, but the London groups disbanded on 22 August. At the Caledonian's half-yearly meeting in Edinburgh on August 31, Hope Johnstone took a relaxed view of the many criticisms: "When the mercantile community was again in activity they would get an ample return for their money"[25].

From the first, the Caledonian had matched the fares charged by the E&G between Glasgow and Edinburgh, and on 10 July it increased the number of trains and speeded up the service with four trains each way, running non-stop between the two cities in two hours. The E&G promptly matched this, but with its best train taking only an hour and a half. Competitive fare-cutting swiftly followed – good news for travellers but disastrous for company revenues – until the boards, both under pressure from anxious shareholders, achieved a truce during August.

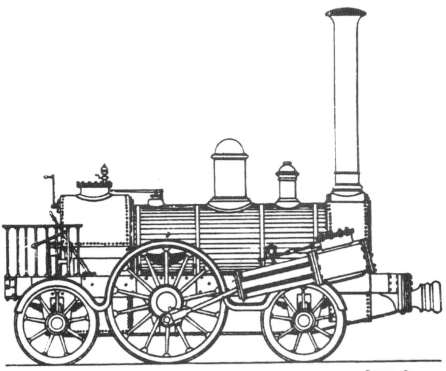

Arbroath & Forfar Railway: a product of Stirling & Co.'s East Dundee Foundry, c.1839-40.

"THE ENGINEER"   SWAIN SC

In August 1848 the Caledonian confirmed the salaries of some key managers, including Robert Sinclair's £700 a year as locomotive superintendent. Mr. Addison, superintendent of the line, got £400, and Christopher Johnstone, goods manager, £250. Locke and Errington were receiving £1,000 a year for enginering superintendence, and their colleague Collister was being paid £500 a year for his services. On 7 August the central main line of the Caledonian was completed to meet the Scottish Central, which had been open since 22 May, at Greenhill Lower Junction, from where the Central also had a link to the E&G, facing Glasgow. The CR line passed beneath the Edinburgh & Glasgow at Castlecary, two miles west of Greenhill, without a junction. A through service to Perth could now begin, and advertisements by the Scottish Central announced "Running of express trains between Perth and London in fourteen hours", at fares of £5 8s. (express), £4 7s. 10d. (first) and £3 4s. 4d. (second); no third class fares were quoted[26]. With the completion of the Scottish Midland Junction's line from 20 August, through services went beyond Perth to Forfar. The flimsy 4ft 6in tracks of the Newtyle and Coupar Angus and Newtyle & Glammiss lines had been converted to standard gauge and relaid with heavier rails. A train journey could now be made from Dundee to London, taking 15 hours. Queen Victoria was a passenger over the new route in September when a sea fog prevented her from taking the royal yacht south from Aberdeen, from her first sojourn at Balmoral Castle. In a first class carriage of the Aberdeen Railway she was conveyed from Montrose to Perth for an overnight stay, then on to Crewe the following day and London after that[27].

From its starting point at Guthrie on the Arbroath & Forfar Railway, the Aberdeen Railway had got as far as a terminus at Montrose, with a branch from Bridge of Dun to Brechin. By an agreement made in late 1845 it had a lease on the Arbroath & Forfar "in perpetuity" from its own formal opening date of 1 February 1848. At the southern end of the line's prolongation to Aberdeen, a triangular link was to be formed between the stations at Guthrie and Glasterlaw, and a point just south of Friockheim, thus providing the Aberdeen Railway with connection both to the coastal line at Arbroath and the inland line via Forfar to Perth. Although the Dundee & Perth & Aberdeen Junction's wooden bridge across the Tay in Perth was not completed until 8 March 1849, that city was becoming an important railway centre, with the Edinburgh & Northern Railway coming up from Burntisland through Fife and Kinross-shire by way of Ladybank and Bridge of Earn. Arbroath, which had had two unconnected stations, became a railway junction in 1848 with the construction of a link line between the Dundee & Arbroath and the Arbroath & Forfar. These lines were re-gauged to the national standard. Financial troubles were hitting the Aberdeen Railway, however. A shareholders' meeting on 26 October 1848 considered two proposals to work the completed line. One was from the London & North Western, presumably in concert with the Caledonian, to pay £80,000 on account, against valuation of the assets, and to work the line for five years. The other was from the Edinburgh & Northern Railway, backed by the North British and York, Newcastle &

Berwick companies, to take all of the Aberdeen company's authorised new stock (£276,000) to be repaid at a rate of £20,000 a month; and to work the line for 20 years for two-fifths of the receipts. Guarantees on dividends would be given. Neither offer was deemed acceptable, and the Aberdeen company was forced to soldier on alone, raising money by issuing Preference shares[28].

The Glasgow, Barrhead & Neilston Direct Railway, worked by the Caledonian, opened between South Side and a terminus at Arthurlie Street, Barrhead, on 27 September 1848. Earlier that month, at the Caledonian's half-yearly meeting on the 15th, it was reported that the Company had renounced the option of incorporating Glasgow, Paisley & Greenock 4% stock with the CR Ordinary stock, "whereby the guarantee of 4% has become absolute"[29]. The dividend rate was moderate compared to some of the other guarantees, but it was another fetter to the Board's chains. It was also committed to paying 4% on Glasgow, Paisley & Greenock Debenture stock of £216,666 and either 7% or 6% on 20,000 new Preference shares at £7 10s. issued by the Greenock company, the rate depending on when the shares were fully paid up[30]. The difficulties over the amalgamation were ostensibly because the Glasgow, Paisley & Greenock objected to the terms of the Caledonian's arrangement with the Scottish Central, but the Greenock management had some shady practices to hide. The CR Board recorded its "great dissatisfaction"[31], but it also had many other concerns. Cash remained extremely tight, and a general instruction went to all departments to exercise "the utmost economy"[32]. On 8 November, an agreement was reached with the Dundee & Perth & Aberdeen Junction Railway to lease its lines at 8%. If the Aberdeen Railway shareholders were alarmed by this move, many Caledonian owners were both alarmed and angry. Disgruntled shareholders, concerned about what seemed an incessant profligate policy of offering substantial guarantees to other companies, met in Manchester at the beginning of November and passed a vote of no confidence in the Board. At a crowded special meeting on 10 November in the Euston Hotel, London, the directors defended the joint lease of the Scottish Midland Junction Railway, with the Edinburgh & Glasgow company. Protesters challenged the competence of the CR, which had been formed to provide a railway from Carlisle to Edinburgh and Glasgow, to bind itself to pay guaranteed dividends on railways to Perth, Dundee and Aberdeen, but the Board got a narrow majority. On 22 November the Edinburgh & Glasgow Board gained approval from its shareholders for the leasing arrangement with the Caledonian, Lancaster & Carlisle and LNWR Companies, in relation to the Scottish Central; and with the Caledonian in relation to the Dundee & Perth & Aberdeen and the Scottish Midland Junction. Traffic would be shared or divided as follows[33]:

1. Edinburgh-Glasgow traffic to the E&G.
2. Glasgow-England traffic to stations south and west of York and Newcastle to the CR.
3. Glasgow-Paisley-Greenock traffic to the CR.
4. Glasgow-Edinburgh-Newcastle traffic to the E&G.
5. Scottish Central traffic to and from Edinburgh to the E&G.
6. Scottish Central traffic to and from Glasgow: goods to the CR; passenger to the E&G, but the Caledonian to receive half the passenger revenue, because the E&G is contributing only a quarter-share of the guaranteed dividends.
7. Traffic from the CR and E&G to north of Fife to go via the Scottish Central.

It was a neat and tidy arrangement, and the Edinburgh & Glasgow directors were apparently willing to accept it even though they were doubtful about the profitability of the Scottish Midland Junction and Dundee & Perth & Aberdeen Junction companies.

In December the General Terminus & Glasgow Harbour Railway, giving much wider access to the southern quays than the Polloc & Govan's line to Windmillcroft Dock, was complete, and it opened on 30 March 1849. Linked to the Polloc & Govan, an Act of 2 July 1847 had also authorised it to form links with the Glasgow, Paisley, Kilmarnock & Ayr and the Glasgow Southern Terminus lines. Its cranes greatly speeded up the business of coal loading. From 1 June 1849 its link to the Clydesdale Junction Railway, the prime artery of coal traffic from Lanarkshire, was also open. Though it remained an independent company until 1865, it was part of the 'Caledonian system'.

A combination of financial worries and shareholder agitation drove the repeated efforts to share traffic and reduce competition. Yet Hope Johnstone's optimism was not unfounded. Commercial prospects were expanding to an extent which the Caledonian's original promoters can hardly have anticipated. By 1848, North Lanarkshire alone was producing 564,000 tons of pig iron a year, compared to 39,000 tons in 1830. Scottish coal output was rising towards 10 million tons a year, with Lanarkshire and Stirlingshire as the prime fields. Owners and exploiters of mineral rights were enquiring about railway access to their mines. Towns as yet unconnected to the rail network were making overtures to railway companies. In such a fluid situation, full of opportunities, it was

Bannockburn Colliery in the late 1890s. All lines have loaded wagons, suggesting that there has been some delay in moving them: the other side of the 'demurrage' issue (see page 170).

tempting to assess the future earnings and value of a company in the most positive way. This made collaboration between companies, hampered by existing rivalries, increasingly difficult. The key relationship was that between the Caledonian and the Edinburgh & Glasgow, and weakened by increasing rivalry and suspicion through the second half of 1848, it cracked. With that the whole structure of the great leasing arrangement collapsed. The Caledonian withdrew the Lease Bill, informing the other companies that "because of obstacles with the Edinburgh & Glasgow it is useless to incur the expense of prosecuting the Lease Bill"[34]. Having sat back in anticipation of the leasing arrangement, the Scottish Midland Junction Board now received a curt letter from Coddington, of 14 February 1849, informing them that "the Directors consider it quite useless to incur the expense of prosecuting the lease bill". A CR advertisement in the *North British Shipping & Railway Journal* of 17 February 1849, signed by Coddington, stated that in consequence of differences between the CR and the Edinburgh & Glasgow, the Bills presented for joint leases of the Scottish Central, Dundee & Perth & Aberdeen Junction, and Scottish Midland Junction Railways were withdrawn. The journal remarked caustically that the SCR shareholders were now in a pretty pickle, as "they will be obliged now to fall back on their own resources for a dividend", and it suspected that SCR stock would have no value at all[35]. The Dundee & Perth & Aberdeen could, and did, feel equally aggrieved. But a new contract was quickly fixed up between the Caledonian and the Scottish Central, also involving the Lancaster & Carlisle and LNWR, backdated to 1 January 1849 and intended to last for 25 years. Under this, the SCR would receive £37,500 each half-year, before the working companies could obtain repayment of their operating costs, which would be claimed in proportion to traffic mileage as recorded by the Railway Clearing House. The CR deputy chairman, John Hodgson Hinde, headed a joint management committee. On this basis the Scottish Central allowed the Caledonian to take over all its plant, on condition that it would be returned "in an efficient state" on expiration of the agreement. At its half-yearly meeting on 27 February, the Scottish Central Board announced its "three great objects": the efficient and economic working of the line; the development of its resources for through and local traffic; and "to obtain for the proprietors such an immediate and secure return for their capital, as the peculiar and commanding position of the line entitled them to expect"[36]. Of these aims, the last undoubtedly loomed largest with the shareholders. Unfortunately for them, 1849 was to be a disastrous year for the Caledonian Company, starting off with a fire at Lothian Road which destroyed a new goods shed and the old passenger shed. The cost of damage was assessed at £5-7,000 and the property was not insured. On 11 February five people died when the mail train derailed near Rockcliffe, after a Lancaster & Carlisle carriage broke an axle[37].

By some way, the Caledonian was Scotland's largest railway company. In 1849 it employed 2,403 staff: four managers-secretaries, one treasurer, three engineers, four superintendents, three accountants-cashiers, 15 timekeepers or inspectors, 42 stationmasters, four draughtsmen, 78 clerks, 33 foremen, 84 drivers, 106 firemen or assistant drivers, 68 guards-brakemen, 318 artificers, 98 switchmen, 61 gatekeepers, 30 policemen or watchmen, 113 porters, 486 platelayers, and 856 labourers[38]. The company's accounts for the second half of 1848 showed traffic revenues of £130,968, and costs and charges of £99,060, more than 75% of revenue. The balance, with that of the first half carried forward, came to £53,641, and a dividend of 3% was declared. Yet the Caledonian was offering a guaranteed 6% and more to the shareholders of lesser lines.

At a noisy half-yearly meeting on 26 February, the Caledonian Board came clean (to a degree) about some shady practices. Hodgson Hinde, presiding, assured those present that the new agreement with the Scottish Central (not submitted for Parliamentary scrutiny) was "according to the best advice they could obtain … entirely free from any legal objection", and that there was no working agreement with the Scottish Midland Junction. As far as the Dundee & Perth & Aberdeen company was concerned, there had been a working agreement since May 1847. Under that, the Dundee & Perth & Aberdeen Junction Railway had applied to the Caledonian to make good the difference between the actual earnings on the line, and the agreed annual dividend of 8%. However, the Caledonian Board, considering that "they had never worked the line, and that no direct communication had been opened between the Caledonian and the Dundee & Perth & Aberdeen Junction, were advised and came to the resolution that they were not bound to make any such payment"[39]. He admitted that the Company had purchased shares in other Scottish railway companies in order to exert influence. These purchases, made by individual directors, were kept secret because otherwise the CR's tactics would have been made known "to those very railway companies to counteract whose plans was the object they had in view"[40]. The transactions were known to the auditors and entered in the account books, but not included in the reports to shareholders. The total sum spent was said to be £381,227. Despite the protests of dissentient shareholders that the company had acted illegally, the board was backed by a comfortable majority, thanks to over 3,000 proxy votes in favour of the directors. An attempt to get an interdict on the new agreement with the SCR was rejected by the Court of Session[41], but the protesters kept on discovering new evidence. By mid-May they had compiled a tally that showed the board had spent £492,004 on secret stock purchases, including £187,186 on Scottish Midland Junction shares, £35,073 on Scottish Central, and £43,110 on the Dundee & Arbroath. Despite the large Scottish Midland Junction holding, there was still no operating agreement. Though the Scottish Midland Junction line had been open since August 1848, many of its stations were unfinished and there was virtually no goods traffic. Its half-yearly report on 29 February blamed competitors: "The Edinburgh & Northern line and its allies have been working in hostility to the Midland"[42]. The Edinburgh & Northern had just installed a "floating railway" over the Firth of Tay between Ferryport-on-Craig and Port-a-Ferry: a three-track vessel capable of holding a normal-length train[43].

In this troubled year of 1849 the Scottish Freemasonry movement set up the Caledonian Railway Lodge, in Glasgow, as a meeting-place for members. Membership of the lodge was restricted to men with a direct connection to the Caledonian Company, and Robert Sinclair was the first master. Among its rules were, "No meeting to be held in any Railway carriages, engine house, booking office or other untieable fabric." It was virtually a standard procedure for railway viaducts and major stations to be started and inaugurated with a masonic ritual. The masonic movement was well established in Scotland and its character had changed from the freethinking and libertarian one of earlier generations to something formal and conventional, linked to the kirk and very much in line with the public *mores* of Victorian society. Mutual assistance was one of the reasons for membership. While it has always attracted conspiracy theories, it is very unlikely that masonic loyalties played any part in the affairs of the Caledonian Railway. In the inter-company battles, there were certainly freemasons on both sides.

The dissentient shareholders, headed by Captain Edward Plunkett, RN, petitioned the House of Lords for a "full and searching inquiry" into the Caledonian Railway's affairs, and their case was taken up by Lords Monteagle and Brougham. Meanwhile, the company itself was dangerously short of funds. An extraordinary meeting had to be called in Edinburgh on 29 May to approve the borrowing of £200,000. Hope Johnstone, in the chair, politely regretted that there should be a dispute with some leading shareholders but their spokesman, Thomas McMicking, a banker from Stirling who had also been one of the Scottish Central promoters, claimed that the £200,000 was needed for relieving the directors of their obligations in illegal share purchases. The board again got a majority for its proposal[44]. Leasing and take-over agreements were still being completed as Acts of Parliament, with the Wishaw & Coltness on 28 July and the Glasgow, Barrhead & Neilston Direct on 1 August. Efforts to improve the terms of the Barrhead Bill, for a 999-year lease, succeeded in getting the guarantee rates on that company's share capital down from 8% and 6% on the original capital of £150,000 to a flat 6%, and agreed on £150,000 of new capital to be raised (for the Caledonian's use) at 5%, and reducing the responsibility for its

Brocketsbrae Station, after 1905. It opened on 1 December 1866. Between 1 June 1869 and 1 June 1905 it was named Lesmahagow. Note the chocolate dispensing machine, and the oil lamps.

mortgage to a maximum of £50,000[45]. It was too little, too late. The Dundee & Perth & Aberdeen company had tried in June to get the Caledonian to pay the difference between its actual half-yearly revenue and the guaranteed amount under the leasing agreement, but the Caledonian had refused[46], claiming that it could not "under existing circumstances" undertake the agreed lease, which – it now emerged – was liable to legal objections anyway; and the Dundee & Perth & Aberdeen Junction was coolly invited to test the agreement's legality if it should wish to enforce it[47]. In this rather shabby manner the Caledonian wriggled off one hook. But it was impaled on many others.

The company was under siege. The protesters provided the House of Lords with sheaves of information. In May 1846, the CR had bought 2,960 shares in the Glasgow, Strathaven and Lesmahagow Railway, sold them again in August at a loss of £1,886, "and in order to obviate the opposition of the latter company, an agreement was made, whereby the deposits were returned to the shareholders, and the expenses incurred, amounting to £10,1810, were paid by the Caledonian Company, and charged to Parliamentary expenses"[48]. By August the reckoning of mis-spending was over £600,000. The CR half-yearly report published in September regretted that no dividend could be paid, and blamed construction delays and reduced traffic because of cholera outbreaks in Glasgow. At the half-yearly meeting on 27 September, Hope Johnstone had to agree to the formation of a committee of inquiry. It was apparent that what McMicking called "as pretty a piece of cookery of accounts as ever was made" had been happening. A new auditor, Donald Campbell, had been appointed and submitted a supplement to the Directors' Report, accusing the board of paying the last dividend partly out of capital, to the extent of £17,235, something expressly forbidden by the Companies Clauses (Scotland) Act, Section 124. Hodgson Hinde's attempt to refute this was dismissed with scornful ease by Campbell[49]. The commitment to the SCR was not sustainable, and the Caledonian simply failed to pay over the sums due. At the October half-yearly meeting of the Central, it was reported that directors had made four visits to the Caledonian offices to seek payment, to be told by Hodgson Hinde that there was neither money nor security available. A promise to pay by instalments of £500 a week was not kept[50]. The Caley was in dire straits, and its creditors were closing in. William Acworth noted that an old resident informed him that he remembered "seeing the engines [at St. Rollox] going about with mortgagees' names on them after the crash of 1848"[51]. Buildings too were pledged to anxious creditors. From 1 December, the Scottish Central reclaimed its locomotives and rolling stock and started to work its line and the Scottish Midland Junction on its own. Relations between the Caledonian and the northern companies sank to dismal levels of tit-for-tat aggression and recrimination.

Seven worthy and impartial gentlemen were nominated to the committee of inquiry, headed by George W. Cram, including Douglas Campbell and the ironmaster James Baird, and they appointed Messrs. Quilter, Ball & Co., of London, experts in the new field of railway accounting, to undertake a thoroughgoing investigation. Many aggrieved shareholders sent in comments about mismanagement. One submitted information to show that the CR freight rates were only half of what comparable railways charged[52]. Stirring the pot, Peter Blackburn of the Edinburgh & Glasgow wrote to Cram proposing once again a merger between his company and the Caledonian[53]. This ignoring of the board was a calculated insult to Hope Johnston and his colleagues, but the chairman replied with dignity and force, pointing out that the Caledonian's business was expanding fast and that the imminent opening of Buchanan Street Station would draw off much of the E&G's traffic. He was not averse to the committee of inquiry considering an amalgamation on suitable terms[54]. Despite his brave words, the board was casting around desperately for a lifeline. In November, it was reported that the Caledonian had put itself up to the London & North Western for a take-over[55].

On 24 December, the committee produced its report, lengthy, detailed and damning. Up to 1 October 1849 the company had spent £1,983,764 11s. 4d. on construction, over £700,000 more than the contractors' bid. The agreements on guaranteed dividends to other companies were itemised. The Wishaw & Coltness traffic was yielding only £9,600 a year against the guarantee of £25,200. The Garnkirk company was receiving 8% on its capital of £156,355, though the traffic only yielded 5%. The Clydesdale Junction Railway was receiving 6% on a capital of £450,000 with a further right for its proprietors to have their shares bought up by the CR at a premium of 50%, giving a liability of £225,000. But in 1849 the traffic on the Clydesdale Junction Railway was bringing in £592 9s. a week. The Glasgow, Paisley & Greenock was due to receive 6% per annum on £150,000 until 1 November 1853, and thereafter 5%, also 4% on capital of £500,000 plus interest on Debenture debt of £216,666. To the Glasgow, Barrhead & Neilston, the Caledonian was committed to pay 6% on £150,000 and 5% on another £150,000: £16,5000 a year on a 999-year lease. Receipts were barely covering the working costs.

The committee estimated the Caledonian's total annual loss on these agreements at £66,164 3s. 2½d. It then looked at the arrangements made with the northern lines, tracking the history of dealings with the Scottish Central. On 3 January 1849 the Caledonian, with the Lancaster & Carlisle and the LNWR, had made an agreement to work the SCR that was intended to last 25 years. In the first half-year of operation, the traffic had

St Rollox Works: a general view from 1898. The works had been rebuilt and extended in 1886. The through tracks from bottom right are the original Garnkirk & Glasgow line to Glebe Street.

Coatbridge Station building, 1904. Monkland Canal in foreground.

amounted to £8,149. The Caledonian's share of losses against the guarantee was £14,149. At the same time an agreement had been made to work the Dundee & Perth & Aberdeen Railway, the Caledonian guaranteeing a dividend of 8% on capital of £450,000, or £36,000 a year. In addition, the Dundee & Perth & Aberdeen Junction had been paid £60,000 for the use of its plant, which it had not delivered up to the Caledonian (keeping it as "security for the performance of the agreement"). With the Dundee & Arbroath Railway the Caledonian had agreed 8% on capital of £266,666 13s. 4d. for working its lines, including the Newtyle Railway. The annual losses on these arrangements were estimated at around £40,000 a year, and the agreements themselves were considered to be probably invalid[56].

Next, the directors' share dealings were laid bare. The CR had purchased 37,744 shares in other railways, the Scottish Midland Junction, Glasgow, Kilmarnock & Ardrossan, Caledonian & Dumbartonshire, Glasgow Barrhead & Neilston Direct, Scottish Central, Wilsontown Morningside & Coltness, Dundee & Arbroath, and Dundee & Perth & Aberdeen; and the total cost involved was £1,011,251 8s. 4d., a stunning amount[57]. At a London meeting on 2 June 1846, the Caledonian directors had agreed with the London & Birmingham and Grand Junction boards to "purchase up one-third of the Stock of the Scottish Midland Junction Railway … 4,000 shares at a capital of £100,000, to be held by trustees. A meeting of the finance committee on 27 February 1847 agreed to buy more, because the Edinburgh & Northern and Aberdeen companies were now making considerable purchases of Scottish Midland Junction stock, and the CR wanted "to facilitate our arrangements for a lease of the line." Looking at the arrangements made with the Dundee & Arbroath and the Dundee & Perth & Aberdeen companies, it was noted that to counteract efforts to divert traffic to the East Coast lines, it was determined that the Caledonian should lease the Dundee & Perth & Aberdeen Junction and that the latter should lease the Dundee & Arbroath – the Caledonian to guarantee an 8% dividend to both. On 3 February 1847 the Caledonian agreed with the Dundee & Perth & Aberdeen Junction board to jointly buy shares in the Dundee & Arbroath in order to outvote shareholders who were trying to prevent the lease arrangement: £84,665 15s. was spent on the purchase of 1,946 shares, whose par value was £48,460. Further dealings approved on 31 August 1847 allowed the Caledonian and Dundee & Perth & Aberdeen companies to pledge their Dundee & Arbroath shares to "sundry parties" for £55,000 at 6.5% and 7% interest, and to use the money to buy Dundee & Perth & Aberdeen Junction shares. Meanwhile the Caledonian directors themselves had reduced their holdings in their own Company to the minimum: from 1,533 shares in December 1845 to 256 in 1848 – hardly a sign of confidence in the future.

From the report and other company reports it is clear that similar tactics were used by other companies, creating a wholly artificial market in the shares of companies like the Scottish Midland Junction and Dundee & Arbroath. The directors were exonerated of acting for personal gain but "the purchases are illegal" and had added to the company's deep financial embarrassments. Proposing that the company's losses should be split between the company itself and the directors, the committee felt that some kind of compromise was the only way out of the morass. It recommended that the board should be reduced to nine and that the present directors should be allowed to remain until due for re-election, when they would retire[58]. Other aspects of the report stated that the company was overpaying its management and that the salary bill could be reduced from £29,718 to £23,529; Captain Coddington's salary in particular was "far beyond the proper scale". Stores were kept at unnecessarily high levels, and working charges were too high. The head office should be removed from Edinburgh to Glasgow, as the company's main business centre, and the capital account should be closed as soon as possible. The report also notes that the Caledonian had given the Scottish Central notice of its intention to quit the Working Agreement[59]. Amalgamation with the Edinburgh & Glasgow, on proper terms, seemed the best solution to the committee. But, as they noted, at 19 December 1849 the Caledonian's debts were £670,744 2s. 3½d. and "there are no funds." For Hope Johnstone's board, the report was a devastating, if anticipated, blow. As the *Times* stated, their actions had been the product of folly rather than crookery, but they were publicly exposed as directors who had failed to run a very large business efficiently and within the law. Railway managers were having a terrible press anyway, as a result of the 'mania' and exacerbated by the exposure of George Hudson's machinations with share prices and company finances on English railways.

Still, the railway was being run, and works were going on. On 1 June 1849, Brassey's gangs completed the Clydesdale Junction line between Motherwell and Rutherglen, enabling trains from Carlisle to run over the former Polloc & Govan tracks and up a new short spur into South Side Station[60]. This station, a high-level one with the lines approaching it on arches, had opened on 27 September 1848 as the terminus of the Glasgow, Barrhead & Neilston Direct Railway, but now for a while it was also to be the terminus of Anglo-Scottish expresses, as well as of trains from Hamilton (from 10 September 1849). In 1849 it was rebuilt to a design by William Tite. At Motherwell, the station was off Brandon Street, at what was later Melville Drive[61]. Work was also going ahead on the two-mile access line from Milton Junction to Glasgow's new terminus on Buchanan Street.

Uddingston Station opened on 1 June 1849. This view is from 1906, by which time it had a bookstall.

Already the imminence of the station was pushing up property prices in the area[62]. The line crossed the noxious Pinkston Bog, reeking with chemical effluvia, and entered a 400-yard tunnel, on a gradient of 1 in 80, to take it under the Forth & Clyde Canal and just above the Edinburgh & Glasgow Railway's tunnel to Queen Street. Designed by John Collister, Buchanan Street Station opened on 1 November, with workmen still busy completing the offices. The passenger shed was of wood, the goods depot was brick[63]. There were only two passenger platforms, serving trains to Stirling as well as to Edinburgh and Carlisle. Stirling trains had to reverse at the Gartsherrie junction. Glebe Street remained as a mineral depot. By November the CR was advertising five trains a day from Buchanan Street to the south, and four a day to Perth; two trains a day to Edinburgh from South Side (both starting from Greenock) and five to Hamilton[64].

Though the Caledonian company might be in dire straits, it still had allies. Far away at Euston, Captain Mark Huish, now manager of the LNWR, had consolidated his position as the country's leading railway manager by forming what was to be known as 'the Euston Confederacy', a powerful though informal alliance of companies associated with the West Coast route and services into Euston Square Station. It was Huish who, in the words of one historian, "got the West Coast service into working order" in July 1848, with a train leaving Euston at 9 a.m., reaching Edinburgh at 9 p.m. and Glasgow at 9.10[65], though his generalship went far beyond timetables, into cajoling or, when stronger tactics were needed, coercing other companies into agreements that would maintain the West Coast interests and freeze out the ambitions of any other company, be it the Midland Railway or the Great Northern, to develop an alternative route to Scotland.

The Caledonian Railway had carried mail from the start. The Post Office officials specified their requirements as to trains, stopping points and timing, in return for carrying charges that were always closely negotiated and often had to be resolved by arbitration. On 28 September 1849, Lord Clanricarde, Postmaster General, wrote to the Caledonian company: "I also require you, at your own costs to provide and furnish from and after the said 31st October [1849] next a sufficient number of separate or Post Office carriages for sorting letters fitted up in such manner as in the said Act [Act to Provide for the Conveyance of Mails by Railways]. The company was also required to "appropriate exclusively one Compartment of a second class Carriage in the Train which will daily (Sundays included) leave the Carstairs Junction Station at 11.34 a.m. (London Time) for Edinburgh". Similar requirements were set out for Glasgow-Motherwell and Carstairs-Glasgow trains. In respect of the services provided, the railway company had to give a bond for security. In October 1849, the Carlisle-Castlecary mail train took 4 hours and 42 minutes for the run of 105 miles, 6 furlongs and 125 yards, leaving at 8.16 a.m., and stopping at Gretna, Ecclefechan, Lockerbie, Beattock, Abington, Carstairs, Motherwell and Coatbridge[66]. A more modest source of cross-border passenger traffic was lost to the Caledonian by the Scotch Marriage Bill of 1 November 1849, abolishing the 'Gretna weddings' which had allowed English couples to marry with minimal formalities.

Wamphray Station opened on 10 September 1847. By the 1900s an additional building flanked Tite's station house, and a footbridge had been constructed.

CHAPTER 4. Storm and Stress, 1850-1854

Revolution

Up until now, Glasgow's richest industrialists had not shown particular interest in the Caledonian Railway, despite the involvement of men like Tennant and Dixon in the Monklands and early Glasgow lines. The choice of Edinburgh as location for the head office had not helped. Now, with Caledonian share prices at far below par, one of the richest, James Baird, fourth of numerous brothers who owned the Gartsherrie and other ironworks, and had a major interest in the Wishaw & Coltness, acquired a large holding. His action certainly was not intended to give lifebelts to the foundering board. The Baird ironworks, as was instantly noted by the Londoners, were a large customer of the company. A member of the committee of investigation, he was a highly successful businessman, noted for "the fine spirit of caution which, first carefully counting the costs, goes boldly forward, and is seldom taken by surprise"[1]. Though he may have been concerned to keep the trains running, voices also hinted that he wanted to keep the mineral traffic rates low.

The demoralised board had indeed made an appeal to the London & North Western Railway to take over the working of the line. Huish and his directors politely refused, but interest was shown by Thomas Brassey. Already intimately aware of the company's affairs, he and Joseph Locke set out to compile a proposal. Colonel MacDonald and Robert Sinclair, with John Copling for the dissident shareholders, went to London to discuss the arrangements. Brassey would advance £250,000 to the company on a sale to him of the working plant. He would operate the line, at a charge for the first 23,000 miles run per week of 1s. 2$\frac{1}{2}$d. per train per mile; after that it would drop to 1s. There would be a charge per first class carriage of $\frac{1}{2}$d. per mile, of $\frac{3}{8}$d. per mile on second and third class carriages, and $\frac{1}{4}$d. per mile on wagons. Revenue above those working expenses would accrue to the Caledonian Company. It was to be a seven-year contract, initially[2]. To the board, the arrangement was not only expedient but "absolute necessity," but it was not to the liking of the English shareholders. The London Central Committee of Caledonian Railway Shareholders, headed by Captain Plunkett, already in high gear, launched into criticism, but their representations were at first sidetracked by the board's complaint that the good faith of certain directors had been impugned, and a requested meeting did not take place. In the last week of January 1850 the London Committee circulated a release to all shareholders, citing their concerns and objections to the board's policies. Brassey's proposal was criticised as too expensive and bringing him excessive profits. A later writer suggested that Brassey was working on "the slenderest of profit margins"[3], but Brassey, upright individual though he was, normally took care that his profit margin was well above the highwater mark of accident or miscalculation. At the board meeting of 2 February 1850, the Union Bank demanded payment on an overdue debenture for £50,000. The directors hoped to replace the debenture with a mortgage agreement.

An extraordinary general meeting was held on 5 February at the Freemason's Tavern in London to consider the committee of inquiry's report, Brassey's proposed contract, various Bills and the raising of £66,000 for branches and a station in Edinburgh. But by then, Brassey had withdrawn his proposal, in the face of the onslaught from Plunkett's Committee, leaving the company without a lifeline. On the 11th, the Commercial Bank's debentures for £195,000, also overdue, were considered by the board, and again, refuge in mortgaging was sought, and Gibson (whose efforts were praised by the board) was given the task of holding off another bank. Such a situation could not go on. The Caledonian could not pay its debts, could not raise capital, and the dissident shareholders were clamouring. At a further meeting in London on 13 February, the resignations of six directors were announced, and further resignations were accepted: including those of Hodgson Hinde and Colonel MacDonald. Within a day or two, all had gone, including Hope Johnstone himself. A new board, chaired by Plunkett, was formed by John Copling, James Baird, John Duncan, Thomas McMicking, T.T. Fawcett, Douglas Campbell, Richard Potter, and William Johnston. Of the two latter, Potter represented the Preference Shareholders, and Johnston the Commercial Bank. Joseph Locke was willing to be elected but withdrew when an alternative name was proposed. It soon became clear that despite Baird's share purchase, he was much more interested in the guaranteed (but deeply in arrears) dividend due to the Wishaw & Coltness than the welfare of the Caledonian.

Operating in a new, loosely-regulated and intensely competitive industry, Hope Johnston and Hodgson Hinde had set out to be deal-makers and fixers whose genuine concern to defend and enlarge their company led them into a succession of over-priced commitments accompanied by some dodgy dealings. At the end of the day they had little to show for all their efforts: a nearly-bankrupt company with no secure agreements. Typical of their over-ambitious approach was their relationship with a rickety company, the Glasgow, Kilmarnock & Ardrossan Railway, originally the Ardrossan & Johnstone Railway, known as the 'Ardrossan', whose aim to build a line from Ardrossan to Glasgow, authorised as early as June 1827, had been overtaken by the more dynamic Glasgow, Paisley, Kilmarnock & Ayr Railway in 1840. It owned only a short line from Ardrossan to Kilwinning, but its chairman, the 13th Earl of Eglinton, owner of Ardrossan Harbour, still hoped to expand it. The Glasgow, Paisley, Kilmarnock & Ayr company was of course a natural enemy, and an alliance with the Caledonian was seen as being of mutual benefit. Hope Johnston, Hodgson Hinde and Col. William MacDonald all became directors of the company. Under their influence the Ardrossan bought shares in the Glasgow, Barrhead & Neilston line, "to stop the Glasgow & Ayr swamping it"[4]. When a large holding in the Ardrossan was acquired by the National Exchange Bank of Glasgow, a survivor of the 'mania' period and itself in financial difficulties, the Bank's representatives condemned the Barrhead share purchase as illegal and obtained a court interdict on the Ardrossan's activities. Another large holding in the Ardrossan (15,314 shares at a value of £57,516 19s. 6d.) belonged to the Caledonian Railway, though this was concealed by having the shares registered in the names of individuals who were CR employees. In 1846 the Ardrossan obtained an Act for new lines, from Crofthead, intended terminus of the Glasgow, Barrhead & Neilston, to Kilwinning and Kilmarnock. This would have spread Caledonian-controlled lines from Glasgow right across Ayrshire's industrial area, and explains the CR's early

William Tite's Cathcart Street terminus for the Glasgow, Paisley & Greenock Railway, opened in 1841.
(*Views and Reminiscences of Old Greenock*)

interest in the Barrhead line. By 1847, the Ardrossan had run out of money, but a majority of shareholdings voted down Eglinton's wish to merge it with the Caledonian. Discord and confusion followed, with open hostility between the National Exchange Bank and Caledonian factions on the board. Neither the bank nor the Caley could afford to pay the balance due on their shares, and the Caley hid behind the names of the various clerks to whom shares had been nominally allotted. The Ardrossan was given a time extension on its Act, but the company was effectively bust. Whatever the CR had actually disbursed on shares, and legal costs, was lost. By April 1850 Eglinton had resigned; at the end of 1851 an Act of Dissolution was applied for and effected on 25 August 1852. The Ardrossan lines were vested in the Glasgow & South Western in 1854. For nearly twenty years, until a new venture with a new Earl of Eglinton, the Caledonian would be kept out of Ayrshire[5].

The *entente* of 1848 between the Dundee & Arbroath and the Dundee & Perth & Aberdeen companies, which had seen many wrangles, fell apart and was terminated on 9 March 1850, from when the Dundee & Arbroath resumed responsibility for its own operations. The planned linking line had not been built and the only connection between their termini at Dundee was a tramway owned by the harbour commissioners, and worked by horses (from 1851 to 1907 this tramway was leased to the Dundee & Arbroath[6]). With its finances far from sound, the Dundee & Perth & Aberdeen again sought a working arrangement with the Caledonian, but although a leasing agreement was drawn up, it was not put into effect and the Dundee & Perth & Aberdeen Junction maintained a rather tottery independence. On 18 March the Caledonian/Edinburgh & Glasgow Amalgamation Bill was considered by the Commons. According to the Radical Edinburgh M.P. Charles Cowan it was now universally acknowledged that the Caledonian line should never have been built. Since the proposal had first been made, he said, the Caledonian had acquired a new board "so busy keeping the door shut against their clamorous creditors", that they had had no time to consider the amalgamation idea. Another member "scarcely considered it necessary to kick the carcass of this defunct and unprincipled Bill". Gladstone also denounced it[7]. The Bill was deferred and it was evident that it would not come back.

With the final completion of the railway to Aberdeen, the first through carriages from London to Aberdeen arrived at the provisional Ferryhill terminus at the edge of the northern city on 1 April 1850. The southern terminus was Euston Square – it was very much a 'West Coast' route and the English East Coast companies were denied through booking rights north of Edinburgh[8]. Caledonian tickets had to be purchased, and the Caledonian route followed.

Ardler Station. A depot in the area was opened by the Newtyle & Coupar Angus Railway in 1837, but this station dates from 2 August 1848 and the Scottish Midland Junction Railway. The wrought iron brackets are a striking feature.

Who Gets Priority?

To be a Scottish railway director in the 1850s was not for the faint-hearted. The new board immediately found itself beset by all the problems faced or created by its fore-runner plus the need to manage the business more intensively than before. Its members had little in common with one another apart from their opposition to the previous incumbents. The Londoners were unfamiliar with the Scottish scene and Scottish procedures, but all knew that the company's affairs had to be taken quickly and firmly in hand before it was declared insolvent. They had been installed to defend the interests of the Preference share and Debenture holders, and one of their first actions was to issue a circular, on 25 February, to affirm that their first consideration, after the working expenses of the company, was the Debenture holders. With a weekly revenue, even in February, of around £6,000, they felt able to reassure the creditors that payment would be made. Meanwhile there was a great deal of prudent housekeeping to be done. Staff cuts and salary reductions were an urgent priority, though even here they were forced to concede some increases: Christopher Johnstone's salary as Glasgow goods manager was put up to £350 a year and he was given an additional clerk, even while economies of all kinds were sought. Mr. Paton the printer was allowed advertising space in the new timetable, if he would produce 50,000 copies free of charge[9]. But problems and additional costs emerged like lurking footpads. When the CR began to charge the Scottish Central 2*d.* a mile for use of a postal carriage, Mr. Tasker of the Central objected and another wrangle began. Shippers complained that a lack of wagon-sheets was delaying the movement of goods between St. Petersburg and Liverpool via Leith Docks, and another hundred had to be ordered. The Inland Revenue was chasing the company for £1,323 12*s.* 2*d.* passenger duty[10].

The Glasgow, Paisley & Greenock Railway had remained independent, though in a close if not always harmonious relationship with the Caledonian. The Caledonian operated the line and ran the locomotive workshops; and since completion of the Clydesdale Junction line on 1 June 1849, through trains ran between Greenock and Edinburgh, three each way daily, via Rutherglen and Carstairs, the service promoted by advertisements and 'hanging cards'[11]. But the Glasgow, Paisley & Greenock was in a bad way. Since March 1850 a committee of shareholders had been investigating the management's conduct and in due course revealed that the Tasker and Turner directorial families treated the business as a private treasury: "Within five years from incorporation the directors squandered more than twice the estimated cost of the line"[12]. On 6 May the Board decided to try to obtain a repeal of its Act of Amalgamation with the Greenock Railway. It had already resolved to put no more work through the Greenock workshops. The Glasgow, Paisley & Greenock would retain all rights to its property and the Caledonian would work the line on a shared-income basis; the Glasgow, Paisley & Greenock to receive £433 a week and the CR to keep the balance. A week later a demand appeared from the Scottish Central for £3,588 13*s.* 4*d.*, for "working expenses under protest since 4 December 1849 to 31 January 1850", for which they held "the Southern companies" responsible. The board determined to resist this claim, on the basis that they did not consider the alleged working contract binding even it was legal, which, they claimed, it was not[13]. The board was promoting a Bill to raise £1,200,000 of which £562,000 was "Clydesdale Redemption", £400,000 to be set against "Floating Debt", and £50,000 for "Barrhead Liabilities". The balance was for engineering and plant, including £105,000 for the badly-needed deviation line north of Motherwell. This Caledonian Arrangements Bill was however rejected by Parliament. The directors were divided on policy towards the Guaranteed Companies, which were pressing for payment both of due dividends and of the accumulated arrears. Heavy overtures were made to them, to obtain a reduction in the guaranteed dividends and to write off the arrears. There was little sympathy, however. The Wishaw & Coltness Company agreed to drop its guaranteed dividend to 7.5% "if paid regularly", but still wanted its arrears. James Baird and other directors linked to the Guaranteed Companies were becoming increasingly restive. By the summer the board was struggling to avoid the imposition of 'Judicial Factors' – court orders obtained by the Guaranteed Companies to freeze all revenue relating to their lines. This was refused to the Wishaw & Coltness, the court accepting the Caledonian's plea that despite the Act authorising its sale to the Caledonian, the Wishaw & Coltness had never sealed a deed of conveyance and had continued to carry on as if it were an independent company. But the Garnkirk company was allowed to appoint judicial factors[14]. The Dundee & Perth & Aberdeen board also suffered a committee of investigation into its conduct at this time, but the Caledonian was identified as the villain responsible for its difficulties. Thomas McMicking attended its special meeting, to defend the Caledonian, or at least to tell the infuriated shareholders that there was no point in pursuing the Caley because it had no money. He questioned whether the Caledonian lease on the Dundee & Perth & Aberdeen Junction was legal: because it had never been sanctioned by Parliament, the Dundee & Perth & Aberdeen Junction had very little chance of enforcing it[15]. Baird, increasingly at odds with Plunkett and the board majority, protested against the September half-yearly accounts and resigned on the 26th, publishing his correspondence with Plunkett. Of the other directors, Wheeler (who had replaced Potter as the Preference Shares spokesman) and Fawcett were also increasingly opposed to their fellows.

**Archibald Gibson, Secretary of the
Caledonian Railway from 1852 to 1890.**

Pulled three ways by the demands of the Debenture holders, the Preference Shareholders and the Guaranteed Companies, the board put the Debenture holders first. Baird immediately allied himself with the Guaranteed Companies. Duncan and Johnston went to London to meet the representatives of the Guaranteed Companies but these failed to turn up. By September Plunkett was wanting to resign but was persuaded to stay on. The LNWR, concerned about the continuing instability of its Scottish ally, offered mediation. On 4 October, at a board meeting to consider the company's affairs "in the present crisis", Plunkett did resign, and John Copling was elected as acting chairman. By now the Guaranteed Companies were mounting lawsuits to recover the unpaid dividends. The Wishaw & Coltness was seeking an interdict against any payment before its demands were met. T.T. Fawcett called for a special general meeting, claiming that the board was favouring Debenture holders over the Guaranteed Companies. In the Caledonian's sorely-pressed management team, the busiest man, apart from Gibson, was Thomas Mackay, its law agent, who had some 85 separate lawsuits to deal with. Lawyers generally did extremely well out of railway affairs. The bills of Hope, Oliphant & Mackay, regularly presented, were paid promptly.

William Johnston resigned from the board on 2 November, which suggests that the Commercial Bank had lost confidence in it. During November, with the company's affairs still in chaos, three new directors were co-opted, 'parachuted' in from the LNWR (At this time the LNWR capital account showed it had £162,684 invested in the Caledonian and £91,363 in the Scottish Midland Junction companies). They were Captain Carnegie RN, William Rotherham, and Henry Booth (George Stephenson's partner in construction of the *Rocket*, back in 1829). Their mission was to sort out an agreement with the Guaranteed Companies and they quickly drew up a draft scheme and arranged a conference with the Guaranteed Companies representatives. Meanwhile, the Dundee & Perth & Aberdeen Railway announced it was applying to Parliament for authority to compel the Caledonian to lease their line, on the agreed basis. Somehow, in their travails, the board also found time to approve a further six porters and two clerks for Buchanan Street Goods Station, and to support an initiative from Mr. Addison, the storekeeper, to start a library for the staff, with £10 from the fine fund. This fund held fines imposed on staff for breaches of the company rules[16].

The London & North Western initiative failed against the obduracy of the Guaranteed Companies. It had involved the writing off of all arrears up to the end of 1850, and a somewhat reduced rate of future payments. Although the CR Board expressed a hope that "in these unparalleled circumstances" the LNWR would not desert them, the co-opted directors announced their intention to withdraw. Copling was too much of a faction leader for anything but a stop-gap chairmanship, and on 28 December John Duncan, a wealthy Aberdeen lawyer, was elected chairman[17], accepting the role as a neutral figure. On the 31st, the company deposited a new Amendments Bill, its preamble noting that guaranteed and preferred claims amount to "upwards of £160,000 per annum, and the same, together with the interest upon sums due under mortgages and bonds ... far exceeds the annual revenue of the company." The Bill's aim was to empower the company, the Guaranteed Companies, and the Preferred interests, to make new arrangements; also to enable the Caledonian to borrow £600,00 in order to settle immediate claims[18]. Duncan and his board worked very hard in the early part of the year to obtain agreement, against a background of resentment and suspicion. Among the investing public, there was still a view that the Guaranteed Companies would have their way; in February 1851 Garnkirk £25 shares were trading for £38, and Wishaw & Coltness for £31, while the market value of shares in real railways was far below par[19].

"Something Wrong About the Management"

On 28 October 1850, the rival route from Glasgow to Carlisle, through Nithsdale, was completed, and the Glasgow, Paisley, Kilmarnock & Ayr and Glasgow, Dumfries & Carlisle companies merged to become the

Glasgow & South Western Railway, ready to do battle for a share of the traffic passing north through Carlisle. From a junction at Gretna it had running powers over the Caledonian track into Carlisle, at a toll of £6,400 a half-year[20], but the Caledonian and Lancaster & Carlisle companies ensured that only local traffic for its own line was routed via the GSWR. In the terms of agreement for the GSWR to run between Gretna and Carlisle, one clause specified that "For the purpose of discouraging the steamers between Annan and Liverpool, and Troon and Fleetwood, or such other ports as the Southern may use, the GSWR will charge upon all traffic to or coming from the vessels as high rates as are charged upon any other portion of the line"[21]. The Caledonian was guarding against the GSWR siphoning off Glasgow traffic by doing cheap deals with steamer companies.

In January 1851 Christopher Johnstone reported systematic thieving by the employees at Buchanan Street Goods Station, and blamed the low levels of pay[22]. Pay rises were out of the question. Duncan issued a circular to shareholders on 25 January, appealing for common sense and asking for support: "Influential shareholders in some of the guaranteed lines adopted hostile proceedings in the courts of law. They applied for the appointment of judicial factors; they sought to prohibit the directors from the ordinary acts of administration ... they arrested the traffic dues of goods carried on the line; and ... exhibited a determination to suspend the whole traffic and operation of the company, to obtain possession of the railway, exclude the original shareholders from any right whatever in it, and also to supersede, if not extinguish, the preferential shareholders"[23]. It would seem that Duncan and some of his colleagues believed that the Bairds and their allies had the intention of driving the company into insolvency and getting hold of it on the cheap. The Scottish Central, despairing of getting its due payments, began a lawsuit against the Caledonian and its English allies, demanding a total of £900,000 damages for non-payment of salaries, losses and breach of contract. Eventually this was rejected, the Court of Session agreeing with the Caledonian's argument that the contract had no legal standing. Meanwhile, the SCR with the two other northern members of the 'Caledonian System' made their own arrangement in February 1851, to maintain their traffic. The SCR had been working its own trains from Perth into Glasgow (Queen Street) at least since December 1850[24]. Now the locomotive establishments of all three were combined and run as a single operation, under the aegis of the Central. As Robert Russell Notman, one of the Aberdeen Railway's auditors, wrote in a pro-amalgamation tract published in 1852, they could well have gone further and saved more[25]. Rather like gold prospectors on a not-very productive field, sharing a hut but digging on their own, the Scottish railway companies had to collaborate as well as compete, but despite the elements of co-operation, competition remained intense[26]. *Herapath's Railway Journal* observed in January 1851 that "There is something wrong about the management of Scotch railways ... comparatively extravagant in large matters, penurious in little, lax and unsuccessful"[27].

The Caledonian's half-yearly meeting in March 1851 could not be other than uncomfortable. Yet the underlying trading figures were good:

	1849 (year)	**1850 (year)**
Gross Traffic	£278,457 16s. 5d.	£322,638 4s. 5d.
Working Expenses	£159,192 6s. 7d.	£171,678 3s. 3d.
Revenue from Traffic	£119,265 9s. 10d.	£150,960 1s. 2d.

A 16% increase in revenue was healthy, but to be set against the total revenue of 1850 (£155,909 4s. 11d. including rents and fees) were the following items:

Debenture interest:	£86,992 10s. 7d.
Feus and ground rents:	£ 9,326 5s. 3d.
Guaranteed and Preferential claims:	£162,370 0s. 0d.

Free revenue from the Greenock and Barrhead lines came to £18,742 14s. 7d., leaving a balance of £142,627 5s. 5d. to be found by the Caledonian. Since its net revenue was £59,590 9s. 1d., that left a deficiency of £84,036 16s. 4d.[28]. Stark revelation of the company's plight was probably the best way to introduce a sense of reality and make all parties realise that the only hope lay in acceptance of the proposals in the Arrangements Bill now before Parliament. What the board wanted was to draw a line under past agreements and make a fresh start, under the provisions of the Bill (which the other side was vigorously opposing).

A Persecuted Railway

In March the Caledonian's Bill was getting a pasting in the Commons debate on its second reading. The Bill was to deal with Guaranteed and Preferential interests, giving no security to the great mass of the shareholders. To William Ewart Gladstone, the CR had "obtained an unhappy notoriety for proceedings of this nature". Some spoke up for the company; Fox Maule, Liberal M.P. for Perth, who had been, and would be again, a CR director, said the Caledonian had been a "persecuted railway" from the beginning, and J.B. Smith said the company had "a class of Shylocks, determined to have their pound of flesh"[29], and the Bill was referred to committee. At the board meeting of 26 March, the company offered to pay £500 on account to 'poinding creditors'; they wanted £1,000, and at the April meeting £750 was agreed. Thomas Brassey was demanding repayment of 35s. per share in 200 shares of the abandoned Caledonian Extension Company, which he held. Another enquirer on the same topic was to be told that "no funds exist"[30].

After intensive debate, in April 1851 two important agreements regulated Anglo-Scottish traffic and revenues. The imminence of London's Great Exhibition, due to open in May, was the catalyst – a huge increase in traffic was anticipated, to be encouraged by extra trains and cheap excursion fares. The Octuple Agreement, between the Caledonian, North British, Lancaster & Carlisle, London & North Western, Midland, York Newcastle & Berwick, York & North Midland, and Great Northern Railways, covered traffic from London to Edinburgh, dividing the revenues between each group on a 50/50 basis. Further subdivision between the companies was made in proportion to their traffic "recognised and acted upon in the Clearing House"[31]. The Sextuple Agreement, which did not involve the Great Northern or the York & North Midland, provided for traffic not covered by the Octuple, in a more complex division of revenues depending on the originating and terminal points between Birmingham and Edinburgh. The GSWR and the Edinburgh & Glasgow were not invited to the table – Glasgow was a 100% West Coast location. The Agreements were to stay in force until January 1856[32].

Strapped for cash as it might be, the Company still had to provide uniform clothing for its workmen. In April the Board agreed that the men should be measured for their year's clothing, and also accepted Sinclair's request that enginemen should be given greatcoats[33]. At this time, even in Scotland, locomotives had little more than frontal screens, 'weatherboards', to protect their crews from wind, rain and snow. Compared to the demands of the 'Guaranteed Interests', such matters were trifles. The Caledonian's transition from bountiful provider of guaranteed working agreements and leases to an impoverished and hungry desire to recant on past generosity aroused no sympathy among the other companies. When it sought to modify the working agreement with the Glasgow, Paisley & Greenock company, or once again to amalgamate, the Greenock replied loftily that while it was willing to listen to any reasonable scheme, it would insist upon its full rights. Its management had already been exposed as a little in-group fraudulently ripping off the shareholders[34] (the company's slogan, not inaptly, was 'The Pleasure Line'). But an amalgamation agreement was signed on 26 May, and was passed by Parliament on 7 August. The Glasgow, Paisley & Greenock Railway was reborn as the Greenock Railway Guaranteed Company. The CR was also being pursued by the Lancaster & Carlisle over arrears of tolls and wages at Carlisle Station[35]. Through 1851 an increasingly tough dialogue was conducted between the board and those who spoke for the Guaranteed Interests, who were also represented on the board itself and indeed sought to become a majority element. Already in April the board had to agree to build no more branches "without the previous sanction of the shareholders", by which was meant the Preference Shareholders' Committee and the Guaranteed Lines. By late May there was a stand-off between the board and the Guaranteed Lines, who declined the Caledonian's proposals for settlement. In vain the board protested that "the proposed arrangements should not contain an obligation on the Caledonian Company to pay for what they have got no value [out of]". The Guaranteed Lines objected to the board taking a tone "incompatible with the embarrassed condition of the Caledonian Railway". In the end a draft agreement was signed by Duncan and Baird committing £54,000 to be paid against arrears of guaranteed payments: £30,000 to the Wishaw & Coltness, £20,000 to the Clydesdale Junction, and £4,000 to the Barrhead & Neilston[36]. In June the Guaranteed Companies held meetings at which the proposals in the Caledonian's Arrangements Bill were accepted: they were to be reincorporated as creditor companies in order to collect and distribute the agreed annuities payable when the Bill became an Act.

Amidst so many distractions, it was perhaps not surprising that there were some hiccups in the train service. On 26 June the Caledonian was fined £2 2s. at Glasgow Sheriff Court for failing to run an advertised train. A passenger had waited in vain at Abington, at the bleak hour of 5.41 a.m., and had to walk 14 miles to Lanark to get the 11.29 mail train, missing a morning's work in Glasgow[37].

Port Glasgow Station opened on 31 March 1841. This image, with its plethora of advertising, is from the 1900s. The station was rebuilt in 1912.

New Dispensations, New Disputes

On the passing of the Arrangements Act on 7 August, with its 81 clauses, new dispensations could at last be made. The board was partially reformed, with John Duncan still chairman, and including William Baird (eldest of the Baird brothers), William Johnston (now returned), Archibald Glen Kidston and Alexander Campbell, representing the interests of the Wishaw & Coltness, Clydesdale Junction, Greenock and Barrhead companies respectively; and including also Thomas McMicking, John Copling, and Douglas Campbell, among others. The Guaranteed Lines directors were to remain until the company should have paid three successive half-yearly dividends of at least 1% to the Ordinary shareholders, and should relinquish their seats within six months of that happening. Earlier a proposal from the Guaranteed Lines to restrict directorships in the company to shareholders resident in Glasgow or within 20 miles of that city had outraged English shareholders, already infuriated by the Guaranteed Interests' insistence on their "pound of flesh". Three committees were formed, for finance, traffic and stores, and it was hoped that the company could now get back to concentration on its proper affairs[38]. The Wishaw & Coltness, Clydesdale Junction, Glasgow, Barrhead & Neilston, Garnkirk, Glasgow & Coatbridge companies, with the Glasgow, Paisley & Greenock, were all re-incorporated as distributors of a guaranteed annuity to their shareholders. John Thomas wrote, rather surprisingly given the state of the CR at the time, that "Caledonian money and managerial skills brought sound prosperity to the Greenock line"[39]; though indeed, properly run, it was a railway that could not fail to be profitable. The Greenock Guaranteed company had £150,000 in Preference stocks and £500,000 in Ordinary stocks, and the Caledonian paid it a fixed annuity of £7,500 from November 1853 and another of £15,000 from 1 August 1854. The Clydesdale Junction was to receive £18,900 in August 1852 and £25,250 annually in perpetuity thereafter. The Barrhead was to receive £10,425 a year for three years, and £11,250 after that. In the hope of raising extra cash, negotiations with the Electric Telegraph Company had been going on through the year, also with the Post Office. The secretary was instructed to ask the GPO for a lump sum payment of £25,000 against the mail contract[40].

Commenting on the Caley's affairs in January 1852, the *Scottish Railway Gazette* observed that now, "the intrinsic value and vast resources of that concern have been generally recognised, and there is no stock more confidently dealt in"[41]. On 2 February 1852 the company was able to pay annuities to the value of £41,000 on the due day. But the board was still split into factions. That month Baird, Kidston and Campbell formed a committee of inquiry and submitted a critical report on the company's operations. Captain Coddington, the manager, made a formal objection to their report on the grounds that it contained grave errors of fact as well as defamatory remarks about himself[42]. At the half-yearly meeting on 12 March, Duncan was up-beat: gross revenue was £220,062 14s. 9d., working expenditure was £102,471 4s. 7d., and liabilities on Debentures and guaranteed annuities were £93,288 19s. 1 ½d., leaving enough over to pay the Preference shares and declare an Ordinary dividend of 2.5%. Much of the floating debt had been converted into Debentures and agreement had been reached with most Debenture holders to reduce the interest rate from 5% to 4%. Traffic was rising steadily (putting heavy pressure on locomotives, rolling stock, siding capacity and operating staff); four fifths of the eighty-plus lawsuits had been dealt with directly by the board; and the company was proposing to erect a new head office block in Buchanan Street, Glasgow, some of which would be rented out in order to provide rent-free space for the Caledonian staff. He challenged the Dundee & Perth & Aberdeen to pursue their 8% lease agreement, when their line "was not worth one penny per cent"; and even claimed that his board was more united than rumour supposed[43].

A further boost came when the Court of Session ruled in March that the contract made by the three 'southern' companies with the Scottish Central was illegal, invalid and therefore unenforceable[44], which, if it did not say much for the abilities of those who had made the contract, was a great relief to the new board. On 10 April the board agreed that telegraph instruments should be set up at Carlisle, Carstairs, Edinburgh, Buchananan Street, and Greenhill for the Railway and the Telegraph company, and at fifteen other places for the Caledonian's use. The partner was not the Electric Telegraph Company (which had an agreement with the LNWR) but its rival, the Magnetic Telegraph Company, whose origins lay in Liverpool. Robert Sinclair, having reviewed the locomotive and rolling stock, advised that he needed 40 carriages, 175 wagons and nine passenger engines, at an estimated cost of £25,700 less £7,450 for "old materials". These items were to be charged to the capital account, and old locomotives were to be advertised for sale[45]. There was a real sense of getting down to the proper business of running a railway.

A long Up goods at Glenboig in June 1922, with 0-6-0 engines Nos. 747 (built 1896, ran until 1959), and 761 (1897). Both are McIntosh Class 711, intended for passenger and goods traffic, fitted with Westinghouse brake pumps and painted blue.

Lamington Station opened in 1848. This view is from 1912.

All Clear for Amalgamation

In the early part of 1852, the Caledonian and the Edinburgh & Glasgow companies were trying hard to form a working agreement to regulate services and fares between the two main Scottish cities. Special meetings were held in the London Tavern in May and June to win support from English shareholders. In June, John Duncan emphasised the merits of the agreement, including a reduction in staff costs and a saving of £10,000 a year for each company in operating expenses. Duncan stated that the E&G's working expenses were 37.5% of revenue; the Caledonian's were significantly higher at 43%, but it expected this to fall, especially after Brassey's 10-year maintenance contract, at £10,000 a year, expired in 1856. On each line, the revenue was around £41 per mile per week. Up to a figure of £364,000 per half-year, it was proposed to divide gross receipts in the ratio of 80/37 between the Caledonian and E&G; above that figure, in a ratio of 91/26. Those present voted unanimously for the scheme[46]. However, it seems there was considerable unease among some shareholders in both companies about the terms of the deal.

The still-precarious state of the Caledonian's finances was laid bare in Notman's pamphlet (1852) with accountant-ish precision. The Company's gross revenue in 1851 (actually for 13 months) was £401,967 14s. 11$\frac{1}{2}$d. Gross working expenses were £187,175 19s. 5d. Net revenue was £199,385 0s. 9$\frac{1}{2}$d. But interest due on Debentures and dividends on Preference stocks amounted to £164,933 17s. 5d. The resultant margin, though slender, was on the right side of solvency[47]. As a working railway, the company was sound, and could pay its way. But the guarantees were a crushing burden. Notman and others were arguing for amalgamation of the Caledonian with the northern companies in the 'system', but the board's attention remained focused on the Edinburgh & Glasgow.

Coddington agreed in July to 'retire' if paid £6,000; his salary was £2,000 a year and his contract had five years still to run. It was resolved not to replace him but to ensure closer board supervision of the departments, and Robert Sinclair was appointed general manager, in addition to his responsibility for locomotives and rolling stock. Archibald Gibson became secretary, a position he would hold for 38 years[48]. In 1852 a Glasgow architect, James Salmon, was commissioned to provide a design for a new station building at Buchanan Street, which he duly produced, only to have it shelved by the board. It was hardly the time for a grand gesture, even though, apart from the inadequacy of the station, the office space in Buchanan Street was very cramped, and it was proposed to move the E&G staff there as well as the Caledonian head office[49]. The shareholders' meeting in September was informed that plans for providing "suitable head office accommodation" at Buchanan Street had not yet been put into effect[50].

The shape of things to come. Caledonian Steam Packet Co. poster, showing turbine steamer
Duchess of Argyll, **off Arran. Launched in 1906, the ship was scrapped in 1970.**

Smoke, soot, raw chemical fumes in the air and untreated sewage in the river were prime contributors to the atmosphere of Glasgow in the 1850s. Small wonder that people liked to live away from all that, or at least occasionally get away for an airy trip down the Clyde coast. These desires were catered for by several private steamship operators. The Glasgow, Paisley & Greenock Railway had also owned steamships for a time, and in 1852 the Caledonian formed a semi-independent enterprise, the Railway Steamboat Packet Company, to work from Greenock in connection with the trains. By the end of 1853 it owned four iron paddle steamers, but in 1854 the CR would dispose of its shipping interests[51]. Its managers had enough on their plate without getting involved in the infighting that was endemic in the coastal shipping trade. But deals were made with shippping operators for regular and excursion tickets that combined train and steamer. Relations between the railway and the shipping companies were not entirely cordial, as the effect of the trains was to push steamer traffic away from the city, shortening their routes.

The half-yearly report in early September 1852 was again positive in tone. The dividend was set at 4.4%. The Magnetic Telegraph Company's line was almost completed. Cordial relations with the Edinburgh & Glasgow were noted, and a Debenture stock at 3.5% was proposed to substitute old mortgage and bond debts. There was a new policy of salary rises to be linked to dividend payments – an incentive to managers to economise on costs, "a principle successfully carried out in many large commercial establishments"[52]. At the half-yearly meeting which followed ten days later Duncan admitted that the dividend was on the small side, but considering the company's previous situation, thought it was reasonable. The sum of £220,000 had been realised on the sale of assets that had been under pledge to creditors, both buildings and plant. He took a swipe at the GSWR which had published a document "which appeared very like a declaration of war". This related to claims on sharing the Anglo-Scottish traffic, but as far as the Caledonian was concerned, the GSWR had made its own bed between Glasgow and Gretna, and could lie on it. Questioners' interest focused on Coddington's departure and settlement.

Duncan seemed very much the man at the helm, but only a few days later, it was reported that he had "retired" from the board, and that William Baird had been elected chairman, with William Johnston as his deputy. Apert from his Commercial Bank position, Johnston was closely involved with the Dixon industrial empire and so with the Clydesdale Junction Guaranteed Company. Disunity over the agreement with the Edinburgh & Glasgow company had intensified, and it may be that Duncan, at first a supporter of the plan, had turned to oppose it. But quite clearly a boardroom revolt had ousted him and put Baird in control. Against the forceful opposition of four Guaranteed Company directors on a 10-man board, he was in a weak position. His health was advanced as the reason for his resignation, sacrificed, along with his own professional business, in his exertions for the company[53].

At the half-yearly meeting in March 1853 efforts were made to persuade the shareholders that order and stability had been restored. Good relations were claimed to exist with the GSWR and the Scottish Central, and it was now proposed that the CR should take over working the Edinburgh & Glasgow, at a charge of 35% of the E&G's gross earnings. Deputy-chairman Johnston informed the meeting that the dividend, 2.5%, was the first one that the company had paid wholly from revenue[54]. But the Edinburgh & Glasgow had many disgruntled shareholders (no doubt many of them also with Caledonian shares) who thought their company's dividends were too low and its management incompetent[55], while the Scottish Central, though dropping its case against the 'southern companies' and prepared to be bought off with £9,000, had resolved to oppose the Caledonian/E&G agreement unless it was given running powers over their lines[56]. Anticipating full amalgamation, in the summer of 1853 the managements of the Caledonian and the Edinburgh & Glasgow were effectively merged, although the companies remained run as separate businesses. Archibald Gibson's name appeared in E&G advertisements, as secretary.

Amalgamation Falls Through

Railways took a positive role in the spread of country villas for well-off commuters. On 17 May 1853 the Caledonian board approved the sale of season tickets at staff rates to owners of houses valued at a yearly rental of £30 and built within a mile of any station not being less than seven miles from Glasgow, Edinburgh or Carlisle[57]. This policy encouraged speculative building by developers, and the company sometimes had to look hard at whether certain 'villa' schemes fulfilled the necessary conditions. In July the board authorised works at 42 stations and locations, mostly station houses, but also sheds, cattle pends, and sidings required by the increasing traffic. The cost was estimated at £43,160.

The new board resolved an old dispute with the General Terminus & Glasgow Harbour company, relating to the original CR board's purchase of 50 acres of ground on which the General Terminus & Glasgow Harbour company were laying tracks to join up with the Clydesdale Junction and Barrhead lines. The General Terminus & Glasgow Harbour company was claiming £90,000, but settled for £73,000, giving the Caledonian ownership of the lines and 20 acres of saleable land. In the summer Sinclair negotiated a new 5-year cartage contract with Pickfords and G. Gordon of Glasgow[58]. After what one historian described as "three years of alarming competition"[59] and despite the swipes made at the GSWR in the shareholders' meeting of September 1852, an agreement on traffic-sharing between Glasgow and Carlisle was made in 1853. Intended to last 21 years, it was a generous one from the Caledonian's point of view, according the Glasgow South Western 40% of the goods traffic and 15% of passenger traffic, though the Caledonian was carrying 95% of the latter[60].

In September 1853 the company had 73 passenger and 57 goods locomotives. Eleven were under repair and many others were in a state of some dilapidation. But there were enough for it to place engines by agreement with some large colliery and factory customers. William Dixon had four, and Lord Belhaven had six. Two CR locomotives were also working on the General Terminus & Glasgow Harbour company's line[61]. In anticipation of future needs for locomotives and rolling stock, the decision was taken to close down the Greenock works and to set up new locomotive and carriage works at a site in Glasgow's St. Rollox district, in the angle of Springburn Road and Charles Street. The company had had a locomotive depot in the area at least since 1849[62]. In particular at this time there was a need for new wagons, as the company was using many belonging to the LNWR, and having to pay substantial charges for demurrage.

Under William Baird's chairmanship, the board was evidently getting on with business and laying plans for the future development. The Caledonian Railway (Crofthead Extension & Amendment) Act of that year, for extension of the Barrhead line to Neilston, also included provision for a hotel to be built at Buchanan Street Station, though like most aspirations for better facilities for passengers there, it remained a paper dream. Dividends on the CR Ordinary shares were paid at 2% for the half-year ending 31 July 1853, and 3% to 31 January 1854. These were not considered sufficient by many shareholders, particularly those in England, and the terms of the new agreement with the Edinburgh & Glasgow Railway were being increasingly criticised by shareholders in both companies. Douglas Campbell claimed that the Caley would lose out to the tune of £15,000 a year[63]. Although the Amalgamation Bill was now submitted to Parliament, it was becoming evident that its acceptance was by no means guaranteed. Parliament in 1854 was in an anti-monopoly frame of mind, and Edward Cardwell's Bill opposing amalgamations and substituting ten-year leases was being considered in the same session. The Caledonian proposed that the merger Bill be withdrawn, provoking from the Edinburgh & Glasgow accusations of bad faith. Once more, too, the Caledonian board itself was split. The London Tavern was again the scene of a meeting of dissident shareholders, with John Copling, one of the directors, in the chair. He insisted that the Bill was "injurious to the original shareholders in its operation". It was said that parties at the head of the board held large quantities of E&G and Forth & Clyde Canal shares, and that Duncan had resigned from the board because of his opposition to the scheme. Under the terms of a 'Wharncliffe Meeting' (after Lord Wharncliffe, see page 25) as required by standing orders of the House of Lords for such transactions – intended to ensure that the shareholders were still in support before the relevant Bill got its final reading – the board would need to have the support of three quarters of the stock represented at the meeting. Copling and Campbell claimed to have gathered enough proxy votes to make it impossible for the board to get its way. But in any case, the Commons rejected the Bill and also a Bill for amalgamation of the Scottish Central and Scottish Midland Junction Railways. Between the two latter companies, however, though they had to abandon joint working, "the most friendly relations subsist in respect to moving the traffic." This was not to be the case with the Caledonian and Edinburgh & Glasgow companies, and the combined management came to an end. At a joint directors' meeting after the Bill's failure, the E&G refused to negotiate unless they were given a share of the Glasgow-London traffic revenues and also of the North of Scotland traffic to the major English provincial cities. Collateral agreements with other companies prevented the Caledonian from complying even if it had wished to[64], but relations very quickly soured. The Edinburgh & Glasgow company, hemmed in on all sides, was truculent, and competition for custom between Glasgow and Edinburgh became intense. Between 1854 and 1855 the Caledonian was running seventeen daily trains, six of them expresses, between the cities, at a third class fare of 1s., subsequently halved to 6d. The Edinburgh & Glasgow was matching this and both companies were making heavy losses on the service.

An Edinburgh-to-Glasgow train crosses the Union Canal at Kingsknowe.
The date could be any time between 1895 and 1913.

CHAPTER 5. Mid-Century 1854-63

London vs Glasgow

On 14 April 1854 the board had approved a 14-year agreement with the Magnetic Telegraph Company[1]. Robert Sinclair proposed to restructure the company's cartage arrangements despite the recent contract with Pickfords and Gordon, with a switch to J. & P. Cameron, whom he considered to be businesslike, well-established, and influential in assigning traffic (an important point where railways were competing). In view of the ending of the agreement with the Edinburgh & Glasgow Railway, it was important to get the best carter, and he wanted to pre-empt Cameron from going to the E&G. He proposed that Cameron should work Lothian Road, Pickfords Buchanan Street, and Gordon South Side. But there was a secret intention for the company to proceed "quietly to appropriate that influence so as not to require extraneous aid in future"[2]. Meanwhile Sinclair assured the directors that increased traffic would pay for Cameron's higher rates, as well as the necessary pay-off to Pickfords and Gordons. As so often with commercial agreements, division of the cartage proved to be contentious, and dispute with Pickfords went on into 1856.

Warfare on the board continued. Copling and Campbell, concerned about dividends, demanded information on share sales since 1851 and protested when a board majority instructed departmental heads not to give them direct information. English Debenture holders and Scottish Guaranteed Interests were again at odds. Copling and Campbell advised dissident shareholders that the four directors placed on the Board by Act of Parliament, to represent the "Guaranteed Interests", were due to stand down in September, and hoped the shareholders would replace them with Englishmen, "as long as three quarters of the shares were held in England"[3]. The retiring directors, Baird, McMicking, Price, Johnston, Kidston and Speirs, were all standing for re-election. William Baird announced his intention to stand down as chairman, publishing a statement in his own defence, noting that the Caledonian was now on a much better footing. In July 1851, Edinburgh & Glasgow stock with a face value of £100 had sold at £57, and Caledonian stock at £23. Now the respective figures were £59 and £64[4]. His adversaries retorted that he should never have been on the board: "Mr Baird announces his decision to quit a Board to which his position as a large trader over the line, with adverse or divided interest to ordinary dividend, and his long persecution of the Caledonian during the troubles he and his 'confederation' had helped bring on it, ought to be a disqualification"[5]. Efforts by some shareholders to get John Duncan re-elected to the board fizzled out, against claims of evidence that he had sought to be a "paid chairman"[6].

The September half-yearly meeting was in London. Another modest 3% dividend had already been declared. Mr. Fenton, in the chair, reported that there would be no attempt to re-present a Bill for joint working with the E&G, that negotiations for a division of the traffic had failed, and that the directors were preparing for a fare war, "to guard your legitimate interests". Everything, it seemed, had reverted to the old enmity. On a positive note, he

St Rollox Works, the erecting shop *c.*1896. In the foreground a Brittain 152-class 2-4-2T is being rebuilt as a condensing locomotive to run on the Glasgow Central Railway. Travelling crane in background.

listed forthcoming works including the expenditure of £10,500 on goods sheds and a locomotive depot at Carlisle, £20,000 on goods and passenger traffic at Carstairs, £19,000 on the new workshops at St. Rollox and £12,000 on a new engine shed there. Re-election of the retiring directors was forced through by directors' proxy votes, against furious opposition and accusations of underhand and illegal methods[7]. Since the Guaranteed Lines directors had been installed rather than elected in the normal manner, the dissidents objected to the Board using proxy votes to re-elect them. They also (with William Baird chiefly in their sights) objected to "the election of mineral and trading carriers on the line to seats on the board." William Johnston was elected as chairman[8]. The Glaswegians remained in control.

A short but strategic link built around this time was the 'Hayhill Fork', completing the triangle of lines between Gartsherrie, Gartcosh and Garnqueen North, laid to relieve congestion at Gartsherrie, though it also saved the Monkland & Kirkintilloch tollage charge on trains running between Glasgow and the north. In September 1853 the half-yearly report had noted that "the short independent junction between the Garnkirk section and the Castlecary branch is in course of construction," and new terms were agreed with the Monkland company for use of the Gartsherrie-Garnqueen section by March 1854[9]. The original Garnqueen Junction was renamed Garnqueen South.

Old Enemies and New Alliances

A disgruntled passenger complained in January 1855 that he had bought a Caledonian ticket from Glasgow to Edinburgh for one shilling, but, choosing to get off at an intermediate station, was promptly charged an additional 2*s.* 6*d.*[10]. The Caledonian and E&G did not even try to defend such practices, and the Caledonian claimed it was making a profit on the Edinburgh trains. A shareholders' meeting on 16 January approved the raising of additional capital and debentures to finance the building of new offices at Buchanan Street, the Motherwell deviation line, and the new 'branch' linking Gartcosh and Garnqueen[11]. Feeling more confident as traffic revenue rose, the board was no longer in an embarrassed state, though still being careful. The spring and autumn dividends in 1855 were both 3%, but, with the 1851 capital of £600,000 largely used up in paying old debts, the company was proposing to raise a further £500,000, this time to buy much-needed new plant.

The attractions of Lanark, promoted by the CR, in the 1900s.

The town of Lanark had been bypassed by the main line, but in 1853, local interests formed the Lanark Railway Company and with the Caledonian's blessing installed a double junction at Cleghorn, three miles west of Carstairs, enabling trains from Edinburgh or Glasgow to run along a short branch to a terminus at Lanark. It opened on 5 January 1855 and was worked from the start by the Caledonian, which would wholly acquire it on 23 July 1860. The Crofthead extension of the Glasgow, Barrhead & Neilston Direct Railway, taking the line as far as Neilston, was opened on 5 October 1855 and remained "a Caledonian arrow pointing in the direction of Kilmarnock". Crofthead would be renamed as Neilston on 1 June 1868[12].

Through 1855 relations between the Caledonian and the Edinburgh & Glasgow companies remained bitter and recriminative, sharpened further by the Scottish Central's decision to side with the Edinburgh & Glasgow, seen by the Caledonian as the E&G "inducing the Scottish Central to abandon their natural alliances"[13]. It became apparent that the SCR and

E&G had made a secret agreement that all English traffic from the north coming via the SCR would be routed via the E&G. The SCR stopped its Glasgow goods trains at the E&G's Sighthill Station instead of Buchanan Street, even when goods were specifically booked through to the Caledonian station. Quite apart from its damaging impact on the companies involved, the dispute also affected other railways both north and south, as well as traders. Extension or revision of the Octuple Agreement on traffic between Scotland and England was under discussion through 1855, and the joint committee set up to review this agreement also took on the task of reconciling the Edinburgh & Glasgow and Caledonian companies, but had to admit failure[14]. The E&G was a tricky company to deal with. While the CR wanted to sort out the whole issue of north-south traffic, the E&G preferred to stick to Edinburgh-Glasgow. Asked if it was willing to abide by the traffic shares set out in the Octuple Agreement, it replied vaguely that "on the understanding that all other points are satisfactorily settled, the E&G most probably would assent to the proportion of traffic assigned to them in the treaty for English and Scotch traffic." Towards the end of 1855 things were looking bad, with the Glasgow-Edinburgh fares war bleeding the profits of both companies, to the fury of many shareholders. Once again the Lancastrians were on the warpath, demanding a committee of investigation. The Board managed to fend them off, and during the winter of 1855-56 the situation improved. A new 14-year "English and Scotch Traffic Agreement" was made, involving the Caledonian, North British, Lancaster and Carlisle, LNWR, NER, GNR and Midland companies, with the GSWR also a party, and with provision for including the SCR (which had walked out of the discussions) and the E&G (which had not been involved) as and when it might be possible. And Lancastrian pressure on both companies managed to bring about an agreement between the Caledonian and the Edinburgh & Glasgow – a ten-year joint purse arrangement for the net traffic of both lines, to be apportioned by an arbiter, Henry Houldsworth of Manchester, a former chairman of the Lancashire & Yorkshire Railway (and whose family had industrial interests at Coltness). A joint committee of the Caledonian and E&G Boards met in London on 20 February 1856 and backdated the agreement to 1 January 1856, "on all traffic of whatever description, passengers, animals and goods or other articles", except coal, coke, etc., and mails, though a year later discussion on the details was still dragging on[15]. With a degree of amity restored between Glasgow and Edinburgh, the Scottish Central was isolated. Perhaps with a twinge of vengefulness, the Caley backed a proposal for a 'Denny Junction Railway' from Greenhill to the Forth & Clyde Junction Railway at Stirling, which would have competed both with the SCR's southern section of main line and its own branch to Denny[16], but the proposal, hotly opposed by the SCR, was rejected by the House of Lords. The Caledonian Board made conventional noises of disappointment but probably was not too bothered; Johnston had noted at the half-yearly meeting of 20 March 1856 that now, "we may consider ourselves quite invulnerable"[17].

In February Thomas McMicking resigned as a director, but the board hoped he might be induced to reconsider, and he resumed attendance at the meeting of 20 March. He was one of the few Sabbatarians on the board, but also a shrewd businessman. Money was tight and the company had to extend the period of some loans: in April £30,000 was borrowed from the Clydesdale Bank against the security of £60,000 worth of consolidated stock in the company's hands. Of this sum, ⁵/₆ths was in extension of an existing loan. The interest rate was 6%. Another loan of £20,000 was extended in May, at 4%. The company already had a £50,000 loan from the Clydesdale Bank, at 5%[18]. Later in the year, rather than pay off a loan from the Commercial Bank, secured on 4% and 5% Preference Half Shares, the bank was asked to sell the shares, if it could do so at par. It seems this was not possible, as a loan of £31,300 from the Commercial Bank was extended, at 5.5% interest, in November[19]. The finances were helped by a new agreement for mail carriage, concluded with the Post Office, at an annual rate of £23,710. Prior to that charges had been at a mileage rate, 1s. 8d. per mile, which had brought in £16,457 in 1853[20].

In July 1856 the "loose amalgamation" of the Scottish Central with the Scottish Midland Junction and Aberdeen Railways[21] ended when the Scottish Midland Junction and Aberdeen companies amalgamated on the 29th to form the Scottish North Eastern Railway. One company now controlled the line between Perth, Forfar and Aberdeen. The Dundee & Arbroath's link between Glasterlaw and Friockheim was now unused and the tracks were lifted in 1857. On 8 July Robert Sinclair announced his resignation, leaving the company with two posts to fill. His last communication to the board was to inform it that the transfer of the locomotive and carriage works from Greenock to St. Rollox was now complete. The September half-yearly report noted "overtures of peace made by the Scottish Central Board, and cordially responded to by this company … may, it is hoped, result in the removal of obstructions thrown for the last two years in the way of the Caledonian Company's North of Scotland traffic"[22]. Christopher Johnstone, the goods manager, was appointed as general manager. Benjamin Conner, who had been works manager at Neilson's Hyde Park Works, took up the post of locomotive superintendent and manager of the new locomotive works from 1 October[23]. By now the company's affairs were being run from Glasgow, though the general manager's office was at 138 George Street, the secretary's at 45 Renfield Street, and the goods manager's at 135 St. Vincent Street[24] – clearly a head office building was badly needed.

William Johnston was re-elected as chairman on 23 September 1856, with Thomas Salkeld, a Cumberland landowner, as deputy. At this time, the board had five permanent committees, for workshops, locomotives & stores; permanent way & traffic; finance; joint lines; and Carlisle Joint Station. The committee for economy had produced a report earlier in the month and was disbanded. At this time, Walker's cartage contract with the company seems to have come to an end, with Walker advertising his horses and equipment for sale. The contract was taken over by J.P. Kidston at the same rate, 6s. 8d. a day per horse and man. Another Kidston was a director of the Caledonian.

New Lines and New Plant

Despite financial stringencies, a round of salary rises was announced on 6 October. George Graham was to receive £350 a year plus £100 for each 1% of dividend; Mr. Galbraith, the accountant, £250 with the same bonus; Johnstone went to £600 with £150 for each percentage point of dividend; and Archibald Gibson was also advanced to £600, with £100 bonus on the same terms. The clerks in the company offices were receiving between £30 and £60 a year. Benjamin Conner was to receive £400 a year and the new Goods Manager, Mr. Mathieson, £250 plus £100 for each 1% of dividend. Senior officials had to pay in a bond of £1,000 to the company (the board agreed to pay Conner's in the first instance, as he had not been advised of it when accepting his appointment). More junior employees who handled money were covered by the Guarantee Society, a national body to which the company paid a regular premium. Defaulting was rare, and whenever it happened, the company reacted quickly, as when James Macdonald, goods cashier at Buchanan Street, absconded with £245 in October 1857, including a cheque for £97 which was immediately stopped at the Western Bank, and a claim was speedily made to the Guarantee Society[25].

A staff circular in March 1856 informed engine crews, guards, porters, pointsmen and bankheadmen – the most likely to suffer injury or death at work – that they were to be insured with the Travellers & Marine Insurance Co., the company paying one third of the premium and the balance to be deducted on a fortnightly basis from their pay packets. But the board resolved on 5 November to leave the scheme. The deductions had not started at the right time and payments were £717 9*s.* 10*d.* in arrears. It was stated that the premiums far exceeded the claims, and the company reverted to its former system of paying compensation at its own discretion (a hint of carelessness or rule-breaking was enough to make it refuse). In most cases, a £10 'gratuity' was offered on death through injury, and the company paid for very many wooden legs and invalid carriages over the years. Through the insurance scheme, £50 would have been payable.

In a curious episode, the record books of the goods station at Edinburgh were checked by Thomas Mackay, the company's lawyer, who concluded that Cameron, the cartage company, had been fraudulently overcharging, taking advantage of the inefficiency of Mr. Millar, the goods superintendent there. What was mysterious was that Mackay exonerated Cameron personally from blame, yet no-one else – including Cameron's clerk, Comrie, whom Mackay accused of tampering with the account books – appeared to have profited. Also Cameron's own records, quite improperly (and surely not accidentally) had been destroyed, "sold for waste paper." Robert Sinclair, now with the Eastern Counties Railway, who had been in charge of the cartage arrangements, might have had some answers, but he does not seem to have been consulted[26].

On 1 December 1856 an important new line was opened. The Lesmahagow Railway ran south from Motherwell to Coalburn, or rather to a colliery site at Bankend, west of Coalburn, by way of Larkhall and Lesmahagow. This line had been proposed as early as 1846, and the CR had obtained an Act for its construction in 1847. It had then fallen victim to the double crisis of a financial recession and the dubious accounting of the Caledonian, which left no capital to fund the works. Coping with the angry recriminations of the original backers took up a good deal of the reformed board's time but eventually the Lesmahagow Railway was re-proposed, and re-authorised in 1851, against counter-proposals from both the Edinburgh & Glasgow and the GSWR companies. Engineered by Neil Robson, a Glasgow civil engineer much involved in railway affairs, who had also been engineer of the Glasgow, Barrhead & Neilston line, it was not a straightforward line to construct, with lofty viaducts needed to cross the Clyde and Nethan valleys, though these were built like the original Jerviston Viaduct on the Wishaw & Coltness, with laminated wooden arches between stone piers (they were rebuilt with steel decks, 1861-62). A single track was laid, essentially as a mineral line, with tight curves, speed being hardly a consideration, and a

**The Nethan Viaduct between Tillietudlem and Auchenheath was rebuilt at a higher level
with additional iron piers in 1860-61.**

passenger service was not provided. For a few months before the opening, the colliery owners had run their own wagons over the line, on payment of a toll. Estimates suggested that there were around 63,000,000 tons of extractable coal in this district, and with substantial traffic from the pit-heads, the Lesmahagow line proved a strong revenue-earner. Motherwell's iron and steel industries were expanding hugely, generating a great deal of goods traffic and causing frequent congestion. Lesmahagow line traffic exacerbated the problems. To the north, the single track Jerviston Viaduct over the South Calder Water had long been a bottleneck, and was structurally weak. On 10 October 1857 a short deviation line on the west was completed between a new junction at Fulwood Row (Jerviston Junction) just south of the then station of Holytown, and the Clydesdale Junction line, including the double track Braidwood Viaduct across the valley. The Motherwell station, then known as Motherwell Junction, was located south of the developing town centre, where the original Wishaw & Coltness and Clydesdale Junction lines met. There was no passenger station in Motherwell on the Lesmahagow line until February 1871. The original Wishaw & Coltness line between Jerviston Junction and Motherwell was not used by through traffic after the deviation was opened, but local goods workings used it at both ends. Just when its viaduct went out of use is not clear; the O.S. map of 1859 shows the original line as still intact.

Motherwell viaducts: The original wooden-arched Jerviston Viaduct of 1847, and the Braidhurst or 'Babylon' Bridge built on the diversion line, 1857.

This 0-6-0, bought from Neilsons in 1858 to test against four-coupled engines, was rebuilt as a 2-4-0 in 1873. Conner built two further trial engines at St Rollox in 1872 (Nos. CR120 and 121) before finally adopting the 0-6-0 wheel arrangement in 1874 with the 631-class (see plate on page 113).

Conner's survey of rolling stock resulted in a clutch of new orders made in January 1857: ten first class carriages at £292 each; 14 thirds at £212 plus £22 extra for "guards' seats and breaks"; 14 composite thirds with a single second class compartment at the same price and with the same extras, all from Joseph Wright of Birmingham; 250 mineral wagons at £50 from John Ashbury, Manchester; and 84 goods wagons at £29 15s. less 5%, from Faulds of Glasgow. While some may have been replacements, it was a sign of increasing traffic, and further large orders for wagons followed in August: 137 mineral wagons at £57 10s., 100 pig iron trucks at £33, and 20 bar-iron trucks at £70, from Ashbury; 20 goods wagons at £86 10s. and 10 cattle trucks at £86 10s. from Wright. In October 19 pairs of timber wagons were ordered from Ashbury, at £116 per pair. It would seem that the St. Rollox Works were not yet building new wagons. The scant provision for second class passengers reflects the standard position on Scottish railways, on which a high proportion of travellers went third class through choice rather than necessity. And second class on the Caledonian was quite Spartan: it was not until 1860 that, following complaints, cushions were provided[27]. In May 1857, Conner was given the go-ahead for five new locomotives, with £2,600 of the cost to be set against the revenue account and the balance to capital.

In February 1857 Houldsworth made his apportionment of the joint purse, 69.36% of the traffic revenue of both lines to the Caledonian, and 30.64% to the E&G. He also stipulated that working expenses for both should be taken as 41% of gross revenue[28]. That month a new agreement with the British & Irish Magnetic Telegraph Company was approved, probably as a formality since the old 'Magnetic' had absorbed the British & Irish Telegraph Company in January. On 1 April it was reported to the Board that the wagon-wrights in the company's workshops were threatening to go on strike in pursuit of a wage claim. The matter was referred to the workshops committee, "with full powers"; at the same time the joiners and platelayers were petitioning for a pay rise, and George Graham was instructed "to exercise his discretion" in the matter. In 1857 Henry Ward, who had been with the traffic department for ten years, was appointed superintendent of the line, a position he would hold for 24 years. In viewing the Caledonian's history, it is essential to remember that behind the board was a small group of highly capable officials, including George Graham, Archibald Gibson and Henry Ward, who assured a degree of continuity, expertise and stability through some tempestuous and controversial episodes, representing it at inter-company official gatherings, and, importantly, at Railway Clearing House meetings, and ensuring that daily business was properly transacted. But the board could assert its authority: when James Stewart, retiring as passenger superintendent at Buchanan Street, was made the subject of a public testimonial (i.e. a cash collection), it did not interfere, but stated that in future company officers who solicited or received testimonials would be dismissed[29].

The joint purse agreement with the Edinburgh & Glasgow was amended to take in the Scottish Central from 9 September 1857, with some alterations to the terms on 3 October. It accorded the SCR 14.988% of the combined net revenue of the three lines, leaving 85.012% to the other two companies, split as before[30]. The arrangement would be modified several times in the following months, usually at the behest of the SCR, but it survived until 1860, helped by a general improvement in economic conditions. That effectively put an end to competition on fares and rates, with no more ultra-cheap tickets, but traffic continued to increase in line with the growth of industry and population.

The Caledonian's original Edinburgh route was to have run via Biggar and Broughton. Now the Symington, Biggar & Broughton Railway was finally proposing to provide a line along the eastern flank of the Pentland Hills. The CR offered a ten-year agreement to work it for 40% of revenue, with a minimum payment of £1,200 a year (equating to its estimate of the working cost). Three trains each way daily would be run. The promoters, with a deficit of £7,500 in their share subscription of £32,000, asked the Caledonian to make up the difference, to which the Caledonian eventually agreed, on the understanding that local capital would amount to at least £20,000: "There can be no doubt of the great importance to the Caledonian to have possession of this district and control of its traffic"[31]. Its demand that the promoters acquire ground for a double track line, though only a single track was laid, suggests a strategic cross-country aim.

Yet another spasm of conscience about Buchanan Street Station prompted the company to announce a competition, on 4 November 1857, for the design of a new passenger terminal and company offices, with a prize fund of £200. How necessary this was can be gauged from passenger statistics: in 1850, 1,949,405 passenger journeys had been made on the Caledonian; in 1855 this number had risen to over three million[32]. But the timing was not propitious. The Western Bank, Glasgow's premier banking house, collapsed on 9 November, with liabilities to the public of more than £9 million. Panic reigned in the

Station staff at Broughton, around 1905.

money market and among the bank's depositors. Huge numbers of Western Bank notes were in circulation, but what were they worth? The CR instructed its staff to refuse them[33]. On the 11th, the City of Glasgow Bank stopped payments, and a general financial collapse seemed imminent. Intervention by other banks, including the more conservatively managed Edinburgh ones, staved off a financial disaster. Western Bank notes were ultimately honoured and the City of Glasgow Bank resumed trading[34]. Over-confident and ignorant speculation in railway stocks had been the prime cause of the banking failure, though the railways were mostly in the USA rather than in Great Britain.

Following receipt of a letter from the Board of Trade on the subject of communication between guards and drivers on moving trains, the company agreed on 27 January 1858 to try out a scheme on the Greenock line. To its credit, the Caledonian was always one of the most responsive railway companies to the Board of Trade's initiatives in improving safety measures. On 17 February the manager's salary was upped to £1,000 a year plus £150 for each 1% of dividend, and the secretary's to £800 plus a £100 bonus on the same basis. On 7 April it was announced that J.T. Rochead, the architect of the Wallace Monument tower at Stirling, had won the competition for Buchanan Street. No less than 63 designs had been sent in. Rochead's drawings were added to the file of unused plans. Little ever happened at Buchanan Street except the addition of more and more goods-handling facilities. Glasgow's magistrates and the travelling public continued to complain about the inadequacy of all the city's termini. At this time, steamers, charging low fares, could still compete with the railway. A bold move by two English companies, the Great Northern and the Manchester, Sheffield & Lincolnshire, put on a Glasgow-Liverpool steamer with a train connection to London in May 1858. By September the steamship operator had withdrawn, and was receiving £150 a year for three years as the Caledonian's traffic agent in Liverpool[35].

'The Caledonian Central Railway'

The North British Railway had long intended to extend its line from Hawick to Carlisle, and when it put forward a Bill for this, the Caledonian responded in July 1858 with its own Bill for a Carlisle, Langholm & Hawick Railway. Thomas Salkeld, the deputy chairman, was one of the prime movers. Capital was to be £350,000, of which local sources were expected to contribute £75,000 and the Caledonian £125,000. The proposed company was to be very much within the CR's embrace: "No compromise to be concluded with the North British Railway by either party without the consent of the other"[36]. On 4 September, Richard Hodgson, the North British chairman, offered the possibility of joint construction of a line from Hawick to Gretna, also from Riccarton to Bellingham, meeting the Border Counties line, and from Bellingham to Hexham, on the Newcastle-Carlisle railway, with joint working[37]. The Caledonian declined the prospect of sharing a Borders network. Nothing was going to be done that might help the North British get access to Carlisle and the lucrative English traffic. But the Caledonian's Bill failed and despite intense opposition from Langholmthe North British got its Act for the Border Union Railway, from Hawick to Carlisle, crossing over the Caledonian at Kingmoor and joining the Port Carlisle Railway (leased by the NBR) so that only the last few chains into Citadel Station involved running powers, and charges, on Caledonian tracks. A NBR branch from Longtown to Gretna was included, making a link, via a short section of the CR line, with the Glasgow & South Western.

Comparative peace made amalgamation seem again a possibility, and the board set up a sub-committee on 8 September to consider the details of a merger with the Scottish Central and the Edinburgh & Glasgow. Progress was spasmodic, and the Caledonian was also tying up executive time in the negotiations with the North British. In December, Johnston went abroad in the interest of his health and discussions came to a standstill until February 1859, when amalgamation talks resumed. Between 6 May and 25 October that year the joint Amalgamation Committee of the Caledonian, Edinburgh & Glasgow, and Scottish Central met and kept a minutes book. The CR members were Thomas McMicking, John Macdowall, and Thomas Hill, with Christopher Johnstone and Archibald Gibson. The E&G team of three directors was led by Blackburn, with John Latham the general manager and John Jamieson, company secretary. The SCR fielded a solitary director, George Gray. It was agreed that in the event of amalgamation, the SCR should receive a minimum annual dividend of 6%, until the earnings rose enough to exceed that level, at which point the 'surplus' would be shared in equal proportions. Most of the meetings were taken up by argument between the two larger companies on the value of their lines. This was resolved on 21 September, with the recommendation that for the first six years after the passing of an Amalgamation Act, the Caledonian should receive a 10% greater dividend than the E&G, and after that the proportions should be equal. McMicking, who had resigned before over amalgamation terms, did so again in protest against these terms, believing that the CR had already accepted too great a disadvantage in the "modified competition" created by the joint purse arrangement. In an exchange of letters with Salkeld, he accused the other two companies of manipulating the system both operationally and financially to the CR's disadvantage, noting that the E&G had insisted that the amalgamation of stocks should be on a basis of "the ascertained actual amount of revenue earned and available during each half-year since 1st of February 1856". However, the E&G had insisted that neither company should have charged any additional plant to capital, but all to revenue. As it happened, the Edinburgh & Glasgow had spent very little on plant, and the Caley had spent a great deal, so that the value of the E&G was artificially increased. In his reply, Salkeld was at pains to make clear that he had nothing to gain by favouring the E&G: his family had £70,000 invested in the Caledonian and nothing in the other company, and he asked: "… shall we refuse a very great benefit to ourselves because it will be a still greater one to them?"[38]. Action for a Bill was put in hand[39]. An eminent civil engineer, Thomas Elliot Harrison, from Robert Stephenson's chambers, was appointed on 11 October to examine the lines and plant "to ascertain their present efficiency" and to do so again once the Act was passed, so that any cost of making good could be deducted from the appropriate shareholders' first dividend[40]. The amalgamated company was to be called the Caledonian Central Railway[41]. With these exciting prospects in view, William Johnston retired as chairman in September and Thomas Salkeld was elected in his place.

Something like an American club-car was introduced in May 1859 for the benefit of Greenock's sugar barons travelling to and from Glasgow, a 'Smoking Saloon' painted in two-tone brown and white, presaging a more universal carriage colour scheme for the Company – at this time the passenger stock was painted brown, with lined-out panels[42]. In 1859, under the auspices of W.H. Smith & Son, an *Official Guide to the Edinburgh & Glasgow and Caledonian Railways* was published. Mostly a résumé of the standard historic tourist sights, natural or man-made, to be encountered near the railway, it interestingly includes descriptions of numerous industrial plants, though whether these places actually offered public access is not clear. They included the huge chemical factories, steel works, cotton mills, pottery works, iron foundries and pipe-works that were drawing thousands of workers as new residents into Glasgow. The Caledonian's route into Buchanan Street was marked by the famous 'Tennant's stalk', the 450ft stack of the chemical works, though an even taller chimney was Townsend's at Crawford Street, at 460ft the world's tallest in 1859[43]. There was a real pride in these constructions, often shown, especially in the more centrally-placed factories, by distinctive architectural styles and a high degree of finish in brick and stonework, at least in the façades.

Expansion and Economy

By 1860 the Caledonian employed 3,647 staff, as many as the North British and Edinburgh & Glasgow combined, and had 64 stations. The GSWR was not far behind with 59 stations, though its staff numbered only 1,990. An Act for branch railways to the Wilsontown mineral field was obtained on 21 July 1859 and no time was lost in laying a track from near Auchengray, on the Carstairs-Edinburgh line, towards Wilsontown (opened on 22 October 1860). At this time the area's deep-lying shale oil deposits were being intensively exploited. A few miles away, at Addiewell on the Midcalder line, five locomotives were running shale trains between the pit and the crushers and extraction retorts of the Addiewell Chemical Works. In this region, as in the other industrial districts, many miles of private track were laid to provide mines, quarries, ironworks and factories with access to the main railway lines and the branches. Ordnance Survey maps of the 1850s and later show hundreds of such access lines, often several miles long and with their own junction points and branches, sometimes tunnels, traversing the landscape between the main railways. Mostly tramways rather than railways, they were often of narrow gauge. For direct links to railway lines, the usual arrangement was that the railway company laid the track to the quarry or colliery gate or boundary at its own cost, and provided the linkage and internal tracks at an agreed price.

The Symington, Biggar & Broughton Railway opened on 6 November 1860, and even before completion it had applied, prompted by the Caledonian, for an extension as far as Peebles, which already was linked by railway with Edinburgh, under North British auspices. The CR was willing to invest £15,000 in the Peebles extension and to buy up the Symington, Biggar & Broughton at cost[44]. This thrust towards NBR territory was aimed beyond Peebles to Galashiels, and would establish a Caledonian presence right across the Borderlands. At the time the NBR was also trying to obtain an Act for a railway from Peebles to Galashiels, and a pact was made whereby, if the Caledonian did not oppose that proposal, it could make a double junction at Peebles, with a northward spur to the North British station and an eastwards one to lead into the Galashiels line. The NBR even offered the possibility of Caledonian goods depots at Innerleithen and Galashiels, to be served at agreed rates by NBR trains.

Once again the Caledonian's effort to absorb the Edinburgh & Glasgow failed. On 15 May 1860 the Amalgamation Bill was thrown out by the House of Commons, which did not consider a single company should monopolise the traffic between the two cities. In fact the joint purse agreement, now four years old, had effectively limited competition anyway, to the annoyance of goods shippers. This time, however, a co-operative spirit remained, and the Caledonian offered to extend the joint purse arrangement without further revision for another twenty years, and to pay the Scottish Central £800 a year, this being the amount that company claimed to be losing under the current terms. At the half-yearly meeting on 11 September 1860 Salkeld gave a bullish report on the state of the company and economic conditions generally, and also "no rupture in the present arrangements" with the E&G and SCR. The dividend of 4.25% on the Ordinary shares showed a pleasing rise after the lean years, and twenty locomotives were under construction, making the total fleet 204. He also noted that "When this railway was first opened, owing to the extreme poverty of the company, the mineral traffic of the line was worked without break vans" and this was still very common. Now, however, with more trains and greater concern for safety, the practice was to be greatly reduced: 25 goods brakes had been delivered in the half-year, and a further ten to fifteen were to be built[45]. Among other events of 1860 was an Act for the establishment of the Lesmahagow Railways Guaranteed Company, confirming Caledonian control for an annuity of £5,885. Making expansive agreements on the one hand, the Caledonian was still pursuing economies on the other. When the platelayers asked for a pay rise in June, they were given an extra shilling a week "until after the harvest" and in December, when the question of uniform renewal came up, the board decided to follow the example of the Glasgow City Police, and buy cloth wholesale in London and have the uniforms made up by inmates of the Glasgow Reformatory[46].

Despite all previous rebuffs, another Bill was introduced to Parliament in the session of 1861 for the dissolution of the Edinburgh & Glasgow and Scottish Central companies, and their amalgamation with the CR into the 'Caledonian Central Railway'. The capital of the three companies was noted as £4,870,684 in the Caledonian, with loans of £2,516,366; while the E&G had capital of £3,128,375 and loans of £1,311,700. The Central's capital was £1,388,400 and its loans amounted to £460,000. Yet again the Bill was rejected, after strong opposition from the Glasgow and Edinburgh municipalities, and the ever-critical *Railway Times* observed that "… the Caledonian retreats for another year into the accommodation derived from a joint purse with the Edinburgh & Glasgow and the Scottish Central"[47]. But the companies were holding together, and the CR was advancing on various fronts. The half-yearly meeting on 12 March 1861 had been told of three new branches in the 'mineral district', and a Wharncliffe meeting (see page 67) on 21 May unanimously approved them: an Act for the enlargement and regulation of Carlisle Citadel Station, a direct line between Rutherglen and Coatbridge, with a branch to Whifflet; an extension from the Cleland branch to Morningside, with branches to Omoa, Drumbowie and Langridge; and an extension from Ayr Road (later Dalserf), on the Lesmahagow line, to Cotcastle, just beyond Stonehouse; and for the amalgamation of the Symington, Biggar & Broughton Railway with the Caledonian[48]. Every shareholder could agree that these were the kind of developments the Caledonian should be making, to tap the apparently inexhaustible mineral riches lying beneath the unrewarding topsoil of Scotland. Money was made available to improve the permanent way, with £40,000 in the half-year, to include 60,000 new sleepers, and £49,000 was also spent on locomotive purchase and repair.

The Caledonian had had a friendly relationship with the fifth Duke of Buccleuch since its earliest days, and allied with him in order to extend its foothold in Edinburgh. Buccleuch owned the harbour at Granton, west of Leith, built in 1835-42, and an Act for an access line from the Caledonian at Slateford was obtained in 1857, with the company putting up half the capital of £60,000. Difficulties with the contractor led to a delayed opening on 28 August 1861. The branch was for goods only, dividing into lines serving the western breakwater and the harbour quay. A North British branch came in from Leith to the east, and Granton became an exchange point for goods, using the ducally owned harbour tracks (owned by the Buccleuch estate until 1948). On 24 June 1861 a short goods branch was opened from Rutherglen to Dalmarnock, with a bridge over the Clyde, to serve the intense industrial development of the area. This branch, only a mile long, eventually had five miles and 579 yards of sidings whereas the 43 miles between Dundee and Perth had 3 miles 510 yards[49]. Sidings were often laid with redundant main line rails and sleepers, following upgrading of the permanent way (if not required in this way the rails were sold as scrap in the company's regular disposals of waste and scrapped plant).

Shunting at Granton Gasworks, the spur built 1901-02. Some very tight curves are evident.

**Benjamin Conner's 2-2-2 design with 8ft 2in driving wheels;
the first locomotive class built at St Rollox, from 1857.**

The outbreak of civil war in the United States in 1861 had swift repercussions on Scottish industry. Blockade of the Confederate states caused disruption in raw cotton supplies and the cotton factories were badly hit. Scottish merchants had long traded with the American South and these links resulted in a boom for Clyde shipbuilding, with a stream of orders for fast steamships which could run the blockade and maintain the Confederacy's imports and exports. Seventeen new shipyards opened between 1861 and 1864. Great Britain's official neutrality was stretched thin by these activities, but the bonanza fed back into the coal and iron industries and the many ancillary businesses to shipbuilding; and the Caledonian Railway, though it still lacked proper access to the north bank of the Clyde, got its share. A dividend of 5.5% was declared for August 1861-January 1862. But the effects were mixed, with a reduction of general trade to the United States, and at the half-yearly meeting on 12 September 1862, Salkeld hoped for a trade increase after the American War ended; and the dividend was down half a percent. At this time the company also built a bullion van to add to the rolling stock[50].

The Hamilton & Strathaven Railway, authorised on 8 August 1857, opened for goods to Quarter Road (Quarter from 1 July 1909) on 6 August 1860 and to Strathaven on 16 June 1862; passenger trains ran from Hamilton from 2 February 1863. A circuitous route between the terminal towns, it was more concerned to take in mineral traffic than to make a point-to-point connection. A branch to Eddlewood Colliery was included. Trains from Hamilton set off in the Glasgow direction before diverging at Strathaven Junction and turning west, then south, through High Blantyre, Meikle Earnock, and Quarter Road. Steeply graded with a maximum 1 in 64, it was not a cheap line, and stations remained rudimentary. Seventeen years later there were protests about the small, fireless waiting room at Quarter Road being filled up with goods packages[51].

Tweedledum and Tweedledee

Inter-company relations were often taut or hostile at board level between the North British and Caledonian, the Tweedledum and Tweedledee of Scottish railways. If the animosity was driven largely by Richard Hodgson, chairman of the NB, the Caledonian was rarely slow to respond in kind. Hodgson and Salkeld were both Borderers (and both Englishmen), which may not have helped. But in the early years of the 1860s, it was becoming steadily more apparent that rationalisation of the Scottish railways was overdue. On 28 January 1862 the Caledonian and Edinburgh & Glasgow companies signed an agreement intended to come into force on

1 March 1866 (when the current joint purse arrangement ended) and to last for 30 years[52], but events in the next few years were to overtake it. Shareholder interests loved such arrangements, as they got rid of loss-making competition, and allowed charges to be fixed at a higher level than might otherwise be the case. For the same reason they were greatly disliked by customers of the railway. But the companies were seeking still closer bonds. From 31 January 1862 the Dundee & Arbroath company was effectively absorbed by the Scottish North Eastern Railway, although the position was not formalised until an Act of 28 July 1863.

A new International Exhibition was to be held in London in the summer of 1862. The Midland Railway, anxious to get a share of the Anglo-Scottish traffic, tried but failed to have the agreement of 1856 rewritten. Reformed arrangements were badly needed. Not only were passenger numbers growing fast, but so were the quantity and variety of goods being exchanged between the manufacturing districts, and distributed nationally by railway. G.P. Neele, superintendent of the LNWR, recorded his experience, and some aspects of long distance travel, at this time:

"The through traffic to Scotland was one of the subjects that early fell to my lot to deal with. There existed at this time, under the 'English and Scotch Agreement' as it was called, an arrangement by which, as between the East Coast route and the West Coast route, the whole receipts were 'pooled' (an imported American expression) and divided in certain agreed proportions. This had the effect of preventing any hostile action between the parties by reduction of fares, or acceleration of speed, but it also resulted in leaving the London and Edinburgh traffic to the East Coast route, and the Glasgow business to the West Coast; a state of things which continued quietly to exist so long as the Midland terminated at Normanton on the one side, and at Lancaster, via Skipton, on the other. All competitive fares were agreed at the English and Scotch Quarterly Conference, while so far as the train arrangements were concerned, those for the West Coast route were regulated at meetings held between the officers of the North-Western and the Caledonian Railways. The first I attended was on the 27th November, 1862. The controlling power at that time on the Caledonian was their Chairman, Colonel Salkeld; Mr. Christopher Johnstone was the General Manager, and Mr. Henry Ward, the Superintendent.

"This 'English and Scotch Traffic Agreement' dated from 1st January 1856, and was the outcome of a conference between the representatives of the English and interested Companies at the close of the year 1855, at which it was reported that as the Octuple Agreement would shortly expire, it was desirable that some steps should be taken to continue or extend its provisions. The Octuple Agreement was an arrangement for sharing the traffic from London to eight principal towns in the North-Midland district of England, based on an agreement which Mr. W. E. Gladstone, then coming to the front in public affairs, had had a very leading part in determining. The conference by which the establishment of the New English and Scotch traffic agreement was first debated was attended by Mr. C. Johnstone for the Caledonian, and representatives of the GSWR, NBR, LNWR, Lancaster & Carlisle, Midland, Great Northern, and York & North Midland Railways. It was agreed to adopt certain percentages for division of traffic, to remain in force for fourteen years; and the agreement was sealed by the seven interested companies, the London and North Western, the Lancaster and Carlisle, the Great Northern, the Caledonian, the North Eastern, the North British, and the Midland. Mr. W. E.Gladstone was named as the arbitrator, failing him, Mr. S. Laing.

"The train service to and from Scotland, judged by present lights, was of a very indifferent character, so far as speed was concerned. There was no 10 o'clock day express till June, 1862; the morning train from Euston left at 9.0 a.m., 1st and 2nd class only. It did not reach Edinburgh till 8.45 p.m., nor Glasgow till 9.10 p.m. The night train for general Scotch traffic left Euston at 9.0 p.m., and took upwards of 12 hours to reach Edinburgh, and 13 hours to Glasgow. The Limited Mail, 1st and 2nd class, then leaving Euston at 8.40 p.m., was limited to three carriages only, so far as passengers were concerned; one running to Perth, one to Edinburgh, and one to Glasgow. The train had no competitive service from King's Cross, and was timed to reach Edinburgh at 7.10, and Glasgow at 7.22. The restrictions on the train at the hands of the Post Office authorities were very close, and the concession of an extra vehicle to accommodate royalty entailed a visit to the Post Office to ask concurrence, and an undertaking that the punctual arrival should be maintained. The LNWR Manager, Mr. Cawkwell, refused to allow the Directors' Passes to be available by the train, and even when I had occasion to travel in attendance on any special parties, I had to take a ticket for my journey.

"'Conductors' were placed in charge of the passenger trains to Scotland; they were a class of men of a higher standing than ordinary guards; at first they were appointed to travel between London and Glasgow, but, in 1865, through a joint recommendation between Mr. Croll, of the Scottish Central, Mr. Ward of the Caledonian and myself, it was agreed they should travel between Euston and Perth instead. The smartest guards were generally selected as conductors, the appointment resting alternately with the Caledonian and the London and North Western. Mr. Preston, late station master at Carlisle, was early in his history one of these conductors. While the ordinary guards were responsible for the proper working of the vans in their own charge, the conductor was specially responsible for the luggage going through to Scotland, and in early days had a waybill of every package. Much of this luggage to avoid change on the journey (for the baggage vans did not run beyond Carlisle) was roofed on the carriages and strapped down under heavy tarpaulins; the night passengers at stations like Preston, with its then very low platforms, experienced very rough thumpings of heavy packages on the carriage roofs. Luggage slides were in use for lowering the articles, and broad steps to enable the men to pass up trunks, etc., from the platform to the men attending to the roofs. Mishaps were not unfrequent owing to striking bridges through careless loading, luggage overhanging and falling off through getting out of position by oscillation while travelling, fire arose from engine sparks, and frequent annoyance was experienced through the carriage roof lamps going out, their supply of air being cut off by close packing of luggage. I had the satisfaction of seeing this roofing of luggage, a relic of old coaching days, gradually but entirely dispensed with, the manager agreeing to my recommendation to adopt the plan of a separate luggage compartment in the centre of the passenger carriages, similar in style to those I had observed in Birmingham on the North Eastern Railway stock"[53].

Such luggage problems became a memory when the new West Coast Joint Stock was introduced for these trains in 1862, with longer carriages and interior luggage compartments.

With the completion of the Border Union Railway – soon named 'The Waverley Route' – at the end of 1861, three main lines converged on Carlisle from the north. From 23 June 1862 the NBR had also opened its link from the Border Union line to Gretna South Junction, converging in a northwards direction with the CR line south of the Caledonian station. The link enabled the Glasgow & South Western and North British to exchange goods traffic from the south west to Edinburgh and the north-east, with running powers over the Caledonian main line between Gretna North and South Junctions. This was regarded by the Caledonian as a breach of faith by the GSWR of their 1853 traffic agreement. On 29 July, the balance of railway power was more significantly altered when the North British took over the Edinburgh, Perth & Dundee company, becoming a part-owner of Perth General station and gaining a monopolistic presence in Fife. In a further development, the Edinburgh & Glasgow Railway absorbed the Caledonian & Dumbartonshire on 14 August. For the Caledonian Board, the message was clear: it too must achieve amalgamations or become dangerously isolated.

Coal output was still increasing and the demand, despite economic fluctuations, was still rising. The search for new workable reserves was spreading west and south-west from the central fields, and large deposits were identified in west Lanarkshire and across the county boundary in Ayrshire. As the colliery operators moved in, so did the railways, and the Caledonian network was enlarged. Most of these lines were envisaged primarily or wholly for mineral traffic, and passenger operations often came later. From the new junction at Dalserf (at that time called Ayr Road, not because of any proximity to Ayr but because here the line crossed the Edinburgh-Ayr turnpike), on the Larkhall-Lesmahagow-Coalburn line, by 1 September 1862 the rails were open to Canderside Colliery, just a couple of miles short of Stonehouse, with a branch from Southfield to Blackwood.

Although the Dundee & Perth & Aberdeen Railway made a junction with the Scottish Central at Perth General Station, its own trains terminated at Princes Street until 1862, when enlargements to the General Station included terminal platforms for the Dundee line, making transfer for passengers much more convenient. This 'Dundee

Lesmahagow: the new station of 1905.
Although there is a crossing loop, it has only a single platform, as at many other places.

Dock' was in use until 1887[54]. Also in 1862-63 the wooden bridge across the Tay was replaced by a stone structure, which, like its predecessor, incorporated a swing span. In Glasgow some improvements were made to the passenger station at Buchanan Street in 1861, when the arrival platform and its canopy were extended[55].

Taken by surprise in March 1863 when the Scottish Central proposed to take over the Dundee & Perth & Aberdeen, the Caledonian announced its intention to oppose the merger. At the half-yearly meeting of 17 March, it was made clear that the Caledonian did not want the Central to "obtain a position which would be more dangerous to the Caledonian than that which they already hold"[56]. The SCR in turn expressed surprise and anger, pointing out that it did not have to tell the Caley everything, and threatening to drop out from the tripartite agreement[57]. By May the spat had been resolved: it seemed likely that the East Coast companies would lease the Edinburgh & Glasgow Railway, and the Caledonian and SCR made a secret agreement to amalgamate if that should happen, and the Caledonian withdrew its objections to the takeover of the Dundee & Perth & Aberdeen Junction, which was duly approved by Parliament on 31 July[58]. With legislators once again willing to approve railway mergers, there was a general feeling that further amalgamations were only a matter of time. But the Caledonian directors were still obsessed by the Edinburgh & Glasgow – Salkeld suggested it was a propitious moment for the CR-E&G-SCR amalgamation, and yet another Bill was drafted.

The Scottish Central Railway in its now-enlarged form had the lease of the Dundee & Newtyle (the latter remained a financially independent enterprise until 1923), and took a keen interest in developing traffic on its two lines into Dundee. Rivalry between it and the Scottish North Eastern Railway became intense. The Scottish North-Eastern Railway reopened the Glasterlaw-Friockheim link, with a single track, giving better access to Dundee from Aberdeen and Montrose, but had also been engaged for several years in planning a direct line of its own over the Sidlaws between Forfar and Dundee, and a Bill for this line was submitted to Parliament in mid-1863. On the Newtyle line, the new leasors had to take over work in progress on a deviation around Newtyle itself, to eliminate the last of its original rope-hauled inclines, at Hatton; and also on new connections with the Perth-Forfar main line and the Alyth branch, which had opened on 2 September 1861. Meigle Station, where the 'Glammis Fork' met the Perth-Forfar line, had been resited as Meigle Junction half a mile west, at the point where the Alyth line joined, in an east-facing junction. Its former site became Meigle Upper Junction, though the rails of the 'Glammis Fork' were lifted in July 1861 before the Alyth branch opened[59]. The Alyth branch also had a Meigle Station, closer to the village.

Earlier in 1863, in March, some excitement had arisen over a "runaway engine" on the Caledonian. It transpired that a driver had fallen asleep at Beattock and his engine had moved off down the line. It had to be chased by another engine, and boarded, in order to be stopped. The errant driver absconded but was caught, tried at Dumfries and sent to prison. Dumfries itself was about to become a Caledonian terminus. The Dumfries, Lochmaben & Lockerbie Railway opened on 1 September 1863, with passenger services from a bay platform in the GSWR Dumfries Station. Though locally sponsored, it was very much a branch of the Caledonian, and travellers from Dumfries to Edinburgh soon had the choice of through services either by Lockerbie and Carstairs, or via Gretna and Hawick[60]. In Midlothian and North Lanarkshire the shale oil industry was still expanding. On 1 December 1863 the *Scotsman* reported that the refining works at Tarbrax had been enlarged, with a siding from the Cobbinshaw-Tarbrax goods branch of the Caledonian almost completed. Although one or two accounts state that Tarbrax had a passenger service, this was not the case. A passenger station was established at Cobbinshaw, though not until 1874, and was resited a little closer to Tarbrax on 4 October 1875.

The Tarbrax oil-extraction works had a rail connection to the Carstairs-Edinburgh line from 1869.

CHAPTER 6 The Great Amalgamations 1864-67

Machinations in Glasgow

Complaints in Glasgow about the inadequacy of the railway terminals made a loud and daily chorus. In each decade after 1847 the city stations experienced a two- or three-fold increase in passenger numbers, while remaining cramped to danger point. Buchanan Street, to which Caledonian passengers from the south were still being taken via Gartsherrie, was not the worst. The South Side terminus of the Barrhead line was described as "a discredit to the city". Bridge Street Station had four platform faces[1] but the site was narrow and handling over two million people a year by the later 1850s. Queen Street Station was also too small for the ever-increasing passenger traffic (in the 1860s, to suit the convenience of both companies, some sharing of facilities was still going on. Caledonian trains to Stirling and beyond used Queen Street Station, and E&G services to Coatbridge, Airdrie and beyond used Buchanan Street). Early in 1864 a scheme was brought forward for a "Union Railway Terminal" on the north bank of the Clyde. Though proposed as a joint station for the Caledonian, Edinburgh & Glasgow, and GSWR, with links to all their incoming main lines, the initiative came from the Glasgow & South Western Railway side, and its offer to the CR was less than generous. For an investment of £250,000, an annual user fee of £25,000, and a toll of 6d. per passenger, the Caledonian was allocated a modest part of the station and two out of nine directors. Unsurprisingly it chose to oppose the scheme, exposing it as a contractors' ramp. John Fowler, Samuel Morton Peto, Brassey and others had combined to put up £400,000 of capital as long as they got the building contract, with a guaranteed 10% profit. After the GSWR's combination with the North British to send trains via Gretna and the Waverley Route, and now this, the Caledonian Board had some reason to feel that their traffic-sharing agreement of 1853 was not being honoured in spirit at least, though the Glasgow & South Western's manager, William Johnstone, piously assured the Commons Select Committee on the Union Railway project in 1864 that his board felt "a strong moral obligation not to break the agreement". Although the City of Glasgow Union Railway was ultimately passed by Parliament (resulting in the construction, twelve years later, of St. Enoch Station) the Caledonian had no involvement, and its opposition forced substantial revision of the Bill[2]. The scheme however convinced the Caledonian board that its own north bank terminus was essential, though it certainly did not rush into action, and congestion of trains, carts, omnibuses and passengers remained the norm at Bridge Street and Buchanan Street. At the latter site the company built a five-storey grain warehouse and a nine-bay goods shed in 1864, at a cost of £43,493, further eclipsing the passenger terminal.

Intense opposition, led by the North British, ensured that the latest Amalgamation Bill joined its predecessors on the waste heap, thrown out on its second reading in February 1864[3]. Among the would-be partners, mistrust had arisen, with the North British active in stirring it. Taking advantage of public hostility to the joint-purse rates being charged between Edinburgh and Glasgow, Richard Hodgson of the North British proposed to build a completely new railway between the cities, and the E&G, alarmed at the prospect, unilaterally lowered its fares and charges, causing the Caledonian to accuse it of breaching the agreement[4]. In May the E&G and Scottish Central companies were discussing arrangements for shared running powers, excluding the Caledonian[5]. The Edinburgh & Glasgow's collaboration with the GSWR over the City of Glasgow Union Railway was seen by the Caledonian as a further betrayal. But at last the Caledonian accepted the fact that it was not going to get control of the Edinburgh & Glasgow company, and adopted a new strategy. "Caledonian Railway envoys went to the North Eastern and Great Northern in turn with the suggestion that one or both take over the E&G"[6]. The Caledonian would not oppose this if it got the Scottish Central. The E&G and the East Coast companies were discussing a union anyway, but the Caledonian was anxious to keep it separate from the North British. The NBR was an integral part of the East Coast alliance, however, and by June it was apparent that this was a hopeless aim. Co-operation between the Caledonian and the E&G petered out, and the Caledonian observed that the E&G was bypassing traffic-sharing by carrying goods from Glasgow to Grangemouth and transferring the loads to a steamship company in which its officials had an interest. The joint purse arrangement ended by mutual agreement at the end of July[7]. Relations between the various railway companies remained fluid, of an acid or sweet nature depending on who was talking to whom, and when. In September, recriminations were still being exchanged between the Caledonian and Edinburgh & Glasgow companies[8] about breaches of the defunct joint purse agreement and the E&G's treachery in first opposing, then backing, the City of Glasgow Union Railway scheme.

In the form of the 'Caledonian Extension Railway' the CR had contemplated a west-east cross-country line from Ayrshire in its earliest days, but having acquired the Lanark Railway in 1860, it was 1864 before it made an extension from the Lanark line southwards below the slopes of Tinto Hill through Ponfeigh as far as Douglas. Beneath this austere countryside of bare hills and steep valleys, there were known to be large coal reserves. But although the aim was to reach Muirkirk, by now a flourishing coal and iron town, Douglas was to remain a terminus for eight years (it may be relevant to note that Muirkirk was essentially a one-company town, and that company was Baird's). On 25 July 1864, an Act was passed to allow the amalgamation of the Hamilton & Strathaven Railway with the Caledonian – which had always worked it – from 1 August. Its capital of £53,090 Ordinary and £16,865 Preference shares was converted to equivalent Caledonian stocks. On 1 September the railway to Stonehouse was completed, to a colliery at Cotcastle, west of the town. In the north of Lanarkshire, too, significant developments were under way. Several branches in the Cleland area, for which an Act had been obtained in 1861, were completed in 1864, opening up a district of ironstone pits and coal mines. The tap-root of this local system was a line running north from Drumbowie Junction, with short extensions to collieries and ironstone pits, past Lanridge up to Drumbowie, where a reverse junction gave a short branch to Duntillan Colliery. Over the next decades it would be adapted and extended, and provided with other links into the main system.

**Ponfeigh Station opened for passengers in December 1865. Note the single platform
and its varying levels. Passenger facilities are minimal.**

The Portpatrick & Wigtownshire Joint Committee ran a three-times daily motor bus from 1907 between Drummore, Scotland's most southerly village, and Stranraer Town station. The 17-mile journey took 1½ hours.

The Port Line

The railway across southern Galloway, from Dumfries via Castle Douglas to Stranraer and Portpatrick, might seem beyond the Caledonian's area of interest, though Mark Huish had alerted the company to it as early as 1846. Indeed, in November 1856 the CR Board had resolved not to make a financial contribution towards the Portpatrick Railway[9], but it was a significant line to the London & North Western, as it connected with the shortest sea route to Ireland, and especially to the growing industrial city of Belfast. In 1859 the LNWR had taken over the Lancaster & Carlisle and was one of the joint owners of Carlisle Citadel Station. The line from Dumfries to Castle Douglas had opened in 1859 and was worked by the Glasgow & South Western. Its continuation from Castle Douglas to Portpatrick was under the auspices of a separate company, the Portpatrick Railway, which by March 1861 had reached Stranraer, and was at Portpatrick, then seen as the steamer port, on 28 August 1862. On 1 October that year it opened a short branch to Stranraer Harbour, and in 1863 another spur led down from Portpatrick Station to the pier. However, the Portpatrick Railway was not a money-spinner. By late 1863, the company was in debt to the tune of £20,000, a large amount for a small concern, and clearly could not manage to operate its own line. From September 1863 the new line from Dumfries to Lockerbie had given the Caledonian a fresh interest in traffic to and from Galloway (a later writer noted that "… the traffic of the Stranraer route is to the East of Scotland and to England, in fact anywhere rather than to Glasgow"[10]). Although the Glasgow & South Western might have seemed the Portpatrick's natural ally, the terms it demanded were considered excessive by the Portpatrick's board; also the LNWR had a substantial shareholding in the Portpatrick line. Deals and counter-deals were wrangled over through 1863 and 1864. A heads of agreement was negotiated and signed with the CR in January 1864, under which the Caledonian would subscribe £40,000 to the Portpatrick Railway and work the line for a maximum of 43% of the receipts. But talks still went on. A growing number of Caledonian shareholders were expressing concern about the company's reversion to an expansionist policy, and in June the Caledonian proposed joint working of the line with the Glasgow & South Western. The Portpatrick and the Glasgow & South Western Railways then began to discuss a merger, but failed to agree on terms. Finally a working agreement between the Caledonian and the Portpatrick Railway, with the LNWR's support, was made on 1 October 1864, and approved by an extraordinary general meeting of Caledonian shareholders on 29 November. The Caledonian undertook to work the line for 21 years, to 1 October 1885. Gross revenue would be divided 38% to the CR and 62% to the Portpatrick Railway as long as the weekly gross traffic receipts were at or under £10 a mile, falling by stages to a 33/67 split if the figure reached between £15 5s. and £19 5s. In addition the CR would pay the

Portpatrick Railway £37,325 7s. 6d. for the plant (it possessed eight locomotives), 5% interest on the cost of its workshops, up to £6,000; and would invest £40,000 in Portpatrick Railway shares. The Caledonian would maintain the line and pay the staff, and a Joint Committee would supervise operations[11]. Relief among the Portpatrick shareholders must have been palpable. The London & North Western management was pleased that the sea route to Northern Ireland had been secured under West Coast auspices. If many Caledonian shareholders thought the terms over-generous, the Board made reassuring noises about the traffic volume and rate of return to be expected. To help in this, unsuspecting passengers booking from Newton Stewart to Carlisle or beyond were liable to be sent round by Lochmaben and Lockerbie rather than by the direct GSWR route between Dumfries and Carlisle[12].

The Caledonian was also concerned with Edinburgh harbours. It had had access to Granton since 1861, but Leith was a far busier port, and on 1 September 1864 the CR completed a goods branch from Crewe Junction, on the Granton line, running through the fishertown of Newhaven to Leith Docks. At the same time two new connections were made: a curve between Pilton West and East Junctions to enable traffic to be worked direct between Leith and Granton on CR owned metals; and another between the Granton line and the main line at Dalry Road, allowing access to the goods station at Lothian Road.

Callander & Oban – A Question

In that extremely busy year of 1864, the Caledonian was invited to interest itself in a large-scale new project. Since 1858, a railway from the Scottish Central at Dunblane had run to Doune and Callander. In July a provisional committee was formed to promote its extension as the Callander & Oban Railway, resuscitating part of the old Scottish Grand Junction project. Thomas Brassey was willing to build it, at an estimated £600,000 for the 71 miles. The Caledonian declined to give support, but the Scottish Central agreed on 17 December to invest £200,000, undertaking to work the line in perpetuity for half the gross revenue: this to be operative as from when the C&O company had built not less than twenty miles of their line. Why should the Scottish Central do this? It was a curious action for a company which had seemed more interested in selling itself than in making major capital investments in new and distinctly speculative railways. Merger talks had been going on with the Caledonian, with terms finally agreed in September; and in November a Bill was promoted for the amalgamation of the two companies. Thus the merger was already confidently anticipated when the decision to invest in the Oban line was made. It is highly likely that some at least of the Caledonian directors, including the chairman, had given tacit approval to a decision which most of their own shareholders would have strenuously resisted.

Dunblane Station opened on 23 May 1848
and was rebuilt as a junction for the Callander line in 1858. This view is from the 1900s.

At the Caledonian's half-yearly meeting on 14 March 1865, Salkeld commented that the number of new projects was so large because the success of new Caledonian branches had tempted "adventurers" to pre-empt the company's plans. As a result it was now proposing new lines that might otherwise have been spread over several years. Almost casually he informed the meeting that the company had bought six acres of land at Blythswood Holm, in the centre of Glasgow, as a potential site for a central station to replace Buchanan Street. He did not mention the cost which, with all charges, amounted to £125,777[13]. But many shareholders were seriously alarmed by the huge amount of capital now required, and the scope of the company's ambitions. At a Wharncliffe Meeting (see page 67) held in Glasgow on 15 May 1865 to obtain approval for the various Bills, it was noted that authority was being asked to subscribe £100,000 to the Dingwall & Skye Railway, "if the Directors should see fit." A shareholder asked how the chairman "could connect the Caledonian with the Island of Skye?"[14] The reply, that it was a permissive power only, was hardly reassuring (in fact the Caledonian never made this investment, and probably never seriously intended to). At this time, almost every railway company in the country was over-extended financially, with debenture and loan interest payments increasingly hard to meet. By August, the newly-formed Highland Railway Company was trying to get itself leased by the Caledonian[15].

A far-reaching strategic arrangement was made on 12 May, when a "Scotch Territorial Agreement" was confirmed with the North British[16]. By the terms of this, the NBR withdrew opposition to the Caledonian taking over the Scottish Central. In exchange, the Caledonian agreed not to oppose the NBR's ambitious plan to bridge the Firths of Forth and Tay (and so gain direct access to Dundee without ferries), nor to oppose the North British amalgamating with the Edinburgh & Glasgow (and so have its own line right into central Glasgow). This was a diplomatic and commercial coup for Hodgson and the North British. To gain the Scottish Central, which it had originally expected to do nearly twenty years before, the Caledonian was conceding free access to Glasgow to the East Coast companies, who could also look forward to a major share of traffic from Dundee and Perth. For the Caledonian Company, and its allies to the south, it was now plain that the Scottish North Eastern must be secured as soon as possible. If that company should fall into the East Coast net, the North British would capture Aberdeen and the Caledonian would be restricted to the area south of Perth.

In May 1865 the Greenock & Wemyss Bay Railway was ready for opening, and the Caledonian worked its 10 mile line from the beginning. It had been involved almost from the start, having agreed at the half-yearly meeting of 7 March 1862 to invest £30,000 in the undertaking. The charge was 50% of receipts, dropping to 45% if the CR's earnings should exceed £4,000 in a year. A Joint Committee of directors and officers decided the affairs of the line, including the frequency of services and the fares to be charged. Relations between the Wemyss Bay company and the Caledonian were rarely cordial; the critical and demanding attitude of the Greenock & Wemyss Bay Railway's chairman (and majority shareholder), John Lamont, put the backs up of the Caledonian management, who sometimes seemed to enjoy frustrating him. The Wemyss Bay company operated its own steamships at first, in what proved to be an unsuccessful venture[17]. In the same year, notice was served on the Caledonian that its monopoly of Greenock was under challenge, with the promotion of a Bill for the GSWR-backed Greenock & Ayrshire Railway, ostensibly to link Greenock with Ayrshire as the name suggested, but also providing a Glasgow-Greenock line, from the GSWR at Bridge of Weir right to the quayside. The Act was passed in July 1865, against stiff opposition from the CR, which reacted by purchasing the pier at Gourock, and entering a Bill for an extension of the Greenock line to Gourock Pier[18].

Meetings of the Joint Committee of the Caledonian and the Portpatrick Railway were held on a quarterly basis, variously in Glasgow, London and Carlisle, with Lord Stair of the Portpatrick Railway as chairman. After 1865 they seem to have become more occasional. In 1867 the Caledonian's habit of sending southbound passengers via its Lockerbie line was still an issue; on 26 April it was minuted that an arrangement should be made with the GSWR "to prevent the Complaints now made by Passengers carried round by Lockerbie." By August the matter was resolved and the traffic went by the Glasgow & South Western[19]. Much of the Joint Committee's time was taken up by steamship business, complicated by hesitation over whether to adopt the Portpatrick-Donaghadee or Stranraer-Larne/Belfast route. Harbour works were still in progress at Portpatrick when the fast paddle steamer *Fannie* began to run between Stranraer and Belfast on 4 December 1865. Passengers were few, there was no mail contract, and the steamship service was sporadic. At the CR half-yearly meeting in September 1866, the chairman noted that new steamers had been put on for the Irish traffic, unfortunately coinciding with the outbreak of cattle plague that was to affect all the country's railways in the course of that year, with a huge drop in cattle traffic. Though he made bullish comments about the prospects for the 'Port line', the steamers were withdrawn and for four years there would be only an irregular locally-run service.

The second Tay viaduct at Perth. The swing span was removed around 1890 (see page 138).

Merger with the Central

In the summer of 1865 the long anticipated major rationalisation of Scottish railways was finally achieved. By a series of Acts of Parliament, the Monklands Railways merged with the Edinburgh & Glasgow, which immediately amalgamated with the North British. The Dunblane, Doune and Callander Railway, worked by the Scottish Central, became a subsidiary of the SCR on 31 July, and on the following day the Central itself was merged with the Caledonian. The Scottish Central might have been conceived as a good girl, meant to play a prescribed part in the spread of the railway network, but she very quickly became a tart, on the lookout for whoever had most money, and with a chronic tendency to switch her affections. By the Act of 5 July 1865 the Caledonian finally made an honest woman of the SCR, but the terms were steep, involving a guaranteed 7% return for the SCR shareholders on the Ordinary stock of £1,113,070, and a share with the Caledonian stockholders in any payout above that level. The Caledonian inherited the SCR's running powers between Larbert and Haymarket East Junction in Edinburgh, and replaced the Scottish Central as a joint owner, along with the Scottish North-Eastern Railway (two-fifths each) and the North British (one-fifth) of the General Station at Perth, which by previous agreement was about to be extended and to be provided with a large hotel. Since the completion of the Dundee line's new bridge across the Tay at Perth, the extension from Princes Street into the General Station had been finished. The former Dundee & Perth & Aberdeen company's installations were in a somewhat decrepit state and the Caledonian also inherited considerable work in progress on this line, including the new Dundee West terminal station, which was opened in October 1866. From the Scottish Central, the CR also acquired a relationship with the cartage company William Wordie & Sons, who as carters to the Scottish Central had had an office at Buchanan Street since 1850[20]. Wordies also worked for the Scottish North Eastern and the Edinburgh & Glasgow at this time, and would remain the carriers at numerous Caledonian depots until the end of the Company's existence. Another inherited SCR commitment was to invest £20,000 (half the capital) in the Crieff & Comrie Railway, which obtained its Act at the same time as the merger. But other investors were few, and the local subscription was very low. Invited to increase the subscription, the Caledonian declined, and Crieff remained a terminus[21] for another 28 years. Far more alarming to the Caledonian's already-anxious shareholders was its embracing of the SCR's commitment to invest £200,000 in the Callander & Oban company, which had obtained its Act on 8 July 1865. Five Scottish Central nominees sat on its board.

On amalgamation, the SCR added 113 miles of track to the Caledonian and contributed 45 passenger and 39 goods locomotives to the CR stock, 26 of them dating back to between 1855 and the beginning of the line. With 352 engines of its own, the Caledonian had if anything a surplus of motive power. Rolling stock from the SCR amounted to 213 passenger coaches, 62 other passenger vehicles (brakes and composite) and 2,102 wagons[22]. On 29 June the Caledonian also took over the General Terminus & Glasgow Harbour company, whose shareholders were guaranteed a dividend of 4%, rising to $4^1/_4$% after two years, on a share capital of £160,000.

In the summer of 1865 the board was thinking of strengthening the manager's office with an assistant manager. The post was offered to Andrew Dougall, secretary and manager of the Highland Railway, but he declined[23], and no-one was appointed. Dougall was known to the Caledonian management through discussions, initiated by the financially-straitened Highland, about the prospect of the Caledonian leasing its lines, or even of a merger. Once again the Caledonian's reputation for wealth had brought a suppliant to the door. But the Highland hopefuls got no more than fair words. At the half-yearly meeting on 12 September, Salkeld, in the chair, could announce that five previously independent companies were now fully merged with the Caledonian: the Scottish Central, Dunblane Doune & Callander, Crieff Junction, Glasgow General Terminus, and Dumfries, Lochmaben & Lockerbie Railways. An Act had been obtained to build a line between Cleland and Midcalder, which would complete a second Caledonian route between Glasgow and Edinburgh. The new line between Rutherglen and Coatbridge was on the verge of opening (it opened for goods on 20 September; passenger services followed from 8 January 1866), and would tap a district of intensive mining and quarrying activity where it intersected the old Drumpellier Railway, as well as providing a north-south link with the Carlisle line at Whifflet. The half-yearly dividend, at $6^3/_4$%, was up on the $6^1/_2$ of the same period last year, and he confidently looked forward to 7% in the next three years. In the general climate of approval, a motion to increase the directors' remuneration amount from £1,100 to £3,300 was passed without a vote (four SCR nominees had brought the board up to 14 members)[24], and the *Railway Times*, usually hostile to the Caledonian, said of it, "The finances, that truest of all touchstones in regard to successful management, are in the best possible condition"[25]. Caledonian Ordinary shares rose to 30% above par. But as one writer observed, there had been a time not so long before when "persons (if of responsible position) were offered Caledonian shares gratis, with a money payment of 30s. added to tempt them"[26]. What went up, might come down again.

During 1865 the board had been considering the possibility of sharing Waverley Station with the North British, which owned it. The Edinburgh town council was keen that the city should have a single principal station. But to agree on suitable terms proved impossible. Hodgson announced to the NBR half-yearly meeting on 28 September that "… unless these terms and conditions are satisfactory to the North British … the Caledonian never will, never shall, enter the Waverley Station"[27], and in the end the Caledonian board resolved to build its own new station in the capital.

Trouble with the Shareholders

Railway shareholders generally were becoming jittery about the scale of the companies' plans. On 21 December 1865 a large meeting of shareholders of the Caledonian, North British and Glasgow & South Western companies was convened in Glasgow, to challenge the new schemes currently proposed. James Hozier was called to the chair, and James White informed the meeting that current schemes required the outlay of £10 millions for hostile and aggressive purposes. The railway directors seemed to be powerless in the hands of "lawyers and engineers". He cited eighteen Caledonian schemes, involving 132 miles of track, and requiring the raising of £4,933,500 in new share capital plus £1,644,500 borrowing powers. The chief item was the proposal for a new central station at Blythswood Holm, Glasgow, with connections to all incoming CR lines, including a tunnel link under the Clyde at Whiteinch to lines on the south side; the estimated cost of £2,000,000 was considered far below what was likely. Another was the proposed absorption of the Scottish North Eastern Railway, about which one periodical had already noted that the terms "indicate on the surface an absolute loss to the Caledonian. It will require no great depth of digging, however, to get at the fact that the whole of the traffic to the North British is intended to be wrested from that Company"[28]. The meeting agreed to form a committee to try to persuade the companies to reduce or withdraw their Bills. The *Scotsman* commented that "… in every district where the one company has projected a new line, the other has followed with a similar and rival one"[29]. In particular it criticised another Caledonian proposal, for its own railway from Larbert to meet the Cleland-Edinburgh line at Dalmahoy, and which would for most of its way be within a mile of the North British line. When the shareholders' committee met the CR directors, the chairman expressed the company's willingness to drop this proposal and indeed every other scheme (except one) if the other companies would do likewise (including the abandonment of the St. Enoch plan). The one scheme he would retain was the proposed Greenock-Gourock extension, because the company had made an obligation to an (unnamed) individual[30]. Intense pressure was put on all three companies to make the boards come to terms, but in Richard Hodgson, chairman of the North British, antipathy to the Caledonian company seemed almost pathological. One historian wrote, "If Hodgson was one-idead, that one idea was to contain and defeat the Caledonian". Hodgson was convinced that the Caledonian, "when pretending to seek peace, seek to cheat"[31]. With such views held by the NBR's top man, the chances of real peace were slender. Nevertheless, the companies agreed to trim back their plans. But the Caledonian shareholders kept their committee in being, under the chairmanship of James White[32].

In open countryside south-west of Glasgow, the Busby Railway, 3 miles 43 chains, was opened on the first day of 1866, having gained its Act on 11 May 1863. Diverging from the Barrhead & Neilston line at a spot designated Busby Junction, it was a locally-promoted company with largely local ownership, and a capital of £36,000. Its prospectus described the area as admirably suited for "villa residences" and a combination of industrial and commuter traffic was confidently expected[33]. Busby in 1861 had a population of about 1,000, and several textile factories. During construction it was resolved to extend the line to East Kilbride, then an isolated village, with the Caledonian contributing a third of the estimated £45,000 cost, an investment criticised by numerous shareholders[34]. Trains began running from the Caledonian platforms at South Side to East Kilbride on 1 September 1868. To the east, the Symington, Biggar & Broughton had reached Peebles on 1 February 1864, and on 16 April 1866 the Caledonian completed the seven-arched skew stone viaduct across the Tweed carrying the agreed linking line between the Peebles stations. But there were no through passenger services, and it was used for goods transfer only. The North British never apppears to have completed the eastwards loop[35], which would have offered the Caledonian the possibility of invoking running powers right across to the east coast. Peebles remained a Caledonian branch terminus.

Neilston, the second station of 1871, for the Glasgow & Kilmarnock Joint Line. Attention to detail in finials and eaves, even the water column cap, is evident.

On 21 March 1866 the Caledonian held its first meeting since the amalgamation with the Scottish Central. Salkeld, in the chair, announced a dividend of 7.5% for the half-year, the highest return on the Ordinary stock since the company's formation. The united lines had brought in £45,000 of revenue with no increase of the working expenses. He went on to say that "they did not close their eyes to the gigantic proportions which a neighbouring company had assumed" – the North British, once "a modest little railway of 150 miles in length, was now a first-rate power, owning above 700 miles of railway, and some of its extensions were manifestly projected in order to cut off, if possible, some of the Caledonian traffic." But he also assured the meeting that the Caledonian and North British had concluded a new traffic agreement and hoped for future co-operation. Hozier and White, from the floor, suggested that the directors should try to bring about an amiable adjustment of all questions either by defining territorial limitations or by appointing an arbiter. The chairman then stirred things up by saying that the directors had been involved in inter-company negotiations anyway and that the protesters had merely aggravated matters. Shouts of "No, no!" were recorded[36].

The financial climate had been deteriorating through 1865. Railways and railway construction were big businesses, but other forms of industry were expanding rapidly and also requiring capital. Investors were looking for security and guarantees and had long since learned not to take the prospectuses and reports of railway companies at face value. The major railway contractors, Peto & Betts, went bankrupt in May 1866, with huge debts to the London banking house of Overend Gurney, which was forced in turn to declare its own insolvency and close down in June. The collapse had more impact on English and overseas railways than on Scottish companies, but for a time it was impossible to raise funds (for three months, the bank rate was set at 10%), and "the great panic of 1866" halted the Caledonian plan to advance to Gourock: "the Company were left *minus* their railway, but *plus* the burden of owning Gourock Harbour, to which, of course, they had no access"[37]. Another casualty of this time was the proposed Balerno Railway, to serve the numerous mills on the Water of Leith, south-west of Edinburgh. An Act was obtained on 29 June 1865, for a double track branch to be built by the Caledonian Railway, and prescribing for opening within five years. Authorised share capital was £150,000, plus borrowing powers of £50,000. But the Caledonian, having raised much of the capital, spent it in other ways and the project went into abeyance[38].

Merger with the North Eastern

During this financial storm, the Bill for amalgamation of the Scottish North Eastern with the Caledonian was being considered by a parliamentary committee. All the other Scottish railway companies, led by the North British, and nearly every municipality north of the Forth had entered objections. After what the *Times* called "a severe contest in both Houses of Parliament", the Commons committee accepted the Bill on 14 June, and the Lords on 27 July. On 10 August 1866 the Act for amalgamation received the royal assent. It was clear from the committees' proceedings that few of its customers considered the Scottish North Eastern Railway to be providing an adequate service, but there was considerable concern, especially in Aberdeen, about a Caledonian monopoly of the city's rail link with the south. Numerous provisions were made to take account of the objections, including the granting of very substantial running powers to the North British. East Coast services could run over any of the former Scottish North Eastern Railway lines and the NBR was empowered to rent space at the Caledonian's Aberdeen Station. At last the original ambition was fulfilled, and the Caledonian company possessed the entire route between Carlisle and Aberdeen (except for the short Garnqueen link), as well as a great many other lines. But if the thick red line looked good on the map of Scotland, there was also a discomfiting shortage of funds. The Scottish North Eastern Railway paid its last dividend on 31 July. John Stirling of Kippendavie, its chairman for the past ten years, joined the Caledonian Board. He and his colleagues had negotiated a good price for their shareholders; by the terms of amalgamation, the Caledonian was committed to a range of guaranteed payments:

> 5% to proprietors of Dundee & Arbroath 5% Preference Stock (to a maximum of £66,700).
> 3.5% to proprietors of Aberdeen Railway 3.5% Preference stock (to a maximum of £73,174 13s. 4d.).
> A minimum of 6% to proprietors of Aberdeen Railway 6% Preference stock (to a maximum of £276,666 13s. 4d.).
> 3.5% to proprietors of Aberdeen Railway 3.5% No. 2 stock (to a maximum of £63,650 19s. 4d.).
> 7% to proprietors of Aberdeen Railway No.2 Preference shares (to a maximum of £150,000).
> 4.5% to proprietors of Scottish North Eastern Railway 4.5% Preference Stock (to a maximum of £192,079).
> 5% to proprietors of Scottish North Eastern Railway 5% Preference stock (to a maximum of £188,500).

Scottish North Eastern Railway staff continued in their posts as Caledonian employees, and soon some were moved elsewhere in the system. The most notable newcomer was the secretary, Irvine Kempt, aged 35, who transferred to the General Manager's staff in Glasgow. The Scottish North Eastern Railway brought to the

Caledonian 162 miles of line, 80 locomotives, 237 passenger coaches, 50 other vehicles "for attachment to passenger trains", mostly fish wagons, and 2,327 assorted wagons. An unusual part of the package was the 4 1/2 mile Carmyllie Railway, begun as a private undertaking by Lord Dalhousie, the local landowner, in 1854 to transport paving stones from the extensive Carmyllie Quarries, and bought by the Scottish North Eastern on 19 June 1865. It met the Dundee & Arbroath line at Elliot Junction, just south of Arbroath. The Caledonian also took over operation of the one-engine-in-steam Montrose-Bervie railway, which had been worked by the Scottish North Eastern Railway since its opening in November 1865. But the Caledonian's demand for 11% of the Bervie company's revenue for the use of its terminus station at Montrose led to the local company stopping short on its own tracks at Broomfield Junction. The dispute was resolved and the CR worked the line until the Montrose & Bervie company amalgamated with the North British on 1 October 1881.

Anticipating, as well it might, a reluctance on the Caledonian Railway's part to make decent provision for competing services on the Aberdeen route, Clause 125 of the Act stated: "The Company shall, for the Accommodation of 'East Coast Traffic', run and carry forward, from Perth to Aberdeen, and from Aberdeen to Perth, a Train in conjunction with every Train which shall run or be appointed to run for the Accommodation of that Traffic from London or York to Perth, and vice versa, via Edinburgh." There was to be no change of carriage, and the speed was not to be less than 35mph, exclusive of stops. The Caledonian, already pledged not to oppose the NBR's forthcoming Tay Bridge Bill, accepted that on completion of the bridge, the Dundee & Arbroath line should be jointly owned with the North British, and agreed not to oppose any NBR application for an Arbroath-Montrose-Stonehaven railway made within the next five parliamentary sessions.

The effect of the amalgamations was to more than double the authorised capital of the Caledonian Company:
1864: Shares £7,977,519 (Ordinary shares were £3,744,434). Loans £2,936,266
1866: Shares £16,268,181 (Ordinary shares of the CR: £4,722,707; Scottish Central £1,112,122; Aberdeen Rly £830,000; Scottish Midland Junction £600,000; Dundee & Arbroath £200,000). Loans £5,513,091[39]

On 5 July 1866 a special meeting authorised the board to raise £540,000 by the creation and addition of Ordinary stock, under powers granted by four Acts of 1865. Current shareholders were allocated £13 of new stock for every £100 they already held, if they wanted to buy. With the last dividend at over 7%, even though the price was above par, most found the money. During that summer, the Caledonian and NBR companies made an agreement, referred to by the CR chairman as "an armistice", that in the next session of Parliament the Caledonian would not promote new lines except in the counties of Ayrshire, Renfrewshire and Dumfries-shire, while the North British would not promote new Bills for any railway in Scotland, except in relation to schemes already committed. Both companies would oppose new Bills from any other source that did not comply with the same stipulations. The NBR however reserved the right to oppose Caledonian schemes in the three reserved counties, if it saw fit. The nine-clause agreement "merely limited the extent to which the railways could expand their systems rather than make any attempt to reduce the competition in which they were so ruinously involved"[40]. A touch of financial realism was reflected in the decision, transmitted to the Highland Railway in August, not to invest capital in the Inverness lines[41]. In September the Caledonian maintained its high dividend level, at 7.25% on the Ordinary shares. For former SCR shareholders, it was a bounty. Salkeld at the half-yearly meeting was still complaining about North British aggressiveness while still assuring the shareholders that the Caledonian was trying to get along with everyone, having formed joint committees with the GSWR and even the NBR[42].

Large-scale alterations to Perth General Station were made from August 1866, involving the demolition of the Scottish Central offices. A new carriage shed for the North British was set up on the site. Construction of the Callander & Oban's first section, 17 1/2 miles from Callander to the head of Glen Ogle, began at the end of October 1866. The contract price was £124,218. If the economy was in recession, there was still congestion of goods traffic around Greenock, where the *Glasgow Herald* noted that wagons were blocking both main line and sidings, with "relays of men and engines" engaged day and night, including Sundays[43].

The Lesmahagow Railway, after ten years of carrying coal, lime, and other mineral traffic, gained a passenger service in late 1866, after long agitation by communities on the line[44]. By this time for most of its extent it had been double tracked and could accommodate additional traffic. From 1 December, trains ran between Brocketsbrae (named Lesmahagow from 1 June 1869 until 1 June 1905 when Brocketsbrae was reinstated) and Ferniegair, and also on the Blackwood branch. From Ferniegair, horse-drawn road transport (Caledonian-operated) took passengers to Motherwell and to Hamilton.

At the half-yearly meeting on 14 September, Salkeld promised that the Scottish North Eastern Railway would be worked in a spirit of liberality and fair play. The Caledonian would have done well to keep John Stirling of

Kippendavie on side. Having led the affairs of a substantial company for a decade, he perhaps chafed at being just another member of the CR Board. Unlike his new colleagues, who were businessmen trying to run a railway company, he was first and foremost a strategically-minded railway director. In that autumn the North British company was distracted by a major crisis in its own affairs. Richard Hodgson was forced out of office by a shareholders' committee of inquiry and on 15 November a new board was formed. On 21 December, to general surprise, Kippendavie, having resigned from the Caledonian board, joined the new NBR board and was immediately elected as its chairman.

Following the amalgamations, the two companies remained of approximately equal size, as the following figures show.[45]

1865		
	Caledonian Railway	**North British Railway**
Track mileage total	494 miles	710 miles
Double track mileage	283 miles 57.3%	363 miles 51.1%
Passengers	6,590,725	7,876,747
Passenger trains	85,986	145,745
Train miles	2,084,683 miles	2,407,039 miles
Gross passenger revenue	£399,883	£491,115
Coal and minerals gross revenue	£429,097	£300,095
General merchandise revenue	£502,768	£443,114

1867		
	Caledonian Railway	**North British Railway**
Track mileage total	673 miles	722 miles
Double track mileage	399 miles 59.3%	363 miles 50.3%
Passengers	9,127,203	8,194,921
Passenger trains	113,512	158,177
Train miles	2,649,330 miles	2,577,614 miles
Gross passenger revenue	£542,744	£511,373
Coal and minerals gross revenue	£484,015	£312,138
General merchandise revenue	£630,214	£476,542

On 1 March 1867 a branch was opened from Carstairs to Dolphinton, 10 miles and 61 chains long. Authorised in 1862, with several bridges including two of three arches, it was quite a substantial undertaking. This Lanarkshire hamlet, with a population in 1867 of 260, was already served from Edinburgh by the Leadburn, Linton & Dolphinton Railway, a local undertaking worked by the North British from Leadburn on the Edinburgh-Peebles line. There were no coal pits, and the only purpose of the Caledonian can have been to prevent extension of the NBR line and the possibility of the NBR gaining running powers beyond Carstairs. A linking line was built from the Caledonian station to a point on the other branch beyond the North British station, and used for the exchange of light freight traffic. For several decades Dolphinton enjoyed the possession of two railway termini, each dealing with three trains each way, Monday to Saturday. By 1881 its population had risen to 292. Just east of Carstairs Junction the Dolphinton Railway passed over a loop line, laid in 1848, variously known as the Float branch or Lampits Curve, making it possible for trains to run between Carlisle and Edinburgh without reversal at Carstairs. By 1858 it was disused and disconnected at the north end; by 1898 it was reduced to a short spur at the south end[46].

Dolphinton Station opened on 1 March 1867.
The connecting line, meeting the North British beyond the NBR station, is on the right.

The Gaining of Grangemouth

Railway workers' claims for more pay were becoming vociferous in early 1867, and CR drivers were conceded an extra 3s. a week, with a 1s. rise for labourers and platelayers[47]. A relic of the old Polloc & Govan line was set to disappear with an Act of 14 March, authorising lifting of the rails along the streets between West Street and the Clyde at Windmillcroft. Another major strategic acquisition came with the Forth & Clyde Navigation Act of 20 June, authorising the CR to acquire the Forth & Clyde Canal, the Monkland and Forth & Cart Canals, the old Drumpellier Railway, and Grangemouth Harbour and the Grangemouth Railway which ran from Grahamston to a passenger station at Grangemouth and a few dockyard sidings. Its capital value was £1,141,333 but the canal revenues were declining. However, it was a Clyde-Forth link and the Caledonian did not want any other railway to have it; Salkeld also expressed the hope that the CR could transfer some goods traffic to the canals, to relieve pressure on the railway between Coatbridge and Glasgow[48]. The canal company had been paying 6.25% to its shareholders, and the price was a guaranteed 6.5% dividend, amounting to £71,333 a year. Now the Caledonian possessed its own east coast port, but could not monopolise its position: the North British was granted running powers over the Grangemouth branch, which it exercised, paying a fixed toll. In return the Caledonian was allowed to use the old Stirlingshire & Midland Junction line through Grahamston to Larbert. A Joint Committee, with a jointly employed manager, oversaw operations on the branch. Both companies ran passenger trains between Grangemouth and Glasgow. As a canal owner the CR behaved conscientiously, reducing tolls and improving the cartage service to loading points[49]. But with a guaranteed dividend to find, it had every reason to develop the traffic. In effect, the Caledonian had now become a transportation organisation rather than simply a railway company, with strong harbour and shipping interests on both sides of the country. Aberdeen's new Joint Station, initiated by the Scottish North Eastern and shared with the Great North of Scotland, came into use on 4 November 1867. Since 2 August 1854, Scottish North Eastern Railway trains had terminated at Guild Street; now at last passengers to and from the north-east could change trains in the same station, and transfer of goods traffic was eased. Concerned about cash reserves, in November the Caledonian tried to enforce a halt to construction work on the C&O, but that company's indomitable secretary, John Anderson, succeeded in getting the work continued, though at a slow pace.

Enlarged as it now was, the Caledonian's income from mail traffic, always the greatest of any Scottish railway's, had risen accordingly. In 1850 the Post Office contract had been worth £16,931; in 1867 it was £28,562 18s. 2d., including a payment for "accelerated and limited service" on the Up and Down Carlisle night mail trains. A further £473 13s. 6d. was paid for the Paisley section. The 4.36 a.m. from Carlisle carried one clerk, six sorters and two stampers as far as Carstairs, one clerk, seven sorters and two stampers to Gartsherrie, and one clerk and three sorters to Greenhill. The 5.45 p.m. Up mail had one clerk and two sorters to Gartsherrie, one clerk, four sorters and two stampers to Carstairs, and one clerk, six sorters and one stamper to Carlisle. On these trains the PO had one sorting carriage and a mail tender, with an extra tender on the Down service when the Australian mails had come in[50].

The wreckage of a goods train which was derailed and fell from the Carron Viaduct,
south of Larbert, on 29 April 1867.

Shale bings rise beyond the station at West Calder, opened 9 July 1869.

CHAPTER SEVEN Crisis Years, 1867-69

A New Revolt

Despite great commercial and geographical expansion, financial storm-clouds were again gathering over the Caledonian. Although it appears that in August 1867 the Highland company signed up to a lease agreement at 4%, the Caledonian backed off from what would have been a major commitment, though it paid the parliamentary expenses incurred, of £1,205 9s. 7d[1]. That summer, a pamphlet was published in London, under the title of *The Caledonian Railway: A Review of Its Financial Position*. The author was identified only as 'A Public Accountant', and his document was both an exposé of the Company's position and a condemnation of the policies and decisions which had led to it. It revealed a heavy imbalance that had developed between Ordinary and Preference or Guaranteed shares in the capital account. In 1865, 65% of the stock was of the latter kind, and with the acquisition of the Scottish Central and the Scottish North Eastern, this had risen to over 75%. To 'Public Accountant' this was "culpable imprudence", though it may rather have simply shown a difference in the ways of raising capital between Scottish and English companies, but he also pointed to some dubious accounting practices. The Caledonian charged the purchase of shares in other railways to its capital account, but if the shares showed a premium, this was credited to revenue. Bridge reconstruction, a substantial item as most of the original bridges north of Stirling had been wooden-decked, had been charged against revenue until 31 July 1866, but since then had been charged to capital. The effect had been to inflate the revenue account, on which dividends were calculated. The pamphlet also accused the company of insufficient investment in maintenance of the track, locomotives and rolling stock. These accusations, authoritatively stated, naturally caused intense concern. But the Caledonian was not without its defenders, and the publishers of the pamphlet were accused of running a 'bear' market (speculators who try to run down the value of a company's shares so that they can buy them at a low price and resell them at a higher one), to force down the value of CR shares.

The half-yearly meeting on 26 September 1867 was a packed and stormy one. Regretting that the dividend had gone down – it was 5.25% against 7.25% – the chairman blamed bad trading conditions, including the recent coal strike, but claimed to be unperturbed: "I stand before you today without the slightest misgivings as to the future …" Turning to criticisms of the board, as voiced by 'Public Accountant' and others, he repeated the accusation of stock market 'bears', and urged stockholders to keep their nerve. He defended the controversial agreement made on 22 March that year with the Solway Junction Railway, to invest £60,000 towards its completion and to work the line (the CR had originally declined to invest in this enterprise). Established in 1864, the Solway Junction Railway had sought a capital of £315,000 to form a line from Kirtlebridge on the Caledonian main line, crossing above the GSWR east of Annan, and traversing the Firth on a long viaduct, to join the Maryport & Carlisle line at Kirkbride. Work had been going on since March 1865, but it had run out of capital. Salkeld told the meeeting that the Caledonian had earned £25,000 in 1864 from carrying Cumberland haematite ore north from Carlisle; and

The Solway Viaduct, designed by James Brunlees and opened on 13 September 1869, viewed from the south.

the potential was much greater. The directors were also proposing to erect a new passenger station at Buchanan Street both because of the nearing completion of the Midcalder line and because the trains currently using Queen Street were costing the Caledonian "many thousands." Evidently the Blythswood Holm plan had been dropped. New offices would also be built, and though the cost would be £70,000, he reckoned the return would be of the order of 20% a year. As often on occasions of this kind, the ire of vocal shareholders was turned chiefly on individuals who seemed to be getting more while the shareholders were getting less. Christopher Johnstone, general manager since 1856, was retiring early at 50, through ill-health, and the board was proposing to give him a retiral present of £5,000 in addition to a pension of £500 a year. It also emerged that the directors had given him £2,000 in 1864, for "special services". Johnstone had certainly worked hard for the company over 20 years, but he was regarded as a prime expansionist, and the motion for the huge pay-off was withdrawn. Speakers from the floor urged the company to pull back from the Solway Junction, from a proposed Kilmarnock line, and, especially, from the Oban railway. Salkeld defended them all. Explaining his difficulties in reaching traffic agreements with John Stirling of the North British, he said that Stirling wanted to divide the goods traffic, whereas he, Salkeld, wanted to share it by the companies carrying "traffic between all competing points at equal rates"; the rates to be set by arbitration if necessary, " … and let the traders and public select their own Railway." Given the previous history of competition between the Scottish railway companies, this was a fanciful notion which cannot have inspired much confidence among a largely sceptical audience. On the Oban line, the chairman insisted that the CR had inherited an obligation from the Scottish Central to invest £200,000. As far as the GSWR and competition for Kilmarnock were concerned, "the Glasgow & South Western now being bound in a certain allegiance to the Midland, if they wished to get rid of the obligation to make an additional line to Kilmarnock, it was for them to intimate that to the Caledonian Company, who would be most happy to meet them"[2].

At a board meeting on 22 October, the directors had to confront the fact that they had bitten off much more than they could chew. A Bill was prepared, listing projects to be abandoned and delayed, as well as authorising yet more borrowing. Among the abandonments were a link line which would have formed a triangular junction between the main line and the Crieff Junction railway just north of Crieff Junction, and a long cross-country branch from Dalmakeddar, between Dinwoodie and Wamphray, to Shieldhill on the Dumfries-Lockerbie line[3]: a revival of an old project which would have provided a north-facing link from Dumfries. The chairman's comments at the September meeting had failed to allay the fears and reservations of shareholders, and a continuing barrage of criticism resulted in the formation of a committee of inquiry to the shareholders. Under the chairmanship of Thomas Richardson, it produced a report on 3 January 1868, with many figures and tables supplied by Alfred Allott and Robert Fletcher, public accountants. Examination of the company's accounts for the two years to July 1867 found substantial amounts improperly charged to capital rather than to revenue, with the effect of inflating the revenue and procuring higher dividends than the company's situation justified. While the published accounts for 1866 and 1867 showed a total net revenue, after providing for Guaranteed and Preference dividends, of £507,624 9s. 8 1/2d., the accountants claimed that the true sum was £288,510 0s. 1 1/2d. The great amalgamations were heavy drains on the Company's resources; the Scottish Central, with its capital of £3,072,289, represented an annual charge to the Caledonian of £158,319. The Scottish North Eastern Railway, capitalised at £3,512,643, represented £182,500, and the Forth & Clyde Navigation, with a capital of £1,269,433, required £76,665 9s. 11d. to service its 6.25% guarantee. Its net revenue for the year ended March 1867 was £2,833 16s. 3d. short of what the Caledonian had to pay under the guarantee. As for the Portpatrick Railway, even though the Caledonian had managed to unload some of its commitment on to the LNWR at the beginning of 1867 (splitting revenues and expenditures two-thirds to the CR and one-third to the LNWR) its loss on the Port Line railway operations was £9,243 7s. 4d., inclusive of interest on the £40,000 share purchase. The Portpatrick's dividend of £1,250 did not even cover the interest, which amounted to £7,000. In all, including a loss of £17,679 17s. 9d. on steamer services, the Caledonian had lost £46,889 1s. 9d. on its engagement with the Portpatrick. And this scale of loss could be expected to continue, yet the Caledonian had a Bill deposited to raise £1,200,000 by stock issue and a further £400,000 by borrowing. The inference was clear. Any needy and greedy railway company could hawk itself to the Caledonian and settle back to enjoy a comfortable income and complain about the standard of the Caledonian's service. Christopher Johnstone was not the only senior manager with well-lined pockets. Seventeen individuals received their basic salary plus 135% in 1866, and plus 92% in 1867. Among them were men responsible for allocating costs either to capital or to revenue. Yet they had let revenue per mile drop from £1,293 18s. in 1866 to £1,262 0s. in 1867[4]. John Duncan's salary policy of 1852, however well-intended, had become a treacle-barrel for the managers, and there were demands for repayment. On a more positive note, the enquiries made by specialists into the civil and mechanical engineering sides, John Hawkshaw and Daniel Kinnear Clark, resulted in favourable reports. At this time, the Caledonian had 524 locomotives at its disposal, eight from the Portpatrick Railway, 84 from the SCR, 80 from the Scottish North Eastern Railway, and 352 of its own, of which almost half, 167, were classified as "mineral engines". Another thirty locomotives were under construction or on order[5].

An aspect of the company's affairs not covered by the inquiry but of extreme concern to the shareholders was the share price. At the end of December 1866, Caledonian Ordinary shares were being quoted at a comfortable 24% above par. Exactly a year later, they had slumped to 71.25% of par. The drop, of 53%, had wiped £2,850,000 from the company's stock-market valuation[6]. The Board and their auditors responded by challenging the Committee's allocations of costs and suggesting that it was too early to estimate the value of the new acquisitions. There was some truth in this, though if the directors had been less triumphalist in 1865 and 1866 they would have been more credible now. They asked what would be the position of the Caledonian company if the lines in question had fallen under Edinburgh & Glasgow or North British control. But they were willing to resign if the shareholders considered it in the company's interest. At an extraordinary general meeting in the City Hall, Glasgow, on 29 January 1868, the report was discussed. The shareholders were far from united. Thomas Richardson's question as to what sort of dividend they wanted: "a larger dividend based on a cheat, rather than a smaller one honestly earned?" was not what some wished to hear. Some felt that the committee was being over-rigorous. All were concerned about the value of their shares. One shareholder complained that the overstated dividends of 1865 had pushed the share price up to £130 or £135 and that he with many others had bought at the high – now they were worth only half that. But James Hozier's motion that the report be referred to a committee to recommend action was carried[7].

Throughout this tumultuous period, the board was also having to run the company and manage its affairs. A new general manager, James Smithells, from the Lancashire & Yorkshire Railway, was appointed to succeed Johnstone in late 1867. Perhaps in the hope of deflecting the torrent of criticism (there was by now a shareholders' committee in Dundee as well as in Glasgow and London), the directors convened another special meeting on 31 January to approve a new joint purse arrangement with the North British. This was carried unanimously but did nothing at all to stem the fury. 'Public Accountant' was still active. He felt the inquiry had been too lenient towards the directors. He had submitted the documents to the auditing firm Price, Holyland & Waterhouse, who had opined that the company should have paid no dividend at all[8].

The Shareholders' Committee

The Shareholders' Committee, chaired by Hozier, had fourteen members. Nine, including the chairman, were from Glasgow, two from Edinburgh, one from Dundee, one from elsewhere in Scotland, and only one from England. Its deliberations were fairly brief and centred on a recommendation, made on 1 February 1868, that six named directors should retire and be replaced by certain members of the committee: William Hozier, J.C. Bolton, James Clerk, John Cowan, James Falshaw, and William Lindsay. The directors responded to this *diktat* by saying they had expected to select the retirers themselves, and that they considered the committee's choice of new men insufficiently representative. They announced their intention to seek support from proxy votes at another extraordinary general meeting, on the 13th. Mingled hisses and cheers greeted Salkeld as he opened this gathering. He had to report that six of his directors had left the board in a dispute centred on the proposed use of proxy votes to defeat the committee's proposal. Because of the urgency of ongoing business, including the agreement made with the North British, he wanted to reconstitute the board immediately. This led to an intense, noisy and thoroughly confused series of exchanges, accusations and declarations, relating to the motives of the committee and the actions of the board. At one point Hozier tried to take over the chair, and with a mass of people trying to push on to the platform, the meeting was adjourned in disarray[9]. At the adjourned session on the 19th, a poll gave the directors a majority by the use of their proxy votes. Actual votes showed a majority for the protestors, 2,944 as against 1,352 for the board, and Hozier presided over a continuation meeting of "Shareholders opposed to the policy of the Chairman". One element in that policy was to raise £540,000 by an issue of 4% Preference stock. The fact that it was to be offered at a discount of 20% showed how weak the Caledonian's financial standing had again become – the maximum that could be realised was £432,000. A further extraordinary general meeting was held on 5 March. Salkeld emphasised the need for the new money: for investment in the Callander & Oban Railway, for the next instalment of investment in the Solway Junction line, and for "works in Forfarshire". Once again the gathering was noisy and acromonious. The Oban railway in particular was criticised: why throw away another £120,000 when £80,000 had already been wasted on it? Once again the meeting was adjourned. On the 11th a poll showed that the board had won the day, with personal votes of 2,918 and proxies amounting to 21,418; while the antis had 1,361 personal votes and 10,416 proxies[10]. Behind the scenes, negotiations were still going on between Salkeld and his rump board, and the committee representing the dissident shareholders. On 24 March it was reported that agreement had been reached: four directors would retire after the half-yearly meeting, to be replaced by James Taylor, J.C. Bolton, James Clerk and John Cowan. The two vacancies already existing were to be filled by Mr. Davidson, a Perth solicitor, and Sir Thomas Gladstone of Fasque, elder brother of the prominent politician William Ewart Gladstone. Peace had not broken out in the Caledonian's affairs, though: some shareholders were seeking a legal interdict against the joint purse agreement with the North British[11].

Strife had been going on for months and showed no sign of abating. At the half-yearly shareholders' meeting on 31 March, the chairman announced that a shareholder, Mr. Alexander Glen (on behalf of the Glasgow law firm H. and R. Lamond) had obtained an interim interdict against the company paying a dividend "which anyway would have been small", but which was still claimed to be artificial. Reviewing the position, he noted that the Caledonian had only one Bill before Parliament, but was also opposing the North British Bill to bridge the Forth at Alloa. Some reform had taken place in salaries, with a dividend-related augmentation now only for goods managers and the superintendent of the line. And Salkeld announced his own retirement from the chair after nine years, with "all personal animosities swept away (except Mr. Alexander Glen)"[12]. He remained a director. Two weeks later Thomas Hill presided over an e.g.m. as chairman of the reformed board. Once a director of the Monkland & Kirkintilloch Railway, he had been a Caledonian director since 1856. Reviewing some past episodes, he admitted that the Portpatrick agreement had been a mistake, and recalled that at the time, the Glasgow & South Western chairman, Sir Andrew Orr, had said "it is no use fighting over an empty hat". The interdict on the dividend had been lifted but the complainants had immmediately appealed. And the Baird family interests, with a reputed £700,000 investment in the Caledonian[13], were seeking a further interdict, to prevent the company from publishing reports and accounts that did not conform with the law. There was still plenty of animosity around. Alexander Robertson, a Glaswegian Ordinary shareholder, demanding more cuts in operating costs and more transparency over salaries, was heckled from the gallery. Shaking his fist, he shouted, "Are you not done yet, Edinburgh? Do you think we are going to lose our money and stand hearing you Edinburgh oyster boys with your £750 Preference stock?"[14]. Throughout 1868, the Ordinary share price stayed under £75.

To the *Railway Times*, the Caledonian was the great disruptor of the Scottish railway system. It accused the Caledonian of fostering agitation in the North British and of waging "a wasteful 20 years' war"; and now, it claimed, the Caledonian was attempting to lock the Highland Railway into its embrace at 4%[15]. In fact the NBR shareholders needed no prompting to investigate the excesses of their own board, and the Highland company was doing its best to get into the Caledonian's arms. But to the *Railway Times*, the Caledonian's financial policy was "rotten to the core."

**The two-horse Ferniegair bus, with clerestory roof and luggage rack,
at the original Hamilton terminus, later Hamilton West. It was in use until 1876.**

While such rhetorical flourishes enlivened the newspaper columns (and 1869 would bring further revelations), real things were still happening on the ground. From 1 January 1868, passenger trains had been running between Ferniegair and Motherwell[16], though this only partially closed the gap, as the Motherwell Bridge Station was some distance from the main line station. Horse buses still plied between Ferniegair and Hamilton, which had a service to Glasgow South Side. If no engine was available for the Blackwood carriage at Southfield Junction "a couple of horses hauled it to the terminus"[17]. Construction of the Edinburgh line via Midcalder was going on. In Forfarshire, works in progress inherited from the Scottish North Eastern included the reshaping of the junctions at Meigle, where the old Newtyle Railway and the new Alyth branch (opened 1861) intersected with the Perth-Forfar main line. The Newtyle line had been greatly altered over the years. Between 1860 and 1868 its inclined planes were replaced by new deviation lines. Balbeuchly was diverted by 1 November 1860, Dundee Law Tunnel by 10 June of the following year, and Hatton by 31 August 1868. New stations were built at Auchterhouse, Dronley, Liff (later Camperdown), Victoria (Lochee West); and at Newtyle a new station was built on a deviating curve, the original serving as a goods depot. The new layout was put into effect on 1 August, making it possible for locomotive-drawn trains to run direct from Dundee to Blairgowrie and Alyth, and the former, in particular, became a busy country terminus over the next few years. The speeded-up line carried considerable commuter traffic into Dundee[18].

Court actions dragged on. A dividend of 1.25% was declared for the half-year to July 31, and was promptly blocked by an interdict. As a miserable year for the company approached its end, the directors announced that the joint purse with the North British was "put in abeyance"[19]. But there was one useful bonus. The Telegraph Act of 1868 put the telegraph companies into state ownership, under the charge of the General Post Office. Since almost all telegraph lines followed the railways and were maintained by the railways for their own purposes as well as for public use, the transfer meant large payments to the railway companies. In the Caledonian's case it was £75,000, plus £1,500 a year for maintaining the lines, and free transmission of all the Company's telegraph messages[20]. The Portpatrick Railway also stood to gain, and on 1 February 1870 the Joint Committee resolved to ask for £10,000, to be split like other income, 62% to the Portpatrick Railway and 38% to the Caledonian.

Interdicts and Openings

In February 1869 Caledonian Ordinary shares stood over 20% below par, at £78.75, and the half-yearly dividend announced in March was 3.75%[21]. But the North British applied for a court interdict against the CR paying any dividend until it had lodged £40,000 as security against any claims the NBR might have under the joint purse agreement. This was followed by the lodging of an interdict claim against both the CR and the NBR by the chairman of the Carlisle & Silloth Railway, which alleged that the joint purse was illegal and the consent to it of the North British had been fraudulently obtained[22] (This was thrown out by the court on 4 June). The Caledonian and North British were each accusing the other of breaking the joint purse agreement. The dispute centred on Carlisle, with the NBR claiming that in the negotiations leading to the joint purse, the Caledonian had concealed an agreement with the London & North Western about traffic through Carlisle. In response the CR pointed out that the NBR chairman, Kippendavie, had been a director of the Caledonian at the time and had been present in October 1866 when the negotiations were going on. The NBR had never asked for details of the Caledonian's agreement with the North Western, and "nothing was said or done by representatives of the Caledonian Railway calculated to mislead." The judge disallowed the North British claim for interdict, but the dispute went on[23], and both companies set up shareholders' committees to help to resolve it. At the beginning of June the Caledonian's committee submitted a report, suggesting that the agreement was more properly a "joint traffic" rather than a "common purse" one. It considered the NBR to be acting intransigently in refusing to allow the matter to be discussed between the two chairmen or the general managers, and disputed the figures on which the North British claim was based. The Caledonian offered to divide the traffic from 1 February 1869 on a basis of 45.75% to the NBR and 54.25% to the CR, but the North British wanted to start at 45.5%, rising half-yearly by half a percent to 47.5%. Neither company would accept the arbitrator proposed by the other, and on 15 June the North British terminated the joint purse agreement[24]. In fact, as was pointed out later, the actual figures of both companies showed the North British share as 44.85% and the Caledonian's as 55.15%, so the offer of 45.75% was a good one[25]. At this time, too, "the agreement regulating division of traffic between England and Scotland was terminated by mutual consent of all parties on June 30"[26]. This was the 'pooling' arrangement dividing the revenues of West and East Coast traffic, which harked back to Captain Huish and the early 1850s. It had stabilised rates and fares but its inequitable division of the 'pool' could not be justified. None of the companies wanted to see a potentially ruinous free-for-all, and a simple agreement on standard charges between competitive points was set up[27]. Despite the areas of dispute, there is also evidence of co-operation. In the summer of 1869 the Caledonian and North British were jointly advertising excursions from Glasgow to Loch Lomond, Loch Katrine and the Trossachs[28]. The relationship between the companies was always a complex one, capable of harmony at certain points and levels while other matters remained contentious.

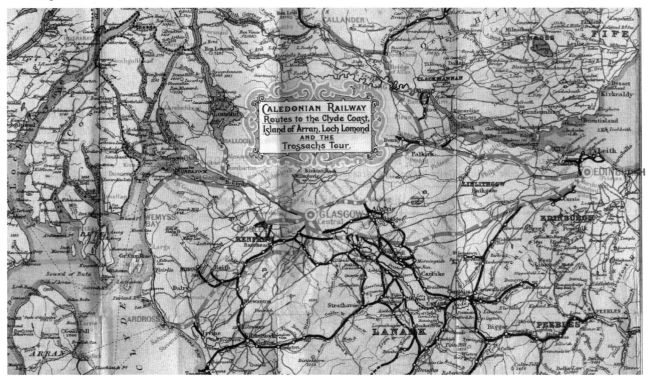

CR promotional map highlighting tourist routes, 1900s.

The Midcalder line, between Holytown and Midcalder on the Carstairs-Edinburgh line, had opened for goods on 1 January 1869. It was essentially an industrial railway, with branches tapping coal, iron and shale oil workings at Muldron, Woodmuir, Benhar and Camps, and a loop section between a point near West Calder and Stoneyburn, bypassing the stations at Addiewell and West Calder[29]. The expansion of the shale oil industry was a bonus – in this small area, over a century-plus from 1853, around 10 million tonnes of oil would be refined from 140 million tonnes of deep-mined shale, whose spoil bings reshaped the landscape. The Caledonian now had a line between the two cities that was considerably shorter than the Carstairs line; at 46 1/4 miles it was almost the same length as the E&G's original line, if not so level. On 9 July 1869 the passenger service between Glasgow and Edinburgh via Midcalder opened. The Act for the line had set the Edinburgh-Glasgow fares at 5s. 6d. for a first class single (9s. 6d. return); 4s. for a second class single (7s. return) and 2s. 6d. for a third class single (4s. return), less than the NBR, which was obliged to lower its fares. Four trains ran each way daily, two of them expresses (at a shilling premium for first and second class), taking an hour and ten minutes for the run. The new stations were built economically, mostly of wooden construction; and with oil or gas lighting and coal fires, the risk of fire was always high. Rather than pay hefty insurance premiums, the company became in effect its own insurer, debiting a sum from revenue each half-year until it reached £10,000. The fire fund was later increased to £20,000[30].

Struggling to reduce its commitments, and to improve its liquidity, the Caledonian introduced a Bill in the 1869 session of Parliament which would allow it to abandon the lines to Balerno and Gourock, and branches in Lanarkshire and Midlothian. The value of the abandoned works amounted to £793.000[31]. At the same time it sought authorisation to divert money raised for these projects, but not yet spent, to other projects. Altogether it wished to raise £355,000 capital and £112,200 by loans. It also sought belated authority for its purchase of Blythswood Holm, along with permission to sell or feu the ground. Shareholder interests, led by Bairds, vehemently opposed the Bill, but the company claimed there were precedents for diverting "surplus capital"[32]. To the objectors, this was "misappropriation" and the CR was compelled to acknowledge that £800,000 or £900,000 had been "applied to the general purposes of the Company" instead of to specific schemes for which the money had been raised. The shareholders' committee put the sum at £1,099,000[33]. The Bill, including the Caledonian's investment in the Solway Junction Railway, was passed, receiving the royal assent on 27 July.

After decades of intensive mining, the iron ore deposits of Lanarkshire were becoming worked out and most of their high-grade ore was already gone. Alternative supplies to the ironworks had been coming from the Cumbrian mines, whose production went up by six times between 1857 and 1863, to reach 150,000 tons a year. Although it was possible to route ore trains from the West Cumberland field via Carlisle, the Solway Junction Railway's 21-mile direct line across the Solway Firth would cut out twenty miles. On 13 September 1869 it opened for goods traffic (passenger trains followed in August 1870). The Solway Junction Railway's most distinctive feature was the viaduct, 1,940 yards long. Hollow iron piles twenty feet long and one foot in diameter had been sunk into the bed of the firth as a support for 193 cast-iron pillars carrying the bridge deck and the single line; and 2,900 tons of cast iron and 1,800 tons of wrought iron, had been used. The engineer was James Brunlees, the contractors Waring & Eckersley. Despite its length, the bridge failed to become a 'wonder'. In the view of experts, it had been a greater feat to lay the line across the Bowness Moss on the Cumbrian side than to build the viaduct. The Caledonian operated the line very much in its own interest, and a few months later, at its half-yearly meeting on 31 March 1870, the Solway Junction Board recorded its regret that the CR had not yet made any of the intended interchange arrangements with the North British or the Glasgow & South Western companies.

CHAPTER 8. The Caledonian in the Seventies 1869-1879

Competition on the Coast, and Elsewhere

Competition came to Greenock on 23 December 1869, when the GSWR-backed Greenock & Ayrshire Railway opened its new line right to the riverside, at Albert Harbour. Transfer to a steamer or ferry was vastly easier than from the Caledonian station at Cathcart Street, which involved a walk through insalubrious East Quay Lane, "Over mud and dubs and stanes"[1] to Custom House Quay, and the new route drew most of the traffic, and the mail contract. The Caledonian had had four years to prepare but seems to have done nothing until the new line had arrived. Efforts to persuade the steamship owners to stick with the Caledonian came to nothing. With an alternative route to Glasgow now on offer, inevitably a fares war started up. The Caledonian already owned the pier at the village of Gourock, where some steamer services already called, though its plan to build an extension line had foundered with others in the storms of 1865-66. Still cash-strapped and in no state to raise loans or capital, the CR could not afford to build what would be an expensive three-mile line, and financial stringency prevented any development for another nine years. Meanwhile for two years the traders and citizens of Greenock enjoyed cut-throat prices on the rival lines, both of which used the heavily overcrowded Bridge Street Station in Glasgow, until in March 1871 a joint purse agreement for the traffic was made, giving 57 $^2/_3$% of the revenue to the Caledonian and 42 $^1/_3$% to the GSWR, and fixed fares were agreed[2]. The third class fare from Glasgow to Upper Greenock went up from 6d. to 9d., and a return from one shilling to 1s. 6d.. Protest came from the Wemyss Bay company, which was not privy to the agreement, and which had agreed in 1870 to accept 47.5% of the profits on its line. Arbitration was sought and on 30 December 1871 the Lord Advocate made an award entitling the Wemyss Bay company to a share of the whole Glasgow-Wemyss Bay fare equivalent to its proportion of the total mileage, plus 50%. This was not at all to the liking of the Caledonian, which raised the rates again and also procured an increase in "the allowances made to them by the steamboat proprietors" without passing any of it on the Greenock & Wemyss Bay Railway. Since 1869 the Wemyss Bay company had ceased to run its own steamboats and the service had been leased first to Captain Gillies, then his son-in-law Captain Alexander Campbell, who would run it for twenty years. Greenock, incidentally, could still be a gateway to the south – in 1870 the shipowners G.&J. Burns were offering a daily steamer service between there and Liverpool, with a train connection to the quay from Glasgow, for 12s. 6d. cabin class (£1 return fare), or 6s. steerage[3].

From 1 January 1870, following extensions made to Buchanan Street passenger station between 1865-69, Caledonian trains to destinations north of Stirling ceased to use Queen Street Station. This was the first time scheduled passenger services used the 'Hayhill Fork' between Gartcosh and Garnqueen North Junction. North British services to Coatbridge, Airdrie and beyond continued to use Buchanan Street until 2 January 1871[4].

With the Caledonian and North British companies back in the familiar posture of mutual rivalry and suspicion, the NBR's plans were being closely watched from the Caledonian HQ. On acquiring the Scottish Central, the CR had become owner of the Newport-Dundee passenger ferry, and a special general meeting on 8 February 1870 approved the drafting of a Bill for the Caledonian to rebuild the jetty at Newport[5]. At this time the new direct line from Forfar to Dundee was nearing completion. On 2 May 1870 the new "temporary" station at Lothian Road in Edinburgh was opened, and renamed Princes Street, to which it was nearer than its predecessor. Given its position at the end of one of the finest streets in Europe, it was not the impressive structure that might have been hoped for. The chairman's speech at the formal opening on 30 April made the best of it. Wood, he suggested, was preferable to stone as it was easier to make alterations. Three tracks and two platforms were considered sufficient (the original station had had a single platform for arrivals and departures). Plans for a fine hotel on the site had long since been shelved.

Back in 1865 the Glasgow & South Western Railway had promoted a Bill for a new line to run from Kilmarnock to Glasgow, a direct route via Stewarton, which would run parallel with the Caledonian line between Neilston and Glasgow. The Caledonian had responded with a Bill to extend its Neilston line to Kilmarnock, which was, rather surprisingly, accepted by Parliament in the same session, and for some time it appeared that there would be two new railways from Kilmarnock to Glasgow. Residents of Kilmarnock might have anticipated some fine racing at minimal fares, but, with loud shareholder objections, both companies realised the absurdity of this and agreement was reached to make a joint line, with an Act of 12 July 1869. A short section of line from Kilmarnock had already been laid by the GSWR, and was extended to meet the Caledonian at Neilston, with a new station there which opened (for Glasgow trains) on 27 March 1871, and the Glasgow, Barrhead and Kilmarnock Joint Railway opened on 26 June 1873, with a branch from Barrmill to Beith, more conveniently placed for that town than its station on the GSWR main line. Its Glasgow terminus remained South Side, inconveniently distant from the city centre. In the extreme south-west, the irregular steamer service to Northern Ireland was improved with the establishment of the Larne & Stranraer Steamboat Company[6], promoted by by the Belfast & Northern Counties Railway, operating from 1 July 1872 in conjunction with the trains.

During 1869 the slow progress of the Callander & Oban line, impeded by lack of funds and bad weather, attracted the attention of the board. By now the Dingwall & Skye Railway was under construction, but the competitive instincts of Caledonian directors were not aroused. The £200,000 pledged by the Scottish Central was still widely resented and it was generally supposed that more would be demanded. The Caledonian resolved to abandon any construction beyond Tyndrum, where the line would meet roads leading north, south and west, and where there were still hopes of developing lead mining; and a Bill was prepared for a Callander & Oban Railway (Abandonment) Act, passed on 12 May 1870. Capital investment was reduced to £243,000 of which the Caledonian guaranteed £162,000 and also agreed to work the line at cost. Meantime the first section of the line, from Callander to a station named Killin, high above that village at the head of Glen Ogle, opened on 1 June 1870.

Callander in the pre-motor era; coaches and gigs await the train.

The Scottish North Eastern Railway's proposal for a direct Forfar-Dundee railway, made in 1863 (a Dundee & Forfar Direct had been one of the lost schemes of 1845), had been overtaken by the series of amalgamations between 1863 and 1866, and with all the lines now under Caledonian ownership, one of the reasons for building it – to have a separate line from the Dundee & Newtyle – had disappeared. Nevertheless the Caledonian resurrected the scheme, and incorporated it in a Bill in 1867 for various works in Forfarshire. The route, 17 1/4 miles long, left Forfar in the Arbroath direction, swinging south and climbing past Kingsmuir and Kirkbuddo, only two miles from the quarries at the end of the Carmyllie line, where a crossing loop was provided, to a summit of 570 ft, and taking a somewhat bendy path past Kingennie to join the former Dundee & Arbroath line at Broughty Junction and so to the terminus at Dundee East. It opened for goods traffic on 12 August 1870, and for passengers on 14 November. Later, stations would be added at Monikie (1871) and Barnhill (1874).

The original Act for the Balerno branch had specified a fine of £50 a day if the line were not opened on time, but the 1869 Act of abandonment spared the Caledonian from this. A new Bill was promoted, which became an Act on 20 June 1870, providing for a cheaper, single track line from Slateford, which instead of terminating at Balerno, would be extended to meet the new Edinburgh-Glasgow line at Ravelrig.

"Ruinous Competition"

Once again, in March 1870, the Caledonian paid only a modest dividend, of 3.75%. Hot dispute had been going on with the NBR on the running rights between Larbert, Perth and Aberdeen conferred by the Caledonian/Scottish North Eastern Railway Amalgamation Act: the CR was detaining North British trains at Larbert and charging passengers extra if they did not have Caledonian tickets. Eventually it was agreed that tickets issued at Waverley would be valid on either line for travel between Edinburgh and Perth[7]. Dundee was another location of acrimony. The CR's application for an Act to build a new jetty at Newport and extend the term of its ownership attracted strong objections from the municipalities on both sides of the Tay, who, no doubt rightly, saw the proposal as no more than a tactical move against the North British proposal to build a bridge. Incidentally, Christopher Johnstone appeared for the Caledonian at the Parliamentary inquiry as its "Consulting Manager"[8], presumably for a substantial fee. Shareholders of both companies, often with holdings in each, were again bubbling with protest, and a meeting was held in Manchester on 15 July to protest against the "ruinous competition" that was consuming the funds of both railways and eroding the dividends. Pressure was still on for a renewal of the common purse or some other arrangement that would end or at least abate the rivalry. The Caledonian was earning more than the North British; its total traffic receipts for the first half of 1869 were £859,474, and for the first half of 1870 £886,834, a rise of 3.4%. The NBR figures were £660,662 and £666,936, a rise of 2.5%[9].

Larbert Station (opened on 1 March 1848) seen around 1900. Despite the through lines, it was a frequent scene of delays, with many trains being divided and re-marshalled here. The under-hung signals control the double cross-over.

At this time, Parliamentary proposals to review the charging of duty on passenger fares was an important issue. Hitherto a flat 5% had been payable on all passenger fares except for 'parliamentary' trains, which charged a standard penny-a-mile and stopped at all stations. It was proposed instead to levy a flat 1% on all railway charges, passenger and goods, without exception. For a predominately goods-carrying railway this was not good news. The CR's passenger receipts in 1869 were £549,604 and it paid duty of £13,653. Its goods receipts were £1,290,604, and the combined duty would have been £18,402[10]. The proposal was denounced at shareholders' meeetings, and massive resistance from the 'railway interest' in Parliament ensured that it never got on to the statute book. In 1870 the Caledonian started its own cartage department, buying up the horses and plant of the contractors C. Robb & Co. and J. & P. Cameron. Wordie's contract was maintained, but the Caledonian (and the North British and GSWR), also became large-scale owners of horses in their own right.

In 1871 the NBR, then just embarked on construction of the first Tay Bridge, invited the Caledonian to discuss the prospect of a jointly owned Dundee Central Station which would replace the East and West Stations. Representatives of both companies met with the Trustees of Dundee Harbour, but nothing was resolved, and Dundee East and West remained as termini. Although further discussions on reducing competition were reported in July[11], there was no agreement on action, and at the half-yearly meeting of 26 September, J.C. Bolton had to report that the negotiations "had come to nothing"[12]. Again in anticipation of the Tay Bridge, the North British in 1871 sponsored a direct railway between Arbroath and Montrose, which would put both towns on an East Coast line to Aberdeen, shorten the North British route to Edinburgh by 40 miles, and reduce its dependence on the Caledonian to the section north of Kinnaber Junction.

By November 1871, with pressure from shareholder groups in both companies remaining strong for agreement or amalgamation, merger talks with the North British were once again being held. John Stirling of Kippendavie, the NBR chairman, was the prime apostle of amalgamation, and it was he who made the sacrificial gesture of letting the combined company be known as the Caledonian, or perhaps United Caledonian, Railway. The amalgamation proposal was accepted by both boards during November. But while the directors approved, the shareholders were restive. A committee of both companies set up to negotiate the terms had made a straightforward agreement that "the basis of division shall be the actual amount of the net receipts of both companies as shown in the accounts for the year to 31st July 1871". The comparative figures produced by Kippendavie for the NBR special shareholders' meeting on 1 December 1871 showed the Caledonian to be both larger and more efficient in the six months to 31 July 1871[13].

	CR	NBR
Revenue	£1,063,000	£762,000
Working Expenses	£448,000	£388,000
Working Expenses as % of revenue	42.61	52.02
Maintenance Costs	£204,000	£193,800
No. of locomotives	532	396

The new board would be formed of equal numbers of CR and NBR directors. They had gone as far as deciding who would be the senior officers in the new company. Smithells was to go, with a large gratuity of £10,000. And item 12 in the agreement invited the GSWR also to become a party to the amalgamation. At the Caledonian's special meeting on 1 December, the amalgamation was approved with only two opposing votes. But at the NBR meeting, opposition was strong, despite Kippendavie's oratory: "Either the Scotch railways will be amalgamated into a large concern, or we shall be cut up and divided among the English lines"[14], he announced prophetically. A prominent NBR shareholder, John Monteith Douglas, disputed the figures produced by the boards, and contended that if the Caledonian adopted the NBR's principles of book-keeping, it would pay out £70,000 less to its shareholders, while if the North British adopted the CR principles, it would pay out £54,000 more[15]. The terms were criticised as less favourable to the North British than the failed joint purse arrangement, giving it only 40% of revenues, just at a time when its future was looking highly promising; and it was forecast that Parliament would throw out the Bill. Virtually every town council served by the companies was opposed. Clearly Kippendavie was not going to get a rubber-stamp result, and on 16 December the boards had to announce the postponement of the Amalgamation Bill to the 1873 parliamentary session. In fact it was dead, and though a new joint purse arrangement was said to be in preparation for 1 February 1872[16], the Caledonian reassembled all its old suspicions and oppositional tactics. *Railway News*, on 10 February 1872, suggested that in looking at the

Traders' wagons behind; the nearest wagon is a CR vehicle leased in a thirling agreement
to John Watson's Meikle Earnock Colliery. CR wagons on the centre track.
Numerous wagons still have dumb buffers. (Caledonian Railway Association)

figures, it had emerged that the CR had been overcharging its customers despite the Acts of Parliament regulating railway charges. This was angrily denied by the Caledonian, though the magazine did not retract .

Although certainly not written with only Scottish railways in mind, a letter in the *Railway Times* from 'Justus' at this time expressed a widely-held view on the morality of railway directors and their apparent freedom from the law, with the ironic comment: "A sure sign of our growing civilisation is found in the ease with which the moral shortcomings of our directors is slurred over"[17].

Happenings to South, West and East

From 1870 to 1872 the Caledonian had been buying steel rails to be laid at busy junctions and other places where traffic was very heavy. It had also been buying up traders' wagons, to be used as, or replaced by, company wagons. Most of these were coal trucks – as many as 10,000 were estimated to have been acquired[18] – and many were in poor condition. But a very large number of traders' wagons remained, inhibiting the flexibility with which the wagon stock could be used, and making the Goods Managers' and Superintendent's tasks more difficult. Along with such evidence of positive action, the board also declared a dividend of 4.75% for the half-year. The *Railway Times*, the prime journal for railway shareholders, was still castigating the Caledonian for "vicious and unprincipled" management, and implying that half-yearly reports and balance sheets still did not represent actuality. But in 1870-71 for the first time the company had earned more than a million pounds in a half-year, £1,050,057 to 31 January 1871. Train mileage had greatly increased, 2,537,415 for passenger trains and 2,814,619 for goods in the half-year, compared to 1,892,491 and 2,086,464 respectively in the corresponding period of 1870. Operating expenses were up from 48.3% of revenue to 49.9%, but many railways might have envied the CR's ability to keep the figure below 50%.

The Caledonian's worst accident until 1915 happened at Kirtlebridge on 2 October 1872, when the 9 p.m. train from Euston, running almost two hours late, hit a shunting goods train which was occupying the Down line although the signals were clear for the express. Eleven passengers and one engineman were killed, and the failures exposed did much to speed up the company's change to block working. A few days later, on 10 October, a connecting loop was opened, the 'Strawfrank Curve', just east of Carstairs, placing the station on the western tip of a triangular layout. Trains between Edinburgh and Carlisle could now pass by without having to reverse, though any Edinburgh passsenger train booked to stop or divide at Carstairs still had to enter the station and leave in the reverse direction. The Lampits by-pass line[19]. was not in use by this time, except perhaps for wagon storage, though it seems to have remained intact until at least 1880. the 1in Ordnance Survey map of that date shows it as intact; the 6in map of 1896 shows it as dismantled except for a short length at the south end. The new curve also gave direct access to the Dolphinton line from the south, though that was surely incidental.

One might suppose that by the 1870s there was hardly any need for another railway to link the Glasgow conurbation with Lanarkshire, but the North British put up a Bill in 1873 for a line through the territory between the Caledonian's Hamilton and Motherwell lines. Vehemently opposed by the Caledonian, it was rejected. Part of the North British case had been the inadequacy of the Caledonian's facilities on the south of the Clyde, and the Caledonian had to commit itself to building a branch from Fallside, on the Rutherglen-Motherwell line, to Bothwell, and, much more expensively, to extend the line across the Clyde from Bridge Street to a new terminus, then known as Gordon Street. A Bill was entered to Parliament which became the Gordon Street, Glasgow Station Act of 1873 (modified in 1875). It incorporated a two-level bridge over the Clyde, railway above, road below, at the Broomielaw. This design, deplored by Glaswegians, was dropped when it proved extremely difficult to get sufficient ground on the south bank, and in 1875 the CR paid £73,000 for wayleave on a site 50 yards downstream[20]. Large-scale changes at another major station were set out in the Carlisle Citadel Station Act of 21 July 1873, in anticipation of the completion of the Midland Railway's line from Leeds and Settle. Joseph Cubitt was appointed as arbitrator to assess what extensions and alterations would be needed. At this time the station was jointly owned by the Caledonian and the LNWR, and articles of agreement with the other companies using the station, Glasgow & South Western, North British, North Eastern, Maryport & Carlisle, and Midland, had been made on 16 December 1872. While eagerly awaited by the GSWR and NBR, the prospect of the Midland at Carlisle was far from welcome to the Caledonian and LNWR, at last facing serious competition for traffic between England and Scotland on 'their' side of the country. The Act also required the CR to provide stabling, at a charge, for Glasgow & South Western locomotives at Carlisle. Other developments in 1873 included the westwards extension of the Lanark line from Douglas to Muirkirk, which was reached on 1 January, making an end-on junction with the 1872 GSWR line from Ayr and Cumnock, and forming what was potentially a cross-country line from Ayrshire to Edinburgh and the Berwickshire coast. Such a line had long been advocated in Ayr. But the CR, more interested in coal and iron, was in no hurry to operate a passenger service over it. Local trains began from 1 June 1874[21] but another four years went by before a through Ayr-Edinburgh service was provided, and it was not a success. The working agreement with the Solway Junction company was altered in June 1873 when the Caledonian purchased the section of the line between Annan and Kirtlebridge, and continued to work the English section. In August, the Oban railway reached Tyndrum, and a small locomotive shed was built there, to service two trains each way daily.

Tyndrum Station, opened 1873 as a terminus, rebuilt 1877. The Loch Tay steamer service is advertised. Note the level change in the platform.

The half-yearly report in July 1874 depicted a generally highly satisfactory situation. A dividend of 6.25% on the Ordinary shares had been announced, and the stock was currently £30 above par. The long delayed Balerno line was on the point of opening. The company also agreed to put another £20,000 into the Callander & Oban. Tyndrum's status as a terminus had been purely to suit the Caledonian, and in February the C&O company had resolved to promote a Bill to resuscitate its western extension. To this the Caledonian somewhat reluctantly acceded. By now the Dingwall & Skye Railway had been running to its western pierhead at Strome Ferry for over three years, without any sign of profitability. The C&O was allowed to push another 12 miles westwards, to Dalmally. Already it was making an economic difference in its thinly-peopled territory. The price of coal at Lochearnhead fell from around £1 a ton to 13s. when the railway came[22]. In the far south-west, Portpatrick was finally deemed an unsuitable harbour for steamships, and in 1874 Stranraer Harbour became the railway and shipping terminal for Ireland, with the Portpatrick section relegated to village branch-line status.

Four years after its new Act was passed, the Balerno loop opened on 1 August 1874, a sinuous line branching off the Edinburgh-Glasgow line at Slateford and following the Water of Leith to rejoin the main line at Ravelrig. The builder was Charles Brand of Montrose, whose bid was £42,143 13s. 6d. There were numerous paper and grain mills on the river and most acquired a siding. A crossing loop was provided at Currie. At Balerno itself the goods station was built at the end of a short spur where the original terminus had been intended. The branch prospered and attracted new residents to the villages it served. Passenger numbers at Juniper Green were 32,280 in 1883 and 166,653 in 1914[23]. In Glasgow, the Clyde Trustees were completing the large Queen's Dock, at Stobcross on the north bank of the river towards the end of 1874. The Glasgow & Paisley joint line had had a branch terminus at Govan, only a few hundred yards away, but on the south bank, since 1868. On the north side, wrangling over railway access to the new dock had been going on since 1864, when the Edinburgh & Glasgow Railway had made an early and successful bid for a branch from the Dumbarton line at Maryhill, down to Stobcross, a project duly inherited by the North British. Both the Caledonian and the GSWR had opposed this, with alternative proposals. With a typical blend of half-co-operation, half-competition, the Caledonian had jointly purchased some of the ground at Stobcross with the NBR, which compelled John Stirling to acknowledge that "the Caledonian Railway had money powers over it [the branch] and certain rights in the station of Stobcross", but in March 1870 it opposed the Clyde Navigation and North British (Additional Powers) Bill to alter the railway access[24]. After high controversy, the best the Caledonian could get was running powers over the NBR tracks and joint ownership, with the NBR, of the line into the dockyard area.

"Beware the Coatbridge Line"

A useful feature of the Caledonian was its through services, enabling passengers to make certain journeys without having to change carriages. These were no doubt appreciated but did not always go quite according to the timetable, as one traveller's account of a journey from Wemyss Bay to Edinburgh, at the beginning of September 1874, suggests. The advertised journey time was 3 hours and 35 minutes:

> "Sent luggage down to station at half-past 11, train time 12. Luggage placed in van for Edinburgh. Stationmaster ordered it into an open truck. Remonstrated as the van, when we started even was quite empty. Got away at 12.30. At Coatbridge tickets were taken. Asked why, and was told it was to save stopping at West Calder. At Coatbridge 35 minutes, as an engine was sent for to Glasgow. Heard a porter say that 'engine-driver didna ken the way and that's why we beguid to gang slow'. The guard also was a common porter. In my first class smoking compartment were two third class men who got in at Paisley on the pretence there was no room in their proper place, one a Cockney shoemaker. Lent them *The Scotsman* and another paper and they said 'it would be all right if only they had a paper'. It was not all right, especially in the case of one of them. Thankful to say they were both extracted and relegated to third class at Coatbridge, leaving a smell behind them. Although tickets were taken at that place 'to save time', we stopped at four other stations to land a single passenger at each. In Edinburgh 1 hour late. Moral '*Cave* Coatbridge line' —I am, &c., D.K."[25]

Through tickets extended to steamer services also. One ticket took the traveller via Buchanan Street and Bridge Street (omnibus between not included) to Wemyss Bay or Gourock, then by ship to Kilcreggan, Cove, Blairmore, Kilmun, Kirn, Dunoon, Arrochar, Lochgoilhead or the Arran piers[26].

Prompted by the belief that certain railways, notably the Caledonian, were charging too much for coal and mineral carriage, a group of Glasgow industrialists in 1874 re-promoted the failed North British venture of 1873 as the Glasgow, Bothwell, Hamilton & Coatbridge Railway, in order to deprive the greedy men of Buchanan

Street of some of their traffic, and this time, despite the Caledonian's promised Bothwell branch (opened in March 1877) and its ongoing work towards a new Glasgow terminus, the scheme was approved. James Baird, never a friend of the CR, was a leading promoter. Its attempt to oppose the project cost the Caledonian £5,700 in legal fees, but the half-yearly meeting on 22 September 1874 was also told of a property bonus – thirty years before, a large area of land in the Blythswood area of Glasgow had been acquired for a terminus, before the plan was abandoned in favour of Buchanan Street. Now 3,352 square yards had been sold for £107,000, twice the original price. The board was more discreet about its purchase of the former Govan Poorhouse (from the recently established Glasgow Tramway & Omnibus Co., which had been going to use it as stables) for the very large sum of £38,000. But it was on Eglinton Street, where ground was required for a new station[27].

South Side had a small locomotive shed in the Caledonian goods yard, but there was obvious need for more accommodation for engines in south Glasgow. In 1873 land was acquired from Dixon's, alongside the ironworks, and on 30 December a tender of £12,750 was agreed for construction of a depot with a great wooden shed over 14 tracks. First referred to as Rutherglen, its name was established as Polmadie by the time it opened in September 1875. It was, and would remain, the Caledonian's largest depot, with workshops for repair and overhaul. A large mineral station was also laid out to the east of the engine shed. A smaller engine shed was opened at Eglinton Street in 1878, primarily for passenger services from Bridge Street.

Shares, Brakes, and Other Matters

In the autumn of 1875 a major effort was made to simplify the company share structure, which by now had 46 different kinds and class of share. Of the Preference stocks 15 were related to the Guaranteed Companies, leaving 29 to be consolidated at 4%. Preference shares which had a right to participate in the Ordinary dividend, if that were to rise above a specified level, were to be split, into one 4% Preference share and one Deferred Ordinary share. An extraordinary general meeting 23 November accepted the proposal. The exercise was a success, with the total value of the relevant stocks rising from £9,673,442 on 8 September 1875 to £10,525,744 exactly a year later. But as one commentator noted, it was now hard to gauge the true capital of the 'True Line'. In July 1881 the notional capital was £36,459,245, of which shares accounted for £29,037,751, with £10,257,074 as Ordinary, £2,783,658 as Deferred, and £15,997,019 as Guaranteed and Preference shares; plus £7,127,936 in Debentures and loans. He reckoned "upwards of £30 millions" as genuine investment[28]. The company's nominal capital had been increased by £5 million[29]. By any standards of the time, it was a vast concern.

4-4-0 No. 128 of the 125-class, the CR's first 4-4-0s, built by Neilsons in 1877, intended to share mainline traffic with the 8ft singles but found to be underpowered. Modified by Drummond, they were relegated to secondary traffic and known as the 'Dundee Bogies'.

Among the more general issues affecting railways at this time was the question of safety, particularly in relation to braking. Trains were heavier and travelled faster, and a succession of accidents caused serious public alarm. The railway companies, though pressed hard by the Board of Trade, seemed reluctant to invest in better braking systems, despite the Westinghouse continuous brake having been successfully demonstrated in the USA in 1869. Benjamin Conner tested the Westinghouse brake on 2-4-0 engine No. 92, on the Wemyss Bay line, but at this time it was not a fully automatic 'fail-safe' system, and the Caledonian went on to sponsor the development of the Steel-McInnes pneumatic reaction brake from 1871. McInnes, a former engine driver, was the company's brake inspector; Steel was a well-known Glasgow engineer and inventor. Their system was worked by compressed air, piped along the carriage roofs, from a compressor on the locomotive, and any sudden diminution of pressure automatically applied the brakes as well as alerting the driver by activating "a huge alarm whistle" mounted on the leading carriage. It was tested on the Garnkirk, Cleland & Midcalder, and Drumbowie lines on 5 February 1875, with apparent success. Going down the 1 in 65 Drumbowie incline at 40-45 mph, the engine coupling was lifted, the brake connection parted, and the train came to a halt in ten seconds[30]. The Caledonian sent a locomotive and train equipped with this system to the Newark brake trials in England, in June, but like other methods tested there, it proved markedly inferior to Westinghouse's automatic version. James Smithells and George Brittain were present at further tests, on the North British, between 12-22 December 1876, when again the Westinghouse brake gave the best result. Two years later, the Caley was still toying with its own method; at the half-yearly meeting on 14 September 1878, Hill said somewhat vaguely in reply to a shareholder's question that "they were getting some carriages prepared for the use of the Steel-McInnes brake, but they had various kinds of brakes upon the system"[31]. Finally on 23 November 1880 an agreement was made with the Westinghouse Company for its brakes to be fitted to 50 locomotives and 500 carriages, and with the advent of Dugald Drummond at St. Rollox in 1882 this programme was accelerated[32]. In 1889 the Regulation of Railways Act required automatic continuous brakes on all passenger trains, and the Caledonian was among the first to comply.

In May 1876 work began on the bridge over the Clyde to the new Glasgow Central and continued until 1 October 1878, when the four track bridge was completed, at a cost of £64,000[33]. The Glasgow & South Western, with no access to the new terminus, insisted that Bridge Street Station should be maintained, and the Caledonian had to pay for its reconstruction. It remained a joint station. South from Bridge Street, a new main line was under construction. Known as the "Gordon Street Lines", it clove its way between foundries and mills to a new station at Eglinton Street, where it divided, with an eastern arm running in a tunnel to meet the Rutherglen line at Larkfield, and a western arm joining the Barrhead and Kilmarnock line at Muirhouse Central Junction. Near Eglinton Street it passed under the City of Glasgow Union Railway, which had been built from Shields Road as far as Dunlop Street in 1870-71. While the Gordon Street lines were being built, the Glasgow, Barrhead & Kilmarnock Joint Railway extended its tracks north from South Side to meet the City of Glasgow Union Railway just beyond a new station, Gorbals, which opened on 1 September 1877. From that date the Joint Line closed its South Side platforms and trains ran to Gorbals. The Caledonian, as joint owner of the Glasgow, Barrhead & Kilmarnock Joint Railway, must have acquiesced, but it continued for the time being to use South Side as terminus of Hamilton trains, though the station was partially demolished. In Edinburgh, at the increasingly complex set of junctions in the Dalry district, a new linking line was opened on 3 July 1876, from Haymarket West Junction on the North British Railway coming in from the west, crossing above the Slateford-Granton branch and joining the spur from that line towards Princes Street at Dalry Middle Junction. Caledonian trains coming in from Larbert now took this route and ceased to use Haymarket Station. On 23 September a line was opened from the original Hamilton terminus, renamed Hamilton West, to a junction at Haughhead, where one loop turned north to link up in the Motherwell direction at Ross Junction, the other crossing under the Lesmahagow line and joining it facing south at Ferniegair Junction. Passenger services began from 2 October. A large new station was built as Hamilton Central, with two platforms and four through tracks, under a wide overall roof formed of iron bowstring trusses, and substantial buildings on each side. Ferniegair Station was resited south of the new junction at the same time. It now ceased to be the terminus of Lesmahagow line passenger trains, and the horse-bus service to Hamilton was replaced by through trains which ran via Hamilton Central to Glasgow South Side (until 1879), then to Glasgow Central[34]. The three-mile line, with a river bridge and a tunnel beneath the Duke of Hamilton's parkland, had cost over £80,000 a mile to build. But the shorter distance saved 9d. a ton on coal and "the travelling public will be enabled to save from an hour to 1½ hours in their journeyings to and from Edinburgh and the south"[35]. By comparison, it was noted that the C&O line required £210,000 for the completion of 25 miles from Dalmally to Oban. Optimistic hopes were expressed that £70,000 of this could be raised in Argyll, by means of 4.5% Preference shares. However, in September 1878 the Caledonian added £140,000 to the £182,600 it had already subscribed, and the LNWR coughed up a further £50,000 to enable the line to be completed[36].

From 1 May 1876 the traffic flow through Carlisle was significantly changed by the full opening of the Midland Railway's new line from Leeds. The station layout and facilities had been substantially enlarged in readiness. The

'Long-boiler' 0-6-0 No. 635 of the 631-class, 1874, at Dundee West.
Introduced to replace the 0-4-2 mineral locomotives, the short wheelbase was achieved by
placing the rear axle in front of the fire box. Most lasted until the mid 1900s.

Midland was determined to gain prestige from its London-Glasgow and Edinburgh passenger services, via the Glasgow & South Western into the imposing new St. Enoch terminal, and the North British to Waverley, and the Caledonian-LNWR West Coast route had a challenge to meet. Compared with St. Enoch, Buchanan Street was a modest, not to say mean terminus. But the Central Station project was well under way. Proposals for another Central, never to be realised, were briefly resuscitated in Dundee in 1876. The Caledonian again joined in discussions with the NBR and the Dundee local authorities. Surprisingly, it seems to have been objections from the latter that kicked the project again into limbo, with no further action after a meeting on 30 December 1876[37]. In 1877 the busy Dalmarnock branch in east Glasgow was extended northwards, from a point south of its terminus to a new goods terminal at London Road, opening on 12 April. Dalmally became the new temporary terminus of the Callander & Oban when the line opened to there on 1 May.

Thomas Salkeld died in January 1878, still a director of the company. He had been a combative and often embattled chairman, and though the achievement of the amalgamations had been overshadowed by dispute over the terms, he had kept the Caley's place as Scotland's largest railway. The year was to be one of trade depression, especially in iron and coal, and the company suffered accordingly, though it entered an ambitious Bill on 21 March for the construction of a railway extension to Gourock and of a deep-water harbour to provide a port not just for Clyde steamers but for the foreign trade, both cargo and passenger. Energetic opposition from the town of Greenock and the GSWR ensured that the Bill failed. The Caledonian came back with a less ambitious scheme for a railway pier handling only Clyde steamer traffic.

New Dispensations in Angus and Glasgow

With the opening of the first Tay Bridge on 1 June 1878, Dundee finally acquired a cross-city passenger service, through the North British Tay Bridge Station. But the East and West termini continued to serve the Caledonian lines. By an Act of Parliament passed on 21 July 1879, the lines of the Dundee & Arbroath Railway were to come under joint NBR and Caledonian management from 1 February 1880, along with the Carmyllie Railway and a short extent of the Arbroath & Forfar as far as as St. Vigeans, where the new North British line to Montrose and Kinnaber Junction would diverge. The Caledonian gained £171,566 in compensation for the loss of revenue. It also sent the southbound mail from Arbroath the long way round via Guthrie and Forfar, to keep it on Caledonian metals, despite local protests[38]. The Arbroath & Forfar was still a separate company, operated by the Caledonian under the working agreement. While the North British line between Arbroath and Montrose was under construction, in the summer of 1878 the Caledonian relaid the link between Friockheim and Glasterlaw, to enable North British services to run between Edinburgh, Dundee and Aberdeen. Opening of the Tay Bridge brought the expected increase in North British passenger numbers, giving it 84% of Edinburgh-Dundee, and 63% of Edinburgh-Aberdeen traffic[39].

The rival line to Hamilton was completed on 1 April 1878; known as "Baird's Railway", it was worked (and eventually taken over) by the North British, making a substantial and of course deeply unwelcome NBR intrusion into 'Caledonian' territory. At Uddingston it crossed over a new Caledonian cross-country link, completed on 1 October 1878, running from Uddingston through Bellshill, crossing the Motherwell-Coatbridge main line at right angles near Mossend and meeting the Cleland-Midcalder-Edinburgh line at Fullwood Junction. This line provided a useful bypass both to Coatbridge-Airdrie and to Motherwell, though Mossend itself was becoming a complex intersection.

The 1870s had been an expansive and generally prosperous decade up to 1878, when there was a sharp economic downturn. During May-June of that year the Caledonian also experienced its first serious strike, when the engineering workers at Glasgow and Perth withdrew their labour for four weeks in response to wage reductions. A compromise was reached, in which a 51-hour working week was guaranteed, though pay went down by 7.5% and 5% respectively, a result seen as reasonable in the current state of the labour market. The half-yearly meeting on 17 September had to note a fall in revenue against the previous half-year, of £77,824. A sharp-eyed and critical shareholder, John McGavin, noted that although the value of carted goods had fallen by £26,000, the cost of cartage had gone up by £300. He observed ruefully that "the horse affair on all the railways was bungled" and that it always cost more to get someone else to do a job[40]. Railway cartage offered many opportunities for low-level graft, pilferage and fraud. At the same time, crisis hit the City of Glasgow Bank, which had teetered on the brink on previous occasions, and it failed on 1 October. The depositors were paid, but the bank's shareholders lost heavily[41]. The collapse led to a general economic slump, particularly strong in Glasgow, with property values falling, and a general slowdown until things picked up again in the early 1890s.

Advertisements in Glasgow newspapers in late June 1879 announced the closure of South Side as a passenger station and the opening of new stations at Bridge Street and Eglinton Street, as from 1 July. Trains from Hamilton, Motherwell and the Edinburgh line were now to work to and from the rebuilt Bridge Street. Trains from Strathbungo, Pollokshaws, Busby and East Kilbride would cease to use "the Station at Gorbals" and work to and from Bridge Street, and "Passenger trains with through carriages between Edinburgh, Paisley, Greenock, Wemyss Bay and the West will be run via Eglinton Street, Bridge Street and Pollokshields"[42]. This was a geographically slightly odd way of putting it, perhaps to conceal the fact that trains would have to leave Bridge Street in the reverse direction (the same had been true at South Side). It also noted that "the Company's omnibuses between South Side and Buchananan Street Stations would cease with South Side's closure" (South Side remained a busy goods centre, for the Glasgow & Kilmarnock Joint line to the west and the Caledonian to the east of the through tracks). Only a few weeks later, when the new Glasgow Central opened, most services were diverted here. But the trains to England did not transfer immediately; CR advertisements noted that: "The Main Line Trains between Glasgow and England and the North and Edinburgh will, until further notice, be worked to and from Buchanan Street"[43]. Wemyss Bay trains continued to terminate at Bridge Street, which had four terminal platforms. But four lines also ran through it and over the new girder bridge across the Clyde, constructed by William Arrol, once a spinner's boy, now proprietor of the Dalmarnock Ironworks and a leading engineer.

Glasgow Central Station opened on 1 August. The architect was Sir Robert Rowand Anderson of Edinburgh and the building has been described as "the first of a sort of Glasgow-Scots vernacular"[44]. Lunch was laid on by the contractors, Watt & Wilson, for 150 gentlemen who took the short ride from Bridge Street to the new Central Station on 31 July. Construction of the foundations had delved through layers of what was not yet known as industrial archaeology – old gas works, a sugar house, and many subterranean passages about four feet wide and five feet high. An impressive range of statistics was assembled. The station had used 80,000 cubic yards of rubble masonry, 20,000 cubic yards of concrete, and 450,000 cubic feet of ashlar stonework. Ten million bricks, 7,000 tons of wrought iron and 1,400 tons of cast iron had been used, and the total cost was £700,000[45]. It was undoubtedly a triumphal occasion for the Caledonian, and passengers could now step out right into the city centre. Work was not complete, however, and the new booking hall did not come into use for another three years[46]. But traffic was increasing all the time and the station, with its eight platforms, was intensely busy and often overcrowded.

Expansion of commerce and industry required ever more investment in Glasgow around 1879 and into the 1880s. Pollokshields Station had been opened by the Glasgow & Paisley Joint Committee in Glasgow in 1863, just to the east of, and above, the General Terminus line of 1849. After many Acts of Parliament, in 1870 the new City of Glasgow Union Railway diverged from the joint line about 300 yards west of Pollokshields, at Pollok Junction and its Shields Road Station was alongside Pollokshields to the south, also over the General Terminus line. Beneath these lines, the Caledonian built a junction westwards off the General Terminus line to a large new goods depot at Kinning Park, alongside the Glasgow & Paisley Joint line. This station may have opened around 1879[47].

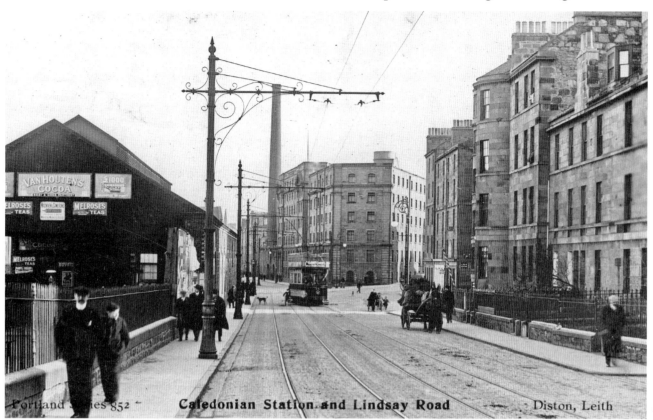

Leith Station on left, opened in 1879, was renamed North Leith in 1903.
Electric trams ran in Leith from 1905 (the one in the picture looks as if it has derailed),
but until 1922 Edinburgh-bound passengers had to change half-way, to Edinburgh's cable-hauled trams.

In July 1885 the GSWR's line from Johnstone and Paisley (Canal) came in parallel to the south of the two existing lines and a third contiguous station, named Shields, was opened above the junction. Substantial works had also been going on in the Rutherglen-Dalmarnock area. Rutherglen Station was resited to the Dalmarnock branch junction[48]. The branch's new terminus on London Road was provided with a passenger station from 1 January 1879, and a passenger service was operated between here and Rutherglen. The original Dalmarnock goods terminus was renamed Bridgeton and a passenger station was constructed on the adjacent through line from London Road. In Edinburgh, a passenger service from Princes Street to Leith (renamed North Leith in 1903) began on 1 August 1879, serving stations at Murrayfield, Craigleith, Granton Road and Newhaven[49]. Expansion of specialised traffic is suggested by orders placed with Brown, Marshall for 18 four-wheel and ten six-wheel 'Fresh Meat' vans at £166 10s. and £183 each, respectively; as well as ten 'Roadside Covered Vans' at £94 10s.[50]

Conscious of the fact that very large expenditures were committed to, the board looked for savings, and in August instructed heads of department to look at ways of reducing the wage bills. Pay reductions were implemented at St. Rollox Works and the board received 'memorials' of protest from the men[51]. Throughout the winter and into the spring of 1880, petitions for pay rises were declined or deferred.

After the Tay Bridge catastrophe on 28 December 1879 the NBR reverted to train ferries, which continued until the new bridge was opened on 11 July 1887. Until its new line between Arbroath and Kinnaber Junction was fully opened on 1 May 1883, NBR trains from Dundee terminated at Bridge of Dun, where passengers transferred to Caledonian trains[52]. The Board of Trade's reaction to the Tay Bridge disaster prompted railways to look anew at some of their bridges, particularly where Sir Thomas Bouch had acted as engineer; and though he had no part in the building of the Strathmore lines, the Caledonian embarked on on a programme of renewal of the wooden bridges which dated back to the original construction, and which were increasingly unsuitable for faster, heavier trains.

CHAPTER 9 The Caledonian in the 80's, 1880-1889

Consolidation

The decades of the 1880s and 1890s were the best time of the Caledonian's 78-year history. The company consolidated its position in Glasgow, developed its services effectively, and ran some of the fastest trains in the world.

Traffic in the area round Motherwell was becoming ever more congested. The multiplicity of junctions and spur lines to collieries and factories, combined with the slow speed of goods trains and the limitations of the signalling system, created delays and acted as a brake on revenue generation. A new line was opened on 1 June 1880, giving the fast-growing iron-smelting town of Wishaw a Central Station, "an ornamental wooden structure"[1] better-placed than the original one, which was renamed Wishaw South, and also providing an alternative route past Motherwell, in a district becoming ever more intensely industrialised. The new line ran north from Law Junction to meet the CR's Glasgow-Edinburgh line at Carfin (Holytown from 1 October 1901). A short intermediate link was also laid to enable trains to run between Wishaw Central and the main line at Shieldmuir Junction. New industry attached itself to the line: between Glasgow and Wishaw were steelworks at Hallside (1871), Dalzell (1881), Wishaw (1885), Clydebridge (1888) and Flemington (1890). The Caledonian had to resort to the Railway

Flemington Station was opened on 2 March 1891. The large verandah valances are a prominent feature.

4-6-0 No. 51, of the second batch of the 55-class, built at St Rollox in 1905, with a westbound train near Taynuilt. The 55s were the CR's first 4-6-0s, and ran until 1937. Ben Cruachan rises behind.

& Canal Commissioners to ensure that these new lines got the maximum traffic. Increasing amounts of pig iron were coming up from England, and, if destined for steelworks on the North British system, were transferred to the NBR at Whifflet. However the North British had begun to refuse to take the traffic there and insisted on its being handed over at Carlisle. The Caledonian won the case, but, in recognition of its expenses in taking over "Baird's Railway" from Glasgow to Hamilton, the NBR was awarded an extra 3*d*. per ton[2]. Far from the soot-laden environs of Lanarkshire, the at-last completed railway to Oban was ceremonially opened on 30 June 1880. Goods trains had been running on it since the 12th. A subscription of £50,000 from the London & North Western Railway, for Preference C&O stock at 4.5%, had made possible the final stage. Special trains brought guests to the opening, and at the usual banquet, civilities were exchanged in numerous speeches. Thomas Hill reflected on the stormy history of the 15-year project, and the "hours of darkness when the board was almost overturned" in its support. Looking ahead to the 1880 tourist season, and with the C&O due to be completed, the board had decided to drop its West Perthshire and Argyll coach services except for Crieff-Lochearnhead, the only profitable one[3].

Hill gave up the chairmanship in November, switching posts with his deputy, Joseph C. Bolton. Bolton's career had begun as "a sailor-boy" but natural ability had taken him up to be director of an East India merchant company and chairman of Glasgow's Chamber of Commerce. A few months later, following Henry Ward's death, in April 1881 Irvine Kempt was appointed general superintendent, at a salary of £1,200 although the official rate for the post was £900, "in consideration of exceptional circumstances"[4], and would hold the post for over 20 years.

The country's Sabbatarians, as well as its advocates of teetotalism (often the same people) had early-on identified the railway as, if not quite a Satanic device, at least a dangerously effective force (albeit unintentionally) in encouraging a secular approach to life. They had been successful in minimising, if not stifling, Sunday train services, and less so in trying to prevent stimulating liquors being sold in railway refreshment rooms. But by 1880 they were routed when it came to Fast Days, in the cities and big towns at least. Once allotted for penance and prayer, these days off work were transformed by the railway into opportunities for jolly excursions, to the Falls of Clyde, or the coast, or even as far as Oban. Newspapers carried enticing advertisements offering special fares, and for the Caledonian it was a useful source of extra revenue.

Bolton's chairmanship, its start coinciding with an improvement in the economy and a boost for industry and commerce, also confirmed a change in the Caledonian's general style and comportment, though it had had been gradually coming for several years. The rackety years were past history. Solid businessmen were in charge, and

The Viaduct, Glenluce.

**A Caledonian train passes over the Glenluce viaduct on the
Portpatrick & Wigtownshire line, in the early 1900s.**

though there were excitements to come, and many challenges, the company was confident, secure and with more than a touch of complacency about itself. As the premier railway company of a large, rich and expansive industrial city, it shared in civic pride and assertion and the desire to be worthy of Glasgow's size and status in the world. If Glasgow was no mean city, then the Caledonian was no mean railway. Its instantly recognisable blue locomotives could now be seen from Aberdeen to Stranraer and from Edinburgh to Oban. Traders in Dundee went so far as to present an Address to the Caley "for the admirable local service given by them"[5]. Addressing the fourth annual soirée of Buchanan Street and Central Station staff, on 26 February 1880, James King, director and future chairman, mentioned the company savings bank, now with 1,600 savers and £100,000 on deposit, and announced that the board was proposing to set up an accident and benevolent fund for employees, to which the Company would give "a large and liberal subscription" each year[6]. From 1880, the civil engineering department was reorganised in two divisions, each with an engineer in charge; George Graham, in overall control, was concerned with new works and extensions. There were other issues to tackle, not least the condition of the locomotive department and the St. Rollox Works, but there was also the will to deal with them. James Baird was dead by now but the Baird Trustees, large holders of Debentures and Preference stock, kept up the hostility to the Caledonian board, lodging a petition with Parliament to look into the company's financial transactions and position, and alleging misappropriation of capital[7]. This caused a flutter in the stock exchanges but the Caledonian put up a vigorous defence, not denying that capital raised for certain purposes had sometimes been diverted to others, but denying that any had been used to pay dividends; and the petition, designed to torpedo the Company's Lanarkshire Lines Bill of 1882, failed[8].

End of the 'Guaranteed Companies'

The winter of 1880-81 was marked by severe weather, intense cold and heavy snow followed by thaws and floods, then snow again. Traffic on the Solway Junction line was stopped when in January 1881, floating ice carried by the tide damaged or broke 45 of the Solway Viaduct's iron piers. The part-collapsed bridge would not be reopened until May 1884. Repairs were estimated to cost more than £30,000, to be raised by the Solway Junction Railway through an issue of Debenture stock, and there was an unusual dispute with the Caledonian, which wanted to take up the entire isssue, while the Solway Junction Railway, fearing perhaps for its independence, refused to sell it any. The Solway company had never felt the Caledonian was fully exploiting their line, and hoped to extend running powers to the North British, which was all too willing to step in[9].

A special meeting had been convened on 20 July 1880 to approve a Bill now with the House of Lords, to dissolve the 'Guaranteed Companies' and replace their stocks with Caledonian Railway Annuity stock at a perpetual 4% from 1 August 1880. Thomas Hill said the initiative came from the companies themselves, seeing their continued existence as "a useless and expensive formality". These dissolutions confirmed that the Caledonian was seen as a sound, reliable and confident concern. With the Caledonian Railway (Guaranteed Annuities Stock No. 2) Act passed on 8 April 1881, the Clydesdale Railway Guarantee Co., the Garnkirk & Glasgow Railway Co., the Wishaw Railway Guarantee Co., the Glasgow, Neilston & Barrhead Direct Railway Co., the Lesmahagow Railways Guaranteed Co., the Dundee & Perth & Aberdeen Junction Guaranteed Co., and the Forth & Clyde Navigation Guaranteed Co. all finally passed into history. The Greenock company, its share records complicated by earlier frauds, would remain in existence until 1 August 1883. A total of £2,751,943 6s. 8d. of capital was to be allocated among stockholders in the dissolved companies. In December 1881 the Board agreed to purchase £2,940 of 5% Preference stock to be given to Busby Railway shareholders in exchange for their shares, so completing the purchase of the Busby company.

Periodically, the minutes of the locomotive & stores committee chart the vast range (and sometimes vast quantities) of materials the Company had to buy, to keep the works and rolling stock going, to maintain its stations and permanent way, to provide the necessary stationery for every purpose, and also to clothe its uniformed staff. For 1882, the committee ordered some 48,800 yards of assorted fabrics, blue pilot cloth, blue-check lining cloth, grey twill, double milled tweed, blue-mix mole, blue olive cord, and many other kinds; along with 944 gross (135,936) of the numerous kinds of buttons needed. Canvas and buckram for caps were ordered, along with collars for various operatives, with 'silver' lettering to specify function, like 'CR Parcel Deliveries'[10]. At a time when economies were being looked for, no attempt at rationalising these items was considered. But in the following year it was decided to close the tailoring department at St. Rollox, and put the work out to contract[11]. Horses were also a responsibility of this committee. A horse cost anything from £20 to £100 and the Caledonian owned over 700. They had no names, officially at least, but were numbered, and deaths, with their depreciated value, were reported each month. With a spirit of improvement possessing the board, it was inevitable that St. Rollox itself should come under scrutiny. Traffic requirements, train loads and train speeds were very much changed from the days of Benjamin Conner. George Brittain, Locomotive Superintendent since 1876, had managed the housekeeping well enough, as the regular disposals of waste materials, scrap iron and clapped-out engines show. Ten old engines, two without their tenders and two without boilers, and four tenders, plus four old boilers, were sold in February 1882 to Thomas Clavering, for £2,045. The retention of tenders and boilers was for re-use on other locomotives. At the same time 240 new trucks and covered vans were ordered at a total cost of almost £18,000[12]. A programme of fitting Westinghouse continuous brakes on the carriage stock was also well under way. But by then the locomotive department was under review, at the board's request.

This one-off well-tank 2-2-2, with Gooch fixed-link motion, was built at St Rollox in 1881 to haul the directors' saloon, and numbered 1. Renumbered 1200 in 1898 and 1001 in 1901, it was withdrawn in 1902.

P.S. *Ivanhoe*, the 'temperance' steamer, in service from 1880.

Thompson and Drummond

James Smithells retired as general manager through ill-health in January 1882 (somewhat tardily, prompted by his family, the board granted him a gratuity of £1,000[13]), and was replaced by James Thompson, who had been Goods Manager, at a salary of £2,000. He immediately inherited a row between the Greenock & Wemyss Bay company and Captain Alexander Campbell, who operated the steamer service. In December 1881 Campbell offered to sell his vessels to the Caledonian, which declined, and Campbell intimated that he would withdraw his service from 1 January 1882. From that date the Caledonian refused to sell through bookings via Wemyss Bay, and when the Greenock & Wemyss Bay Railway company proposed to engage Captain Williamson's steamers, the Caledonian refused and wanted Campbell's agreement to be restored. This finally happened in April[14], but wrangling between the companies went on. There seems to have been little reason for the Caley's attitude other than to do the opposite of whatever the Wemyss Bay company wanted. There was dissatisfaction too in Ayrshire, when requests for reinstitution of the Ayr-Muirkirk-Edinburgh service, put on in 1878 and soon removed, were refused.

On April 25 the board accepted the locomotive committee's recommendation that a new locomotive superintendent be appointed and a "readjustment" made of Brittain's duties. Brittain was in poor health and frequently absent. At the end of May there was a brief strike at St. Rollox, over pay; resolved when the board offered an extra shilling a week. While committees usually met in the boardroom at the company offices, there were occasional meetings, for participants' convenience, in London; and one of these was held by the locomotive & stores committee in May 1882, a perfectly routine affair, but which again shows the scale of operations at this stage. For locomotive coal it ordered 25,000 tons of Stravenhouse Main coal at 3s. 9d. a ton, plus 5,000 tons of splint coal at 4s. 2d. a ton, and another 5,000 tons from Waddell & Sons at 4s. a ton. Orders for office coal were always lumped in with the locomotive coal to get the best bulk price.

A large new engine shed came into use at Hamilton from 30 May 1882, with ten stabling roads and capacity for 60 engines, as well as repair facilities for engines and wagons. It was anticipated that work in the district would now be more economical; "all overtime will be done away with, and fewer locomotives required". The man in charge was McInnes, "of the Steel-McInnes patent brake fame"[15]. But the great event of that year was the opening, on 3 June, of the Carron Dock at Grangemouth. The modest harbour of 1867 was now a modern port, specialising in timber, coal and grain, and capable of accommodating large steamships. Hydraulic hoists speeded up coal loading. J.C. Bolton, local M.P. as well as Caledonian chairman, presiding over the ceremonies, offered some interesting statistics: in 1867, 1,639 ships had called at Grangemouth, with an aggregate registered tonnage of 286,691; in 1880 the number of ships was little greater, at 1,725, but the registered tonnage was 481,000. In 1880 the port had handled 794,832 tons of cargo: now it was capable of dealing with a far greater amount[16]. Although the Act did not allow the Caledonian to use Grahamston Station, the NBR conceded use of it to the CR from 1 August 1883 after threats from the Caledonian to build its own connection between Larbert and the Grangemouth branch. With its great spread of new sidings, its docks and its railway tracks and canal leading back into Scotland's industrial viscera, Grangemouth summed up what the Caledonian company was chiefly about.

Modernisation was going on in other ways. In November 1881 electric lighting had been approved for Glasgow Central, Buchanan Street (goods and passenger) stations, and Grangemouth Docks; telephones were also coming into use, with a line installed between the carting offices in Glasgow[17]. A key appointment was that of Dugald Drummond as locomotive superintendent from 14 August. Drummond, now 42, had reformed the North British locomotive department and its Cowlairs Works, and the Caley offered him a salary of £1,700, £700 more than he was getting from the NBR, and double that of George Brittain. Soon new tools were being ordered, but his main task was to produce recommendations for the expansion and re-fitting of St. Rollox, which were accepted in November (not to exceed £60,000)[18], and the work was immediately put in hand. To cope with demand, a stream of board decisions through the 1880s approved new sidings, additional rolling stock, and new or extended locomotive depots. At Greenock, where the sugar-refining industry was being modernised with vastly greater output, a shed for 30 engines was authorised at Bogston[19]. At the same time, a spirit of frugality ensured that plant was re-used when possible. When the new locomotive depot was built at Hamilton, the old Hamilton shed was transported to Bridgeton as a goods shed. Turntables were often transferred; when Perth got a 50ft table at the end of 1885, its old 45-footer was moved to Montrose.

One way of helping to pay for improvements was of course to put up fares, but experience showed that this was a two-edged sword. On the Leith line from Princes Street, the return fares went up in 1882 from 5d. (first class) to 6d., and from 3d. to 4d. in third. Passenger numbers promptly fell, from 35,344 (first class) in 1881 to 28,244; and from 164,429 (third) to 143,813, resulting in a drop of revenue of £1,093. The old fares were restored. Instances like this made sure that on most Scottish routes, the fares, especially third class fares, remained lower than on comparable routes in England. Back in 1866 more than three quarters of Scottish railway journeys were third class, 77.04% compared to 57.58% in England and Wales[20], and this remained a distinctive difference. For the employees of the company, there was ample evidence of increasing traffic, revenues and investment. Parcel carriage for the Post Office, a relatively new but hugely increasing business, had been agreed on a basis of 55% of receipts for the CR and 45% for the GPO[21]; another 360 assorted wagons were ordered in July, and in August new carriage sidings, with large sheds and repair works, were authorised at Larkfield Junction, west of Polmadie, abutting the Glasgow, Barrhead & Kilmarnock Joint Railway line leading towards South Side, and known as Gushetfaulds Depot. Upturns in the economy meant more traffic, and more demands on the workforce. It was easy for the employees to see that the Company was doing well, when they were pressed into more overtime – but this did not mean more pay. Early in 1883, simmering discontent among the Caledonian's workmen boiled over. Meetings in the company's main and secondary centres were virtually unanimous in wanting to make a stand; the main reservation was to be sure that the others would come out too. On 16 January the men in Leith stopped work, and Perth, Dundee, Forfar, Glasgow and Carstairs followed suit. The claim was for a working day of nine hours, for overtime at time-and-a-half, and double time on Sundays. Although the strike was not observed by everyone (Thompson put it at only three or four hundred men), few trains moved. Newspapers and other perishable items were not distributed. But the action was brief. By the 20th it was over. Thompson and Drummond, on the Company side, offered no compromises, though offering to discuss grievances; and received deputations from the workforce. The strike was later described as "a partial failure" but which had resulted in "a considerable modification of the conditions of employment"[22]. Although some concessions were said to have been made, it is hard to see what they were. No change was made to pay and conditions. Of 66 men at Glasgow Central who stopped work, it was reported that only 12 had been received back by the station master.

In late 1882 the general managers of the Caledonian and North British had been working on the terms of a mutual agreement, and this – the first real 'peace agreement' between the companies – was approved in principle by the board on 26 December 1882, heralding a few years of comparative tranquillity, up to the end of 1888, with many issues thrashed out at meetings held two or three times a year, from Parliamentary Bills and rebates to bulk shippers, to traders' tickets. The minutes[23] suggest a frank and reasonable relationship between the two general managers, Thompson and Walker, with give and take on each side, though agreement was not always achieved.

While most of the larger locomotive depots were capable of making light repairs, Perth had also undertaken heavy repairs for the northern districts, but one of Drummond's proposed reforms was to close the works, which

Beattock Station was remodelled with construction of the Moffat branch in 1882-83.

caused a great outcry in the city; and a civic deputation went to see the CR directors in Glasgow. In 1885 heavy repairs at Perth ceased, and though the works were retained, it was on a scaled-down basis.

Local interests in Moffat, which was growing in popularity as a spa and holiday resort (it had once been Joseph Locke's favourite recreation place), frustrated by the Caledonian's refusal to build a branch line, promoted their own short rail link to the CR main line at Beattock, in 1881, at a cost of £16,000[24]. It was opened on 2 April 1883, in good time for the season. The Caledonian, which already stabled locomotives at Beattock to bank trains up to the summit, consented to work the line. In May 1886 it announced "A fast train for the convenience of summer visitors" from 1 June, serving Moffat and Peebles, leaving each of these places at 7.50 a.m. and arriving in Glasgow and Edinburgh at 9.50. The return service was the train from Glasgow at 4.20 p.m. and Edinburgh at 4.30, "to be accelerated to reach Moffat and Peebles about 6.30 p.m."[25]. This was the service known as the 'Tinto Express'. The trains were combined and split at Symington. At Montrose the Caledonian branch and harbour line at Erskine Street lost its monopoly of the town when the North British station opened on 1 May 1883. The NBR's new line from Arbroath crossed above the Caledonian in its climb to meet the Aberdeen line at Kinnaber Junction, soon to be a crucial staging point in the 'race to the north'.

Lanarkshire & Ayrshire

Ardrossan, served by the GSWR, was well established as a coal port by 1880. Much of its traffic came from Lanarkshire pits and the Caledonian carried the coal to Gushetfaulds, where the GSWR took over. The 'three towns' area of Ardrossan, Stevenston and Saltcoats, along with nearby Irvine, were also of growing importance industrially, and the Caledonian management was determined to reach them directly. With the old 'Ardrossan' company a distant memory, an Act for a new line was obtained on 20 August 1883. Diverging from the Beith branch at Barrmill, it was to meet the GSWR at Kilwinning, six miles from Ardrossan. Known first as the Barrmill & Kilwinning Railway, by 1884 this scheme had been enlarged into the Lanarkshire & Ayrshire Railway, whose chairman was the 14th Earl of Eglinton. Instead of making a junction at Kilwinning with the South Western, the Lanarkshire & Ayrshire was to be extended from Kilwinning to Ardrossan, with branches to Kilbirnie and Irvine. The Caledonian was to work and manage the line, and an Act of 16 July 1885 enabled it to invest up to £150,000 of the £375,000 capital. Among the conditions imposed with the CR investment was that the traffic of certain companies be thirled to to the new railway for 20 years, including the Mossend Iron Co., Cadzow Coal Co., J.&W. Beardmore, Merry & Cunningham (from expiry of their current agreement with the NBR and GSWR), and Archibald Russell. This practice of 'thirling', tying up a customer's traffic for years ahead, was a regular practice and equally regular source of dispute among the railway companies.

Ardrossan Station, opened 4 September 1888, and renamed Ardrossan Town in 1906, was designed to reflect the town's role as a holiday resort.

Dugald Drummond's 171-class 0-4-4T of 1888 was designed for light branch work, but later 0-4-4T types, notably the 439-class, displaced them. No. 225 is seen as station pilot at Carlisle Citadel.

While the Caledonian was pushing for more access to the coast, it was also involved in a controversy with the Wemyss Bay company, as usual over fares and rates. The Wemyss board wanted an adjustment of the Glasgow-Rothesay fare to 3s. 1d., of which 8d. would go to the steamer operator. The Caledonian held out for an overall fare of 2s. 6d., of which 8½d. would be for the steamer. The dispute went to the Railway & Canal Commissioners, who ruled that the 2s. 6d. fare should stand, as it had to be "a competition rate"[26].

The Busby Railway company, with its line to East Kilbride, was absorbed by the Caledonian by an Act of 18 July 1881, though it was not effected until 2 February of the following year. The Busby was always a modest affair; in the half-year to January 1876, its total revenue was £4,383, with £1,423 available for dividend[27], but in 1883 the CR proceeded with an extension from East Kilbride to meet the Hamilton-Strathaven line at Hunthill, just east of High Blantyre. In the same area, in order to simplify the workings and reduce the mileage of mineral trains, a cut-off was opened on 1 May 1882, from Auchinraith on the Hamilton-Strathaven line, to Blantyre, allowing coal trains to run north towards Glasgow. This potentially made a 'circle' service possible through Busby, Blantyre and Newton, and back into Glasgow, but traffic beyond Busby was always sparse, and the East Kilbride-Hunthill section was to be an early closure, in 1914. Another connecting line was laid in 1883 between the Lesmahagow railway at Alton Heights, south of Brocketsbrae, and Poneil on the Lanark-Muirkirk line. This enabled coal trains from the Douglas field to use the Lesmahagow line to reach the marshalling yard laid out at Ross Junction.

Amenities for Passengers

Glasgow's Central Hotel opened for business on 19 June 1883, under the managership of Charles Lord, who got £600 a year, later amended to £500 plus 5% of the establishment's net profits[28]. Much of the building was converted from the offices designed by Robert Rowand Anderson. Well advertised, with notices in every station, "Central Hotel, Glasgow, now open"[29], it was a vast establishment, with over 200 rooms, and electric lighting in its public rooms. Active rivalry with the St. Enoch Hotel, a few streets away, kept both establishments on their toes. Though existing hoteliers protested, the railways led the way in providing large quality hotels in city centres; with a steady supply of first class passengers, they were well-placed. But they also played a useful part in trade, with exhibition rooms which could be hired by companies and commercial travellers to put on a display of their wares. Passengers now expected to find a range of amenities at any large station, such as refreshment rooms and bookstalls, as well as toilets (gradually provided at almost every station. The trains, of course, being non-corridor, had no lavatory facilities). Automatic vending machines and self-weighing scales were placed even at smaller stations, at a small rent plus a percentage of the takings for the railway company. The Caledonian had inherited a relationship with the John Menzies company from the Scottish Central, going back to its first bookstalls at Perth, Stirling and Bridge of Allan in 1857, and in February 1883 a new five-year contract was

A placard for the *Oban Times* rubs shoulders with *Truth* and the *Tatler* at John Menzies' bookstall in the enlarged post-1913 Stirling Station.

**The other Forth Bridge: the Alloa Viaduct, built in 1882, from the
control cabin on top of the rotating span, of which one end is visible.**

signed, at £910 a year for three years and £1,000 for the final two. Another major improvement was the gradual provision of passenger footbridges. By the end of 1883, 72 double-line stations had footbridges and 74 did not. An iron bridge cost £205 and a wooden one £80 or so, and for smaller stations the cheaper option was taken, as with Fordoun, Laurencekirk and Drumlithie, all provided in early 1884[30]. Safety combined with economy as a concern: compensation on behalf of passengers hit by trains while crossing the lines between platforms was regularly claimed. At the same time platforms, often only nine inches high in their original form, were being raised to two and a half feet, and lengthened to accommodate longer trains.

From the late 1870s the Caledonian had been increasingly concerned about getting access to the coalfields and developing industry of the Fife peninsula. The natural entry point was from Stirling, but the North British had long since gained control of the Stirling-Alloa-Dunfermline line. There was however the former SCR branch from Plean to Alloa South, making a modest living from the ferry and harbour traffic, and pointing in the right direction. Local interests in Alloa, with Caledonian encouragement, promoted a Bill for a bridge to extend the branch across the Forth into Alloa, and this became an Act on 11 August 1879. The distance involved was only about three quarters of a mile, but involved the construction of a viaduct 568 yards long, with a swing span. There was also a short spur to a a munitions factory a little way upstream, at Bandeath. A contract for the bridge was let in 1882, by which time it was understood that the Alloa Railway Company would be taken over by the Caledonian. The North British Railway's response to these developments was to propose a bridge of its own, a little way upstream. Diplomatic talks followed, in which it was agreed that the North British should have running powers over the Alloa Railway's viaduct, and the Caledonian would use the North British passenger station in Alloa. On 14 August 1884 the Caledonian obtained a portmanteau Act enabling it to

> "construct certain Railways and other Works in the counties of Renfrew, Forfar, Stirling and Clackmannan, to acquire and complete the Alloa Railway and to take in lease the Moffat Railway, for extending the time to complete the Alloa Railway, for dissolving the Alloa Railway Company; for abandoning the Larbert and Grangemouth connecting lines … and confirming an Agreement between that Company and the North British Railway Company with respect to the Stirling & Midland Junction and Grangemouth Railways, and other matters."

Nobody supposed that the Caledonian's purpose in building an £80,000 bridge was just to get a station in Alloa. In 1883 it promoted a Bill for an Alloa, Dunfermline and Kirkcaldy Railway, to run more than 29 miles from a proposed new Alloa Station through Clackmannanshire and Fife, serving the coalfield and ending in a coal-loading dock at Seafield, by Kirkcaldy. A branch would run inland from Kirkcaldy to serve collieries between there and Lochgelly. Of course the North British moved to oppose, pointing out that the Caledonian line simply duplicated its own Stirling-Alloa-Dunfermline-Kirkcaldy connections. The Caledonian withdrew its proposal for coal docks which would compete with the NBR at Burntisland, but the proposal came to nothing. Fife remained a North British dominion. Though the Alloa Bridge was well-used, it was also a memorial to the Caledonian's failure to break into Fife.

The North British Railway's directors and managers appear to have been better tacticians than the Caledonian's at this time. The two companies were equal in size. While the NBR had successfully kept the Caledonian out of Fife, and held the majority of Edinburgh traffic, it was also well entrenched in Glasgow, where it controlled access to the Queen's Dock at Stobcross, was building a cross-city line, the Glasgow City & District Railway, and also had its Hamilton line right into the Caley heartland. For the Caledonian's hotel and station frontage at Glasgow Central, a cast iron verandah was ordered from Walter MacFarlane's Saracen Ironworks at Possil, at a cost of £1,939. At the time there was a dispute going on about the route of the proposed Hamiltonhill branch from Balornock, intended to serve the Saracen Works and end in a goods terminal by the Port Dundas branch of the Forth & Clyde Canal. MacFarlane demanded £15,500 for traversing his ground. The line was never completed, defeated by excessive property prices and by the fact that the North British already had access to the works[31]. James Thompson seems to have been less than adept here. But it was doing well in Renfrewshire. Between Hillington West and Paisley Gilmour Street, the joint line was made quadruple track in 1883 to cope with the increased traffic, and the 209-yard Arkleston tunnel was opened out as a cutting. The expansion of Gilmour Street was completed in 1888, with four platforms.

Alloa and Perth

Among other events of 1884, the Caledonian took over the Alloa Railway, still under construction, from 1 September. Perth General Station, its ownership shared since 1866 with the NBR and Highland Railways, needed a complete remodelling, and an Act was procured in 1884 for a new layout of the station. Much enlarged and improved for operating purposes, it comprised nine platforms, paved rather than planked as before, including two very long main platforms at 557 yds 1 ft and 471 yds 2ft, able to accommodate two trains at once. Two curving through platforms replaced the old Dundee dock, and through tracks for north-south goods trains were laid on the west side, outside the train shed. Inside, the buildings were substantially altered and enlarged. A great all-over roof was built[32], its girders transverse to the platforms. The architects were Blyth & Cunningham of Edinburgh. Reconstruction took two years and though the new station lacked the charm of Tite's original design for the Scottish Central, it coped with vastly greater traffic and provided excellent facilities. A joint committee continued to operate the station, and details of the agreement were altered occasionally; a minute of 3 December 1892 reallocated the station's working expenses in the ratio of 64% to the Caledonian, 26% to the North British, and 10% to the Highland[33].

Some time before 1884 the Caledonian had set up a sleeper creosoting plant at Greenhill, a central location for the whole system, and in that year 50,000 sleepers of Baltic redwood were ordered at 2s. 4d. each[34] for treatment there. Dugald Drummond, seeking efficiency and cost savings, got authority to convert the recently-built Eglinton Street engine shed to a carriage depot and transfer the engines to Polmadie[35] – in the same spirit a few years later, he proposed to build all the needed iron footbridges at St. Rollox and hold them there, with the cost debited to each half-year until paid off. At £120 each, this was much cheaper than buying bridges piecemeal, and no doubt encouraged the board to raise his pay by £400 a short time later[36]. An indication of how new technology was being applied to the mineral traffic comes from the decision for a "speaking wire" to be installed between Earnock Colliery, the junction of its branch with the Caledonian line, and the Hamilton Engine Shed signal box, along with an electric repeater in the signal box for the distant signal on the branch[37].

From 1 July 1885, a special mail bag train, for Post Office use only, was laid on between Perth and Carlisle. The Post Office paid £14,000 a year for this service, on a ten-year contract, over and above the existing agreement[38] The Caledonian was quite adept at making customers pay when special timings were needed; a couple of years later it threatened to withdraw the 6 a.m. train from Edinburgh and Glasgow to the south, but kept it on when the Post Office agreed to pay £1,250 a year, and the newspaper proprietors of the two cities contributed £500[39]. On 6 August 1885, with the Caledonian-Portpatrick Railway working agreement nearing its end, there was some rationalisation in Galloway. The independent Wigtownshire Railway had operated from a junction at Newton Stewart since 3 April 1875. Now the Portpatrick and the Wigtown Railways amalgamated. The merger and the resulting arrangements had been under discussion for two years, and a proposal for joint ownership by the

Caledonian-LNWR and GSWR-Midland Railway had got as far as a Parliamentary Bill at the end of 1883 before it was withdrawn following disagreements. By 1885 these had been resolved and the Portpatrick and Wigtown became a Joint Line, managed by an operating committee which included two directors each from the Caledonian (J.C. Bolton and Hugh Brown), LNWR, GSWR and Midland Railway companies. The joint enterprise also owned four-fifths of the Larne & Stranraer Steamship Joint Committee, with the Belfast & Northern Counties Railway. The Caledonian continued to work the line until 31 October, after when alternate services were operated by the CR and the Glasgow & South Western, which had absorbed the Castle Douglas & Dumfries company. Caledonian locomotives and stock were still very much to be seen between Dumfries and Stranraer, and it provided a through service between Whithorn and Edinburgh, using the Dumfries & Lockerbie line[40]. On 1 October the Alloa Bridge was completed across the Forth, 1,600 feet long, supported on twenty pairs of stone piers, linked by cast iron braces, and with a swing section powered by a steam engine.

Sugar and Jute

Greenock's 18th century sugar industry had expanded to make it the largest sugar refining centre in the United Kingdom, apart from London. Withdrawal of duty on sugar in 1874 boosted demand, and by 1881 the town's annual production had peaked at 260,229 tons[41], making sugar an important item in the Caledonian goods accounts. The town was building a new dock, named after its most famous son, James Watt, and the Caledonian laid a connecting branch and sidings in 1885. In 1890, William Acworth noted that "nowadays the raw sugar comes mainly from the Continent, and is imported either through Leith or Grangemouth". In 1889, when the price of raw sugar went up from thirteen to 23 shillings a ton, "there were literally miles of trucks loaded with some 6,000 tons of raw sugar standing in every siding in the neighbourhood of Greenock waiting for the refiners to take delivery"; the reason being that the refiners were holding back until retail prices should rise (no wonder the Caledonian was concerned about its trucks being held up). "Not so many years back, the railway rate for sugar from Grangemouth to Greenock was 6s. 8d. per ton; from Leith it was 7s. As the sugar trade became more and more depressed, the Company made reduction after reduction in the rate, till finally they had brought it down to 3s. 6d .and 3s. 9d. But when sugar almost doubled in value last spring, they thought they too had a right to a little better terms, so they advanced the rate by 3d. a ton all round." Acworth also noted what he called a probably unique instance: "When the agitation against the new classification and schedule of maximum rates first began last spring, a deputation of the Greenock sugar-refiners waited upon the general manager of the Caledonian, not in order to demand any concession, but to express their gratitude for the treatment they had received in the past, their readiness to support the Company to the utmost of their power, and their confidence that their relations with it would be equally amicable in the future"[42].

If Greenock was 'Sugaropolis', Dundee was expanding and prospering as 'Juteopolis' and a tender of £11,232 17s. 2d. for a new locomotive depot at Dundee West was accepted, and the old site at Seabraes was abandoned[43] when the new shed opened in 1885. That year a proposal for a Dundee Suburban Railway was drawn up in 1885, to provide a circular system round the city[44]. It came to nothing, but the Caledonian was building a new Dundee West Station, large enough to cope with additional traffic, and with a goods station alongside.

Carriages and wagons were included in Dugald Drummond's remit. In 1882 a unique vehicle, a prison van, was built, at a cost of £350[45]. From 1883 all carriages, including third class, were routinely fitted with gas lighting, usually on the Pritsch system, and continuous air brakes. Some were dual-fitted for air or vacuum braking, to work on the Highland Railway and on West Coast traffic. Carriage trucks, horse-boxes and fish trucks, regularly attached to passenger trains, were also included in this programme. In April 1885 he reported that 756 vehicles were on order, at a total cost of £46,750: ten third class brakevans, eleven six-wheel brakevans, 15 goods/mineral brakevans, 20 meat vans, 100 rail wagons, 400 goods wagons,100 swivel-bar wagons, and 100 round timber or iron wagons[46], and in 1886 he introduced the CR's first bogie coaches, followed by an improved version in 1887. Used on the Glasgow-Edinburgh route, these carriages, "with seventeen springs" weighed 22 tons (first class) and 20 1/2 tons (third class), carrying 56 and 140 seated passengers respectively. They had continuous brakes, steam heating and gas lighting. The trains were normally of three carriages, an easy task for the rebuilt Conner 2-4-0 engines and even more so for Drummond's new 66-class 4-4-0s. Drummond was a pioneer of steam heating, piping exhaust steam from the locomotive's Westinghouse brake pump to radiators under the carriage seats[47]. Before that, and for some twenty years after in many cases, Caledonian longer-distance passengers had to rely on acetate of soda foot-warmers, the stock of which was replenished occasionally – 250 were bought in 1885 and 700 in 1899[48]. At least the Caley, unlike some railways, provided them free of charge[49]. But there was also need for new rolling stock: from the Forfar-Dundee direct line there were complaints about the "boxes" substituted for cushioned carriages in the winter[50]. Always averse to paying out insurance premiums, the company decided to

Railway Viaduct ... ... , Killin

An early example of a concrete-arched viaduct, over the River Lochay, on the Killin branch (1886).

be its own insurer for the St. Rollox works, valuing them at only £20,000 despite the recent large investments, and setting aside a premium of 1%[51]. At this time a government-imposed valuation of railways was going on, and the assessor valued St. Rollox workshops and depot at £49,812.

On 13 March 1886 a locally sponsored railway was formally opened from a new exchange station, Killin Junction, on the C&O, to Killin village and beyond it to a pier station named Lochtay. The C&O's original Killin Station was renamed Glenoglehead (closed from 30 September 1891, though remaining in use as a crossing loop). Passenger services began on 1 April. The moving spirit was Lord Breadalbane (the Marquis of Breadalbane, so closely associated with the Scottish Central, had died in 1862; his successors, distant relatives, had the title of Earl until 1885 when the 'Marquis' title was revived). It was one of the first railways to have all its bridges made of concrete, which apart from being cheaper than stone or iron, also minimised the need for skilled labour[52]. As with the C&O, it was worked by the Caledonian, initially at 55% of the gross revenue, with a guaranteed minimum of £2,377, though after three years this was revised to working the line at cost. On 25 May 1886 the Cathcart District Railway, authorised on 7 September 1880, opened as far as Cathcart, a new residential suburb to the south. Three schemes had been proposed but this was the one which prevailed, not least because of Caledonian support: the CR was to subscribe 50% of the capital and to work the line at 45% of gross income[53]. Trains served it from Glasgow Central by way of Mount Florida, and commuter traffic grew rapidly. In 1887 an Act was obtained to continue the line, in a western loop back towards the city, rejoining the original line at Muirhouse Junction and creating what was always known as the Cathcart Circle, though it more resembled a mis-shapen pear. Although half-yearly reports through 1885-86 refer to depressed trading conditions and lower traffic figures, the Cathcart line showed confidence in Glasgow's continuing expansion. Bridges were provided over open fields in anticipation of a street layout still to be built[54]. The city's population, 587,000 in 1881, was 658,000 in 1891.

Ostentation and Display

Pride of place in Edinburgh's grand International Exhibition that opened on 6 May 1886 was taken by four new locomotives placed in the great central corridor. Two of them were resplendent in Caledonian blue (CR Nos. 123 and 124; see Chapter 16). For the exhibition, excursion trains were laid on from Glasgow, at a return rail/exhibition fare of 5s. 6d. (first class) and 2s. 6d. (third), inclusive of reduced-price admission from 9d. to 6d., on which the Exhibition paid the Caledonian 10% commission. Railway support for such mass events was crucial to get the crowds coming.

The one-off Dübs 4-4-0 No.124 of 1886, named *Eglinton* in 1890, at Buchanan Street.
Note the wood-planked platform: Buchanan Street was always the Cinderella of CR major stations.

On 1 June 1886 a branch was opened from Langloan, on the Rutherglen-Coatbridge line, to a terminus at Airdrie. An intermediate station was built at Whifflet, above and at right angles to the (now rebuilt) station on the old Wishaw & Coltness line. Airdrie was already served by the North British, but the townsfolk hoped for "honest competition"[55] and lower fares. A south-eastwards extension, via a three-way junction south of Airdrie, was begun, reaching Chapelhall Ironworks on 1 September 1887 and joining the Lanridge branch of the Drumbowie line by 2 July 1888. Though primarily a coal and mineral line, with spurs to collieries, a passenger service was also operated between Airdrie and the Caledonian station at Morningside, which (unlike Airdrie-Glasgow) did not duplicate any other.

Large-scale industry was still expanding on the east side of Glasgow, and the Caledonian, having built a branch from the Buchanan Street main line into the Blochairn Ironworks in 1884, and another from a junction on the London Road extension into the massive Parkhead Forge in 1885, made a connecting line between the two in 1886, providing a north-south route between the old Garnkirk and Clydesdale Junction lines. At its north end it passed under the main line and bent to a west-facing junction, enabling goods trains to run from Buchanan Street and St. Rollox to Rutherglen and on into Lanarkshire. At some time this section, traversing a hummocky district, acquired the name of the 'Switchback' ('scenic railways' were becoming popular in fairgrounds). To the west, seeing the Caledonian's Gourock extension under construction, the board of the Wemyss Bay became anxious around the end of 1886 about the impact the new steamer link would have on their own service, especially as the Caledonian would no doubt find room for the Gourock trains at Central Station, while the Wemyss Bay services still started and stopped at Bridge Street. But the CR did not yield to the importunings from Wemyss Bay[56].

If the company was earning large amounts, it was also spending heavily on new works and through 1886 and later it regularly took out and renewed short term loans, mostly from the Commercial Bank, £100,000 for one month and £150,000 for two months at 2.5% in April, and another of £200,000 at 3% in May[57]. An increasing source of expense, as coal workings spread, was the need to 'buy' coal that lay under or close to the lines, in order to preserve it from being dug out, with a resulting risk of subsidence. Often the company preferred to take the risk, or shore up the line, but when underground workings came near its bridges and viaducts, it had no option but to buy. Disputes between railway and mining companies on this issue frequently ended up in court. Though many pits were worked out, new shafts were being sunk and rail links requested. Typical was the connection to

Dunn & Brothers from the Motherwell-Coatbridge line. Partly on Caledonian ground and partly on the colliery's, it was laid by the railway company at a cost of £2,600. Dunn's share was £1,350 and they paid the Caley 2.5% a year on this sum while the connection was in use[58].

On 11 July 1887 the new Tay Bridge was opened. The Caledonian lost a useful income of £25,000 a year for North British goods services between Perth and Dundee[59]. Looking at its Perth traffic, the company also reviewed a twenty-year old agreement made with the Highland Railway, in December 1867, by which the Highland's annual toll of £5,000 for use of the Perth-Stanley line was waived, so long as it handed over at least two-thirds of its traffic to the Caley at Perth. Doubt was cast on the HR's figures, and the toll was restored[60]. A spirit of rivalry in services to Aberdeen resumed. For some years, the West Coast route's service between Edinburgh and London had taken ten hours, compared to nine on the East Coast. But the CR-LNWR expresses carried third class passengers, while the other side did not. In November 1887, the East Coast also began to carry third class passengers on the 'flyer', prompting the West Coast to speed up their best service to match the nine hours from 1 June 1888. This sparked off the first of successive periods of 'racing' from Euston and Kings Cross to Scottish cities. From 1 July, the East Coast companies cut the time to eight and a half hours; the West Coast responded by matching that time from 1 August, whereupon the other side cut the Kings Cross-Edinburgh time to eight and a quarter hours. On 3 August the West Coast announced eight hours flat, to begin from the 6th, though to achieve this they had to cut capacity to four eight-wheel carriages, in the peak of the holiday season. On 13 August, the East Coast accelerated to seven hours and forty-five minutes. On the same day the West Coast train ran from Euston to Princes Street in seven hours and thirty-eight minutes. Next day the East Coast express knocked the timing down to seven hours and thirty-two minutes. A temporary truce followed, fixing the West Coast timing at eight hours and the East Coast's at seven and three quarter hours. This was soon trimmed back to a "best time" for either route not to be less than eight and a half hours. There were other smart Caledonian services, including an Edinburgh-Greenock 'West Highland Express', leaving Edinburgh at 7 a.m. and reaching Greenock at 8.41, and a 'Belfast Boat Train' leaving Edinburgh at 5.05 a.m. and stopping only at Holytown[61]. Much more reluctantly, after vigorous local agitation, the company provided a passenger service between East Kilbride and Blantyre, three trains daily each way, with an annual mileage of 12,732 and considerable doubt about its profitability[62].

Ostentation and display were rampant in early summer 1888, led by the Glasgow International Exhibition at Kelvingrove, into which the city poured vast resources, not least to outshine Edinburgh's show of two years previously. The Caledonian and other lines laid on many special cheap trains, as well as the one that conveyed the Prince and Princess of Wales from Carlisle to Motherwell and on to Glasgow; from Motherwell, "the engine used being a powerful locomotive exhibited by the Caledonian Company at the Edinburgh Exhibition, and reserved for special occasions"[63]. This was No. 124 with a Prince of Wales feathers emblem.

Expanding the 'System'

On 10 August 1882 an Act had been obtained for the 7 ½ mile Kilsyth & Bonnybridge Railway, which had been first promoted in 1862, and which finally opened on 2 July 1888. Linking the town of Kilsyth, terminus of the NBR-worked Kelvin Valley line, with Bonnybridge, terminus of a CR branch from Greenhill, it was set up as a locally-managed private company, operated by both railways as a "common line", a relatively unusual system in which both companies provided staff, sharing operating expenses and a proportion of revenues: 20% of local traffic or traffic off the operating companies, and 40% of 'foreign' traffic. The Kelvin Valley line would maintain its joint status even after the LMS/LNER Grouping of 1923. The NBR ran trains from Glasgow Queen Street through Kilsyth to Bonnybridge, from where the CR provided connections to Larbert on the main line. Running powers to Larbert were granted to the NBR. Before the Kilsyth & Bonnybridge opened, the Caledonian rather sneakily laid a short branch from Greenhill Lower Junction to Bonnybridge (Canal) on the Forth & Clyde Canal. This opened on 2 August 1886 and offered an all-Caledonian alternative route to Glasgow. At the same time as the Kelvin Valley, the Caledonian completed the multiple junctions south of Larbert by opening a west-to-south link, and building a short spur to set up its own Falkirk goods station at Camelon.

Ardrossan gained a second station when the Lanarkshire & Ayrshire opened on 3 September 1888 (renamed Ardrossan Town in 1906). A short branch to Ardeer was opened on 3 November, serving ironworks and the Nobel explosives factory, and a temporary spur to the GSWR line gave access to Ardrossan harbour from 30 November, while the Lanarkshire & Ayrshire's own harbour works were still in progress. Coal was the staple of the Ardrossan railways, and though the Glasgow & South Western at first invoked running powers for its own coal trains over the North British lines from Glasgow to Bothwell and Blantyre, it could not compete with the Caledonian rates. Work continued, albeit slowly, on the Lanarkshire & Ayrshire pier, and, foreseeing competition soon from here as well as Gourock, in January 1887 the Wemyss Bay company, still stuck at Bridge Street,

Industrial debris and colliery tracks at No. 7 Pit, Coalburn, *c.*1890s.

unsuccessfully applied to the Railway & Canal Commissioners to compel the Caledonian to use Central for Wemyss Bay trains[64].

Following an agreement with two landowners, Charles Howatson of Glenbuck and Sir Windham Anstruther of Carmichael[65], early in 1888 the Caledonian extended the Coalburn line from Bankend to a remote colliery at Galawhistle, 1,000 feet up in the fells, with a short spur to a nearby pit at Spireslack. Retrospective authority for building this line (referred to as the 'Glenbuck line'), was obtained in the Company's Act of 1889, along with numerous other projects. Its cost was £12,300. The coal was worked by the Cairntable Gas Coal Company, which had additional sidings laid at Galawhistle; they were willing to pay 6% over ten years on the cost of £632 if Howatson and Anstruther considered it as outside the agreement[66]. The extra traffic from the Coalburn line required new siding capacity at Alton Heights Junction.

In the summer of 1888 an important Act was passed, authorising the construction of the Glasgow Central Railway, an underground cross-city line passing beneath Central Station. The Bill had been put forward by a private group, headed by the prominent Glasgow civil engineer Charles Forman, but the Caledonian had been involved from the start[67] and the Glasgow Central Railway's nominal independence was brief, as it was absorbed by the CR on 31 May 1890. Work began on 11 June[68] on what was to be a massive eight-year construction project.

Management – Perks, Pay and Problems

In April 1888 most senior officials got a salary rise. If they worked hard, they also had their occasional perks, as G.P. Neele of the London & North Western Railway noted:

> "I have previously stated the whole of our gatherings at the Clearing House were not unbroken toil: the needed relief to prevent our becoming 'dull boys' generally accompanying the July or summer meetings. Our Scotch gatherings in friends vied with each other in affording us gratification. Now it was the Caledonian introducing us to the Falls of the Clyde at Lanark; the North British exploiting Melrose and Abbotsford; the Great North of Scotland, Peterhead and Balmoral; the Highland, Inverness and Wick; the Glasgow & South Western, Ayr and Arran. In

return the officers of the Companies South of the Tweed would invite those North of the Tweed to entertainments at the Crystal Palace or on the Thames. One of the most pleasant of these took place at the Palace in October, 1888, Mr. Cockshott in the Chair, Mr. Dawson, Railway Clearing House, and Mr. Gardner, Great Eastern, Vice-Chairmen. Sixteen Scotch guests were at the head of the table; sixty of the hosts, including Goods Managers and Superintendents occupied the two sides of the long horse-shoe table … Pipers marched, skirling round the table at intervals, and those who liked haggis could partake of it"[69].

In 1887 James Thompson was ill and Edward Eddy, of the LNWR headquarters staff, moved to Glasgow as Assistant General Manager. Eddy was a vigorous character and his behaviour during his brief tenure suggests he had been put in as a "new broom" and was determined to do some scouring. His one-time boss noted later:

"In July 1888 we learnt that Mr. Eddy had decided on leaving the Caledonian Line, and that he had accepted the terms offered to him for becoming the Chief Commissioner of Railways for New South Wales. … Mr. Eddy's stay with the Caledonian Railway Company had been but short. In the period during which he had acted as chief, through Mr. Thompson's illness, he had carried out many improvements in the local working : simplified the shunting arrangements, reduced the number of engines employed, and had made himself felt in all departments. A story was current among the officers that the brusque language and demeanour of the men on the line much annoyed him; and on one occasion, when he and Mr. Kempt were conducting an enquiry, an off-hand gruff 'Yes' or 'No,' as reply, was given by an inspector to questions by Mr. Kempt. 'Is that the way you speak to your superior officer?' thundered Eddy, who proceeded to deliver a sharp lecture to the delinquent.

It was a new experience for the inspector, but the lesson was quickly appreciated. To the next query, 'Did you then do so and so?' the inspector first touched his cap with his right hand, then with his left, and replied : 'Yes, please, gentlemen both!' The soft answer turned away wrath."[70]

Another new recruit had a longer stay. In 1888 a 28-year old architect, James Miller, joined the engineering department and was soon at work on the new building at Bridge Street Station in Glasgow. In 1893 he would set up his own practice but keep close links with the Caledonian. Up to 1925 he would be responsible for the design, or redesign, of almost seventy CR stations.

In common with other railway companies, the Caledonian clerical staff were given a heavy extra work load by the Railway Rates Act of 1888. This piece of legislation, intended to clarify, harmonise, and exert a degree of control over the rates charged for haulage of merchandise, was anything but welcome to the companies, each of which had to produce a rate-book with a full set of charges for every conceivable kind of goods, per ton-mile. The Railway & Canal Commission was set up to supervise and adjudicate. Through 1889 and 1890 the company had to study an official draft classification of merchandise traffic and charges, which was to replace the Railway Clearing House list. Users and traders were also invited to contribute. Finally in 1893 the government set maximum rates in all categories, then appeared surprised when the companies proceeded to charge the maximum. A Royal Commission resulted, whose findings brought further constraints on the railway companies' freedom to charge. A further Railway & Canal Traffic Act in 1894 tried to stabilise the position. Although coal (itself of various grades) was by far and away the Caledonian's principal freight item, the company carried a vast range of other materials and products, and its rate-book was a formidable document. The effect was to keep freight charges at their 1892 levels right up to 1922. With inflation very slight between 1892 and 1913, the impact of this was not as great as it might have been, and the Railway Rates Act might get some credit for compelling the railways to improve their efficiency in order to maintain or increase their profitability. Railway managements saw them as an infliction, holding down charges while operating costs were rising. The board meeting of 5 March 1889 noted a vast amount of work going on right acrosss the system, in extensions, renewals and improvements. Although short-term loans were still prominent in the accounts, a dividend of 5.25% was approved.

CHAPTER 10. The Caledonian in the 90s, 1889-1899

Competition on the Coast

The Lanarkshire & Ayrshire constructed its branch from Giffen (known as Kilbirnie Junction from 4 September 1888 until 1 October 1889) to Kilbirnie, opening it for goods on 1 November 1889 and for passengers on 2 December. Though just over four miles long, the line had taken three years to build because of its deep cuttings and the late delivery of ironwork. It also served the iron and steelworks at Glengarnock, with a spur diverging southwards and bending under the branch to an extensive spread of sidings right up to Kilbirnie Loch. These places were already served, a little remotely in Kilbirnie's case until 1905, by the GSWR's line to Ardrossan, but the Lanarkshire & Ayrshire offered a shorter route to Lanarkshire. No attempt was made to run through passenger services from Kilbirnie (population in 1881 3,405) to Glasgow; passengers changed trains at Giffen.

After several years during which competition among the Clyde steamer companies was growing (the North British had opened Craigendoran Pier on the north bank in 1882), Gourock's railway extension and pier were finally opened on 1 June 1889, with a panoramic view of sea-lochs and mountains that soon became famous. Parliamentary sanction had been got on 28 July 1884, despite objections from the GSWR and the town of Greenock, and work had been going on since 1886. Though only three miles long, it included the Newton Tunnel, between Greenock West and Fort Matilda, 1 mile 350 yards long, and double tracked. The total cost was £620,000, one-third more than the original budgeted cost. The terminus at Cathcart Street in Greenock was rebuilt as a through station and renamed Greenock Central. The Caledonian's heavy investment in Gourock caused anxiety to the Wemyss Bay company, whose relationship with the Caley had always been fractious, with regular recourse to the High Court or the Railway Commissioners to resolve disputes over rates and fares. But on 29 August 1889, the *Glasgow Herald* reported that the Greenock & Wemyss Bay company had been acquired by the Caledonian, which already owned £70,000 of the Greenock & Wemyss Bay Railway stock of £200,000. The terms were ten Wemyss Bay £10 shares for one CR £100 share. At the time, Caledonian Ordinary shares were trading at £128, while the price of ten Greenock & Wemyss Bay Railway was £124 7s. 6d. In fact the report was in anticipation of events: formal take-over would not be achieved until an Act of 27 July 1893, but from 1889 the Caledonian acted far more co-operatively towards the Wemyss Bay company. Now serving two steamer piers, Wemyss Bay and Gourock, with Ardrossan imminent, and familiar with the commercial and administrative difficulties of dealing with the independent steamboat operators, the CR inclined towards operating its own ships, and in early November 1888 had bought two, *Madge Wildfire* and *Meg Merrilees*, and commissioned the building of two more. This plan was scuppered by rejection of its Caledonian Railway (Steam Vessels) Bill in March 1889, following intense opposition from the independent steamship operators. Something had to be done quickly to retrieve the situation. A marine superintendent, Captain James Williamson, had been appointed in January. On 7 May, the Caledonian Steam Packet Company was formed, a nominally independent corporation but intended to work

C.R.C. S.S. "Galatea"

39986.

P.S. *Galatea*, launched November 1889, in a vigorous backing maneouvre.

hand-in-glove with the railway company. Capital was £64,000 in £10 shares. Its chairman, the Marquis of Breadalbane, had been a Caledonian director since 1882, and was chairman of the Killin Railway, but the key figure was Williamson, who became the secretary and manager. The house flag was a yellow pennant with a red lion rampant, and "The smartness of Caledonian steamers soon became a byword"[1]. The new ships were *Caledonia* and *Galatea*. *Madge Wildfire* served Kilcreggan and Kilmun, the others worked a new Gourock-Rothesay route. Gourock's rail service (40 minutes to Glasgow Central) quickly became popular with regular travellers from Cowal and Bute, and by the end of the year almost 700,000 passenger journeys had been made on the Gourock line[2]. The independent boat operator at Wemyss Bay, Captain Campbell, found his trade to Rothesay and Millport slumping. Efforts to sell his ships to the Caledonian Steam Packet company failed. The Caledonian had long backed him against the efforts of the Wemyss Bay company to replace him, but now the Caledonian Railway and Caledonian Steam Packet Company were deliberately forcing him out. Soon after formation of the Steam Packet Company the CR offered to co-operate with the Wemyss Bay company in terminating Campbell's agreement and "making other arrangements", and after a financially disastrous winter he pulled the service abruptly from 30 April 1890. The Caledonian smoothly accepted his resignation, reserving any claims for "irregular termination of contract"[3]. On 1 May, *Caledonia* and *Galatea* were transferred to Wemyss Bay, and Wemyss Bay trains, which hitherto had always terminated at Bridge Street, at last ran to and from the far more convenient Central. As a result, traffic improved again, but the Caledonian was operating services which to a large extent duplicated each other, even though extra traffic was created. Excursion trips, linked to cruises with music and grand firework displays, were organised to boost the revenues[4]. At Ardrossan, after long nagging of the Lanarkshire & Ayrshire by the Caledonian, the Montgomerie Pier and Station were finally opened on 30 May 1890, a two-platform terminus with 15 iron-framed bays clad in wood, and with an overall roof supported by lattice girders. The inevitable contest with the GSWR for passenger traffic ensued, given an additional dimension by the steamer connections both to Arran and to Belfast, the latter run by G.&J. Burns. The other Edinburgh Exhibition locomotive, No. 124, was given the name *Eglinton* and used on the 'Arran Express Boat Train', Glasgow Central to Montgomerie Pier. To serve the Arran trade in rivalry with the GSWR's contractor, the Caledonian Steam Packet Company, which had already added *Marchioness of Bute* and *Marchioness of Breadalbane* to its fleet, provided a splendid new paddle steamer, *Duchess of Hamilton*, "the finest and most successful steamer engaged in the Clyde passenger traffic"[5], to which almost all the passengers deserted.

The opening of the Gourock line, and the establishment of the Caledonian Steam Packet Company, inaugurated an era of railway and steamer competition into which the Caledonian, the Glasgow & South Western, and the North British all threw themselves with fervent zeal. The railway and steamer racing of the following years has often been chronicled. The record for travel from Glasgow Central to Dunoon, via Gourock, was 45 minutes[6]. But passengers, if they liked speed, did not like being hustled. One writer observed that: "On the Caledonian no luggage was permitted at all on the Clyde boat expresses. When no more than 2 minutes was scheduled at Gourock between arrival of the train and departure of the boat one cannot be concerned with such trifles as luggage!"[7]. Most passengers were commuters but many had to send their luggage on ahead.

An Amalgamation Contest

The arrival of a competing railway company was usually welcomed by local commerce and industry. Any railway with a monopoly position was regarded with suspicion, as likely to overcharge on rates and economise on service. Noting that the Caledonian was now competing with the GSWR in nearby Ardrossan, in August 1889 the chamber of commerce and town council of Ayr made strong representations to the company for an extension of its system, promising at least half their traffic and offering a central site for a new station. The Caledonian investigated the possibility of extending the Lanarkshire & Ayrshire Kilwinning-Irvine branch (opened 2 June 1890) to Ayr, with links to Troon harbour and to the GSWR Mauchline line, which would lead through to Muirkirk and the CR's own Lanarkshire lines. It could have been a neat scooping out of much of the Glasgow & South Western's trade, but the Caledonian did not follow it up. The cost, estimated by John Strain, the Lanarkshire & Ayrshire engineer, as £440,000, would have been very difficult to recoup, as the GSWR would certainly have battled to keep its traffic.

A few months after Gourock the rebuilt Dundee West was opened in September 1889, a spacious station with four terminal platforms under an overall roof, behind an imposing Scotch baronial frontage. From 1 November the Moffat Railway was absorbed by the Caledonian, with £75 of CR Convertible Preferred for every £100 of its

The new station building at Dundee West, completed in 1889.
The architect was Hippolyte Blanc, of Edinburgh (once James Miller's employer).

shares. New lines for which the Caledonian sought an Act in 1889 were the Barnton Railway in Edinburgh, an extension from Bridgeton North to Carmyle, and a goods line "from near James Hill to Dalzell" serving the Dalzell Ironworks at Motherwell from both the main line and the stump of the old Wishaw & Coltness from Jerviston Junction.

The stock market was astonished in 1889[8] by a proposal for the amalgamation of the NBR and the GSWR Railways: "The Glasgow & South Western, whose board is presided over by the Midland chairman, has been a Midland dependency for twenty years past"[9]. The merger was to date from 1 August 1890. The Caledonian was certainly surprised. Archibald Gibson wrote to the GSWR on 26 September 1889 to express regret at not being informed and asking for a copy of the proposed terms; the South Western declined his request as "unusual". Gibson responded by asking if the GSWR would consider joint ownership, which again was declined[10]. The proposed union would leave the Caledonian pincered by a greatly enlarged North British, and on 24 October the board resolved to "secure that the whole case be brought before Parliament", and began preparation of a Bill which would enable the Caledonian to acquire the Glasgow & South Western from 1 February 1891, with an option for the North British to become joint owners[11].

The Caledonian's half-yearly report to 31 January 1890 showed only a modest increase in revenue, £1,589,916 compared to £1,583,943 for the equivalent period of 1888-89. But working expenses had risen from £681,116 (45.46%) to £732,828 (47.4%). Sir James King, deputy chairman, commented on how a large increase in passenger numbers had not fed through to revenue. Second class carriages had now been withdrawn from all local trains, as part of a phased abolition.

Faced with these figures[12], the company was seeking to reduce the number of train miles by 4,000 a week. Around

Passenger numbers	1889	1890
First class	629,919	637,842
Second class	208,846	131,782
Third class	8,945,760	9,776,429
Season tickets	11,232	12,556

50 passenger trains had been cut from 1 February. But £150 was found to build a new four-wheel car for the horse-drawn Inchture Branch, with 6 first class and 22 third class places[13].

The terminus, and motive power, of the Inchture Tramway, opened 1 February 1848, closed 1917.

After some peaceful years, the proposal for amalgamation of the North British and the South Western caused rivalry to flare up again at the end of the 80s. Old suspicions resumed. The Caley repaired Eddlewood Colliery sidings, on the Hamilton-Strathaven line, at its own expense for £900 "with the view of keeping the North British Railway out of the district"[14]. Such hints of NBR ambitions may explain why at Aberdeen in the summer of 1890, "the Caledonian deliberately and blatantly intensified the war of nerves against the NBR"[15]. This related to the NBR's use of the Joint Station and of the Caledonian's locomotive shed.

External Perceptions

In 1889 Foxwell and Farrer published their survey of express train services and noted that "the Caledonian has within the last year or two been strung up to a very much finer pitch of efficiency", and although "Scotch railway officials appear to either lose their head or to become helplessly rigid in the face of a traffic emergency", the Caledonian and GSWR are perhaps the most exempt. But still, "the former is liable to hysterics at Oban, and the delays at Larbert are an insoluble conundrum." The Caledonian's best train was noted as the 4.08 p.m. Carlisle-Edinburgh, which reached Edinburgh at 6 o'clock, having travelled $100^3/_4$ miles at an average 54 mph[16].

In preparation for rebuilding, Princes Street Station in Edinburgh was in a partly-dismantled state when fire broke out on 16 June 1890, leaving the buildings half-destroyed. After some patching-up, work continued on the new terminus. Work had also been going on to build a new Bridge Street Station in Glasgow, still shared with the GSWR. Despite some improvements to the Central Station, Bridge Street, relocated a little way south of the original buildings, still had four terminal platforms. A long terrace of offices was built alongside, to the design of James Miller.

William Acworth, a keen-eyed observer of the railway scene, published *Railways of Scotland* in 1890. "One thing is clear," he declared, "the effect of the opening of the Forth Bridge will be felt right away to the extreme north of Scotland"[17]. A not uncritical writer, he praised the facilities of Perth Station: "Even the very dogs are not forgotten, and after their hot night in the train, should enjoy their roomy kennels with fresh water and clean straw … For their masters there are comfortable dressing-rooms with hot baths all complete," as well as excellent breakfasts. But another station jointly owned by the Caledonian, Aberdeen by contrast had no scruples about charging "twopence for a penny bun, and threepence for a sandwich composed of equal parts of gristle, fat, and sawdust"[18]. The Station Hotel at Perth opened in August 1890. It had been authorised as early as 1865 but the company's situation in that year certainly did not allow for such ancillary items. Designed by the Perth architect Andrew Heiton, it set up Perth as a sort of caravanserai for the first class traffic heading northwards and southwards from the Highland line. Buchanan Street Station was described by Acworth as "a low wooden shed, put up by Joseph Locke as long ago as 1849 as a temporary structure, but still standing, and to confess the truth, except for its looks, by no means a bad station even now"[19]. In at least one respect, "Scotland is distinctly in advance of England": the Caledonian's train heating system using "the waste steam of the engine – or rather of so much of it as escapes from the cylinder of the Westinghouse brake pump. Iron pipes, connected between the coaches by pieces of old worn-out india rubber brake hose, run from end to end of the train. In each compartment there is, under the seat and connected with the train-pipe, a pipe four inches in diameter which serves as as radiator." He found it in use even on the Glasgow suburban trains; the only objection was that passengers could not adjust the temperature "as the carriage often gets unpleasantly hot"[20]. Visiting St. Rollox Works, he found "… for the use of its 45,000 goods trucks the Caledonian railway manufactures some 600 or 700 tons of grease per annum" in its own factory, the ingredients being "palm oil, soap, soda, tallow, and a small quantity of an extremely fluid white oil which looks not unlike the finest castor-oil"[21].

Like all English visitors, Acworth found Scottish railway fares to be agreeably low: "the Glasgow fares are certainly less than half of what we are accustomed to in the south", and noted that "Alone of all the great towns of the kingdom, the Glasgow Chamber of Commerce has not appeared as an objector before the Board of Trade at the Railway Rates Enquiry". He admired the boat train schedules: "In all, 11 trains, and 13 boats in connection, run for the accommodation of passengers leaving Glasgow in the half-hour after four o'clock"; and also the excursion programmes: "Probably nowhere in the world, certainly nowhere in the United Kingdom, are so many pleasure-tours organised with so much intelligence and forethought. Coaches and steamers are independent of the railways, but it is always possible to obtain through tickets at the railway booking offices"[22]. He believed he had put his finger on the reason: "… in universal and ubiquitous competition is to be found the keynote of the Scotch railway system"[23].

Stock Conversion – or 'Watering'?

Acworth did not comment on another Caledonian ploy of early 1890, an exercise in what the *Railway Times* called "stock watering" and the board defined as "the optional transfer of Ordinary stock to Converted stock (Preferred and Deferred Ordinary stock). The holders of Ordinary stock could convert their shares into Converted Preferred at a maximum dividend of 3%, with the same number of Converted Deferred, which would earn any dividend over and above 3%. The potential effect was to double the number of shares. Preferred and Deferred shares did not have voting rights. A Wharncliffe meeting (see page 67) was called on 4 February 1890 to gain approval for the presentation of a Bill to Parliament, a measure which, J.C. Bolton insisted, was merely a nominal duplication, an option for shareholders. All existing rights of Preference shares would be preserved. At that time, Caledonian £100 Ordinary stock stood at £127.5. At the same meeting, approval was sought for the CR to present its Bill for the acquisition of the Glasgow & South Western company, and for the North British company to become a joint owner. Both schemes were approved by the shareholders[24].

The two Bills competing for control of the GSWR were considered by a single Commons Committee, which in May rejected the Caledonian proposal but granted the preamble of the North British one[25]. But on 11 July 1890 the House of Lords threw out the North British Bill. As a result the Glasgow & South Western Railway, Midland Railway protectorate though it might be (the Midland had backed the NBR Bill) would remain independent until the post-War grouping. It had been a costly campaign: the CR's parliamentary expenses were £21,168, an increase of £14,763 on its parliamentary costs in the February-July period of 1889[26].

Running on a parallel track before a different committee was the stock conversion scheme, which was objected to by holders of existing Deferred shares, as the new Preferred would get priority for payment. To some observers there was a more sinister aspect. Stock conversion was a fashionable concept, and companies had been formed specifically to deal in converted shares. One such was the Stock Conversion and Investment Trust Co., which was said in May to have secured transfers of £600,000 worth of Caledonian Ordinary stock. At any meeting of shareholders of the Trust Company, one-fiftieth of the shares constituted a quorum, which enabled the meeting to proceed. A simple majority could decide any issue. Of a holding of £600,000, a quorum was £24,000, so that £12,001 could carry a resolution. In fact, since the shares were duplicated, this meant that £6,000-worth of Caledonian shares could, in theory, bring £600,000 worth of influence to bear. For those who scented conspiracy at every corner, the fact that the chairman of the Stock Conversion & Investment Co. was the Marquis of Tweeddale, who was also chairman of the North British Board, was deeply significant. The Caledonian Board pointed out that its Bill was a duplication of the stock, not a splitting, and that voting power in the Caledonian was not increased at all. They were simply securing power to do what the Trust Company was already doing. The Bill was passed, and gained the royal assent in August[27]. In the same month the Caledonian issued £750,000 of new Ordinary stock, at a premium of 15 per cent.

In April 1890 Dugald Drumond, ambitious for new opportunities, resigned as locomotive superintendent, to the board's expressed regret. In eight years he had modernised the works and set the basis for a locomotive policy that would last for twenty years. Under his regime 287 locomotives had been built. He had spent a lot of money, but Drummond estimated that he had reduced operating costs per train mile from 12.28*d.* to 10.56*d.* between 1883 and 1887, which if correct meant a saving of £50,000 (train miles run in 1887 were around twelve million). Greater locomotive power and sterner discipline in departmental management (Drummond's word was law) combined to reduce double-heading on trains: in January 1883, 69 engines were in use as pilots; in 1887 this was down to 29, and the mileage done by assisting engines was down from 882,680 to 274,990. The board made him a parting gift of £1,000. His final salary had been £2,400; his successor, Hugh Smellie, poached from the GSWR, got £1,500.

The swing-span of the Tay Viaduct at Perth was finally removed around 1890, having been out of use since mid-1886, when the Dundee, Perth & Newburgh Steamship Co.'s vessels had to lower masts and funnels to reach the harbour. The CR Board refused to pay £400 in compensation[28]. An agreement on sharing receipts of passenger traffic between Glasgow and Edinburgh, and between these cities and Aberdeeen, was signed by the Caledonian and North British in late September[29]. Peace was not breaking out on the lower Clyde, where the GSWR was hoping to regain its advantage with a new terminal at Princes Pier, alongside its Albert Harbour Station. On the south side of the Clyde, the immense volume of coal and iron ore traffic, combined with inter-company rivalry, was creating almost chaotic conditions, with neither the harbours nor the railways able to cope. It was claimed before the Railway & Canal Commissioners that in 1890-91, 200,00 tons of iron ore from Bilbao, plus 380,000 tons of iron ore, pig iron and limestone from other ports, had had to be discharged at Port Glasgow or Greenock because of lack of facilities at Glasgow, but the GSWR also alleged that the Caledonian was deliberately trying to get ships to use its own port of Grangemouth, or Ardrossan or Port Glasgow[30]; however, by the end of 1893, coal companies were also demanding more quays at Grangemouth because of congestion in that port[31].

View over St Fillans Station, opened 1901, looking west: the railway integrated into the landscape.

Archibald Gibson, the long serving secretary, died in November 1890, aged 71. For decades his name had appeared in all Caledonian advertisements, and his knowledge and steadiness had been invaluable. His widow received a year's salary. George Jackson, the company's solicitor, was temporary secretary until John Blackburn was appointed in 1891.

Its familiarity with the Oban railway's affairs might well have made the Caledonian feel dubious about cross-country routes through thinly-populated districts, and for a long time it fended off overtures from the promoters of a railway west from Crieff towards Loch Earn. In the late 1880s the company was running a regular coach during the tourist season through the scenic region between the stations at Crieff and Balquhidder (then called Lochearnhead) but even the growing tourist traffic did not encourage it to invest in the Crieff and Comrie line, though Gibson wrote to the promoters on 7 March 1888 to confirm that if they built the line at their own cost, the CR would be prepared to work it, a position re-affirmed in May 1889.

Commenting on the Caledonian Railway's operations in the later 1880s, a Scottish economist of the period was critical about some key aspects. He considered the perpetual and apparently unresolvable competition between the Caledonian and the North British to have many bad effects. While both companies offered cheap fares wherever their lines competed for the same traffic, they tried to compensate for their losses by pushing up the rates on lines which they monopolised, thus forcing a "tax" on some sections of the population to subsidise others. Again, in order to pay for the costs of competition, he regarded both companies as seriously undermanned, resulting in an over-stretched and resentful workforce. Taking the Caledonian's Carlisle-Glasgow goods service as an example, he observed that in earlier years this had been worked by enginemen as a 'single trip'. Twelve engines were stationed at each end, and the journey took nine hours, with the crew sleeping on alternate nights in Carlisle and Glasgow. Now the service was operated as a 'double trip', and the locomotive and its crew went each way within a single 18-hour shift. This required only six locomotives. The men's pay was increased, but the workload, and the strain on their strength and health was vastly greater. He could see no benefit for anyone in such a "pinched and straitened" service, except perhaps future stockholders: "it is a question as to how far this is justifiable from any point of view"[32]. This kind of paring away in the name of efficiency and saving, in ways invisible to the public, is a counterpoint to the opulence usually put on when the Caledonian was showing a public face.

Strike

In the course of the 1880s the trade union movement had made considerable progress. Previously, unions had been mostly among skilled tradesmen, with a strong 'friendly society' aspect providing benefits and an element of security to members. Railway workers had various levels of skills and few could be regarded as wholly unskilled labourers. The Amalgamated Society of Railway Servants for Scotland was formed in 1872, and as its name suggests, was a fusion of earlier groups. Any attempt at 'organisation' of their workforces was regarded by railway companies with extreme hostility. The Caledonian Railway refused to recognise the existence of the Amalgamated Society of Railway Servants for Scotland, which by 1890 had around 7,000 members. It could not prevent its workers from joining, but it could, and did, make life difficult for anyone who was known to be a union activist. Rule 15a of the company's rule book was seen to cover the position: "Should any servant think himself aggrieved at any time he may memorialise the Board; but in such cases the memorial must be sent through the head of his department." Discussion of working practices and workers' pay was entered into unwillingly and seen as something to be achieved between a manager (under direction from the board) and his men. But the self-awareness of the working man was changing. Since 1867 the urban working classes had been able to vote in Parliamentary elections. New political ideas were widely discussed. Far more information was available to the reading public than in previous decades, about the wealth of the nation and of its major enterprises. In 1888 James Keir Hardie and Robert Cunninghame Graham had founded the Scottish Labour Party, whose programme included the national ownership of railways and banks, the biggest businesses of the time. Meanwhile, on the Caledonian as on other railways, working conditions and pay were imposed by the company without discussion. Since the railway ran 24 hours a day, at least on its busiest lines, shift working was essential. A signalman's or a driver's shift could last for 14 hours and sometimes longer. If he had to do extra, there was no overtime pay. Exhausted men were much more likely to experience, or cause, accidents, and there was some public anxiety about this. A Regulation of Railways Act was passed in 1889, one of whose clauses required railways to "make returns of overtime worked by their servants whose duties involve the safety of trains or passengers", but the definition of overtime rested with the companies.

In October 1890 the Amalgamated Society of Railway Servants for Scotland made an approach to the Caledonian, the North British and the Glasgow & South Western companies, with a request for a reduction of working hours to 10 a day, overtime at time plus a quarter to be payable after 60 hours; time and a half for Sunday work, a maximum 8-hour shift for men working in busy shunting yards, and more signal cabins to be worked on an 8-hour rather than the 12-hour system. Altogether ten points were listed, including the request for a set annual holiday. It is notable that in some respects the men were asking for less than had been requested in the Caledonian strike of 1883. The companies' response was that any grievances could be brought up "in the usual manner". Strikes were not illegal but the Amalgamated Society of Railway Servants for Scotland followed a set procedure which involved giving advanced notice of the action, and the men giving their 'resignations' to the union officers, which would then inform the company of the numbers about to strike. While branches in the Glasgow area were militant, railwaymen in country centres were less so, and the union leaders, in successive meetings, recommended delay. They were pushed by their members, however, when a meeting in Glasgow on 21 December voted overwhelmingly for immediate strike action. Of the Caledonian men present, 356 voted for a strike, 22 against[33]. That same day the strike began, supported by the vast majority of the Caledonian workers. James Thompson was authorised by the board to take the necessary steps to prosecute the strikers. A letter from him, instructing the men to return to work on Monday or they would be dismissed from the CR's service, was burned in one meeting. Few contingency plans had been made by the railway companies. Rail services were almost completely halted, and by Christmas Day it was estimated that 8,500 to 9,000 men were on strike. Picketing of the main depots was immediate and effective. But the Caledonian board began to fight back. Drivers and other workers were drafted in from Ireland and England. Motherwell, as the centre of operations for much of the coalfield traffic, was a key location. Its locomotive depot, protected by police, became a camp for the imported blackleg workers. Many of the strikers lived in company-owned houses and on Christmas Day about a dozen families were served with warrants to appear at Hamilton Sheriff Court on the 27th. Effectively these were eviction notices. The company was taking the view that these were tied houses and the tenants had left the Caledonian's employment. Though legally valid, it was a deliberate exercise in intimidation. On 31 December Thompson was instructed to put the decrees of ejectment into force, but efforts to make the evictions on 3 January failed, and on the 4th, two cavalry troops from the 13th Hussars arrived to back up the police and Sheriff's officers in evicting people from houses in Muir Street, right by the station (which was still relatively new, having been opened in August 1885 to accommodate all the town's passenger traffic). A hostile crowd estimated at 20-30,000 assembled. Blackleg workers in the station received abusive shouts, then stones began to be thrown. As the crowd became increasingly unruly, the Sheriff read the Riot Act and the police made several baton charges. In the violent scenes that followed the station's glass roof was smashed and the buildings were damaged.

Damage was also done to the signal box at Lesmahagow Junction. Disturbances went on through the day and even after dark. More police arrived from Glasgow and on the 5th a special train brought 100 from Lancashire. But there were no more serious disturbances. Later the damage was estimated as costing £882 12s. 9d., and the company's solicitor was instructed to take steps to recover this sum[34].

The Caledonian Board did not order further evictions. The Motherwell riot showed strong popular support for the railway workers, and this continued even though many people were laid off because their factories and yards could get no coal. In Greenock, three of the sugar works stopped production after three days. Three hundred Greenock railway workers were on strike[35]. The huge Singer works at Clydebank laid off 5,000 workers, and it was estimated that 100,000 people's jobs were directly or indirectly affected[36]. The price of coal, when available, shot up. Miners and steelworkers joined the railway pickets and there was a fracas between steelworkers and police at Polmadie Locomotive Depot in Glasgow, with several injuries. Accusations and counter-accusations of violence and intimidation were exchanged in the press and in parliamentary debate. Train crews with no experience of the line were hired and put straight on duty. In a collision outside Buchanan Street Station on 7 January, William Hunter, stationmaster at Bishopton, was killed. He had been acting as 'conductor' to a driver hired from England less than a week before, on a coal train from Ross Junction to Sighthill. The engine ran out of its own coal and came to a stop. It then appears to have been pushed forward by a passenger train from behind, down towards Buchanan Street, against signals set at danger, until it collided with a goods train coming out of the Goods Station[37]. There were many less serious incidents of a similar nature. But the board remained obdurate. Joseph Bolton, the chairman, though a Liberal M.P. was not on his party's radical wing (his final utterance in Parliament, on 21 June 1892, would be to challenge Board of Trade figures on "unduly long hours" for railway workers). Sir James King, for the company, announced that he "desired to make it clear that the company did not see their way to concede a ten-hours day all round, and that they could not agree to recognise the Executive of the Amalgamated Society, but on the men returning to work, the directors would be quite ready to consider and remedy any grievances … so far as these were reasonable"[38]. James Thompson is quoted as saying that "The working class must never be allowed to taste power"[39], but that is exactly what the railwaymen were doing. They had paralysed the country's economic life. Professor Mavor noted a "coming and going" of strikers, who would turn up for work and then withdraw again[40], but there was a steady drift back. The Amalgamated Society of Railway Servants for Scotland issued strike pay of 10s. a week, which many of the strikers did not take. By the fifth week of the strike, there was still virtually no mineral traffic moving, and no sign of a settlement. The Glasgow & South Western men had returned to work on 31 December. But the end came quite quickly. On 29 January the North British men returned to work. On the 31st, the Caledonian management met "delegates of the men" and it was agreed that normal working would be resumed. There was a certain pride among the Caledonian employees that they had stuck it out longest, and bronze medallions were cast, 'I stood firm to the last'. For its part, the board praised the "ability, firmness and kindness" of the general manager and top officials in dealing with the strike[41].

On the face of it, the strike had gained little or nothing for the workers. But the board was not triumphalist. Public opinion had not been on its side, even when the men were being urged to go back to work because they had made their point. The government was making noises about a Select Committee inquiry, and further legislation regulating railways was clearly going to come. The Caledonian's loss of earnings was estimated at over £36,000[42], and expenses shot up, due to damage by inexperienced blackleg workers as well as the cost of their hire and protection. One contemporary view of the strike was that it "is best described as a revolt of labourers against the inefficient Organisation of their industry"[43].

Another Go at Fife

Encouraged by invitations, hints, even promises of custom from the industries and businesses of Kirkcaldy, the Board resolved in March 1891 to promote a new Bill for a line into Fife, branching off the main line at Larbert, passing beneath the Firth of Forth in a long tunnel, and linking with the Seafield Dock Railway at Kirkcaldy, with a passenger terminus at Kirkcaldy Sands. Despite much support in Fife, in the hope that a competitor to the North British would result in lower rates and fares, and much talk about the undesirability of the North British monopoly, the Bill was rejected. An equally contentious Bill was passed on 5 August, for an additional railway to serve the north bank of the Clyde Estuary. The Caledonian had owned the canal terminal at Bowling since 1867 but had no railway access to it. Now a body of industrialists and businessmen formed the independent Lanarkshire & Dumbartonshire Railway, with strong Caledonian support, to break the North British hegemony of the district. Since 1874 the Caledonian had exercised running powers over the North British lines from Sighthill via Maryhill to the Queen's Dock at Stobcross, though the NBR was rarely co-operative[44]. For more than 20 years, the CR had no share in the north bank traffic west of Stobcross. In 1886 the Glasgow City & District Railway had been completed, giving the North British a cross-city route, part underground. It seemed as if the NBR was gaining the advantage in the Caley's own stronghold. But in Glasgow, a still-spreading conurbation of densely-packed housing and industry, the Caledonian still saw valuable opportunities, among which the Lanarkshire and Dumbartonshire Railway was an important element of what may have been an ambitious planned strategy or simply a series of separate decisions and deals, some of which fell neatly but fortuitously into combination. Certainly suggestions and proposals came from people outside the company who had influence with the CR directors, like Charles Forman, chief promoter of the Glasgow Central Railway. At the heart was the Glasgow Central line, still digging its great cut-and-cover trench across the city, with five out of seven miles underground. On 18 June 1891 the Board authorised the issue of £975,000 of Glasgow Central Railway stock, offered to current shareholders in a ratio of £1 for every £14 of their holding, at a premium of 10% on the face value. Half was to be paid within a month and the balance by the end of January 1892. This may have eased the temporary loan position: on 30 June 1891 the company had £11,500 from Glasgow University Court, £7,000 from the Royal Infirmary, £10,000 from J.C. Bunten, one of the directors, £40,000 from the Anderston Foundry Co. in which Bunten was a partner, and £420,000 from the Commercial Bank in London and Glasgow, at rates varying from 2.25% to 3%.

The Lanarkshire & Dumbartonshire Railway, under construction in the early 1890s, had two arms, or perhaps wings to lift the Caledonian into new levels of prosperity. Converging on a new Maryhill Central Station, they were the Dumbarton line from the west, and the Lanarkshire line from the east. Apart from the section between Bowling and Dumbarton, the North British Dumbarton line was some way from the river, and the planners of the Lanarkshire & Dumbartonshire set their line as close as possible to the new shipyards and factories clustering along the riverbank at Yoker and Clydebank. East of Partick it was to make a junction with the Glasgow Central line, providing a direct route from Dumbarton to Coatbridge and Motherwell. The Lanarkshire line ran from Maryhill Central through the Possil district, crossing the North British line to Edinburgh north of Cowlairs and making a wide arc to join the Caledonian's first main line, the old Glasgow, Garnkirk & Coatbridge, at Balornock, from where there were links to south and east. From Possil it used the track of the CR's Hamiltonhill branch, providing that ill-conceived line with a useful role. Work began on 6 October 1891, with several contractors on different sections. The consulting engineer was Charles Forman. Its capital had been readily subscribed by local industry, though the Caledonian contributed £82,000 and was to work the line for a minimum 4% guaranteed dividend[45].

In other developments, on 2 November 1891, Coalburn finally acquired a passenger service when trains on the Lesmahagow line were extended to there. An agreement with the North British confirmed that there would be no more invasive schemes into each other's territory, and provided for exchange of traffic at Crianlarich when the West Highland Railway should reach that place[46].

Coalburn had a passenger service from 2 November 1891.

Hugh Smellie died in April 1891, it was said through fatigue and illness under the stresses of the strike. The board gifted £500 to his family and appointed John Lambie, currently assistant locomotive superintendent, to the top job at St. Rollox, at £900 a year.

On 1 February 1892, the GSWR finally vacated Bridge Street Station, awarded £129,251 compensation for giving up its joint ownership. The Caledonian was now free to decide what do with Bridge Street, and to rearrange the access lines to Central Station. A link line was laid to complete the triangle at Rutherglen, allowing trains and engines from the Polmadie direction north towards London Road and the 'Switchback' line. Much of the Caledonian's planning and preparation of Parliamentary Bills was taken up by short industrial lines, often less than a mile, to join new factories and coal pits to the system, or to create new connections at junctions. From the Drumbowie branch, extensions were made to Legbrannock No. 2 Colliery (off the Airdrie line), and to Legbrannock 4 and 5, fron North Linrigg Junction, and from Turdees branch Junction west to Springbank and Blackridge Collieries, and the eastwards line past Kirk o' Shotts to Duntilland was extended to a colliery at Dewshill (all 1896-98). In the far south-west a boost was given to the jointly owned Portpatrick & Wigtown line and Larne & Stranraer Steamship Co. when a mail contract for Northern Ireland was awarded at the end of 1892, worth £13,500[47] a year.

Even in far-off New Zealand, the effect of the Scottish diaspora brought news of the Caledonian Railway's affairs. The *Otago Witness* of 9 February 1893 carried a report "from our own correspondent", of a social gathering of servants from the Central and Buchanan Street Stations, with James Thompson, General Manager, presiding. Thompson observed that in 1850, the whole staff numbered 1,600, and now was 16,000, while the wage bill of £80,000 had risen to £800,000 (no increase in average earnings, incidentally). He also noted that the Caledonian had been the first company to use the electric train tablet system on single lines, one of the first to use continuous brakes, and to carry third class passengers on all trains. Here was a company whose 'servants' might be proud to work for it. Thompson also dwelt on the benefits the Caledonian had brought to Glasgow. A few years before, he confided, it had been proposed to relocate the St. Rollox Works to "a country district", but "we preferred to enlarge and retain them", adding to the prosperity of "the second City of the Empire". And construction of the Central underground line had enabled the city to acquire "a vast new sewerage system" at the expense of the Caledonian[48].

No More Second Class

Early in 1893, the conversion of the Great Western Railway to standard gauge had repercussions in the Caledonian timetable, when in February through carriages began running daily between Glasgow Central and Plymouth, the longest daily run in Britain. From May of that year, having already eliminated them on some lines, including the Clyde Coast (except Wemyss Bay)[49], the Caledonian also abolished its second class fares completely and offered first and third class only. In Scotland, barely 10% of passengers travelled second class while in England over 30% did. Several other companies made the change, including the Highland Railway and some English lines. The London & North Western continued to operate second class carriages but it was no longer possible to book through to Scotland in Second. It has been wondered why third was not abolished instead, but 'second' conveyed certain intimations of superior comfort and also of higher fare levels. Nevertheless the effect was to make further improvement to third class facilities, at least on express trains. In July, the West Coast route inaugurated its ten-carriage 'Corridor Train', with dining facilities and lavatory accommodation for both first and third class. This new West Coast Joint Stock, built by the LNWR at Wolverton, was the joint property of it and the CR, and the Caledonian officers were very much involved in the planning. The first all-corridor train to run in the British Isles, the new stock initially ran only between London and Glasgow, on the 2 p.m. train from each city, but in August it was used on an Edinburgh express, and also on services between Edinburgh and Glasgow and Liverpool and Manchester[50].

In Upper Strathearn, the committee of the Crieff & Comrie Railway had obtained an Act on 25 April 1890 and their four-mile line was completed on 1 June 1893. The "collection of wooden huts called the Crieff railway station"[51] became a goods depot and the Caledonian built a new through station alongside. Improvements were also being made in Angus, where the junction station at Bridge of Dun was rebuilt and enlarged in 1893. Back in 1890 the Caledonian had introduced a Bill to enable it to take over the Greenock & Wemyss Bay Railway, which was finally passed on 27 July 1893 in a portmanteau Act with numerous other provisions. On 1 August the Caledonian formally absorbed the Wemyss Bay company, and the long wrangling about quality of service at last came to an end.

Through 1893 and 1894, the spacious new nine-platform terminus at Edinburgh Princes Street gradually came into full use. At last the company had an Edinburgh station it could be proud of. The cost was over £250,000 including £65,000 for property compensation. In 1894 an Act was obtained for building a hotel, but it would be

Davidson's Mains Railway Station.

Edinburgh suburban: Barnton Gate, opened 1894, was renamed Davidson's Mains in 1903.

almost ten years before this was completed. Potential residential areas west of Edinburgh were tapped with a branch from Craigleith, on the Granton line, to Barnton Gate and Cramond Brig (Davidson's Mains and Barnton from 1903), built in collaboration with the local landowner, who was interested in housing development. It opened on 1 March 1894. Some of the major new works in Glasgow were also near completion. On 19 March 1894 a new station at Cathcart opened, no longer a terminus but on a through route, with the completion, two weeks later, on 2 April, of the full 'circle' back to Muirhouse Central Junction. The Caledonian had expanded its investment in the Cathcart District Railway, with an Act of 1889 enabling it to invest £100,000 and to guarantee the interest on the Cathcart company's Debenture stock, up to £94,330; and further authority in 1890 to lend it £100,000 against Debenture stock[52]. On 26 November the Glasgow Central Railway, mostly underground, opened between Maryhill Central and Stobcross, through the Kelvin Valley, for goods and mineral trains, and the Lanarkshire & Dumbartonshire opened for goods traffic between Maryhill and Balornock Junction, where it met the Coatbridge line and the 'Switchback' line of 1886. A remnant of the Hamiltonhill branch[53] now diverged east of Possil towards Hamiltonhill, serving eventually as a goods line for the large new Ruchill Hospital built in 1901-4.

Fighting back against the Caledonian's advantageous location at Gourock, the GSWR replaced its Albert Harbour terminus at Greenock with a fine new pier and terminal, Princes Pier, on 25 May 1894, and reclaimed some of its lost traffic. The North British had no presence on the south bank but served the same steamer destinations from Craigendoran on the north side, where it had no competition.

From 26 June to 15 October 1894 the Scottish miners were on strike, bringing severe repercussions on industrial and commercial life. Coal was the universal fuel for every purpose, and the prime source of goods revenue to the Caledonian. Train services were cut back. Around 160 goods engines, and their crews, were laid off. Although the company used 21,000 tons less coal than normal during the strike period, the consequent hike in prices meant that it paid £3,611 more for its supplies[54].

After a gap of several decades, new railway development was going ahead in the county of Forfarshire. The old town of Brechin had been at the end of a branch of the Aberdeen Railway from Bridge of Dun since 1847. Now the Forfar & Brechin Railway was promoted in 1889 and obtained its Act on 4 August 1890. It was very much a rural line, but intended to serve a wide agricultural district, with anticipated traffic in livestock, grain, potatoes,

THE STATION, BRECHIN

The terminus at Brechin, around 1920. It opened on 1 February 1848 and was enlarged when the Forfar & Brechin line was built, in 1895. The North British exercised running powers to here and a NBR poster can be seen.

manure and lime. In the harsh winter of 1894-95 the 13-mile railway opened formally for goods traffic on 7 January. Passenger services began from 1 June. On 31 July 1894 the Caledonian acquired it, having made an undertaking to work the line in perpetuity from its opening. Capital was £330,000 and the Forfar & Brechin was entitled to borrow up to £110,000[55]. The lines from Forfar and Bridge of Dun converged in a rebuilt terminal station at Brechin, with a bypass line (little-used, this was closed in 1917). On 27 August a train ran through the buffers at Brechin and the engine landed in the street, provoking jocular press comments about "the unauthorised extension of the Forfar & Brechin"[56].

John Lambie died in February 1895 and again a 'running' man was appointed as locomotive superintendent, the 50-year old John Farquharson McIntosh, who had spent 35 years rising in the Company's locomotive hierarchy, having joined the Scottish North Eastern Railway's Arbroath Works in 1862. McIntosh's salary was £700, but by 1900 he was earning £1,500 a year. Like most such 'self-made' men, he was a vigorous personality as well as a man of ability, and after a few uncertain years, a firm hand was again felt at St. Rollox.

The half-yearly report published in March 1895 was the first since the complete phasing-out of second class fares. It was evident that everyone had traded down. Compared with the same period for the previous year, there were fewer first class passengers, 602,156 against 607,232. There had been 100,280 second class passengers in August-January 1893-94. But the number of third class passengers had risen from 11,396,410 to 11,695,747. The number of season ticket holders was almost unchanged, at 16,355 compared with 16,349. Though total operating costs fell slightly, from £827,156 to £808,490, the drop in revenue was sharper, from £1,719,032 to £1,588,812, and the dividend fell below 4% for the first time since 1886.

Racing Again

Since 1888 there had been no change to the agreed eight and a half hour schedule for London-Edinburgh expresses, though the Caledonian had made considerable improvements to its timings to Perth and Aberdeen. By 1895, when the North British had enlarged Waverley Station, conditions were right for another round of speed competition. Since 1893, the three routes, including the Midland-GSWR, were running mid-day departures from London to Edinburgh, with dining car accommodation for all classes. Since 1894 the East Coast had been running to Aberdeen in eleven hours and thirty-five minutes for 523.7 miles, beating the West Coast time by fifteen minutes. From 1 July 1895, the West Coast's overnight express to Aberdeen, leaving Euston at 8 p.m., was due to make the journey in eleven hours and forty minutes for 539.7 miles. The East Coast, with a departure from Kings Cross at the same time, cut its time to eleven hours and 20 minutes. This broke the 8½-hour London-Edinburgh pact, and the Caledonian and LNWR responded with an eleven-hour timing to Aberdeen from 15 July. In fact, the crews and station staff were encouraged to beat the timetable, and on 17 July the train reached Aberdeen at 6.21 a.m. From then until 22 August, there was nightly competition. The East Coast companies set a timing of ten hours and forty-five minutes, and kept punctiliously to booked station stops. But the Caledonian train was always first in Aberdeen, by the simple expedient of ignoring the published timetable. The 'Tourist' was run in two sections, with a lightweight flyer ahead of the main train. Engines stood by for a 3-minute change at Carlisle and Perth. On 31 July it reached Aberdeen 61 minutes before the scheduled arrival time of 7 a.m. It was not until 19 August that the East Coast train was first to Kinnaber Junction, by a whisker. But on 21 August, it reached Aberdeen at 4.40 a.m., with the Caledonian coming in 14½ minutes later. After that demonstration, the East Coast resumed working to the timetable, but the LNWR and Caledonian made one more run, the fastest of all, on the following night, doing the entire journey in 8 hours 32 minutes, at an average speed of 63.3 mph. These excitements and achievements were enthusiastically reported for the most part; the *Glasgow Herald* noted that the Euston-Aberdeen train had beaten the Empire State Express to be the fastest long distance train in the world, running 540 miles in 538 minutes. But of the run, behind locomotive No. 17 from Carlisle to Perth, "it would be incorrect to say that the motion was altogether pleasant", and there had been some really alarming lurches[57].

Dramatic and exciting as they were to the participants, it is now accepted that the 'Races to the North' of 1895 were of no real importance in the development of train working. Their record-breaking runs were only possible with lightweight trains and official backing both to ignore the timetable and to provide a clear line. Passengers might have preferred to leave London later than 8 p.m. and not seek vainly for early morning amenities at Aberdeen Joint Station.

The CR's published tabulation of "the Record Railway Run of the Century"

CALEDONIAN RAILWAY.

Five Hundred and Forty-One Miles in 512 Minutes constitutes the Record Railway Run of the Century in this Country. This was accomplished on night of August 22nd, 1895, when the West Coast Tourist Express ran from Euston to Aberdeen in 8 Hours 32 Minutes, as under:—

STATIONS.		Distance from London.	Booked Time.	Actual Time.	Minutes Early.	Intermediate Distances.		Time Running.	Speed Per Hour.		REMARKS.
		Miles.	P.M.	P.M.		Miles	Chains	Minutes	Miles	Chains	
London (Euston),	depart	...	8 0	8 0	...	138	...	147	64	39	
Crewe,	arrive	158	...	10 27	...	138	...	147	64	39	} Station duties
	depart	..	10 46	10 30	16	...	...	...	...	..	
Preston,	pass	209	11 34	11 16	22	51	...	46	66	42	
Shap Summit,	,,	268	A.M.	A.M.	32	59	...	51	65	44	
Penrith,	,,	281¼			35	13¼	...	11	72	22	
Carlisle,	arrive	299¼	1 15	12 36	39	18	...	15	72	0	Average speed per hour 65 60
Carlisle,	depart	299¼	1 18	12 38	40	..	...	..	...	..	Station duties
Lockerbie,	pass	325	1 44	1 5	39	25	63	27	57	24	
Beattock,	,,	339	1 58	1 17½	40½	13	75	12¼	66	72	
Summit,	,,	349	..	1 31	...	10	1	13¼	44	40	
Symington,	,,	366¼	2 43	1 46	41	17	10	15	68	40	
Carstairs,	,,	372¾	2 54	1 52	42	6	53	6	66	50	
Holytown,	,,	389	3 10	2 7½	42½	16	27	15½	63	19	
Greenhill,	,,	405½	3 7	2 11½	43½	16	23	16	61	6	
Stirling,	,,	417	3 21	2 14½	46½	11	48	11	63	22	
Perth,	arrive	450	3 55	3 7½	47½	33	2	33	60	4	} Station duties.
	depart	...	3 58	3 9½	48½	..	...	...	...	..	
Forfar,	pass	482¼	4 55	3 39	52	32	40	29¼	66	8	
Kinnaber Junction,	,,	501¾	4 57	3 47	54	19	25	18	64	30	
Stonehaven,	,,	523¾	...	4 6½	...	21	68	19½	67	18	
Ticket Platform,	arrive	.	..	4 30	..	..	...	...	...	...	} Collecting Tickets.
	depart	540	5 33	4 31	62	16	12	13½	71	62	
Aberdeen,	arrive	.	5 35	4 32	63	...	...	...	...	...	Average speed per hour 62 69

L & N.-W Engine "Adriatic" from London to Crewe.

     ,,   ,,   "Hardwicke" from Crewe to Carlisle.

C R. Engine No. 90 from Carlisle to Perth, A. Crooks, driver.

     ,,   ,,   17 from Perth to Aberdeen, John Soutar, driver

Driver John Soutar applies a little oil to a glistening No. 17. A CR publicity picture, taken at Dundee some time after the record run of 22-23 August 1895.

There was no resulting increase in traffic. In fact at least one train had only a single passenger; another reached Aberdeen with none at all[58]. If the Caledonian had been seriously interested in operating long distance non-stop expresses, it could have installed water-troughs at two or three points between Carlisle and Aberdeen (as was later done by the LMS). But there was a certain glow of prestige, with both groups able to claim unprecedented records for such a distance. There was never a 'Race to the South', but the Caledonian timetable from 1 July 1895 offered an improved overnight service, leaving Aberdeen at 7.05 p.m., Edinburgh at 10.40, Glasgow at 10.20; and arriving at Euston at 8 a.m.[59]. The reality of the shorter East Coast route had to be accepted. In the timekeeping truce which followed the racing phase, the West Coast had to concede an advantage of 35 minutes to the rivals. Modernisation and improvement of the coaching stock had nothing to do with the races. By 1896 all the company's passenger vehicles had been fitted with Westinghouse automatic air brakes, and 367 locomotives had brake pumps. And the race publicity prompted grumbles from other parts of the system. Querulous correspondents wrote to the press about the dismal service from Larkhall, and the slow-down of Moffat-Glasgow trains: the 'express' in summer 1895 took two hours and ten minutes, if on time, whereas the journey used to take "under two hours"[60]. Not that the Caley was slower on all routes: *Bradshaw's Guide* in 1896 noted Britain's first-ever start-to-stop timing of a train at 60 mph. This was from Perth to Forfar, 32 ½ miles in 32 minutes. An improbable anecdotal tale relates that Kempt, as general superintendent, put on this schedule without consulting McIntosh, whose response was "Och aye, juist like that beggar Kempt! Aye, weel, we'll have tae do it somehow"[61].

On 22 June 1895 the CR acquired the English side of the Solway Junction Railway, despite opposition from the NBR, GSWR and Maryport & Carlisle Railway companies. By that time the iron ore traffic was diminishing as the Cumbrian deposits in their turn were becoming worked out. It was an expensive line to operate because of the maintenance cost of the long viaduct. The Caledonian, which held £122,500 of the Solway Junction Railway's capital, totalling £467,153, was to pay a perpetual annuity of £4,500 to the company[62].

For ten years from 1895, Broughton on the Symington-Peebles line was a junction, for a railway built up the Tweed valley to serve the construction of a dam for Edinburgh's new reservoir at Talla. A public passenger service was operated, but on the completion of the works in September 1905, the line was closed, despite local protests[63]. Another rural line opened between Brechin and Edzell in March 1896; its six miles cost £37,000. A boost

**Glasgow Cross Station on the Glasgow Central Railway, opened on 1 November 1895.
The statue of King William II, erected in 1735, was later moved to Cathedral Square.**

to the tourist trade was hoped for and "many hotels" were anticipated in Edzell[64]. But the advent of the railway did not increase the population of the village, which fell from around 950 in the mid-1890s to under 900 by 1905. Another tunnel section of the Glasgow Central line was opened on 1 November 1895, between Glasgow Cross and a new junction station named Dalmarnock, on the site of the former Bridgeton Station between London Road and Rutherglen. The 'Bridgeton' name was now applied to the intermediate station of Bridgeton Cross. London Road ceased to be a passenger station when the Glasgow Central line trains began to run to Rutherglen.

Between 1890 and 1895 a contract for the acceleration of mail was reached with the Postmaster General, intended to last until 1900, and amending previous contracts of 1887 and 1873. Clause 2 (i) provided that on the 3.28 a.m. Carlisle-Aberdeen train, "The Company shall provide Special Trains consisting of not more than 7 Post Office tenders or Sorting Carriages and 2 Guards' Brake Vans and no other vehicles except 4 passenger vehicles from Stirling to Aberdeen on weekdays and any number of vehicles the Company may think proper from Motherwell to Aberdeen on Sundays." The train was due in Aberdeen at 9.00 a.m. Similar arrangements were made for mail south from Aberdeen, on the 3.40 p.m. (weekdays) and 1.10 p.m. (Sundays). Sorting carriages also ran from Motherwell to Glasgow and between Carstairs, Glasgow, and Edinburgh. Many other trains carried mailbags, in the charge of the company's guards; Glasgow and Edinburgh to Stirling, Glasgow to Greenock, Perth to Dundee, Crieff Junction to Crieff, Forfar to Kirriemuir, Guthrie Junction to Arbroath, Bridge of Dun to Brechin, and Dubton Junction to Montrose, are all specifically noted in 1895. In 1900 the Post Office paid £211,000 to the Scottish railway companies, with the Caledonian receiving £68,000[65].

Speculative Schemes, and Others

At this time, the Caledonian was also looking speculatively at the country to the south, in mid- and west Lanarkshire. Coal mining was already established but further expansion was anticipated. It was not easy country for railway building, hilly and threaded by rivers, but the GSWR was also known to be interested in exploiting it. The Glasgow & South Western line from Kilmarnock to Darvel pointed straight at the region and could readily be extended. The Caledonian obtained a Mid-Lanarkshire Extension Lines Act in 1896, for new lines around Stonehouse, Strathaven and Muirkirk. Considerable shoulder-heaving was going on with the GSWR, in efforts to open up more territory for coal mining, but also an independent company was projected in 1895-96 to build a Muirkirk, Mauchline and Dalmellington Railway, which tried to keep open the option of being worked by either of the established companies, although both opposed it[66]. The Caledonian had put in a counter-proposal for its own line from Muirkirk to Sorn, three miles short of Mauchline[67]. Parliamentary approval was given to a revised Muirkirk, Mauchline and Dalmellington Railway Bill in 1896, but neither this nor the Caledonian's Sorn line was built. But the Caledonian did build a new mineral line from a junction at Auldhouseburn, just east of Muirkirk, in 1896, climbing up to meet the 'Glenbuck line' at a point between Spireslack and Galawhistle. For a coal railway, it required three substantial viaducts, at Glenbuck, Ponesk and Crossflats[68], built with iron girders on stone piers. From Muirkirk it ran for a couple of miles close to a tramway laid by the Baird company to their own pits, but it was intended to serve collieries owned by the rival Cairntable Gas Coal Company. Giving evidence to the parliamentary select committee on the Mauchline and Dalmellington line, William Patrick, assistant general manager of the Caledonian, claimed the purpose of this line was to link the Coalburn coalfield more closely with the Glasgow & South Western system[69]. It gave the Caledonian an alternative route between Muirkirk and the four-way junction at Alton Heights, but the Muirkirk-Spireslack section was never put into use.

In vastly more urban surroundings, the Lanarkshire & Dumbartonshire's Clydeside line opened on 1 May 1896. West of Stobcross it diverged from the Glasgow Central Railway in a finely-engineered underground junction, crossing the Kelvin at Partick and the North British line to Whiteinch at Victoria Park (Scotstoun from 1900) and on to Clydebank. Completion to a junction with the North British at Dumbarton, where a new joint station to serve both companies was being built, followed on 15 June. The Lanarkshire & Dumbartonshire also opened from Maryhill Central, via Kelvinside and Crow Road, to a triangular junction at Partick, on 1 May. Passenger services came later. Maryhill had passenger trains from 10 August 1896, Possil Station opened for workmen's trains on 1 February 1897 and for the general public on 1 October[70]. On the same day the Caledonian began a passenger service from Dawsholm, on a branch from the Lanarkshire & Dumbartonshire Railway line at Bellshaugh, up beside the Kelvin to Glasgow Corporation's huge Dawsholm and Temple Gasworks[71], serving also a paper factory and a chemical works. Perhaps the company was hoping for the same success as the NBR branch to Hyndland, not far away, which had opened in 1874; but the Dawsholm branch passenger trains lasted only until 1908. Dawsholm also had a locomotive shed, opened on 10 August 1896, of six tracks plus two repair roads, to serve the new lines. Glasgow at the turn of the century was a vibrant centre of architecture, fine art, and arts and crafts, and the new Lanarkshire & Dumbartonshire stations reflected this in a range of eclectic and usually striking designs. Kelvinside's building, by J.J. Burnet, with its balcony, frieze and curved pediment, could have been a stately home rather than a railway station. The Glasgow Central Railway did likewise, with its little Kremlin-style station at Botanic Gardens particularly admired.

The now-demolished Botanic Gardens Station, Glasgow, opened on 10 August 1896.

Continuation of the Lanarkshire & Dumbartonshire line beyond Dumbarton to Aber Bay (near Ross Priory) on Loch Lomond had been proposed in 1891, following an earlier attempt to promote a rival line to the Caledonian (no relation) & Dumbartonshire Railway's line to Balloch, but common sense prevailed over the idea of two competing railways in the Leven Valley. Instead, the Caledonian & Dumbartonshire line between Dalreoch and Balloch Pier, now part of the North British system, was put under the management of a joint North British, Caledonian and Lanarkshire & Dumbartonshire committee from 1 October 1896 (as provided by an Act of 27 June 1892). The NBR's four Loch Lomond steamships were also now jointly managed. Despite having more than four years to prepare, the arrangement was not without its stresses, especially in the early days. Hamilton Ellis related that "Each company ran a fast morning business train to Glasgow, and officially they left Balloch at the same time. As this, of course, was physically impossible on a single up road, the two companies had a gentleman's agreement that each should start its train first on alternate weeks"[72]. Between Dumbarton and Glasgow traffic – both freight and passenger – was so heavy that both the Lanarkshire & Dumbartonshire and the North British lines were intensively used. But despite its best efforts, the Caledonian got no freight traffic from the huge Singer factory at Clydebank; the NBR had cannily made a thirling agreement with the management that would not expire until 1907[73]. On 10 August 1896 the central section of the Glasgow Central Railway was opened, including the new Central Low Level station, with two island platforms. More than 260 passenger trains a day passed through, and the new cross-city route was heavily used despite the soot and smoke which became a permanent feature. Suggestions, even pleas, for electrification were soon being made, but this formed no part of the Caledonian's plans. Already an eastern extension of the Glasgow Central line was being built, diverging at Bridgeton Cross, and passing beneath the 'Switchback' line in a tunnel as far as Parkhead, from where it ran above ground, with a station at Tollcross, to Carmyle, where it intersected the Coatbridge line, and on to Newton, to meet the lines from Carlisle, Hamilton and Edinburgh (completed 1 February 1897). Newton, by this time a busy four-way junction station, had opened in November 1852, been resited in December 1873, and would be rebuilt again, the job completed by 23 January 1901.

Now both the Caledonian and North British Railways had lines which encircled Glasgow north of the Clyde and to a great extent duplicated each other's services. None of the established railway companies attempted a Clyde crossing west of the Caledonian's bridge into Glasgow Central, and it was the deep-tunnelled 4 ft gauge cable-worked line of the Glasgow District Subway Co. which provided an inner-circle passenger route linking both sides of the river, from 4 December 1896. The Caledonian's half-yearly report in March 1897, though it declared a 5% dividend, also noted that one effect of the Central Railway was a drop in passenger receipts per mile, from 40.85d. to 39.11d., caused by the combination of shorter journeys and the low fares charged. Passenger receipts were up by £25,474 to £684,289, but the number of passenger train miles had risen by 453,119 to 4,362,307. In June the general manager, James Thompson, was the first Scottish railwayman to be knighted, and the new Sir James received illuminated addresses and gifts from the company staff. Though such tributes could often be forced through by one or two officious executives, Thompson, with his rather old-fashioned patriarchal style, seems to have been genuinely well-regarded by most of the Caledonian staff. Later in the year, when there was considerable agitation among the locomotive men, guards and shunters for shorter working days of ten or eight hours, depending on the job, Thompson gave the standard response, that any man with a grievance should go and see his departmental head. Though a mass meeting recorded its dissatisfaction, no further action was taken by the men[74]. At the end of the year, when railway companies were combining to resist the efforts of the Amalgamated Society of Railway Servants to get a nationwide wage and hours agreement, the Caledonian stood aloof, explaining loftily that "the most amicable relations existed at the present moment between the company and their employees"[75]. In the summer J.C. Bolton retired from the chairmanship, after 17 years, though he remained a director until his death in 1901, and James C. Bunten, an industrialist, partner in the Anderston Foundry company, took over. At his first half-yearly meeting as chairman, Bunten informed the shareholders of the inevitability of increased expenditure. Shorter hours meant taking on more men, and a bigger wage bill. The Workmen's Compensation Act, passed that year, was likely to cost money (better news for the workmen than for the shareholders). The prolonged national engineering strike of that autumn, though it did not involve the Caledonian's engineering workers, had reduced goods traffic for all railways and caused some lay-offs of staff. But there were encouraging signs: dividends were now coming through from the Lanarkshire & Ayrshire company; the £19,798 noted in the accounts as "dividends on shares held for the Company" was mostly from the Lanarkshire & Ayrshire. And the dividend was slightly up, at 5.25%. Locomotive capacity had to be increased at some key points: Stirling's 4-road depot shed was converted into a 'through' shed in 1896, and Motherwell's engine shed was enlarged in 1897 at a cost of £11,000.

Towards the Turn of the Century

Strategic plans for the Ayrshire coast are suggested by the Caledonian's purchase of Largs Pier, for £8,000, in November 1897. Plans had been made by various parties for a Largs-Wemyss Bay railway in 1865 and 1876[76]. Largs was served by the GSWR from Ardrossan but the terminal station was in the town. At this time the Wemyss Bay line was being widened to double track, and an extension down the coast to close the gap between Wemyss Bay and Largs seemed a natural next step. Some surprise was expressed that the GSWR had let the pier purchase happen[77], but nothing came of the extension scheme. No railway was to be built between Wemyss Bay and Largs.

By 1897 the Caledonian had been working the Crieff-Comrie line for four years and felt sufficiently confident to invest in a further westward extension, the Lochearnhead, St. Fillans and Comrie Railway, which would complete a direct cross-country link from Perth to the Callander & Oban line. The CR subscribed half its capital of £165,000 in £10 shares, with an option to take over the whole capital at par, within five years[78]. But in October 1897 the Crieff and Comrie company was in dire straits, partly due to a dispute with the contractors who had laid the line. To the evident relief of the shareholders, the "generous, just and kindly" Caledonian bought it out, agreeing to repay the capital of £45,000, to take over a £10,000 mortgage, and to settle the contractors' claim for £5,000[79]. The transaction was complete by 1 August 1898. Eight months later it was reported to the CR Board that the Lochearnhead, St. Fillans & Comrie had run out of money. The other half of the capital was nothing like fully subscribed. The promoters desperately hoped that the Caledonian would take over the whole enterprise, but the board was in no hurry to do this. Several other large and expensive projects were in hand. An Act for constructing a large new dock at Grangemouth had been passed in 1897 and the Caledonian obtained powers to raise £950,000 to fund this, along with six short mineral branches. The Lanarkshire & Ayrshire's new line between Giffen and Newton would need capital of £502,000, of which the Caledonian was to subscribe £152,000; for the Paisley & Barrhead District scheme £132,000 was earmarked, and the Glasgow & Renfrew District Railway, a joint venture with the GSWR, would require £142,000. Works at Oban and Ballachulish would take up £42,000[80].

The old harbour town of Bo'ness had been struggling to develop its port against the Caledonian's heavy investment in improving Grangemouth. An extension of the Slamannan Railway from Causewayend on the Union Canal, back in 1846, had linked it to the rail system, but despite some improvements to the port, its fortunes had languished. In 1895 the town and the North British Railway agreed that the NBR would take over

Work in progress at Grangemouth, 1905. The swing bridge is at the inner end of the new Western Channel, over the entrance to Carron Dock. River Carron is on the left.

the harbour, but the Caledonian raised objections unless it had running powers into Bo'ness just as the NBR had for Grangemouth. The NBR then dropped its proposal and the Caledonian obtained an Act in 1898 giving it running powers into Bo'ness. For a few months it operated trains to Bo'ness but the whole exercise was little more than routine muscle-flexing, and its Glasgow-Bo'ness passenger service was withdrawn at the end of June. There really was no reason for the CR, already planning for further substantial expansion at Grangemouth, to spend either money or management time on Bo'ness; and eventually it left the North British in sole possession. Among the more unusual workings of 1898 – and a reminder of the railways' continuing virtual monopoly of travel between cities, with canals the only competition – was the conveyance of Barnum & Bailey's Circus from Leeds to Glasgow, in June. Five trains were needed, one of them incorporating three 'elephant cars'[81].

From its days of working the Montrose & Bervie Railway, between 1866 and 1881, the Caledonian had retained running powers on the branch. Now, in August 1897, in a renewal of rivalries with the North British who were running trains to Brechin, it began to exercise the powers, providing an alternative goods and passenger service from its own station in Montrose. When it withdrew all services at the end of September 1898, there were local protests, and the CR restored the goods trains from October until June 1899, when the goods service finally stopped. Twenty men were employed by the Caley on the line, but most seem to have been transferred to other places on the system[82]. Further north, the company's plans (in association with the Great North of Scotland Railway) to rebuild and enlarge the Joint Station at Aberdeen encountered objections from the town council and the harbour board, who objected to the Caledonian's plan to load fish from the passenger platform. Fish vans regularly went by passenger train and the CR did not want to engage in avoidable shunting and marshalling from a dedicated loading bank. Opposition to the Aberdeen Station Bill also came from the North Eastern and Great Northern Railways, who demanded free access, but this was dismissed and the Bill went ahead[83]. Also in 1899 George Graham, who had driven the very first Caledonian train, a prominent figure in the company for over 50 years, died (on 30 June, the day of his retirement), and his post as chief engineer was taken up by the 39-year old Donald Matheson, who had been in charge of engineering for the Central Low Level lines.

During the previous half-century, occasional peace agreements had punctuated the rivalry of the Caledonian and North British. In the 1890s, a more consistent sense of mutual interests became apparent, with successive agreements in 1892, 1896 and 1899. Both companies realised that external forces – government, customers, different and increasingly competitive transport technologies – were now more threatening than each was to the other, and that it would be desirable to stand together against them. From 1896 a Caledonian and North British Peace Agreement Committee was re-established, to review and resolve problems between the companies.

By the end of the century, Glagow's population exceeded three quarters of a million and was still mounting towards its million-plus peak of the 1920s. In 1899, 16,841,070 passenger journeys were made via the Central Station at High Level, and 6,415,936 through the Low Level platforms. By then Buchanan Street had five platforms, though one was used mostly for milk traffic. The goods station had grown vastly and was handling around a million tons a year[84]. Around 100 workmen's trains were operated by the Caledonian every working day. Glasgow was unusual in that the flow of workers was out of the city and back in again, and "the Caledonian was most active in the provision of cheap services … with 8,000 passengers paying between 2d. and 7d. a day"[85] for transport in wooden-seated, unlit and unheated four-wheel carriages.

CHAPTER 11. The Caledonian in the Twentieth Century (1) – 1900-1908

Industrial Nation

In 1900, around 15% of the workforce in Scotland was employed in heavy industry[1], with the proportion a great deal higher in the Lanarkshire and Stirlingshire areas. Advances in technology and the increasing diversification of manufactured products had encouraged the development of steelworks and specialist metal producers. For railway companies, there still appeared to be substantial opportunities. As industry became more complex and interdependent, more machine parts were moved from site to site, by railway, for completion. And basic freight traffic was still rising. Coal output in Scotland rose from 10,300,00 tons in 1859 to 28,792,700 tons in 1895[2]. In the latter year, 1,048,774 tons of pig iron were smelted in Scotland, from 2,331,664 tons of ore and 1,971,731 tons of coal[3]. Confident forecasts were made about coal reserves; even a conservative expert put the figure at 7,807,640,000 tons in 1897. Yet there were warning signals, for those who cared to look for them. The most accessible and richest seams were already close to being worked out. Lesmahagow's gas or cannel coal was almost gone. The Ayrshire field was also largely exhausted. Much of the estimated reserves lay in deep and narrow seams, often in areas of disturbed geology which would make them difficult and expensive to work. Other parts of the world were beginning to export high-grade coal at low prices, and Clyde-built tramp steamers, looking for inward-bound cargoes, offered cheap bulk transport. In central Scotland, the railways and the coal industry were locked in interdependency. While it might be supposed that railway extension might wait on the confirmation of workable coal seams, this does not seem to have always been the case: "Frequently the possibility of a railway being constructed led to a geological survey of the district involved"[4]. Often the rail promoters were landowners, keen to maximise the value of their acres of heather and tussocky grass, like Mr. Somervell of Sorn who had hoped to play off the GSWR against the Caledonian in order to get the Mauchline & Muirkirk Railway over his ground[5]. Generally, confidence in the industrial future remained high. The iron and steel industry had survived the depletion of Scottish ore reserves not only by turning to Cumberland. In 1879, 42,471 tons of foreign ore had been imported; by 1899 it had risen to 1,403,899 tons, the great bulk of it from Spain. The steel plants at Hallside, Blochairn, Wishaw and Glengarnock were as modern as any in the world. In 1900, 115 open-hearth furnaces in Scotland produced 960,581 tons of acid steel and 2,764 tons of basic steel. Around Coatbridge and Motherwell, ironworks smelted 325,000 tons of malleable iron a year[6]. Heavy industry and mining did not have the permanence of location that cities and harbours had – many of the older plants had been closed and dismantled, their rail sidings taken up for scrap or re-laying elsewhere. It was their overall presence in the landscape and the economy that counted as permanent – and still expanding. A railway built to serve a major industrial site or mining district would not be expected to last beyond the productive period, but by then it should have repaid its capital cost many times over. It was against this background, and with such considerations in mind, that the Caledonian made its plans for future operations. As ever, the company was striving to maintain a balance among conflicting demands and requirements: the need to pay a reasonable dividend to the

No. 100 Newmains Station

**Newmains Station looking south. It opened for passenger services on 15 May 1867.
The line curving up and off to the right, with one signal post serving for both directions,
is presumably a connection to Coltness Ironworks, but is not shown on any O.S. map.**

shareholders, to maintain the track, stations, locomotives and rolling stock, to keep the network up to date with new lines where it appeared necessary, to provide a service that broadly satisfied the customers and encouraged use of the railway, and to polish up its own image of Scotland's premier railway. Not every announced intention resulted in action, however. On 14 February 1899 a special shareholders' meeting endorsed the board's proposal to support the 'Douglas & Sanquhar Railway', sixteen miles across the empty moors, with a further nine miles from Douglas to link it to the Muirkirk-Lesmahagow line at Coalburn. The CR was to subscribe £200,000 – two thirds of the capital – and work the line, which was expected to open up "important new coal fields"[7]. The project never became a reality. Nevertheless, huge sums were being spent, not only in building new lines: in four years between January 1895 and 1899, the company had charged 192 locomotives to the capital account: a total of £442,466. From 1899, this stopped, and for six years new locomotives would be charged to revenue[8].

New Kinds of Competition

Around the turn of the century deaths and retirements brought considerable change at the top level of management. Sir James Thompson retired as general manager at the end of 1899 and almost immediately afterwards was appointed a director. His deputy William Patrick succeeded him as general manager. The board in 1901 consisted of J.C. Bunten as chairman, Sir James King as his deputy, Hugh Brown (Glasgow), Lord Newlands (of the Hozier family), Walter J. Houldsworth (Coltness), Sir James Thompson, Lord Breadalbane, Charles Bine Renshaw, Sir R. Jardine of Castlemilk, Lockerbie, J.C. Bolton, James Neilson of Bellshill, Edward Cox, and the Hon. G.R.Vernon of Auchans, Kilmarnock. Bunten died in 1901 (as did Bolton) and the company acquired a new chairman in Sir James Thompson, its one-time junior clerk. It was not unknown for a distinguished official to be invited to join a company board, but to so rapidly assume the chairmanship of a major railway was unprecedented. The Caledonian directors were mostly industrialists or businessmen, and most had close connections with Glasgow. Cox was a Dundee jute millionaire. Several were or had been members of Parliament. Vernon, Liberal-Unionist M.P. for Southern Ayrshire 1886-1892, served on the select committee which investigated the 1890-91 railway strike. Bolton was Liberal M.P. for Stirlingshire from 1880 to 1892, and Renshaw was Conservative member for West Renfrewshire 1892-1906. Throughout the company's history, some Board members had also been associated with major customers, and at shareholders' meetings in the 1900s, the chairman more than once had to insist that their interests as customers did not conflict with their roles as directors, especially in the matter of goods charges. Also in 1901, William Patrick died and Robert Millar, who had joined the company in 1873 as a goods clerk, now traffic agent in Northern Ireland was appointed interim General Manager and confirmed in the role in 1902. Another significant new appointment came in 1902 when Irvine Kempt retired. One of the company's elder statesmen, always a courtly figure, he was presented by the Railway Clearing House Conference of Superintendents, which he had chaired in 1886 and 1900, with a service of silver plate; and yet more silver plate in Glasgow at "an influential public meeting" plus a cheque for £500 (the old edict against testimonials appears to have been overlooked). His son, with the same name, was a senior manager at St. Rollox Works. His successor as Superintendent was a young manager recruited from the LNWR, Guy Calthrop, who "considerably shook up the Caledonian, on English lines" with particular emphasis on punctuality[9].

By 1900 the motor car was well-established, but primarily as a rich man's machine and used very largely for short distance travel. Roads between even the major towns were often in a very poor state. The railways were indirectly responsible for this, since traffic which might have gone by road went more swiftly and efficiently by rail. But of course the railways' own existence had been responsible for a huge rise in transportation of people and goods, in line with the growth and diversification of industrial output and commercial business. This cannot be said to have been stolen from the roads. People still looked to the railway as the prime carrier, and the few villages that had no rail service were anxious to be linked in. The Caledonian was still willing to construct or support lines in districts which had no railway and where the only competition remained the horse and cart. Some were branches, others linked up points in the 'system', like the line which opened on 1 October 1901 from Wishaw South Junction past Cambusnethan to Newmains, which had had a station since 1867 on the Cleland-Morningside line (the Wishaw Central-Newmains passenger service lasted only until October 1909, a few months after the Lanarkshire Tramway began their service to Cambusnethan and Newmains on 29 June 1909)[10].

Cambusnethan Station, on the connecting line laid in 1901 between Wishaw South and Newmains Junctions. Freight was by far the main traffic, and the passenger station here closed in 1916. The Coltness Ironworks rear up massively in the background.

Glasgow suburban: Maryhill Central shortly after opening in 1896. It was a terminus for trains to Rutherglen either via Partick and the Glasgow Central Railway, or via Possil. Mineral traffic from the Lanarkshire collieries is represented by the train in the centre. (Caledonian Railway Association)

By now the pickings to be obtained from such extensions were relatively slim, but other factors also influenced the board's discussions and decisions. With the merger proposals of former years abandoned, the always-latent spirit of competition prompted new building in the hope of gaining a share in existing heavy traffic. Such duplication of service was encouraged by town councils and chambers of commerce, which hoped to see more train services run at a cheaper rate as a result. Most of the Caledonian's new lines fell into this category, and most, viewed in a wider context than the interests of the CR, were unnecessary. John Thomas, referring to the Lanarkshire & Dumbartonshire's great loop round the north of Glasgow, suggests "That the Caledonian facilities duplicated most of those already provided by the North British scarcely mattered; there was traffic enough for both"[11], and the extent of siding capacity provided at points like Maryhill and Dawsholm bears this out; but the traffic could have been coped with by enlarging the North British depots and yards, at far less cost. But that would not have benefited the Caledonian company, whose business was to maximise its own revenues and dividends, not to be concerned with wider economic issues. Relations between the two biggest Scottish railways continued to be a blend of aggressive competition and attempts at market-sharing and rate-fixing. The same was true between the Caledonian and the Glasgow & South Western.

Lower-than-anticipated earnings by the Cathcart Circle line, due to competition from the widening tramcar network (Glasgow's tram fares were the cheapest in Britain), should have signalled a warning to operators of urban railway systems. But it did not deter the Caledonian from embracing the Paisley & Barrhead District Railway. These towns were only three miles apart and both already well-connected to Glasgow. The Paisley & Barrhead District , though locally sponsored, was a Caledonian project from the first. While the line was seen as a useful north-south link on the west side of Glasgow, the Caley was certainly not uninfluenced by the fact that the GSWR was concurrently extending its Paisley West to Potterhill line towards a new Barrhead Central terminus. During the parliamentary inquiry on the Paisley & Barrhead District Bill, the representative of the GSWR observed that, "There is a smack of the Caledonian Railway about the line"; and in fact the CR had agreed to subscribe £132,000 of the £188,000 capital required[12]. Powers were duly obtained on 8 August 1897 to build one railway round the west of Paisley from St. James Station on the Greenock line, and another, from Arkleston on the joint line to Gilmour Street, down the east side of the town. These were to meet at Blackbyres Junction, Barrhead, with a new station in that town, and continue to join the new Lanarkshire & Ayrshire line at an eastwards-facing junction at Lyon Cross. Substantial stone-arched viaducts were needed both north and south of Barrhead. In all it amounted to 12 ³/₄ miles of line. Charles Forman was the engineer, and building began in

Connel Bridge under construction, 1902-03.

The never-opened 'classical-modern' style Barrhead (New) Station, built in 1905.

August 1898. The Caledonian Railway invested a further £80,000 in the Paisley & Barrhead District company in 1900[13], and took it over completely in 1902, while construction was still in progress. The Glasgow & South Western's Barrhead Central opened on 1 October 1902. With the CR's Barrhead (New) and South, the town, with some 9,000 inhabitants, would have four railway stations. Also concurrently, the Paisley tram system was being extended. In May 1905 the Caledonian and GSWR both raised objections to the proposed tram-line to Barrhead; Robert Millar, the CR's General Manager, stated to the inquiry that the Caledonian's new station was to open on 1 June and that the Caledonian, which "made a feature of workmen's trains", had expended £720,000 on the Paisley district lines. All was in vain. Having drastically reduced its traffic forecast, the Caledonian abandoned the plan for a passenger service, and its ready-built Barrhead (New) Station remained unused[14]. The western section was opened in 1905 and the eastern arm was never completed to Arkleston, stopping short at a goods depot named Paisley East (opened 1906). Goods services, primarily coal, kept the line in operation.

A new line to Renfrew was more successful, however. Renfrew had appeared early on the railway map, with the 4ft 6in gauge Paisley & Renfrew Railway of 1837 (later part of the GSWR), running to Renfrew Wharf with a ferry connection to Yoker. This gave it a somewhat roundabout route from Glasgow and even while the CR and GSWR were vying for Barrhead, they collaborated in supporting the proposed Glasgow & Renfrew District Railway, with a capital of £210,000 plus borrowing powers of £70,000. Authorised in 1897, this was absorbed in 1901 as a branch of the Glasgow-Paisley Joint line, from Cardonald, following the south bank of the Clyde, crossing above the old Paisley & Renfrew line and turning south to run parallel with it to terminate at Porterfield. The two companies shared the building cost of £134,000, and the line opened on 1 June 1903. Until 1907 its passenger trains were operated alternately by each of the owning companies for six months at a time; after that they were worked by the GSWR only[15]. Another important development on the south bank of the Clyde was the very large Prince's Dock, completed by the Clyde Navigation Trust in 1900, just across from Queen's Dock, and well-equipped in its day for bulk handling. A jointly owned access branch from near Ibrox on the Glasgow & Paisley Joint line allowed the Caledonian, NBR and GSWR all to share in the Prince's Dock traffic. During 1902-3 Rutherglen Station was reconstructed on the triangular layout, with joined platforms on each arm, twelve in all[16].

A Tunnel to Ireland? And a Transatlantic Trip

Glasgow, one of the world's handful of engineering metropolises, was host to the International Engineering Congress in 1901. Among the events laid on for delegates was a visit to the Caledonian Works at St. Rollox, and the company produced a souvenir brochure. It was rich in statistics. The works employed 3,130 men and boys, and covered 24 acres, of which 13 were roofed over. In a year, 52 locomotives, 104 carriages and 3,000 wagons could be built on the site. The company's overall statistics were impressive. In 1901 the staff numbered over 21,000. It owned 902 locomotives, 287 first class carriages, 1,205 thirds, 304 composite and saloon carriages, five Post Office vans, 116 horse boxes, 41 carriage trucks, 93 fish and milk vans, 207 luggage vans, and one prison van. For goods traffic it had 14,644 open trucks, 1,459 covered vans, 857 cattle and sheep trucks, 523 brake vans, 1,853 swivel wagons, 43,542 mineral wagons, 11 gunpowder vans, and 13 tank wagons. In addition it had nine travelling cranes and 245 ballast wagons. In 1900 it ran a total train mileage of 16,857,547. Passenger numbers (excluding season ticket holders) were, first class, 2,219,215; third class, 42,084,022. Its associate, the Caledonian Steam Packet Company, owned ten paddle steamers, with a combined capacity for 10,994 passengers.

One of the papers presented at the congress touched on a project that had first been proposed to the Caledonian (and ignored) in 1886[17]. This was "the Tunnel between Great Britain and Ireland", a scheme under serious discussion at the turn of the century. From Stranraer a line would run five miles north west to Ebbstone Beacon, then dive beneath the sea to emerge at Island Magee and link with the Belfast & Northern Counties Railway. Electric motors at each end would provide traction through the tunnel. Not technical considerations, but the difficulties of funding, ensured it remained as a paper scheme only.

A passenger service began over Lord Dalhousie's old branch from Elliot Junction to Carmyllie on 1 February 1900, under the terms of the Light Railway Act of 1896. On 1 October 1901 the central Perthshire line was extended west from Comrie to St. Fillans by the Comrie, St. Fillans and Lochearnhead Railway, its construction and route through an area of particular natural beauty and historic interest having been very carefully planned. The Caledonian, having already acquired the Crieff & Comrie company in 1898, and working the line for 50% of the gross revenue, absorbed the floundering Lochearnhead, St. Fillans & Comrie company on 1 August 1902. Away to the south, again using the provisions of the Light Railways Act, a line was opened from Elvanfoot, on the CR main line, to Leadhills in the bare fells above the headwaters of the Clyde, on 1 October 1901. Lead mining had been carried on here since medieval times, and the railway was intended, hopefully, to stimulate a revival of interest in the mineral deposits. It was the highest standard gauge railway in the British Isles, reaching 1,498 feet at its final terminus at Wanlockhead, 7 miles and 1,200 yards from Elvanfoot, opened on 12 October 1902. A revival of mining did not occur, nor did the hope, expressed by the promoters, that Leadhills might become a health resort[18], and the line maintained only a sparse service.

Having failed to take over the GSWR in 1890, the Caledonian with its associate, the Lanarkshire & Ayrshire, set about completing its own route from the Ayrshire coast to the Lanarkshire mines. An Act was obtained on 1 July 1897 for a 21-mile line between Giffen and Newton, situated at the heart of a railway-industrial complex south-east of Glasgow, with connections to the Hamilton and Motherwell lines. The purpose was in part to ease congestion on the joint Caledonian-GSWR Glasgow-Kilmarnock line, especially on the "notorious length between Neilston and Shilford summit"[19], climbing the valley of the Cowdon Burn towards Loch Libo. At the CR's half-yearly meeting on 18 September 1900, Bunten claimed the new line was necessary so that heavier trains could be moved with less power, but G.R. Vernon, a Caley director and chairman of the Lanarkshire & Ayrshire,

Leadhills Station opened on 1 October 1901, and was the highest in Scotland until the Wanlockhead extension was finished in 1902. 0-4-4T No. 171 is fitted with a cowcatcher to work the unfenced branch.

undermined him by agreeing with a questioner that it was absurd that the two railways should be within a stone's throw of each other, "but the Glasgow & South Western Company … declined to agree, and they were obliged to make a separate line"[20]. The Lanarkshire & Ayrshire did not have to pay tolls on its own track. From Giffen to Lugton the new line ran more or less parallel to the Beith branch. At Lugton it crossed above the Kilmarnock Joint line, and a connecting link was laid so that trains from Beith and Kilmarnock could run on to the Lanarkshire & Ayrshire track; and at Clarkston, a south-facing junction was made with the Busby Railway (this lasted only to 1907). On 1 April 1903 the Lanarkshire & Ayrshire opened for goods between Giffen and Cathcart West, and a passenger service from Glasgow Central to Ardrossan was operated from 1 May via Mount Florida and Cathcart West. Neilston now had two competing services to and from Glasgow Central, though the more frequent Kilmarnock trains did not lose much traffic to the new line. On 6 January 1904 the line was completed to Newton, forking at Kirkhill Junction to join the Caledonian's Glasgow Central line at Westburn Junction, and the south and east main lines at Newton, giving access to the Caley network. Unlike some earlier country lines, like the Hamilton & Strathaven, the Lanarkshire & Ayrshire intermediate stations, designed by James Miller, were quite commodious, with his typical care for detail and finish, built of red brick, with green slates, red tile ridges, wide eaves, timbered gables and elegant finials.

In March 1903 Donald Matheson, with J. Stoddart, the Carriage & Wagon Superintendent, joined a group of LNWR officials to visit the railways of the north-eastern USA and Canada. Matheson's subsequent report leaves no doubt that he had been greatly impressed, even though "Since returning from America, we have frequently been asked, in a kindly but rather incredulous tone of voice, if anything had been learned, and what advantage was gained". For him, it "marked an epoch" in his life[21]. Not only the scale of North American operations, but the modernity of their systems and the amount of investment going in, struck him profoundly. He looked at American practice with one eye back on the Caledonian, particularly in relation to electric traction and the operation of marshalling yards and coal docks. Considering electrification in three ways: underground working, suburban-interurban services, and new fast lines planned as electric from the start, he mused on what its effect would be on the lines to Leadhills, Ballachulish or Lochearnhead[22]. Having seen Baltimore's underground Belt Line (opened 1892) he speculated on how the Glasgow Central line might be, with electric locomotives for goods and "multiple-unit systems" for passenger services. At Cleveland Harbour he saw tower hoists lift bogie wagons of 17 tons tare, holding 45 tons of coal, and tip the load into a steamship's hold[23]. He saw new forms of signal working, electric and electro-pneumatic, admired the running of US Pullman cars: "… with a train of American railroad carriages on the best parts of the CR permanent way, the 'running' would 'lick creation;" learned that the Pennsylvania Railroad was capable of paying a 15% dividend but deliberately restricted it to 6%, the rest going to a reserve fund for extensions and improvements, treated as working expenses, and returns again to the comparison between Glasgow's tunnel lines, "smoky and dirty and damp, with everything dismal and dark" and US subway lines, "beautifully light and bright"[24]. His trip left the Caledonian's future general manager with visions of things to come, some of which came about while others did not: "One need not need the gift of prophecy to foretell … a half-hourly service of electric high-speed passenger trains between Glasgow and Edinburgh". He also took on board an American dictum: engineering is "the art of making a dollar earn the most interest." Little more was heard of electrification, though evidently Matheson did test the issue, since in 1923 the company's chairman told the shareholders that some years previously, electrification of the Central Underground and Cathcart Circle lines had been considered, and estimates obtained. "But the capital cost made us hesitate …"[25]. The Caledonian was not, after all, the Pennsylvania Railroad.

Still Developing the 'System'

The Callander & Oban company had once hoped to build a line from Oban to Inverness, without any help, but in more realistic mode it recruited the support of the Caledonian Railway for a branch from Connel Ferry to Ballachulish, which obtained its Act on 7 August 1896. The Caledonian agreed to contribute £150,000 of the total capital of £210,000. The line, 25 miles, five furlongs and 2 chains, incorporated two large viaducts, across Loch Etive and Loch Creran, and opened on 21 August 1903. The Loch Etive Bridge, a cantilever structure engineered by Sir John Wolfe Barry, was the largest single steel span in Britain at 542 feet. The Caledonian worked the trains, but the long dispute over pedestrian and motor usage of this bridge, which had a narrow roadway adjoining the railway, was the C&O company's affair. Slate quarrying at Ballachulish and the new hydro-electric powered aluminium factory at Kinlochleven, linked by boat with Ballachulish, promised an unusual amount of goods traffic for a branch in the West Highlands. Among improvements to existing lines, the CR completed double tracking of most of the Greenock-Wemyss Bay line in June 1903; work had been going on since 1899. Plans for a much-enlarged station at Wemyss Bay had been approved by the board in November 1897, and the Caledonian Railway (General Powers) Act of 9 August 1899 gave the go-ahead. The stations at Upper Greenock, Inverkip and Wemyss Bay were rebuilt. The new terminus was formed on a grand scale with five platforms (one a 'luggage platform') replacing the original

Connel Ferry Junction, around 1910. The station was enlarged for the Ballachulish branch, opened in 1903.

Country house architecture for a railway terminus: the new Wemyss Bay Station of 1903.

two, on an enlarged site, curving towards the pier. The village of Wemyss Bay itself did not generate much traffic, and the station was planned as a kind of valve through which passengers flowed from train to ship, and vice versa, though a purely decorative 'Italianate' clock tower rose above it as a landmark. From the platforms travellers entered a wide semi-circular glass-roofed concourse, from which a covered walkway led in a downwards-sloping curve to the pier. Much thought was put into the details of construction, and a great deal of the design's appeal comes from the sinuous curves of its general lines. Opening on 7 December 1903, the station was widely admired. For its main designers, Donald Matheson and his former Perth Academy schoolfellow James Miller, engineer and architect respectively, it was a triumph[26]. In all, the work put in on the Wemyss Bay branch between 1898 and December 1907 cost the Caledonian Company more than £267,000[27].

The example of the NBR's south Edinburgh circle line may have prompted the Caledonian to develop a "New Lines" plan for north Edinburgh. From a new junction west of Newhaven Station, on the Leith line, a branch was built across Leith, to Seafield, where it divided into a line to South Leith Dock and another to a station named South Leith. As usual in cross-city lines, substantial engineering works were needed, including a 15-arch viaduct between Halmyre Street and Easter Road. It opened to goods traffic on 1 August 1903 and was also intended to be a passenger line, with South Leith as the terminus. But, as in Barrhead, the passenger stations never opened[28]. A locomotive shed built at Seafield in 1902 was little used and closed for twelve years before being leased to the North British in 1916[29]. Further plans existed for a largely underground line across Edinburgh's centre, and were the subject of much discussion, but the combination of civic opposition, capital cost, and the improvement of Edinburgh's tram system, meant that these were never activated, and the Caledonian remained a peripheral presence on the west and north of the city. Ever since 1866 the company had planned for an Edinburgh hotel, and in December 1903 the Caledonian Hotel opened alongside Princes Street Station. A year before, the North British had opened its vast and palatial hotel rising above Waverley Station. Challenged as to the cost (£200,000) and value of the project by a shareholder at the half-yearly meeting on 18 September 1900, J.C. Bunten had replied that the company would have had no thought of going on with the hotel, "if their opponents, the North British Company, had not put up an hotel"[30] – a revealing indication of a still-competitive attitude. And in fact the Caledonian's hotels turned in a consistent profit to the company. The Caledonian Hotel was not so strikingly placed as the North British, but it was widely admired, though a modern architectural critic describes it as "built of machine-cut red sandstone shipped by train from Dumfries, arrived like an overblown baroque bookend to mark the West end of Princes Street"[31].

On 1 July 1904 the railway between St. Fillans and Lochearnhead was opened (18th for goods), and on 1 August a connecting line was opened between Kirkhill and Westburn Junction, south of Carmyle, providing a link, via the Glasgow Central line, between the Lanarkshire & Ayrshire and the Lanarkshire & Dumbartonshire railways. A short-lived railway ran from Coulter, on the Peebles line, up into the hills at Culter Waterhead, in connection with reservoir construction. Between 1903 and 1907 it provided a passenger service for schoolchildren and a few others[32]. On 1 May 1905 the line from Crieff and St. Fillans met the Callander & Oban and the new junction at Balquhidder came into operation. Its layout, joining in the Stirling direction, did not allow for west-east running. A small brick and wood locomotive shed was built and the junction was treated as the terminus of trains from Perth. By now the Lochearnhead, St. Fillans & Comrie company was fully integrated into the Caledonian, having been acquired in a bankrupt condition on 1 August 1902. Meanwhile the Caledonian had also been constructing lines in Lanarkshire in accordance with the Act obtained in 1896. On 1 May 1902 a line westwards from Strathaven Central to meet the GSWR's Kilmarnock-Darvel line was completed, and ground was purchased for a transfer yard at 'County Boundary', which was never set up[33]. The line's Act gave the Glasgow & South Western Railway the option of buying the Darvel-County Boundary Junction section, which it exercised in 1904. Strathaven Station was renamed Strathaven North on 4 July 1904, and resited alongside and below its original position, which became Flemington Goods Yard. This was in anticipation of the opening of Strathaven Central on 1 October, on the new line. The Hamilton & Strathaven line was joined to this new cross-country line by a short section from Whiteshawgate Junction, and the townscape was enhanced, or disfigured, by a series of girder viaducts carrying the converging lines at different levels. In 1905, the line was extended eastwards from

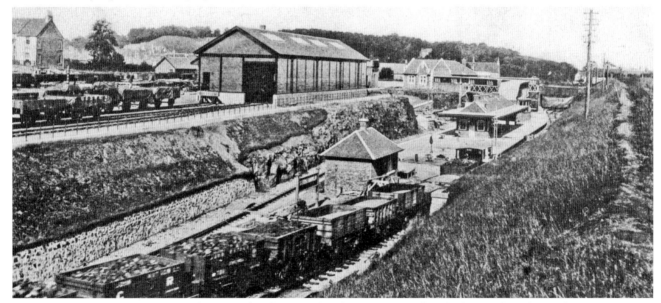

Strathaven Central, soon after its opening in 1905. A coal train is passing through.

The converging lines east of Strathaven Central: Pomillion viaducts (1905), the farther one on the
Meikle Earnock-Hamilton line, the nearer on the Stonehouse line.

Stonehouse Viaduct, over the River Avon, an 8-span steel truss bridge, 158 feet high, built 1904.

Strathaven to meet the former terminus at Cotcastle, near Stonehouse. Traffic requirements at the time hardly justified another Ayrshire-Lanarkshire railway link, and the origin of this line has been elucidated by David Stirling as a reaction (perhaps an over-reaction) to a proposal by the Duke of Portland to build an 'Avondale Railway' between Lesmahagow and Darvel, with the aim of getting traffic to his harbour at Troon. It was also proposed to join this line to the terminus of 'Baird's Railway', now owned by the North British, at Peacock Cross, Hamilton. This was the most grandiose of several proposed 'landowner's lines' at this time, and the suggestion of the NBR spearing through South Lanarkshire and into Ayrshire bounced the Caledonian and the GSWR into a territorial alliance. An agreement on 19 November 1895 had committed the Caledonian to build the Darvel-Cotcastle line and new lines from Blackwood to Stonehouse and from Stonehouse towards Motherwell, with running powers available to the GSWR[34], and reciprocal powers for the Caledonian to run trains between Darvel, Kilmarnock and Troon.

In connection with these developments, Stonehouse Station was transformed (completed 1 July 1905) with three through platforms and a bay. It was now positioned between two junctions, operative from 1 June: from Stonehouse West Junction the line ran to Blackwood, which ceased to be a branch terminus and acquired a through station, with the new line continuing past a new Lesmahagow Station to Alton Heights Junction. This rustic spot, where the Coalburn and Muirkirk lines diverged, was now a meeting point for four railways. The former Lesmahagow was renamed Brocketsbrae. From Stonehouse East Junction the new line continued north through a new Larkhall Central to meet the Coalburn line at Merryton Junction, two miles south of Ferniegair. At Stonehouse, an embankment was raised for a line to enable trains to run between Strathaven and Blackwood. Doubt has been expressed whether rails were laid on it, but the Ordnance Survey map of 1905 shows the triangle completed. By 1926, however, and probably long before, the western curve had been lifted[35]. The former Larkhall Station was renamed Larkhall East. Crossing undulating country and intersecting the winding River Avon, these lines required substantial engineering works. Between Stonehouse and Larkhall the Avon was crossed twice: at Stonehouse by a curving girder viaduct 450 yards long, of eight spans, and west of Larkhall by the variously named Morgan Glen, Millheugh, or Broomhill Viaduct, 170 feet above the river. These viaducts used 2,273 and 1,399 tons of steel respectively, produced by the Arrol steelworks at Dalmarnock. Contractor for the line was Adam Hall Boyle of Glasgow, who had done much work for the Caledonian and its associates. Despite the new lines, congestion was still a problem in some places, and Company Rule 149A allowed for two mineral trains to be worked as one, with the locomotive of the second coupled to the brake van of the first, "in clear weather when authorised"[36].

The branch terminus at Bankfoot, opened on 7 May 1906, with a mixed train at the platform.

Outer commuter lines like that to Wemyss Bay were proving more profitable than those traversing urban areas where electric tramcars now ran. In an initiative to compete, the Caledonian tried the experiment of "zone tickets" between Gourock and Port Glasgow in 1904. Unlimited travel was allowed between the stations for 1s. a week, third class, and 1s. 6d. first. But the scheme does not appear to have been extended. Trams were not a problem when on May 1 1906 the locally promoted Bankfoot Railway was opened from Strathord, south of Stanley, to Bankfoot, and worked by the Caledonian, which took over the company on 1 August 1909. A special session of the half-yearly meeting in September 1909 agreed to subscribe £4,620 for Bankfoot Railway shares[37]. Most of its trains ran to and from Perth.

The 'Grampian Corridor' and the New Central

On 6 April 1905 a 12-coach special train of new stock was hauled from Glasgow (Buchanan Street) to Aberdeen by the 4-6-0 locomotive No. 49, itself "the embodiment of Edwardian locomotive elegance". J.F. McIntosh was on the train and according to one account, he proposed the name 'Grampian' for the new service which was to begin on the 10th[38]. The 'Grampian' carriages ran on six-wheeled bogies. In the third class compartments, comfortable seating was provided for passengers sitting four abreast – the first such arrangement in Great Britain. First class passengers sat three abreast. All carriages were lit by electricity and steam-heated. The first carriages in British use to have hot water in the lavatories, at least while the heating was turned on, the CR's new rolling stock was among the most advanced in the world. The 'Grampian Corridor' left Buchanan Street at 10 a.m. and Princes Street at 9.25. The trains were combined at Perth. The return service left Aberdeen at 5.25 p.m. From 1906 it had dining cars from the West Coast Joint Stock, until the Caledonian's agreement with the Pullman Company in 1914. Newspaper ads claimed it as "The finest train in Scotland", though some shareholders complained about money wasted on unnecessary luxury[39]. Even on unglamorous extra services, the Caley could sometimes pull off a spectacular: "… on February 17, 1906, a football special ran from Coatbridge to Dundee, 77 2/3 miles, in 74 minutes. The load was of five bogies, about 140 tons, and the engine was McIntosh 4-4-0 No. 902 (driver Ranochan)"[40]. Ranochan was one of a group of Caledonian 'top-link' drivers imbued with the urge for speed, including James Currie, George Mackie, 'Cuddy' Mitchell, William Stavert, and William Todd, maintaining the style set by John Soutar on the Lambie 4-4-0 in 1895.

At the other end of the spectrum for passengers, the CR was accused of operating dirty, unlit, unheated workmen's trains. Speaking to a 1905 Commons Select Committee enquiring into workmen's trains, Robert Millar denied that the Caledonian's were dirty, overcrowded, and too expensive. Informing the committee that the CR kept 130 carriages for workmen's use, mostly oil-lit, made up into seven trains of 14-15 vehicles, with the others in reserve, he said they were swept out daily and washed out weekly or fortnightly "depending on the class of men who used them". Listing instances of smashed windows, severed window straps, and damaged furnishings, he turned the criticism on the passengers: "The company had good cause to complain of the way in which cars were treated. The damage was scarcely credible"[41].

Late in 1905 the company enlarged its Peebles Station, forming an island platform and installing a 60ft turntable and extra sidings, in anticipation of traffic to the Royal Highland Show, to be held there in 1906. On a much larger scale, between 1901 and 1906 a major rebuilding and extension programme was also going on at Glasgow Central Station. Piecemeal alterations had been made in the 1880s but now the whole project was systematically tackled. Bridge Street Station, rebuilt less than fifteen years earlier, was now to disappear (the office buildings remained) and its terminal tracks were extended across a second bridge over the Clyde, giving a total of thirteen access tracks, serving the same number of platforms. Donald Matheson supervised the engineering work and James Miller was responsible for the interior design. At last Glasgow had a really worthy Central, "the best-designed terminus in Britain", "the finest station in Great Britain, both from the passenger and the operating point of view"[42]. Matheson's 1903 visit to the USA, in which he visited many of the great stations, was not too late to have some impact on the design, which represented a triumph over the limitations of even the enlarged site, 14,000 square yards compared with 6,250 square yards in the previous station, though his American report shows he also knew, and rated very highly, the terminal stations of Paris. Matheson offered a practical reason for the curved and flowing lines of design: "In planning, the probability of crowding and the tendency of people to spread like flowing water and travel along the line of least resistance was kept in view. It was therefore thought desirable to have curved building lines and rounded corners …"[43]. The result was one of the most sophisticated station concourses of any city in the world. The hotel was extended, to Miller's plans, in 1907. One of the station's features by 1909 was a large illuminated screen, on to which images could be projected. When a display of political cartoons was mounted, however, protests were made, and the company ordered the display to be stopped. Unionism appear to have been the problem: the Irish confrontation was very much a live issue in Scotland, especially central Scotland.

Glasgow Central: the enlarged concourse after 1906, looking towards the Gordon Street entrance. Although the roof is part of the original 1879 building, the entire concourse area has been rebuilt and reconfigured, with the platforms re-numbered from the eastern side rather than from the west. The general layout of the station has altered little in the intervening 100-plus years. (Caledonian Railway Association)

The pier at Wemyss Bay after 1903, with Duchess of Rothesay berthing.

The summers of 1905 and 1906 marked the peak of the Clyde steamers and their railway services. The Caledonian Steam Packet Company was running eleven steamers on regular routes from Wemyss Bay, Ardrossan and Gourock, and excursions as far up the coast as Oban. From 1907, under pressure from shareholders, the degree of competition lessened. In 1909 the three railway companies introduced a "Clyde Coast Pool", along with some private steamer operators, based on their proportions of traffic in 1906-7. Co-operation went as far as allowing GSWR trains to run to Wemyss Bay[44]. From 1908 Sunday steamer services were introduced on some routes and became immediately popular. In the summer of 1909 Sunday excursions to Rothesay and Dunoon were introduced and well-patronised despite the pubs being shut[45].

On 10 October 1906, the new Grange Dock opened at Grangemouth, ten years after its authorisation by Parliament. Ships of 7,000 tons plus could use the new entrance lock, the harbour capacity was doubled, and the dock area had over 60 miles of sidings and running lines, apart from the Fouldubs marshalling yard. Eight hydraulic coal hoists could tip 32-ton wagonloads. That year the port handled 3,100,000 tons of cargo[46]. A quayside passenger platform was constructed in 1907 for occasional use, replacing platforms originally placed at the Carron Dock for use by passengers on Carron Line ships to London[47].

One of Scotland's worst railway accidents happened at Elliot Junction, on the Caledonian/North British Dundee & Arbroath Joint line, in the course of a blizzard on 28 December 1906. The North British 7.37 a.m. Edinburgh-Aberdeen express had been turned back at Arbroath because of snow blocks, and, with its engine running tender-first, passed a signal set at danger and crashed into a stationary Dundee & Arbroath local at the junction station. Twenty-two people died on the scene or shortly after. Public interest fastened on whether the NBR driver was drunk or not, but the shock caused the railways to look again at their arrangements for running in fog and snow[48].

Sir James King was elected chairman of the board in 1906 following Thompson's death; a banker by profession, he was described as a "lifelong conservative, but of the mild and hereditary sort"[49]. At the March 1907 half-yearly meeting, he declared that capital expenditure had been reduced to a minimum. Nevertheless, labour costs were bound to rise, with new legislation on working hours and overtime pay. Also, the company proposed to "abolish" 4,800 six and seven-ton mineral wagons for new ones of 16-ton capacity[50]. Dividend was 3.5%. The government-imposed ceiling on goods rates was having a mixed effect on the company. The Caledonian had always striven to provide a good dividend to its investors, and, conscious of the Scottish Railway Shareholders Association's beady eyes, was treating this as a priority. By later in the year, however, the board appeared to weary of Scottish Railway Shareholders Association nagging, and circulated a letter to shareholders deprecating interference by third parties in the company's affairs and asking for proxy votes at the half-yearly meeting. It duly assured itself of a massive majority against any Scottish Railway Shareholders Association amendments to its policies[51], though

Mr. Macdonald of the Scottish Railway Shareholders Association remained a vigilant watcher and commentator on the company's doings.

The Clyde Navigation Trust's continuing efforts to build up Glasgow's port facilities resulted in the opening of the huge Rothesay Dock at Clydebank on 25 April 1907. Capable of berthing sixteen 3,000 ton steamers at once, it was specifically intended for coal export, and much coal that would have been shipped via Ardrossan was diverted here, dealing a blow to the profitability of the recently-finished Lanarkshire & Ayrshire line as well as to Ardrossan Harbour. For the Caledonian company it was not wholly bad news, since to coincide with the opening, the Lanarkshire & Dumbartonshire Railway built a branch (much of it parallel to the NBR access line) from Scotstoun West, diving under its own main line at Yoker Ferry to reach the dockside marshalling yard.

The Glasgow Fair always placed exceptional demands on the city's railways, with many special trains and duplicate services, and a large number of the Caledonian's substantial fleet of 0-6-0 goods engines diverted to passenger working (many were classified as 'Passenger-Goods', fitted with Westinghouse automatic brake pumps, and painted blue). The *Railway Magazine* for July 1907 noted that on a Fair Thursday, the 10 p.m. northbound from Buchanan Street was run in three sections; the third, bound for Oban, being formed of 18 coaches, of which 15 were borrowed from the Great North of Scotland[52].

As the number of Labour members of Parliament grew, the Caledonian (not alone) found its actions under greater critical scrutiny in the House of Commons than ever before. When its Confirmation Bill, with a whole range of provisions, was considered by the House on 7 August 1907, one member pointed out that the company was seeking to alter its annual contribution to the superannuation fund of the clerks and officers, whose 3,200 members were compelled to pay contributions. In 1866 the company had agreed to match the members' payments; now it wanted to replace this arrangement with an unspecified annual contribution. There had been no consultation with the members, who not surprisingly assumed the contribution would be smaller than the previous payment. The Board of Trade took this up but sided with the company, leaving the clerks to protest[53]. Such Parliamentary discussions allowed members to bring up other considerations, and for almost two decades members protested sporadically about the CR's failure to provide sleeping accommodation for third class passengers between London and Scotland. The company's reply always was that third class sleepers would not pay.

The Rothesay Dock at Clydebank, opened in April 1907, with travelling cranes and loaded ore wagons.

Diamond Jubilee

Sixty years of the Caledonian were celebrated in a special edition of the *Railway Magazine* in September 1907. A series of articles described various aspects of the company's operations. The *Railway Magazine*'s attitude to the railway companies was deferential to cringing-point, and the survey reveals only unmitigated excellence in every respect. But there is much of interest to be found in the accounts of some departments. Company advertising was a responsibility of the head of the time table department, and by 1907 it was producing a stream of printed material, illustrated in colour. Apart from its own advertisement boards at stations, the company embarked on a nationwide use of hoardings for the 'Grampian Corridor Express' in 1905, and by 1907 congratulated itself that "there are no better known trains in the British Isles". Apart from large format posters, the company produced millions of bookmarks, some of them intended to help 'railwayacs' to calculate the speed of the Carlisle-Glasgow expresses, and a wide range of picture postcards, calendars, maps and other ephemera. Guide books were issued, including *Oban and the Land of the Gael, Homes and Haunts of Scott and Burns, and Holidays on the Scottish Fjords*, and distributed in North America as well as in Britain. The Caledonian was not alone among railways in discovering the arts of sales promotion – "Don't be content to share traffic with another, but create it – make business that does not exist" was its ad-men's motto – but its efforts, including the early use of illustrations in newspaper advertisements, were more assiduous and effective than most.

Giving an account of his domain, the Goods Manager, Matthew Waddell, noted that goods revenue for the year to 31 January 1907 was the largest ever at £2,675,535, split almost evenly between general goods and mineral traffic. By this time, apart from Buchanan Street (currently undergoing a massive extension), the Caledonian had ten other goods terminals in Glasgow. Marshalling yards for general goods were at St. Rollox, Robroyston, Polmadie, Carmyle, Mossend, Fouldubs, and Gorgie; and for minerals traffic at Ross Junction and Strathaven Junction. Robroyston and Ross by this time had very up-to-date hump-shunting, in which wagons ran by gravity into the appropriate sidings. Capstan working had been introduced in dock areas to reduce movement of wagons by horses, and Grangemouth Docks now had 120 capstans, and its eight coal hoists each dealt with 50 wagons per hour. Here too gravitation was used to feed wagons on to the hoist and off again. Ardrossan had two coal hoists and they were also installed at "the various Glasgow docks". In that pre-computer era the railway employed a large staff to record the movements and loading of its 65,731 wagons and trucks, with "several thousands of traders' wagons" in addition. For incoming goods, "the checked invoices are passed into the various down offices marked in such a way that the clerical staff can make out the delivery sheets for the various loads, and the accounts for collection from parties who do not have credit accounts with the Company. These sheets and accounts are handed to the carters, the lorries are passed over the weighing machine, and, with the safe delivery of the goods, the transaction so far is at an end. But then begins a complicated series of clerical transactions necessary for the proper accounting of the traffic, not only as far as the Company's own treasury is concerned, but also for the correct division of receipts between all railways concerned in the case of through traffic." The central office for the huge coal and minerals traffic was at Motherwell, and "there is a system in vogue which works with clockwork regularity day by day, and has proved to be most satisfactory. The detailed weights – gross, tare and nett – of all the wagons which have been dealt with at some 20 weighing offices planted in the various convenient points through the Lanarkshire district are forwarded several times daily to the central office … where the charges are made up and the traffic invoiced to its destination." The business of weighing wagons was costly and time-consuming, and in the following year the Scottish railways, chasing ways to cut costs, proposed to cease weighing coal wagons in their yards and to require a consignment note from the colliery, giving weight, destination and route for each wagon[54]. An item Waddell did not mention, modest by comparison, was the running of theatrical specials, taking touring companies and their props about the country. In 1885 the Caledonian had run only thirteen of these, with an average of five vehicles each. In 1908 it ran 123 such specials, with an average of $14\frac{1}{2}$ vehicles each[55].

A section of its own was devoted to the carting department, still with Wordies as the main contractors, as they had been since the amalgamation of the Scottish Central with the Caledonian in 1865. In 1907 Wordies were installed at 28 Caledonian stations and depots, mostly in larger towns. The company's own Carting Department worked from 55 stations. It had around 1,000 horses working in the goods depots and the dockyards.

On the Argyll coast, a more remote segment of Caledonian operations saw the company's only railway service to be operated by internal combustion engine. The village of Eaglesham, two miles south of Busby, had never had a rail service, despite several initiatives. But around 1905 a 'Caledonian Motor Service' provided a connecting service between Eaglesham and the stations at Cathcart and Clarkston, using petrol-engined motor-buses. One of the vehicles used on this service, a Durham-Churchill, was fitted at St. Rollox with flanged wheels and despatched to Connel Ferry, from where between 1909 and June 1914 (when the bridge was opened to motor use) it operated a 'rail-motor' or car-carrying service, with two car-floats, across the Loch Etive Bridge. There were ten booked services each day, of which four went as far as Benderloch[56].

In September 1909, the Lanarkshire & Dumbartonshire Railway published its final report before becoming part of the Caledonian: the amalgamation Bill had been given the royal assent on 16 August. Receipts were £46,213 and the balance after charges was £28,740. A dividend of 4% was paid. Ownership and deployment of wagons was still a major issue. The report to shareholders noted that, as the chairman had forecast, between September 1907 and and 31 July 1909, 4,419 old six- and seven-ton wagons had been broken up, to be replaced by 950 sixteen-ton wagons. Other examples of specialised modern rolling stock include ten 'refrigerator' vans built at St. Rollox in 1906, to carry meat or other perishable items. The demurrage problem had been referred to the Railway & Canal Commissioners. Perhaps as a result of the officials' US trip, the CR took an interest in high-capacity mineral wagons. In 1903 the company had only one 50-ton capacity wagon. Now it had ordered 50 bulk wagons, of steel construction; 30 from Leeds, England, and 20 from St. Louis, USA. The American trucks were supplied in kit form, and once assembled, were rejected as of insufficient quality for the work. Subsequently the Caledonian ordered 300 all-steel wagons from British builders, Birmingham Railway Carriage & Wagon, Hurst Nelson, Metropolitan Amalgamated Railway Carriage & Wagon, R.Y. Pickering, and W.R. Renshaw[57]. St. Rollox also built 70. The 30-ton bogie mineral wagons were fitted with automatic brakes, making the Caledonian one of the first British railways to run fully-fitted goods trains. The interest in larger wagon-loads coincides with building of the large new docks at Grangemouth and the lower Clyde. But as on all British railways, the effort to carry bigger wagon-loads was largely frustrated by the limited clearances and capacity of the yards and sidings where loading took place. In 1898, about a third of the mineral wagons on the Caledonian did not belong to the railway company; and in 1920, a Ministry of Transport enquiry found that only four out of over 200 Lanarkshire collieries could accommodate 20-ton wagons. But there was also a reluctance on the part of railway companies and collieries to provide enough wagons to cope with peaks of demand, since outside peak periods the surplus stock would just stand around, depreciating in value and using siding space without earning its keep.

The Demurrage Dispute

In December 1907 the Caledonian obtained powers to construct its own line to bypass the one-time Monkland & Kirkintilloch (now North British) section between Gartsherrie and Garnqueen South Junctions, which had been a foreign element in its northern route since the earliest days. But no work was ever done on this Gartsherrie-Glenboig link. Early in 1908 another link-line, between Friockheim and Glasterlaw, long unused by scheduled

The Eaglesham bus offered a rather draughty ride. The vehicle was later modified at St. Rollox to operate the Connel Bridge car-train.

trains, was shut, though the rails remained *in situ* until 1917. The North British had no need to exercise its running powers, and anyway, at the beginning of the year, the last of many 'Peace Agreements' had been concluded, this one due to last for twenty years, extending the current 1899 agreement, which was due to expire in 1916. Its main points were the pooling of all competitive traffic between the two companies (within Scotland), and the rationalisation of competing train services which ran at a loss, with staff reductions at competing stations[58]. A letter to the *Scotsman* three months later noted that between Balloch and Dumbarton there was still a train from each company scheduled for exactly the same times, apparently taking turns as to which went first[59], and it may be that the impact of the agreement was political as much as practical. The surviving minutes of the Caledonian and North British 1908 Agreement Committee show very few substantive issues. In May 1908 they agreed that neither would spend over £5,000 on advertising. A 'Standing Arbitrator' was appointed to rule when neither side could agree, and in 1914 he overruled Caledonian objections to the NBR reducing coal rates between Niddrie Colliery and Leith[53]. Often the six-monthly meetings were skipped. A formidable gathering of directors and officials convened in Edinburgh on 23 January 1911 in order to discuss such matters as Caledonian workmen's tickets from Yoker, and the terms of the Greenock Shopkeepers' Excursion to Oban in September 1910. Some issues like 'Free Collection of Parcels in Glasgow' were deferred from year to year[60]. The true value of the 'Peace Agreement' lay in an improvement of attitude between the companies, with a growing appreciation that they needed to make common cause against the vastly-increased powers of modern government, and the new confidence and power of organised labour.

The Scottish Railway Shareholders' Association held a meeting on 22 August 1908 at which it was noted that members accounted for around £12,000,000 worth of Scottish railway stocks. Demands for higher fares and fewer trains formed the basis of their speeches. It was noted that there was now a pooling arrangement between the Caledonian and the North British but it was not regarded as going far enough, and the chairman complained that the steamboat competition on the Clyde "is but little abated"[61]. The CR and the GSWR had each withdrawn one steamer during the summer. Railway shares were still at a market value well below what the Scottish Railway Shareholders' Association wanted to see, but most of its ire was directed at the North British, whose dividend rarely matched that of the Caledonian. But in 1908, the Caledonian had to bring in £17,000 as a special credit in the accounts in order to maintain even a 3% dividend, and a need for substantial economies was proclaimed[62]. In August 1908 Sir Charles Bine Renshaw was elected chairman, on King's retirement at 78. He had been a director since 1895. Robert Millar died in September 1908, and Guy Calthrop took over as general manager. Renshaw's entry in *Who's Who in Glasgow* (1909) noted that "The anxious period which succeeded saw the agitation for economy in railway working, organised by the Scottish Railway Shareholders' Association, which brought about the co-operation of the various railway companies". One important area where the companies saw opportunities for extra charges and for economies was in wagon demurrage (the period when a wagon was held for loading or unloading). In their view, industrial customers were retaining railway company wagons too long, in effect using them for storage, and trying as much as possible to use their own wagons for transport (at a lower charge than the railway's vehicles). On 1 August 1908 the Caledonian, NBR and GSWR issued a joint circular, announcing a scale of demurrage charges to take effect from 1 February 1909. The traders promptly appealed to the Railway & Canal Commissioners, and Renshaw represented the Scottish railways' case in this and other proceedings of the Board of Trade in London. He and his board were highly conscious of the Scottish Railway Shareholders' Association's constant monitoring of the company's doings, and calls for economy, and the half-yearly meeting in March 1909 indicated that service cut-backs were having some effect. Traffic revenue was recorded as £2,038,090, down by £59,874 on the previous six months, but although gross revenue was down by £63,200, the working expenses were down by £85,000 and the net profit was up by £21,800[63]. The North British figures showed a similar trend, testifying to the spirit of co-operation. Train miles for both companies were lower. But for the half-year to 31 January 1909 the dividend on Ordinary stock was still a modest 3%, and share prices remained depressed, with Caledonian £100 Ordinary at £88 in June 1909, unchanged from June 1908[64].

CHAPTER 12. The Caledonian in the Twentieth Century (2), 1909-14

Curlers' Convenience, and Goods Charges

A halt for non-scheduled services had long been established at Carsebreck, about two miles south-west of Blackford, on the Stirling-Perth line. On the adjacent loch the Royal Caledonian Curling Club (no relation to the CR) held its bonspiels, and trains are recorded to have used the halt when the ice was firm at least 25 times between 1853 and 1935. The Caledonian maintained a shed by the pond and in November 1879 it was resolved to repair it "as economically as possible"[1]. In 1909 it was noted that there used to be no platform at Carsebreck, but "three or four years ago the Company built a long platform. In November 1908, 16 special trains ran to it and about a dozen regular trains stopped there"[2].

A special shareholders' meeting in February 1909 approved the company's application for a Provisional Order to absorb the Lanarkshire & Dumbartonshire Railway. The Caledonian already owned half of the Lanarkshire & Dumbartonshire Railway's £1,437,000 capital, and was committed to a guaranteed 4% dividend on its stock. A takeover giving Caledonian 4% guaranteed stock in exchange was seen as the most economical course[3]. A letter in the *Times* on 9 March drew attention to an oddity in the accounts. In September 1908 the 'Small Wagon Replacement Account' stood at £115,520 to be charged to revenue; by March 1909 this sum had risen to £198,393, yet the number of wagons currently owned by the company was 62,585, less than the 63,742 recorded in the previous set of accounts, and only 1,003 were noted as under repair. The writer did not speculate on what this account might actually represent, but suggested that it might be looked into at the next meeting. At the half-yearly meeting a week later there was no mention of small wagons, but the item perhaps related to the acquisition of private trader wagons. The chairman was quoted a few days later as saying that these would fill a line over 300 miles long. Renshaw, at the meeting, emphasised the friendly relations with the North British. Train and steamer traffic to Clyde resorts now used tickets that were interchangeable on CR and GSWR services, and though the NBR was not included, it "had agreed to arrangements without which it would have been difficult, if not impossible, to secure this long desired change"[4]. There were still a few needle-points of inter-company aggravation. At Aberdeen, the Ferryhill engine shed, also used by the North British, had long been inadequate despite enlargement in 1894, and a new 10-road shed, with repair facilities, was opened in 1908. For a year the NBR locomotives used the old shed while negotiations for lodging fees went on, down to the cost of a bucket of sand (3*d.*). Agreement was finally reached between Calthrop and W.F. Jackson on 16 July 1909[5].

The most contentious matters in the 1900s were between the railway and its largest industrial and commercial customers, who pressed continually for reduced charges. In 1909 the Scottish Co-operative Wholesale Society joined with other major users to form another pressure group on railway managements, this one concerned with goods rates. At a Board of Trade Departmental Committee on Railway Agreements and Amalgamations in 1911,

Caledonian rolling stock, at Aberdeen. Note the dedicated Lipton's van, presumably for carrying tea chests or other items, including sausages (also a Lipton speciality) which could be attached to passenger trains for fast delivery. (Caledonian Railway Association)

the coal industry's spokesman made it clear that his side believed it was carrying the burden of cheap passenger fares and under-paying lines: "Scotch railway companies have much cheaper passenger fares than the English railway companies. In the last twenty years the Caledonian, for example, has increased its capital by about fifteen million pounds for passenger railways which have not been of any service for the mineral traffic … some of these lines have never been opened"[6]. The Caledonian was still enlarging its goods facilities, completing a vast potato shed at Buchanan Street on 29 March 1909, in which space was rented to six wholesale merchants[7]. And on its side, the Caledonian complained about the greatly increased price of coal. Renshaw informed another Parliamentary committee that the Caledonian's coal bill in 1897-8 was £151,000, and in 1907-8 was £360,000, through price rises rather than greater usage[8].

Passenger services on the the Muirkirk-Strathaven section of the Kilmarnock-Strathaven line were few, but also thinly patronised, and to save costs, the Caledonian and GSWR applied to run mixed trains from the summer of 1909. This was refused by the Board of Trade, and a local petition also objected. In response the companies withdrew the passenger service between Muirkirk and Strathaven altogether. Questions were asked in Parliament by the local MP, and finally it was agreed that mixed trains were better than no trains. After discussions with the Board of Trade the companies provided two daily mixed trains, each way, from 1 November[9].

Pay Disputes, and Pullmans

Unrest among railway workers over pay and conditions was again becoming an issue in 1909. Railway companies, including the Caledonian, were still unwilling to negotiate with trade unions. But the unions had become larger and more confident since 1891 and especially since 1905. Conciliation boards to deal with labour disputes had been introduced by the Liberal government despite opposition from the railway companies. In August 1909 sectional boards on the Caledonian agreed on a number of reforms, including a 66-hour working week for passenger guards, with a maximum working day of 12 hours (or 14 with two meal-breaks). Overtime was payable at standard rate for the first six hours, then at time plus a quarter. All porter-guards earning less than £1 a week were to receive a 1s. a week pay rise. Greasers and carriage-and-wagon examiners were to work an 11-hour day, with overtime pay on the same basis as the guards. Starting pay for a greaser was nine shillings a week, rising by a shilling after a year. Ordinary surfacemen were to receive between 19s. and £1 1s. depending on length of service[10]. But the unions were dissatisfied with the limited powers of the conciliation boards. After vain attempts to arrange discussions, the Amalagamated Society of Railway Servants, The Amalgamated Society of Locomotive Engineers and Firemen, the General Railway Workers' Union, and the General Society of Signalmen and Pointsmen issued a joint ultimatum on 15 August. The companies were given 24 hours to decide if they would meet representatives to negotiate a settlement, or there would be an all-out strike. Naturally, the various boards objected to being 'railroaded', and preparations for a strike went ahead. Railwaymen in Glasgow were said to have a "militant spirit"[11]. It seemed that a damaging stand-off was inevitable, but the government intervened. A Royal Commission was to be set up to make a report on the railways, and the unions withdrew the strike call.

Up to 1909, for many years the board had been formed of fourteen directors. Now it was decided to reduce the number by two. The directors' remuneration, unchanged at a shared £5,250 since March 1896, was reduced proportionately. Their prime perquisite was of course free first class travel on almost every railway in Great Britain, through reciprocal agreements, and they were also entitled to claim living expenses when engaged on company affairs. But they were wealthy men, and the prestige of a Caledonian directorship was cherished more than the rewards. Share prices remained low. In November 1909 Caledonian £100 Ordinary were at £87. The share duplication scheme had not created extra value: Preferred Converted Ordinary shares were at £63 10s.; Deferred Converted Ordinary were at £24 10s. Caledonian Deferred Ordinary No. 1 shares could be picked up for a few pence[12]. Confronting the fact that some very dubious decisions had been taken little more than a decade before, the company procured an Abandonment Act of 1910 for some lines, including the Glenbuck line's never-used Muirkirk extension. Such actions, naturally, were not given any prominence. But the Caledonian's strong public image was shown in the same year when 30,000 tinplate *Cardeans*, replicas of the iconic 4-6-0 of 1906, in 1 1/4 inch gauge, ordered by the company from the toy and model-makers Basset-Lowke, to sell at 2s. 6d. each, with a matching coach, sold out quickly.

The long running demurrage dispute between the Scottish railway companies and their main industrial customers was finally resolved in early 1911 when the Railway & Canal Commissioners gave a judgement in favour of the railways. A day was allowed for loading and unloading (two days for coal) after which charges

4-6-0 No. 903 *Cardean*, at Gretna. Built in 1906, and superheated in 1911 (as seen here), it ran until 1930.

**Twelve-wheeled Pullman buffet car *Mary Beaton* at the Craven Works in Sheffield,
one of the seventeen delivered to the Caledonian in 1914. (Caledonian Railway Association)**

could be imposed, from 1*s.* to 3*s.* a day depending on the wagon's tonnage; plus 6*d.* a day for sheets. The commissioners had been startled to discover that the Caledonian had 37,873 mineral wagons and its customers had 25,342. In fact, the circular of August 1908 had done a lot to free up wagons, to the point that in February 1909 the Caledonian found itself with a surplus of 15,000[13]. With the NBR and the GSWR, it was examining the workings of the German Railways' wagon-pool, in the hope of organising something similar[14]. But while the German companies achieved pooling and standardisation, the Scottish railways never reached the same level of co-operative success.

Grangemouth traffic was becoming ever more intense, with oil, an increasingly important fuel, added to the mix, and in 1911 one of the last lines to be built by the Caledonian was laid from Fouldubs to meet a North British branch (1908) at Bainsford, providing an access loop that avoided Grahamston and the Falkirk industrial lines.

Pullman cars, the epitome of railway luxury, had run on the Midland-GSWR services from the 1870s. In 1913 the Caledonian made a 12-year contract with the Pullman Car Co. for the construction of 17 cars, at Pullman's expense, 12 buffet, four dining, one buffet-observation car, to be delivered by 1 March 1915. The Pullman Company was to receive a supplementary fare plus the catering profits. By August 1914 ten had been delivered and eight were put into service on trains between Glasgow and Edinburgh, Aberdeen and Gourock. All were named after famous ladies of history or myth; the observation car, 'Maid of Morven', ran on the Oban line[15].

Scottish coal production reached its peak in 1913, when 42 1/2 million tons were dug out, plus many millions more of spoil, piled up and looming over the pit-heads and mining villages. Goods and mineral traffic had to be moved promptly to avoid congestion, and at the city goods depots, handling facilities were generally very good. Dundee West Goods Station handled around 360,000 tons a year. The main goods shed was equipped with capstans, two three-ton, eight 30cwt hydraulic cranes and two further one-ton cranes mounted above the tracks to transfer goods to and from an upper-level store. Wagon traversers moved empty tucks and vans to adjacent tracks for re-marshalling. Around half its traffic was 'mineral', chiefly coal. In addition to Wordie's services, the CR in Dundee had 34 one-horse and three two-horse carts for delivery of goods.

Station improvements went on. Alyth Junction was enlarged and re-signalled in the course of 1912, with lengthened platforms and new waiting rooms. Stirling Station was substantially enlarged in 1913, though its building style remained in the baronial mode employed by the Scottish Central. Five through platforms replaced the original three, and six bay lines replaced the original two. As a result the station became much less of a bottleneck. Aberdeen Joint Station was also being enlarged, and Carstairs was being rebuilt. Its old roof was demolished in an unusual way, pulled down by locomotives with cables attached to the pillars; the work was done on a Saturday night and cleared in time for Monday trains[16].

Donald Matheson was a man capable of vision but also of the practical planning of large-scale ventures. During a holiday in his native Perthshire in 1909, he was taken with the idea of establishing a high class golfing resort close to Crieff Junction, where there was already a golf course (the GSWR had already provided a model at Turnberry, from 1906). In the following year a company was formed, to build and operate a large, luxury hotel, with the more fetching name of Gleneagles, and in 1913 the Caledonian Railway was empowered to invest £25,000 in the project. Crieff Junction, one of the company's more charmless stations, was rebuilt in an opulent manner to serve as the access point. Work on the hotel site continued until 1914, and then the project went into suspension.

On 9 December William Pickersgill was appointed as successor to J.F. McIntosh when the latter should retire in May 1914. McIntosh had unquestionably brought distinction to the Caledonian. He had been a President of the Association of Railway Locomotive Engineers and had received membership of the Victorian Order from the King. Pickersgill, aged 48, had begun his career with the Great Eastern Railway in London, but had been locomotive superintendent of the Great North of Scotland Railway for 20 years, and had overseen the development of that company's new works at Inverurie. At St. Rollox he took over workshops that had seen little modernisation since Drummond's time. The locomotive stock ranged from 2-4-0 types going back to the Conner era (but with new boilers) to McIntosh's new 2-6-0 goods engine of 1912. Modernisation was an element in Pickersgill's brief. But on 4 August 1914, everything changed.

Pulling down the old train shed at Carstairs, 27 April 1913.

CHAPTER 13. The First World War

Requisitioned

As far back as 1871, legislation had provided for the government to take control of the railways in the event of an emergency, for a week at a time, but indefinitely renewable. The same Act provided for compensation to be paid for "any loss or injury" sustained while these powers were in operation[1]. For some years before 1914, the prospect of a European war had been looming, and a certain amount of anticipatory action was taken. A communications board was established between the War Office and the Board of Trade, with ten senior railway managers on it. One of them was Donald Matheson of the Caledonian. With the outbreak of war with Germany on 4 August 1914, this board was rapidly constituted into a Railway Executive, with powers inconceivable in peace-time. The Caledonian received a letter from the War Office in London on August 4-5 to inform it that it had been taken over by the government, and that "you will carry on as usual, subject to the instructions of the executive committee." For the next eight years the Caledonian Railway's board was only partly in charge of the company's policies and fortunes.

An immediate requirement was a large number of special trains as troops were mobilised. In the course of August the CR provided 342 military and naval trains. These conveyed not only men but often horses, trucks and large amounts of equipment. "In the course of one Saturday afternoon and Sunday forenoon … no fewer than 34 military trains were loaded and despatched from Perth, ten from Stirling, and eleven from Blairgowrie"[2]. Perth Station was the first to have a free tea service for troops in transit, set up by the Perthshire Women's Patriotic Committee on 7 August 1914, and rapidly imitated at most major stations. Eight days after the declaration of war, Grangemouth Docks were declared a military area, and a special pass was needed to enter. On 13 November 1914, the Admiralty took over the port entirely. The focus of the naval war was very much on the North Sea, and the Caledonian had two strategic ports in Grangemouth and Aberdeen. The Grand Fleet, based at Scapa Flow in Orkney, required massive amounts of coal and other supplies. This traffic was far beyond the capacity of the Highland Railway to carry north from Perth, and of the harbours of the far north to handle. Coal for the fleet went from Grangemouth, and 'Jellicoe trains', named for the commanding admiral, were routed up from South Wales with prime steam coal from 10 August.

For the Caledonian Railway, the war meant business as usual – only much more so. Like other railway companies, its operation was made more difficult by staff volunteering to join the forces. By November 1918 5,229 Caledonian men were in the army or navy, almost 22% of the total numbers employed in August 1914. More would have joined, but certain railway jobs were 'reserved occupations' and the company could prevent them from enlisting (a special token could be worn by such men to show they were not 'shirking' the trenches). Many joined a Railway Companies' Special Volunteer Force, to be called up in the event of invasion. Overtime was a necessity. While men or youths were recruited whenever possible, for the first time there was an influx of women into the workforce. Prior to the war the company had employed around 80 women, mostly as cleaners, though some as 'typewriters'. In the course of 1914-18, 1,911 were taken on. Clerk-typists numbered 387, clerks 281, passenger porters 239, ticket collectors 106, parcel porters 89, guards 21, porter-guards 16, cleaners 204, signalwomen 16, porter-signalwomen 20. In the workshops and locomotive depots, 166 women were employed, some of them carrying out such husky tasks as engine-coaling (8) and engine-tube cleaning (4)[3]. Of Caledonian men who joined the colours, 706 were killed in the course of the war. A memorial in Glasgow Central Station commemorates the company's war dead.

In early 1915 the War Office requested that ambulance trains be provided to carry injured soldiers back from the Channel ports. Seventeen such trains were built that year, including one built and outfitted by the Caledonian. Between August 1914 and November 1918, ambulance trains would run 962 times on the CR system, 763 from Southampton and 199 from Dover. Several large hospitals in the Glasgow-Paisley area were taken over for military use, and some asylums were converted to military hospitals, including the Perthshire Asylum at Murthly, on the Highland line just beyond Stanley. Towards the end of the war, the Caledonian began work on an ambulance train for the US Government, authorised on 20 August 1918 "subject to suitable conditions of payment". Monthly instalments were agreed, but the train was cancelled.[4]

The Worst Disaster

Like every railway company, the Caledonian suffered numerous accidents, caused mostly by human error or fatigue, and metal or mechanical failure. Victims were mostly company staff, and both by its own record and in the public view, the Caledonian was as safe as any other line. There was nothing to prefigure the catastrophic smash at Quintinshill, a mile north of Gretna North Junction, just after 6.30 a.m. on Saturday 22 May 1915. Quintinshill was a block post, with passing loops both for Up and Down trains, and on this occasion a goods train was occupying each loop. A special troop train from Larbert, bound for Liverpool, of 15 coaches and six assorted trucks and vans, carrying half a battalion of the 7th Royal Scots, 417 men and fifteen officers, was coming south. The 6.10 a.m. local from Carlisle to Beattock was heading north. Close behind it was the overnight express from London to Glasgow, running late. In order to allow the express to overtake it, the Beattock train was instructed by the signalman to shunt on to the Down line. This was a permitted manoeuvre when the crossing loops were occupied, and if the signals had been set to halt the troop train, nothing would have gone wrong. But this was

Spectators' bicycles line the fence as recovery work goes on at Quintinshill on 23 May 1915.

**Locomotives No.121, of the troop train, and 907, of the northbound local, re-mounted
on the rails for removal. Both had to be scrapped. The number 131 was given to
a Pickersgill 4-4-0 in 1916; 907 was not re-used.**

not done; Signalman Tinsley, by his own later admission, having "forgotten" the local train. The troop train, running at 60 mph under clear signals, crashed head-on into the local. Wreckage was heaped across both lines, and burning coal set fire to some of the goods wagons as well as to gas-lit coaches belonging to the Great Central Railway. A minute later, into this horrific scene, despite efforts by some individuals to halt it, crashed the express, thirteen carriages hauled by two engines, also under clear signals. The troop train engine's tender, lying across the track, was carried thirty yards forward in the collision. In the mound of debris and wreckage, now burning furiously, 227 persons were killed and 246 injured, many with terrible burns. As soon as the news reached Glasgow, Sir Charles Renshaw and his senior officials hurried south on a special train, with some city doctors and a stock of medical supplies.

A full account of events and the aftermath is given by John Thomas in *Gretna: Britain's Worst Railway Disaster*. The immediate investigations of the Company, and of Lt. Col. Druitt for the Board of Trade[5], revealed not only appalling negligence on the day, but an established culture of casualness and regulation-dodging at the Quintinshill signal box. The man most responsible, James Tinsley, was jailed for three years for culpable homicide, and his colleague George Meakin got 18 months. It can reasonably be assumed that in many other signal cabins, and not only on the Caledonian, a new respect for the rule book was found, and district inspectors instructed to monitor procedures closely.

Wartime Pressures

Despite intense pressure on its own resources, the Caledonian sent seven locomotives to help out the hard-pressed Highland Railway in the autumn of 1915 (one did not come back until 1922), and twenty-five 0-6-0 engines were loaned to the War Department for work in France. Additional sidings were laid at many points to accommodate wartime traffic, like the new new exchange sidings at Perth North, able to hold 144 wagons. Locomotive facilities at Carlisle were greatly improved by the rebuilding, on the same site during 1915-17, of Etterby Engine Shed, now renamed Kingmoor, with a brick structure replacing the wooden one; and on 13 November 1916 a completely new shed for 80 engines was opened at Balornock to replace the old St. Rollox shed, with 12 roads and two repair tracks, at a cost of £27,997 7s. 6d.[6].

Heavy pressure on wagon capacity made it vital to get more intensive use of the rolling stock. On 5 June 1916, the Caledonian entered a wagon-pooling system with the North British and the GSWR. This was not an entirely new scheme: the *Glasgow Herald* on 5 November 1913 noted that the country's three principal railways were operating a wagon pool for general purpose wagons, and the other two Scottish companies, the Highland and the Great North of Scotland, joined it on 2 January 1917. A conference of railways, coal-owners and other owners of private user wagons was convened in Glasgow on 12 January and provisional pooling agreement was reached[7]. A census of Scottish owned wagons was done, and general pooling of wagons was intended to begin on 5 February, but had to be postponed because the Board of Trade had not given its approval. The extent and effectiveness of this attempt to ensure more effective use of the rolling stock is not clear, but it seems that the CR passed on 231 wagons to other companies, as well as supplying 309 for military use overseas[8]. Submarine warfare, the loss of ships, and the escalation of shipping rates, meant that much goods traffic that had gone by coastal steamers now was transferred to the railways – good for revenue but greatly increasing the pressure on goods handling. In the autumn of 1917 the Caledonian carried over 93,000 tons of potatoes from stations in the Perth area, much of which would formerly have gone by boat from the quay at Perth. By the end of the war it was estimated that the company's freight traffic to and from England had doubled as a result of the transference. Among this range of traffic was a regular service of cordite trains from the chemicals factory at Ardeer, to Holton Heath, near Wareham in Hampshire, and other munitions factories. The trains were normally composed of ten wagons, each loaded with three tons of cordite paste.

Passenger services were maintained as much as possible but were frequently disrupted by sheer pressure of traffic. Express services were cut back, and the company's plans for operating luxury Pullman cariages on some trains had to be suspended. There was difficulty in making up trains because not enough third class carriages had steam heating. Thirty bogie thirds, and ten bogie brake thirds were fitted at a total cost of £2,890, authorised by the board only on condition that the government accept it as special war expenditure[9]. Two heavy-load 28-ton ingot bogie wagons were adapted to support a 'Cradle for 100-ton Gun' with a bogie flat wagon to support the barrel. A 165-ton wagon-set was built at government expense by Hurst, Nelson & Co., of Motherwell, for transporting the heaviest guns. Eighty-four large naval guns were transported south between August 1914 and June 1916, as well as other items, like propellor shafts for battleships[10]. No new carriages were built and intensive usage led to dilapidation at a time when maintenance facilities were stretched to the utmost. St. Rollox Works were making gun carriages and mountings, mine cases, gun barrels and other items of military hardware as well as continuing locomotive maintenance and repair. Although some lines were closed to passengers in order to make economies, they were naturally the most lightly-used, or duplicated other services, and the release of staff and rolling stock was hardly significant, compared to the demand from other parts. Forty-seven Caledonian stations closed from 1 January 1917; among them were Strathaven North, the Town and Montgomerie Pier stations at Ardrossan (the GSWR continued to serve the town), and Neilston Station on the Lanarkshire & Ayrshire line. No passenger trains ran between Langloan and Airdrie, and Whifflet High Level was closed, but an Airdrie-Newhouse service continued. Most stations reopened on 1 March 1919, some on 1 February. In 1917 the link line at Brechin was lifted, and the Carmyllie-Elliot Junction line was closed to passengers for most of 1917[11]. Despite wartime austerity, the "best-kept station" awards were maintained[12]. Track was removed from the never-used line between Auldhouseburn, near Muirkirk, and Spireslack. It was briefly relaid, in part, to facilitate removal of bridge ironwork, in June-July 1918. £115,126 was charged to the displacement account for the Spireslack line[13]. Another permanent casualty was the Inchture Tramway, from the Dundee & Perth line to Inchture village, acquired by the Caledonian with the Dundee & Perth, which was shut on 1 January 1917[14]. Long

Three 35-ton wagons coupled to form a set with cradles for transporting 100-ton naval guns. Other configurations were also made, depending on the nature of the load. (Caledonian Railway Association)

**Aberdeen: south end of the old Joint Station (pre-1905) with CR and GNSR trains;
Caledonian carriages and fish vans to left and right.**

distance train services were rationalised and the Caledonian could no longer book passengers between Edinburgh and London. Another consequence of wartime traffic was the reintroduction of mixed trains on numerous branch lines, in order to economise on locomotive movements. In September 1916 the Caledonian requested permission to run further mixed trains, and although the Board of Trade disapproved of mixed trains, it had no option but to sanction the request.

Aberdeen Joint Station was already in process of enlargement and when completed in 1915, it covered $11 \frac{1}{2}$ acres with 13 passenger platforms. The Caledonian sidings at Craiginches had capacity for 600 wagons, and those to be taken to the docks were hauled by Great North engines. From 15 January 1915 Aberdeen was designated as the prime railhead for all bulk supplies to the Grand Fleet except fuel. Foodstuffs, clothing, ammunition, guns, trucks, cars, spare parts and apparatus of all kinds were handled. Aircraft were part-dismantled and shipped in 40-ft cases (around 50 seaplanes were delivered). In each six month period of the war years between 35,000 and 50,000 tons of naval stores were taken to Aberdeen, in addition to normal goods traffic. The number of loaded wagons taken into the dockyard area between 15 January 1915 and 28 February 1919 was 67,283, with an estimated total load of 297,900 tons[15]. Grangemouth, in addition to the coal traffic, handled a similar diversity of cargo. Between March and June 1915, 8,000 tons of flour was stored in seven sheds; and in 1915-16 19,000 tons of hay were delivered by rail. In the course of the war a victualling yard, oil depot, and mine and ammunition depots were set up. The three largest warehouses at Grange Dock were requisitioned by the Admiralty as a mine depot from January 1916, and to the end of 1918 would take in a tonnage of 57,600, of which 45,875 tons was sent out again. Mine trains came in to the Fouldubs Yard, and from there to newly-laid exchange sidings where Admiralty owned locomotives took over. In June 1916 a victualling yard was opened at Carron Dock, occupying five sheds. Up to the end of May 1919 it would receive 51,000 tons of supplies. Grangemouth was also a timber port, trans-shipping some 30,000 tons from train to ship during the War. But of course the overwhelming tonnage was of coal. Between August 1914 and 30 April 1919, the docks received 2,306,000 tons of coal by rail, and shipped out 2,092,000 tons. The workforce had to be greatly enlarged, and a temporary station was built in the dock area, served by up to four daily workmen's trains from Grahamston. After the Armistice of 11 November 1918, this station despatched 27 "liberty men's" trains in December and January, carrying men on leave from the Grand Fleet. The port was handed back to the Caledonian Railway's control on 25 December 1918, though the Admiralty presence continued for another three months.

Aerodromes and Filling Factories

Aerial warfare was very new, but 'aerodromes' were laid at Montrose, Renfrew and Edzell, and a seaplane base established at Dundee, all supplied by rail. Traffic in certain other places was also greatly increased. The Colville Steelworks in Motherwell, employing 2,800 workers in August 1914, had almost 9,000 in 1918[16] and its traffic virtually doubled between 1914 and 1916. A huge 'National Factory' for explosives was set up at a site known in Lloyd George's (or possibly the King's) honour as Georgetown, on the Gryfe Water near Paisley, where a predominantly female workforce produced 20,000,000 shells, 26,000,000 cartridges, and 32,000,000 assorted small components. The total output of this installation was 459,000 tons. In the case of Georgetown, labour was readily available fairly close by. A station was built on the Greenock line, and Houston Station was enlarged to cope with workers' trains. The factory paid the fares, with each worker having a ticket stamped for use on a specific train. The trains, each carrying 800 passengers, arrived at 15-20 minute intervals, and the workers' shift starting times were adjusted to the trains. At the other of those mushroom 'Filling Factory' sites, at Gretna, an entire township had to be constructed in order to house the workers. Work commenced in September 1915 to construct a factory zone spread over a nine-mile area between Annan and Longtown, with 12,000 resident workers. Linked to the Caledonian, NBR and GSWR lines, it had 40 miles of sidings and 40 miles of its own running track. Up to the end of March 1919, the Caledonian carried 529,957 tons of freight in connection with the Gretna ammunition works, and the GSWR and North British also shared in the traffic. Passenger traffic through Gretna, 10,747 persons in 1913, was 2,932,814 in the peak year of 1917, and 1,348,637 in 1918. This included passengers using a temporary station at Mossband, two miles south of Gretna. From here three miles and 68 chains of additional track was laid to Rockcliffe[17].

In September 1918 it was proposed that the Muldron mineral branch, long disused, should be reopened to give access to a sand pit. The cost was estimated at £7,460 and the Caledonian was willing to undertake the work, so long as "the Government pays the whole cost of the work with no guarantee that the Company will take over any part of it at the end of the period of Government Control"[18]. The Caledonian's smallest locomotive shed, a one-line wooden hut at Loch Tay, burned down on 24 October 1917. In due course an estimate was presented for building a replacement, totalling £560. The prewar cost for the same job was noted as £280, and it was again recorded that "The difference between these figures will be a specific charge against the Government. That is to say, the expenditure by the Company will be £280." As the shed was insured for £120, in fact only £160 was

Munitions workers, mostly women, disembark at the Gretna "Township Station" at Mossband, in 1917 or 1918.

A CR 6-ton dumb-buffer wagon, laden with coal. From the chalked message on the side, it is due for repair. Six- and seven-ton mineral wagons, many not fitted with spring buffers, formed 23% of the Company's wagon stock in 1907.

payable[19]. Throughout the period of government control, virtually every piece of expenditure, large or small, by the Caledonian was noted by the same formula, with the current cost being measured against the 1913 cost, and the difference stacked up to the government's account. When a water closet was installed at Gretna signal box (another on-going improvement programme), for £34, the prewar price of £11 was charged to the arrears of maintenance account, and £23 to the government. But fares and goods rates had doubled in the course of the war and there is no suggestion that the company was measuring these against 1913 revenues and proposing to repay the difference[20].

In early 1918 the officers' saloon, usually hauled by the now-venerable No. 123, was found to be decrepit, and saloon carriage No. 41 was converted for their use. Some Edinburgh-Glasgow express services, withdrawn in 1917, were restored in March 1918, two daily each way, taking 1 hour 18 minutes for the journey[21]. Certain on-going projects were continued through the war, including the refitting of dumb-buffered wagons with spring buffers. The board approved the conversion of the last 3,800 on 28 May 1918.

All the Caledonian Steam Packet ships were requisitioned by the Admiralty, primarily for use as minesweepers. *Duchess of Hamilton* and *Duchess of Montrose* were lost, on 29 November 1915 and 18 March 1917 respectively. The others were returned, somewhat the worse for wear, at the end of the war.

In October 1918 Sir Charles Bine Renshaw died, and Henry Allan, his deputy, a director of the Clydesdale Bank, became the company's thirteenth and last chairman. There was still plenty of vigour in the Caledonian's management. Matheson, who in 1917 was elected as Chairman of the General Managers' Conference of the Associated Railway Companies of Great Britain, presented the new chairman and the board with a major proposal in October 1918, by which time victory in the war was evident: the immediate reconstruction of Polmadie Locomotive Depot, extra tracks between Gushetfaulds and Rutherglen Junctions, and a new marshalling yard to be built alongside. The board deferred a decision but authorised research into land purchase[22].

CHAPTER 14. The Last Years, 1919-1923

Workers, Shareholders, and the Future of Railways

By 1918 the Scottish Railway Stockholders' Protection Society had 32,000 members[1]. Public speeches and letters to the press regularly vented its view that in the course of the war the railway workers had gained immensely, to the detriment of the shareholders' interests. The dividend declared in February 1919 was 3.75%[2]. The officials had not done too badly, either, salaries fixed for 1919 included Matheson's, £3,500, Blackburn's, £1,600, and Pickersgill's, £1,650.

In the course of the war, the provision made for company "losses or injuries" incurred under government control had been, as already noted, very closely monitored. The basic arrangement, arrived at in September 1914, was that a company's aggregate net receipts for the first half of 1913 should be taken as the yardstick. Any shortfall on these would be reimbursed by the government (with a proportionate reduction if the receipts for the first half of 1914 were less than in the same period of 1913). Some further modifications were made, allowing companies to claim for arrears of repairs and maintenance, to receive interest at 4% on capital expenditure, and for replacement of stores and materials. Before the end of the war, it became clear that the period of troop demobilisation, removal of wartime installations, etc., would make it desirable to extend the "emergency" powers beyond the actual emergency, and the government decided to prolong the Railway Executive's control for two years after the end of hostilities. But the long-term future of the nation's railways was also under consideration. General agreement existed that the pre-war system, with its 100-plus companies, was no longer effective, and that a new structure would have to be imposed. Nationalisation of the railways, often mooted in previous decades (not such a political football as it was to become later) was a serious option. In August 1918 the government appointed a Select Committee to consider "what steps, if any, it is desirable to take to develop and improve the internal facilities for transport within the United Kingdom … and to ensure such developments and improvements shall be adequate and suitable to meet the national requirements." This committee produced an interim report in November 1918 which stated, "That unification of the railway system is desirable under suitable safeguards, whether the ownership be in public or private hands." The implication was clear: the national railway system, which for more than 80 years had largely avoided government control, was now to be reorganised in the national interest. Just how this was to be done was still undecided. Without the four years of all-out war, the government might have lacked the will to press forward. But the railway companies, run-down, having lost five years of mechanical development, requiring vast amounts of capital to replace worn-out stock and modernise their facilities, were not in good shape to face the upheavals required in adjusting to post-war conditions, and a government machine far more wide-ranging in its powers than ever before. By no means least, they were bearing far higher labour costs than in 1913, due to nationally-established wage rates and increases in the course of the war years and afterwards. In addition, from 1 February 1919, an eight-hour working day was conceded to all grades of railway staff, a change resisted tooth and nail by the companies, the Caledonian among them. In fact the Scottish companies were the most vociferous in their opposition. Although taking the railways into state ownership seemed likely for a time (the Caledonian Board had no great objection if the terms were right), it ultimately became clear that the government's aim was to force the companies into big new commercial concerns by large-scale amalgamation.

In August 1919 a Ministry of Transport was established for the first time, with far greater powers over the railways than the Board of Trade had ever possessed. Despite the pay and hours awards won over the previous few years, there was great unrest and dissatisfaction among railway workers. The government-supported war time pay deal was about to end and the National Union of Railwaymen, determined to maintain nationally-agreed pay levels against equally determined company desire to scrap them, called a national strike from 26 September 1919. On the Caledonian it was largely observed, and the management concentrated on moving perishable goods, using the few non-striking workers plus around a thousand naval men drafted in by the Railway Executive, and a motley range of volunteers[3]. Economic life was disrupted for a week, until a settlement extended the "war wage" for another year, and on 5 October the strike was called off. A legacy of hostility and mistrust between management and workforce was maintained, not helped by a bonus paid to "loyal staff", approved by the board in December. Hostility and mistrust also affected relations between the railway companies and the government, with the Caledonian chairman Henry Allan one of the most vocal critics of government policy towards the railways.

Ground bought for the never-finished Hamiltonhill line was sold in May 1919, 51 acres at £500 an acre. The Bankend-Galawhistle line was still in use and it was agreed to extend the shunting head at Galawhistle to hold 18 rather than ten wagons, at the South Ayrshire Coal Co.'s cost[4]. Much of the company's non-routine activity was connected with the dismantling of wartime systems. The Caledonian turned down the opportunity to purchase the now-vacated Gretna factory, but agreed to buy three of Georgetown's locomotives at a maximum of £1,000 each[5].

Pullman car services resumed on the Caledonian from 1 March 1919, between Glasgow-Edinburgh, Glasgow-Aberdeen, Glasgow-Carlisle and Aberdeen-Symington, after resolution of a dispute with the Pullman company, which had claimed £5,248 for each year in which its cars had been withdrawn. The CR resisted, but eventually paid £8,500[6], reclaimed from the government through the Defence of the Realm War Losses Commission. Revised contracts were made with the Pullman Co. on 28 July and 19 August 1919, covering cars ordered before the war but not delivered. Ultimately the full original order of 17 cars was supplied, and Pullman services included the morning and evening Wemyss Bay and Moffat expresses. In 1921 the Pullman Company informed the

Official NBL photograph of a 'Wemyss Bay tank', 4-6-2T No. 950.
Built in 1917, it ran until 1950. These engines also ran a fast train to Balloch
and did banking duties at Beattock. (Stephenson Locomotive Society)

Caledonian that it was supplying two further dining cars under the terms of the 1913 agreement. The Caledonian refused, as it already had four diners, but took them in the end, without acknowledging liability to do so, and 'Bonnie Jean' and 'Lady Nairne' were placed on show at Buchanan Street in March 1922[7].

1919-20 was a difficult trading period, with a fall in commercial activity and much unrest among the labour force. At the shareholders' meeting on 24 February 1920 it was announced that expenditure, for the first time ever, was greater than revenue, £8,052,000 against £7,350,000. Still, a dividend of 3.75% was again paid, backed by government funds on the basis of the wartime agreement. Inchture village asked for its branch horse-car back, in vain. The viaduct at Alloa was put out of action on 14 August 1920 when two old destroyers, *Vigilant* and *Mallard*, moored at a breakers' yard, broke loose, drifted upstream on the tide and knocked down two spans of the bridge. The Caledonian successfully sued South Alloa Shipbreakers for the repair cost of £18,000[8], but the company's longest bridge was less fortunate. Imported iron ore from Spain and elsewhere had largely killed off the ore traffic from Cumberland to central Scotland, and though war conditions restored it, imports resumed in 1919. By 1921 the Solway Viaduct was carrying very little traffic and needed major renewal work, at an estimated cost of around £70,000. It was officially declared closed from 20 May 1921, a decision reaffirmed by the board on 24 January 1922. Passenger services continued between Kirtlebridge and Annan. The bridge was not demolished until 1934-35. Labour disputes in the coal industry impacted on the railway, with reduced services during the miners' strike of October 1920. The political troubles of the time in Ireland were reflected in numerous incidents in central Scotland. Stolen ammunition and explosives were found in the Wishaw station yard, an attempt was made to blow up the Braidhurst Viaduct between Motherwell and Mossend, and "a number of young men in the Motherwell district are said to be tampering with explosives"[9]. In the winter of 1920-21 staff were being laid off because there was not enough work[10], though Donald Matheson's pay rose by almost 15% to £4,000. At the opening of the new hostel for railwaymen at Motherwell, in January 1921, which had cost £10,000, he criticised the current proposal to group the Scottish railways together, and argued for a West Coast and East Coast division[11].

As part of the government's efforts to get to grips with the railways, an official enquiry was going on in late 1920 into railway goods rates. John Ballantyne, the Caledonian Goods Manager, produced evidence to show that rates in Scotland were well below those in England. For general merchandise, the comparative rates were 222.41 and 180.9 pence a ton, and for minerals 63.4 and 44.95 old pennies a ton. Asked how this difference had come about, he could only say that it was a long standing situation that went back far before his time[12]. Scottish business and industry were apprehensive about their freight charges being scaled up to a pan-British level. For the Caledonian Board, it underlined the case that its operating conditions were different and it should not be subjected to wages and working hours regulations drawn up with English railways chiefly in mind.

Compensation, and Grouping

The question of compensation for the railways' wartime service was still unresolved. A parliamentary committee led by Lord Colwyn, appointed to investigate the claims, made its report in February 1921. Lamenting the ambiguities and imprecision of the original agreement of 1914 and its various later modifications, the committee was well aware that the railway companies had interpreted it in their own interest and taken advantage of its lack of clarity. No company was named, but the Caledonian, as has been noted, routinely charged every excess cost over 1913 levels to the government. The Colwyn Committee estimated the railway companies' total claim at £156,000,000, but did not recommend that this be paid, and clearly implied that it was far beyond what was reasonable.

A dividend of $3^2/_3$% on the Ordinary shares was declared in February 1921. At the annual meeting on the 22nd, Henry Allan denounced government-imposed awards on hours and wages. The eight hour day had meant an extra 6,000 staff, and the Company's wages and salaries bill, £1.5 million at the end of 1913, was £6.5 million at the end of 1920. He accepted that the cost of living was 165% above [2.65 times] the 1913 level, but even if the 1913 level was adjusted to the later one, "lowest grades' wages would still be at 55s. per week, or 175% above [2.75 times] the pre-war rate." The Caledonian might have 29,000 staff, but it also had 37,000 shareholders, who were urged by the chairman to unite, like the workers, in their own defence. For Allan, the Colwyn Report was a shoe-horn to ease the government out of its proper obligations to the railways, and he insisted that the Caledonian would claim for reinstatement of property, full provision for all arrears of maintenance and renewal work, and for the replacement of stores and plant[13].

At the same time, active planning for the future of railways in Great Britain was going on within the Ministry of Transport, with intensive discussion and negotiation between July 1920 and May 1921. Interested parties included local councils, chambers of commerce, trades unions, special-interest groups like the Scottish Railway Shareholders' Protection Association, major manufacturers and distributors, and the rapidly-growing and increasingly vocal motor trade. The Railway Companies' Association co-ordinated the response of the companies. But both press and public were taken by surprise when Sir Eric Geddes, Minister of Transport, announced on 3 May that a settlement with the companies had been reached. A total of £60 million would be made available for division among the railway companies, in two instalments, with income tax deductible on any amount used to pay interest or dividends; and the companies had to agree to the amalgamation proposals set out in his Railways Bill, of which the first version was published on 12 May. In Scotland, strong opposition emerged to the proposal of an all-Scottish railway group. Customers feared higher rates. Staff feared pay cuts, and the company boards had no enthusiasm for an isolated grouping. Old links and loyalties, going back to the earliest days of 'East Coast' and 'West Coast', were much stronger. Despite this, the Bill dealt with Scottish objections by proposing two groups, one to consist of the Caledonian, GSWR and Highland Railways, the other formed by the North British and Great North of Scotland. This was immediately assailed and by 17 June it was accepted that cross-border mergers were possible.

In a small extension to its vehicle range, the company arranged for eight four-wheel vans to be fitted with ice tanks, for the transport of fresh fish from Aberdeen to London and Southampton (the weight of the ice was to be paid for by the fish merchants)[14]. The CR seems to have been rather slow in providing chilled transport; at that time it was reported to have only four "refrigerator vans", though in 1918 it had been nudged by the Ministry of Food into fitting 51 vans with insulation to carry frozen meat: the cost, £65 each, being duly billed to the government account[15]. All operations in April-June 1921 were made difficult by strikes in the coal mines. One railway writer recalled a journey on the Oban line that year with the locomotive "burning slack and logs mixed"[16]. Caledonian workers refused to unload coal sent from Wales and were suspended, causing a sharp dispute between the National Union of Railwaymen and the management[17]. The locomotives sent on war service were returned in varying states of disrepair, and the company had to sue the War Department for the cost of their repair at Beardmore's Works. The War Department offered £10,000 but was eventually compelled to pay the full £11,919 15s. 11d. required to make the engines roadworthy[18].

A 6-ton refrigerator van, double-walled and insulated.
Note the piping for both vacuum and air brake systems, enabling it to run in
passenger trains between Aberdeen and London. (Caledonian Railway Association)

McIntosh and Pickersgill 4-4-0s on an Up special fish train at Glenboig,
around 1921-22: No. 138 (1910) pilots No. 88 (1921).

A Brief Independence

On 15 August 1921, Government control of the railways came to an end. The Caledonian company was theoretically free to conduct its own affairs, but in reality it was closely bound in by current legislation and future intentions. The Railways Act, given the royal assent on 19 August, was very substantial and wide-ranging, embracing both the grouping and the compensation issues. The Caledonian, Glasgow & South Western and Highland Railways, together with the small independent companies whose lines they worked, were to be merged with the London & North Western, Midland, Lancashire & Yorkshire, North Staffordshire, and Furness Railways. Terms of amalgamation were to be agreed with the new company, and the date for completion was set at 1 January 1923, with provision for disputed cases to be resolved by a special Amalgamation Tribunal, before a final deadline of 1 July 1923. In addition, the Act provided for the regulation of railway rates under a new charging body, the Railway Rates Tribunal, and for a conciliation system to keep wages and conditions of service under review. The Caledonian could not ignore the trade unions or impose its own pay rates. There was a Central Wages Board, with company and union members in equal numbers, and a National Wages Board to consider appeals.

Of the £60 million agreed between the Government and the railway companies for war compensation, the Caledonian received £3,264,788, or 5.2%, plus £3,663 interest, paid in two instalments at the end of 1921 and 1922. The North British received £2,778,866, an allocation against which it vehemently protested. Some of the Caledonian's associate companies also received payments: with £67,821 to the Lanarkshire & Ayrshire, £27,586 to the Portpatrick & Wigtownshire, £21,019 18s. 3d. to the Cathcart Circle Company, and £1,119 0s. 3d. to the Brechin & Edzell[19]. Of the CR's second instalment, £35,000 was due to be passed on to the Callander & Oban[20].

Railway freight charges were widely seen as excessive, and the prospect of grouping the companies did not diminish this. A speaker at a Scottish Motor Trade dinner in Glasgow in January 1922 criticised "railway companies' attempts to get by private Bills what the 1921 Act did not give them." This included powers to operate road vehicles, and some people suggested that the railways were out to stifle the motor trade. He added that, "It was now recognised that the motor vehicle in the hands of the private contractor was the most effective check we had on excessive railway rates and unsatisfactory railway services"[21]. The road haulage industry at the time saw itself as a doughty David facing a railway Goliath. The railway companies were vastly bigger and had far greater resources. What they lacked was flexibility of operation. Already since the 1890s the extension of electric tramway systems had hit the suburban railways very hard. Now the motor bus was adding its erosive effect on rail traffic. In 1919 Rankin Brothers had begun a bus service on the primal route from Garnkirk Station into Glasgow, soon extended into a Cumbernauld-Glasgow service. In the early 1920s the Caledonian management reckoned it was paying £55,000 a year in local rates towards the upkeep of roads (and thereby assisting its new competitors).

On 15 November 1921 the board agreed to acquire the Loch Tay Steamship Company, which had given up operations that year, for £1,750, and announced that steamer services on the loch would resume by 1 March 1922 at the latest. The passenger boats, *Lady of the Lake* and *Queen of the Lake*, respectively 40 and 15 years old in 1922, plied between Lochtay Station Pier and Kenmore at the eastern end. Two small cargo boats also operated, though one was withdrawn in 1923. The prime beneficiary of the purchase was the Killin Railway Company. A few months later the Caledonian bought the Loch Awe Steamboat Service, with its little ship *Countess of Breadalbane*, and the connecting Oban & Ford Motor Service, with two motor cars, for £1,550[22]. The preservation of these almost moribund ventures shows the Caledonian's appreciation of the tourist trade as one of the mainstays of the line west of Callander. On a larger financial scale it approved orders for 20 locomotives from the North British Locomotive Co., at a total cost of £111,340, and 300 covered vans from the Government's Disposal & Liquidation Commission at £210 each. After negotiating to buy 500 or 1,000 new 16-ton mineral wagons, it settled for 250[23].

With the other Scottish companies, the Caledonian asked the National Wages Board in January 1922 to approve a reduction of weekly wages by 5s., to abolish special payments for night work, and to raise the age at which boys were paid men's rates from 18 to 21. Considering that in the previous month it had received £1,125,277 as its first instalment of war-compensation payment, this might seem rather mean-spirited, but the wage rates were linked to the cost of living index, which was falling. The National Wages Board refused the reduction unless the cost of living (then 88% above the 1913 standard) should have fallen to 75% above, or less, by 1 April[24]. Allan made a gloomy speech to the annual general meeting of 28 February 1922, about the need to reduce the wage bill and not reduce fares and charges. Compared with January 1913, the company's tonnage of iron and steel carried in January 1922 was down by 70%. A dividend of 3.5% was declared. He reported that the combination of increased traffic and fares had brought gross revenue up to £9,828,000, to which was added government compensation of £1,636,000, paid to bring the net receipts up to the 1913 standard. Bemoaning the increased operating costs caused by pay increases and the eight hour day, he pointed out that the actual net receipts of 1921 were only £534,952 despite the huge gross revenue. In 1913 terms, the company had made a trading loss of almost a million pounds. Despite the chairman's downbeat remarks, that year the shareholders did rather better, with an interim dividend of 4.5% declared in August: 3% on the Ordinary and 1.5% on the Deferred Converted Ordinary shares.

Improvements to services were made. Half an hour was cut from the schedule of the 1.30 p.m. express from Glasgow and Edinburgh to London, which now arrived at Euston at 10 p.m., and the International Sleeping Car Company opened an agency at Glasgow Central, where through bookings as far as Istanbul or Baghdad could be made[25]. The *Railway Gazette* on 17 November 1922 carried a descriptive article on six Caledonian marshalling yards, mostly concerned with coal and mineral traffic, including the Gorgie yard in Edinburgh, with 25 tracks handling 1,500 wagons each day. The others were at Ross Junction, between Motherwell and Ferniegair, handling mineral traffic only, with track capacity for 1,400 wagons and handling around 10,000 a week, Mossend, with capacity for 2,000 wagons and handling 20,000 a week, the new yard at Polmadie, with capacity for 2,300 wagons and handling 16,500 a week, Strathaven Junction, holding 2,200 wagons, its weekly handling total not noted; and Robroyston, with tracks for 1,100 wagons and handling 10,000 a week. The Caley had facilities, and a degree of efficiency, that could stand comparison with any British railway.

The Gleneagles Controversy

But it had its critics. Construction of the huge Gleneagles Hotel had been in abeyance during the war years but Matheson had not abandoned his pet project. In 1923 the Caledonian Railway promoted a Bill to take over the hotel company and complete the work. During its Second Reading various Scottish MPs asked why the Caledonian was spending money on a luxury hotel and why Crieff Junction had been sumptuously rebuilt as 'Gleneages' for a few wealthy visitors in 1919 while Buchanan Street Station remained a slum for the multitude. Others thought the company should be building sleeping cars for third class passengers, or electrifying the sulphurous tunnel of the Central line, or improving the standard of workmen's trains, "as bad as they were sixteen or seventeen years ago". For another member, "There is probably no place [even] in Ireland where such archaic rolling stock survives as that which is being used between Lugton and Beith" (perhaps one of the disadvantages of a joint line). According to Tom Johnston, a future Secretary of State for Scotland, "... the present railway system in Scotland is a standing monument of inefficiency and stupidity"[26]. But the Bill was passed, and the 'Gleneagles Ltd' project went on. Already the company had laid out a championship standard golf course, complete with clubhouse, and was planning an airstrip. Oddly, there was no hotel committee for Gleneagles, unlike the Glasgow and Edinburgh establishments, and everything went through the board and the finance committee.

Integration

It soon became clear that integration of the Caledonian Company into the new grouping was not going to be an easy matter. Of the associated companies which had remained independent, the Callander & Oban, Dundee & Newtyle, and the Arbroath & Forfar, were absorbed into what was now known as the London, Midland & Scottish group (LMS) at the end of 1922, leaving the Killin Railway and the Caledonian. Arbroath & Forfar shareholders got £146 of LMS 4% Debenture stock for every £100 of Arbroath & Forfar they held; Dundee & Newtyle shareholders were issued with stock to match the value of the annual £1,400 rental (their lease had 950 years still to run). The Killin (whose shareholders got £8 for every £100 of their stock[27], was merely late in agreeing, but the Caledonian was making real difficulties over the terms of amalgamation. The key issue was the valuation placed on its Ordinary stocks. The LMS was offering to convert Caledonian Debenture and Preference stocks at par, on which there was no dispute. But for every £100 of the Ordinary stock, of which £3,364,284 had been issued, it was offering £75 of LMS 4% Preference stock and the same for CR 'Preferred Converted Ordinary Stock', of which £15,101,750 had been issued. For £100 of the Caledonian's 'Deferred Converted Ordinary', also £15,101,750, it offered £8 of LMS Ordinary stock. For the CR Deferred Ordinary stock, Nos. 1 and 2, with a nominal combined value of £2,784,692, on which a dividend had been payable only if the Ordinary dividend rose above 7% and 9% respectively, which had never happened, it offered nothing at all. The offer was made on the basis that the return would be comparable to the earnings of the Caledonian stock in 1913. The Caledonian held out for a better deal, and although it participated in LMS group working from 1 January 1923, on the basis of "preliminary amalgamation", it claimed retention of all its powers, even though its accounts would be merged into those of the new company. With the two sides failing to reach agreement, the case went to the Amalgamation Tribunal, which modified the terms, offering £50 of LMS 4% Preference stock plus £23 6s. 8d. of Ordinary stock for £100 of Caledonian Ordinary; and £50 of LMS 4% Preference plus £13 6s. 8d. of Ordinary stock for £100 of Caledonian Preferred Converted Ordinary. For the CR Deferred Converted Ordinary, £10 for every £100 was proposed. On the two sets of Caledonian Deferred Ordinary stock, the tribunal supported the LMS's proposal to cancel these shares and pay nothing[28]. But the Caledonian insisted that they were worth *something* and requested a further review. On 25 June the tribunal rejected the Caledonian's objections. Though there were threats of taking the matter to the Court of Appeal, in the end the Caledonian Company and its shareholders accepted the terms[29], and on 1 July it became the last company (along with the North Staffordshire) to be merged into the LMS.

From 1 January 1923, Donald Matheson was also a Deputy General Manager of the new mega-company, in charge of its Scottish operations, and on 28 December 1922 the board voted him £5,000 for his services to the Caledonian. Robert Killin, once a Caley telegraph-boy, departed for Derby to become General Superintendent of the Midland Region. At the company's last shareholders' meeting, on 22 February 1923, a pay out of £2,452,839 in interest and dividends was announced. All classes of share were paid except the Deferred Ordinaries. Holders of Ordinary shares got $5^3/_8\%$ and the Preferred and Converted Ordinary got $2^3/_8\%$.

The Caledonian board's last executive decision was on 26 June 1923 when it proposed to take 1,000 shares in the Kinlochleven Road Transport Co., which was to operate a bus on the new road between Ballachulish and Kinlochleven. At its final meeting, on 24 July 1923, it fixed its own compensation for loss of posts. The directors' fee pool was £4,500 a year and in addition the chairman and the eleven other directors received a fixed annual amount of £525 and £105 each, respectively. Retiring directors were awarded a sum equivalent to four years' remuneration, sharing a total of £13,920. The chairman had already pronounced the company's epitaph, in rather muted fashion, at the shareholders' meeting in February: "It is with some regret that we see the end of our old Company, which has grown during so many years till it has become almost a national Institution of Scotland." The hovering shades of Locke, of Hope Johnstone, Duncan, Salkeld, Hill and all the others who had done their utmost in the years of struggle and competition to maintain the Caledonian's identity and security, can only have nodded in silent assent.

CHAPTER 15. Caledonian Style and Substance

A Happy Family?

Donald A. Matheson, the Caledonian's last general manager, was an affable as well as able figure, who liked to lace his speeches with Scotticisms and occasionally referred to the company, with its 29,000 staff, as a "happy family". During the Wages Board's enquiry, in the winter of 1921-22, into the company's proposal to reduce its employees' pay, he was confronted, from the union side, by James Kiddie, a Caley locomotive driver for 28 years. Kiddie was also a Glasgow town councillor, and it was no unequal match. Asked if the Caledonian was a happy family, he replied that that was "a bit of a Scottish joke." The Company had dragged its heels over implementing the eight-hour day and there had been walk-outs at some depots because of this. Matheson's case was that trade had declined, wages in other industries were going down, and the railway workers, having shared in the wartime boom, should now share in the belt-tightening. Kiddie's response was that pre-war wages had been at "starvation" level, and that the Scottish railwaymen, having struggled to get their pay rate up to those of their English colleagues, were not going to let it fall back. "What if the money is not there?" asked Matheson. "Oh, there is never much money in Scotland – not when we are wanting any," was the reply, to general laughter[1]. It was a good-natured exchange which nevertheless revealed two very different sets of attitudes.

In the 19th century, the management had been able to regard manpower as a resource among others, like fuel. A kind of informal labour market existed. At expansive times, men were sought and hired, and pay rates went up because businesses competed, especially for skilled workers. If trade contracted, then men were laid off at instant notice, and wages went down. 'Servants' had no say in this process. All reforms in workers' conditions and extensions of their rights, made in the late 19th and early 20th centuries, were strongly resisted by the companies. Like all directors and managers, the men who ran the Caledonian Railway saw their prime responsibility as being to the shareholders, who required the best possible dividend. To provide this, it was essential to keep the business in viable and competitive form. Provision of a service and welfare of the company's staff were secondary. Perhaps the worst aspect of this attitude is seen in the board's response to the continuous toll of deaths and serious injuries among its workers. Nine fatal injuries to staff were reported in the single month of February 1885. As with an army in action, casualties seem to have been regarded as inevitable. £10 was the standard payment made when a workman was killed on duty, and even this was refused if there was a suggestion of careless behaviour. The widow of Driver Paterson who fell from his engine in January 1852 received nothing, because he was "killed while acting in breach of the rules and regulations"[2]. The relative unimportance of workers was shown on 21 June 1898, when the Royal Train was running south from Aberdeen, drawn by two engines. The driver of the train engine, David Fenwick, was killed as it passed under a bridge at Cove. Thomas Macdonald, the locomotive department's chief running inspector, made the dangerous (normally strictly forbidden) traverse from the pilot engine to the train engine and took charge, "in order to avoid stopping the train and causing unavailing

The Crawford derailment, 2 April 1909. *Cardean*'s driving wheel lies against the snow-fence,
following the fracture of the crank axle.

commotion." The train did not stop until it reached Perth, some 80 miles on[3]. Contemporary attitudes, and strict obedience to regulations, are apparent rather than callousness on the part of the Caledonian.

Matheson could scarcely have made his "family" comment without feeling some justification, and James Thompson had made similar remarks before him. It would be wrong to see the Caledonian Railway's employees as an exploited and repressed group. Compared to some others, notably the farm workers and the coal miners, the railwaymen and boys (work began at 14) were well-treated, and railway jobs were always sought after. The railway was the first mass employer to have a public face, and it needed workers who were intelligent, literate and capable of showing initiative. Emergencies especially showed the value of this. When on 2 April 1909 locomotive No. 903 *Cardean*, hauling the 8.13 a.m. express from Carlisle, broke a crank axle just past Crawford, derailing its tender and train and running on for three quarters of a mile, the signalman at Abington, Henry Brownrigg, sensed something was amiss and held back a train on the Up line even though it had been accepted by Crawford. A major collision with the derailed train was averted. The subsequent report noted that all staff had acted "in a prompt and intelligent manner"[4], and this was typical. Railwaymen had various advantages – uniforms were supplied, reduced price tickets were given once or twice a year, and many lived in subsidised housing, at least while working. The Caledonian was happy to ballot its workers on non-contentious issues, as when in 1883 the St. Rollox men voted to choose a pay day: Saturday was picked, with 806 for and 71 against, out of a workforce of 1,338[5].

Self-improvement was a theme of the 1850s, and later. In April 1853, the sum of £53 12s. 2d. was found in the directors' allowances account. From this, £10 each was given to the Edinburgh and Glasgow Infirmaries, and the balance to the already-established "Library of the Company's servants"[6]. The library was housed at St. Rollox Works and was clearly a source of pride to the workmen and perhaps also to the directors. How it operated is not clear. By 1861 an annual donation was being made, and the directors, perhaps concerned about what the men might be reading, requested that "lists of proposed additions are submitted from time to time"[7]. Again for educational purposes, in 1857 the company gave a donation of £10 to the Buchanan Street Station Evening School for Carters' Boys[8]. Apart from contributions to the worthy cause of "getting on", relaxation was also allowed for: St. Rollox Works had its own golf club and bowling green, the latter being situated at Mount Florida, on land given by the board.

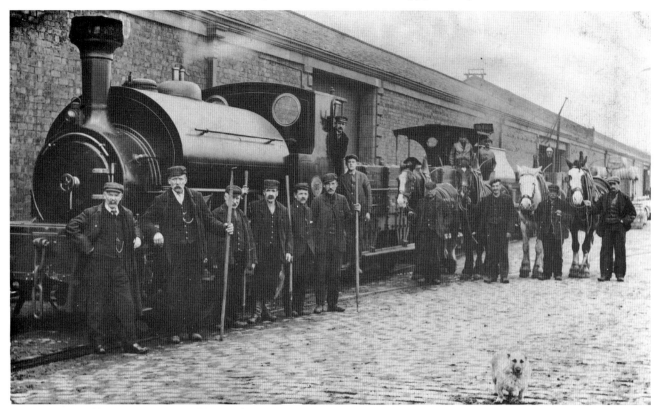

Shunting pugs and horses, with drivers and shunters, at Dundee. The engines are
Neilson 0-4-0STs of 1876, with spark arrestors. The nearer is No. 503, rebuilt with a conventional saddle
tank and full cab; the other still has its original canopy-type cab and 'piano' saddle tank.

In 1866 an Act for new Lanarkshire branches included a clause allowing the establishment of a provident fund for company servants, though this may not have survived the financial crisis of 1867. Later, the CR administered a 'Sick Fund' for employees of the locomotive and carriage & wagon departments. Founded by Dugald Drummond during his time as Locomotive Superintendent, it was a Friendly Society, which everyone had to pay into, from 2d. a week upwards. In 1896 it paid £1,727 sickness allowance and £305 funeral allowance to members, and also gave a rebate of £619 to non-claimants, equivalent to 26% of contributions. As well as clerical assistance, the company contributed £50 a year to it. For salaried officials, a superannuation scheme was provided, to which they and the company paid contributions. Sometimes the figure was topped up; when George Brittain retired in 1882, he was awarded an additional £300 a year "at the company's pleasure"[9], and in 1886 Irving Ferguson, retiring as Minerals Superintendent after 38 years' service, had his superannuation of £176 a year topped up by £226 from the company[10]. Waged employees usually retired only if incapable of further work; with no pension arrangements, they had no choice. Drivers aged into their 70s were not unusual. When disability or illness forced a man to leave work, he might become destitute. John McCallum, head porter at Lanark for 30 years, was given a gratuity of £5 when he had to retire because of poor health in 1880[11].

Like some other railway companies, the Caledonian ran an employees' savings bank, partly for the convenience of staff in remoter places and partly because men with savings were thought less likely to entertain 'socialistic' ideas, or to have to petition for assistance in old age. *Railway Engineer* reported in April 1897 that deposits were £515,005, equivalent to £109 for each depositor. The annual rate of interest at the time was 4%. By 1922, deposits amounted to £1,208,050 18s. 4d., and there were 9,933 accounts. Around one in three of the staff was a depositor[12]. Cohesion among the staff came also from the prospect of promotion. Most of the company's station masters, inspectors, district superintendents, and some top officials, had started as telegraph boys, lamp boys, or engine cleaners. Though their job was to represent and implement the authority of the board, their progress through the ranks ensured that they knew the organisation from the ground up and were part of it. Family loyalties also were important. Other things being equal, the son of a good Caley man had a much better chance of a job with the company than someone with no connection.

But aside from company-sponsored schemes, there is ample evidence (not exclusive to the Caledonian of course) of the workers organising their own events and organisations, usually with the tacit or open approval of the board. Servants' soirées were regular annual events. The gatherings of the Central and Buchanan Street staff raised money to keep ten beds at the Seaside Convalescent Home in Dunoon. From 1906 the head office staff held an annual smoking concert in the Glasgow Trades Hall. On 19 March 1909 400 attended, and Colonel Denny, one of the directors, presided, with Guy Calthrop also in the platform party. Concerts were also put on in Glasgow by the Railway Guards' Friendly Society, with "music and artistes of the highest class". In every town with a concentration of railway staff, including Perth, Forfar and Arbroath, annual 'Railway Festivals' were held, with the platform party usually graced by a director or two. Speeches extolling the company and its staff were followed by tea, music and dancing 'into the small hours.' It was unusual for controversy to be raised in such gatherings, though at the passenger department's soirée in Glasgow on 19 February 1879, the evening's chairman, George Farquharson, Central Station Superintendent, chose to inveigh against trade unions: "a greater slave than a trade unionist was not to be found in the backwoods of North America"[13]. At the time, the company was seeking to extend the working week to 54 hours.

The greatest company occasions around the turn of the 19th century were the annual excursions for St. Rollox workers and their families, organised under J.F. McIntosh's aegis. A multiplicity of special trains would head for the chosen destination city, carrying thousands of excursionists for a day's relaxation. Tickets, at a low price, were sold out far in advance. Aberdeen, Dundee and Carlisle were the venues, and the outings were carefully planned, with huge teas laid on, and dignitaries invited to address the gathering. Souvenir programmes were printed. Perhaps the largest of these events was the visit to Carlisle in September 1899. Fifteen special trains, each of 18 carriages, were scheduled to run from Glasgow, arriving at Carlisle between 7.35 and 10.15 a.m., carrying around 13,000 people, and it was said to have been the largest excursion trip the country had ever seen. Sports were organised, including cycle racing, and a performance by the 'Geisha Boys' of Scarborough was presented at the racecourse, while organ recitals were given in the cathedral and the presbyterian church. The band of the Glasgow Highlanders and the Glasgow Male Voice Quartet also performed. Some 170 gentlemen lunched at the County Hotel, and later Lord Rosebery made an open-air speech on 'The Railway Interests of the United Kingdom'. In the evening the fifteen trains steamed home again, the last one leaving Carlisle at 10 p.m. and reaching Glasgow in the wee hours of Sunday morning[14].

In the 20th century, there is more evidence of the company appreciating the dedication of its staff, and special payments for services beyond the call of duty were made from time to time, as when following a 'mishap' at Wemyss Bay on 22 October 1920, certain employees shared £160. Great pride was taken in the ambulance brigade, which was divided into nine district sections, and which taught and provided first aid for the many kinds of injury, major and minor, that regularly occurred. A competitive spirit was fostered both among the districts and with the brigades of other companies. In 1909 it was noted that the general manager had offered a two guinea prize for the best essay on 'Simple Fractures of the Long Bones'[15]. The Company's 'Christmas Annual', sold to the public, which appeared in 1909 but does not seem to have been repeated, was produced in aid of the ambulance Brigade, and was a volunteer effort, not a production of the advertising department. A reminder that many of the company's employees were teenagers comes from Glasgow's Caledonian Railway Rovers & Boy Scouts' Association. They had been paying £20 a year for the use of a football field on company ground at Cathcart, but the board made it free in 1920[16]. They had a pipe band, which turned out for special occasions.

Company loyalties were powerful. David Smith's *Tales of the Glasgow & South Western Railway* give ample evidence of how rivalry with the Caledonian motivated the engine crews: "We beat the Caledonian with the 259." Thomas Middlemass recorded how his father, a goods guard, "served the North British Railway, and scorned the Caledonian Railway, with equal devotion". Caley men naturally reciprocated these feelings. It was like a regimental loyalty, with the pride and comradeship of being part of a great operation which required teamwork, and such men "found no difficulty in equating an inborn inability to doff their caps with genuine pride at being 'a Company servant'"[17]. The downside of such an attitude could be the assumption that passengers were there for the railway, rather than *vice versa*, and if such a view was far more common in the early decades of railways than later on, it never quite disappeared. At jointly-run stations, inter-company rivalry often showed itself in petty ways. During the 1900s, the Caledonian and North British were supposedly co-operating, but in 1903 the NBR complained to the Railway & Canal Commissioners that the Caledonian was despatching trains from Perth, particularly on the Crieff line, without waiting for the NBR connection, sometimes even when passengers were running along the platform. Robert Millar's response was that the North British should start its trains sooner, or run them faster[18]. Aberdeen, as already noted, was another source of complaints about Caledonian obstructiveness.

Like all railway companies, the CR disliked having to pay ancillary charges for its property and rights of way. As a property owner it was required to contribute to local poor rates and road funds. Especially when short of cash, it often neglected to pay, and had to be chased to pay up. Frequently it contested the amount due, and was taken to court for arrears, as by Carluke Parish in February 1851, when it paid £50 on account pending a judgement[19]. Considering its railway service to be its benefit to the community, the company almost invariably gave a negative answer to the constant stream of requests for charitable donations, special fares or free tickets, which reached the board. Its donations to hospitals were on account of the frequent treatment of accident victims. In a few places, too, it accepted responsibility for maintaining local schools. On occasion it could make a graceful gesture, especially if a little extra income accrued fom it. In March 1851 it responded to a plea from the proprietor of the Gretna Hotel, who wanted to employ destitute handloom weavers from Carlisle to clear an area of moss. The CR agreed to attach a third class carriage to the 5.45 a.m. from Carlisle and to a returning ballast engine in the evening, for a return fare of 3*d*. a head[20]. But a purely humanitarian spirit was evident when, in one of the Dixon company pits at Blantyre, a huge underground explosion killed 240 men and boys on 22 October 1877, shattering the community. None of the underground workers survived, but "The Caledonian Railway, it may be mentioned, kept a train of first class carriages and an engine at the pits during the whole of the day and all night, to be ready to convey to the hospital in Glasgow any men who might be brought to the surface alive"[21].

To the public eye, the character of a railway company is determined by a range of factors, both abstract and physical. Appearance is important: the buildings, the trains and the staff. Aspects of the service, punctuality, a sense of safety, politeness, comfort and convenience all combine to form an overall impression. Measured against these criteria, the Caledonian company scores more than respectably. Competition probably played a part: among the large towns it served, the only one where it enjoyed a monopoly was Motherwell, and many much smaller places had an alternative railway within a relatively short distance. The Caledonian never employed a 'public relations' manager but the men who ran it always had a keen sense of the commercial value of good appearance. From the beginning it had an architect who aimed high: of Carlisle and the first Caledonian station in Edinburgh, as well as Perth (built under the auspices of the SCR), William Tite said, "I have done my best to mould the forms and modes of thinking of medieval architects to the unusual requirements of railways"[22]. If the standard fell back during the 1860s and 70s, Tite eventually had a worthy successor in James Miller. Staff were encouraged to embellish their stations with flowers. By 1909 the directors were awarding £350 annually for "best-kept station", with a total of 190 prizes ranging from £50 to £1. In 1909 Mr. Prentice of Wemyss Bay, with its fine floral displays, was overall winner[23]. Eventually Wemyss Bay had to be excluded, to give the others a chance.

Balquhidder Station opened on 1 June 1870 as Lochearnhead; it was renamed on 1 May 1904, and became a junction with the St Fillans line from 1 May 1905. Only the area under the verandah is paved. The station had an underpasss rather than a footbridge.

William Wallace and Robert I's victory of 1314 are both remembered in this patriotic floral arrangement at Bannockburn Station (opened in 1848 by the SCR). (Caledonian Railway Association)

The spirit of the Caledonian was closely linked with that of the city of Glasgow, which grew in the course of the 19th century from a modest-sized commercial town to "second city of the Empire" and a population exceeding one million by 1921. Civic pride was displayed in an architectural extravaganza of styles not only in public buildings but in company offices and even factories, at least in their façades. Glasgow of course also possessed some of the vilest slums in Europe. Prosperity was deeply unequal, but the spirit of the people was vibrant, encouraged by the sense and possibility of progress. The sheer scale and magnitude of Glasgow's transformation struck awe into those who lived through it. If the citizens were capable of defiance, disrespect and violence when pushed too far, they also knew how to enjoy and express themselves, and to appreciate and indeed expect a certain dash and style in the way their city's managers and grandees presented Glasgow to the world. As Glasgow's major railway company, the Caledonian had to be part of this, and Sir James Thompson's comments, already quoted, show its acceptance. One of its chairmen, Sir James King, had also been Lord Provost of the city. This urge to do things with style, even *panache* at times, was something the staff could relate to and make their own contributions to, whether it was Driver Ranochan's exuberant run from Coatbridge to Dundee, or the adornments made to *Cardean* by Driver David Gibson, "almost a demi-god to boys, who used to speculate on whether the two brilliant coins mounted, among elaborate brazen filigree, on her regulator, were bright ha'pennies or in very truth sovereigns"[24].

It is the fate of railways to be taken for granted by most people, except when running late. For all its colour, the Caledonian was not depicted by the talented painters of Glasgow, and it scarcely features in literature. Perhaps it is the railway company in George Douglas Brown's famous novel *The House with the Green Shutters* (1903) which graphically records the excitement and controversy around a new country branch line: "The question agitating solemn minds was whether it should join the main line at Fechars, thirty miles ahead, or pass to the right, through Fleckie and Barbie, to a junction up at Skeighan Drone. Many were the reasons spluttered in vehement debate for one route or the other"[25]. Jules Verne set three novels in Scotland, and the Caledonian and C&O lines feature in his *Backwards to Britain* (1890). Patrick McGill, 'the Navvy Poet', born in Northern Ireland, worked from 1909 for a time as a surfaceman between Greenock and Wemyss Bay, though he did not write about the Caledonian. But the Company also had its own home-grown bards, who, if not up to the standard of the GSWR's

Alexander Anderson ('Surfaceman'), made their own additions to *esprit de corps*, like 'The Green Corduroy'[26]:

I lo'e my porter laddie …
Oh, ye should hear his manly voice when cryin' ilka day,
"The ither side for Wilsontown, Carnwath and Auchengray!"
An' then he's aye sae cheery, aye the foremost i' the ploy:
My bonnie porter laddie wi' the green corduroy.

A poet who chose anonymity also celebrated the nonchalant style of the Caley railwayman:

He's a big strappin' chiel, everybody declares,
An' he looks quite a toff in the claes that he wears,
He's the new simmer gaird, an' he comes frae Carstairs,
An' he rins wi' the paurly to Gourock[27].

Non-prestige services on the Caledonian often left much to be desired, and occasionally aroused humour as well as complaint. In 1897 the average speed of the passenger trains on the Strathaven line was 12 mph, and a letter to the *Glasgow Herald* pretended that a man had lost his hat from the moving train, got out, retrieved it, and walked back to climb into his compartment again[28]. Others found the restrictions on tickets and special fares irksome: "You are liable to be pounced on by the company at all times, and then you find that the ticket for which you have paid good money is invalid and that you are called upon to pay again"[29]. Even occasional vestiges of that rare thing, an official sense of humour, can be picked up: in 1910 the general manager's telegraphic address was 'Caley, Glasgow.' The superintendent's was 'Donian', the engineer's, 'Theodolite', the locomotive department, 'Powerful'. The front line staff could laugh at themselves on occasion, as a couple of 'baurs' in the 'Christmas Annual' show:

Station-master to doubtful-looking lady who has sat in first class: "Are you first class, ma'am?"
Lady: "Yes, fine. How are you yourself?"

Guard to passenger: "Smoking's not allowed in this compartment. You'll have to get out."
Man: "I'm not smoking."
Guard: "Your pipe's in your mouth."
Man: "Yes, and I have my fut in my boot but I'm no' walking."

At one of the many pleasant annual soirées held in most places with a large Caledonian staff, Lord Breadalbane entertained the Perth employees in February 1895 with the tale of a man who, while the train was waiting at the ticket platform, could not find his ticket when the inspector asked for it, though he looked everywhere. Eventually a fellow passenger said, "Did you not put it in your mouth?" Sure enough, it was there, and the man handed it over to the inspector, who then moved on. When another passenger grumbled about the delay, the man said, "I'm no' sic a fule as I look, for I was busy working off the auld date"[30].

Whose Caledonian was it? Railway companies always meant different things to different people, and often also to the same people. Shareholders, workers, directors, goods shippers, passengers – all had their own take on the company that paid their dividends or their wages, carried their coal or took them from place to place, in grand style sometimes, or in no style at all between Lugton and Beith. Poised around and above all these views and interests, there was something called 'the Caledonian', which everyone shared a sense of, even though it was impossible to define with any precision, combined as it was of buildings and behaviour, grandeur and grime, dash and delay, Pullman fliers and penny-a-mile crawlers. If it did not lack critics, it also attracted strong loyalties. But few tears were shed for it in 1923; there was a feeling that the Scottish railway companies had reached the end of their useful existence, and that change was desirable as well as inevitable.

CHAPTER 16. Rhapsody in Blue (and Green, and Black) – Caledonian Locomotives

This summary account of the company's locomotive history is intended to give an outline of developments and to relate them to the railway as a whole, though it picks up a few salient points along the way. For detailed consideration of design and performance, readers are recommended to Cornwell's *Forty Years of Caledonian Locomotives*, and other specialist works listed in the bibliography.

The Crewe Legacy

> "From the beginning of the history of the Caledonian Railway until the year 1853 the general design of the locomotive stock presented well-marked features and peculiarities that distinguished this line from most railways,"

proclaimed William Pickersgill in 1920, but this was not the case; essentially similar types could be seen on many Scottish and English railways. At the beginning, provision of locomotives was the responsibility of the engineers, and given Joseph Locke's Grand Junction connections, it was natural for him to specify the kind of locomotives being built by the still-new Grand Junction Railway works at Crewe. Robert Sinclair, installed by Locke as the Glasgow, Paisley & Greenock's locomotive superintendent in 1844 at the age of 28, later had his brief extended to the Caledonian and the Scottish Central. He had been apprenticed at Scott, Sinclair of Greenock, where an uncle of his was a director, and had learned locomotive engineering with the Grand Junction Railway. Scott, Sinclair built some of the early Scottish Central and Caledonian engines, and other builders used in 1847-9 were Jones & Potts and the Vulcan Foundry, both in Lancashire, George England of New Cross, Surrey, R.&W. Hawthorn of Leith, and Neilson, Mitchell of Glasgow. But 87 of the 167 engines built for or bought in by the CR in Sinclair's time came from the company's own works at Greenock[1]. All were four- or six-wheel engines, the majority with a single pair of driving wheels, though 23 with coupled wheels were built in 1847-50, and many 2-2-2 types were later converted to 2-4-0. A fifteen-strong 0-6-0 class built in 1849-50 were "very soon rebuilt to 0-4-2"[2]. Typical were two 2-2-2s built by the Vulcan Foundry for the Caledonian in 1847, one of which was in service until 1874. These locomotives weighed around 19 tons and while they could reach a speed of over 50 mph, they could handle only lightweight trains[3]. Sinclair was responsible for introducing the Caledonian's 'stovepipe' chimney[4] which in various styles would be a recurrent St. Rollox trademark for many years, and probably also for the original locomotive liveries of light blue for passenger engines and light green for goods[5] (Glasgow, Paisley & Greenock locomotives were crimson).

In the course of 1847-48 the Caledonian took over 32 locomotives, mostly of 2-2-2 wheel arrangement, with some 0-4-2 and 0-4-0 types, regauged in some cases, from the Glasgow, Garnkirk & Coatbridge, Glasgow, Paisley & Greenock, Polloc & Govan, and Wishaw & Coltness companies. They came from a variety of builders in Scotland

Scottish North Eastern 0-4-2 No. 75, built by Neilson in 1859, became CR 515 in 1866.
Renumbered 681 in 1877, it was withdrawn in 1888.

This 2-2-2 was built by Vulcan Foundry in 1866 to an order from the SNER but delivered to the
Caledonian (who had just absorbed the SNER) as CR463 and renumbered as CR317 in 1877. Put on the
duplicate list in 1887 and seen here at Perth, it was withdrawn in 1898. (Stephenson Locomotive Society)

and England, including Barr & MacNab of Paisley, Murdoch & Aitken of Glasgow, and the St. Rollox Foundry Co. Most were named but the names did not survive the transfer of ownership[6]; the Caledonian was never much concerned to name its engines. Sinclair's responsibility for Scottish Central locomotives ended in 1853 when Alexander Allan moved from Crewe to take charge of the SCR's Perth works. Allan had been collaborating with Sinclair from the start, and his influence on Caledonian locomotive design continued with Sinclair's successor.

The Greenock Works were active until mid-1856, and some of the new locomotives of that year may have been begun in Greenock and completed in Glasgow. From then on, if the Buchanan Street offices housed the Caledonian Railway's head, St. Rollox Works, a couple of miles up the hill, formed the heart of the organisation. Here the company built the majority of its locomotives, carriages and wagons, here they came for repair and overhaul, here were the central stores that replenished every locomotive depot on the system. St. Rollox was unusual in being an integrated works, locomotives and rolling stock being dealt with on the same site. After Sinclair's departure, Benjamin Conner, formerly works manager at the nearby Neilson & Co., was to be locomotive superintendent for two decades from January 1857. The Caledonian's financial travails through much of his time in office restricted his opportunities. Inheriting a stock of lightweight 2-2-2 and 2-4-0 locomotives, he produced more powerful versions rather than attempting anything very different. He maintained the 'Crewe style', and indeed the general design of Caledonian locomotives, as Pickersgill remarked, remained much the same until the advent of Dugald Drummond in 1882. In 1859 Conner introduced a new 2-2-2, with 8ft 2in driving wheels, probably the largest and heaviest (30 tons 13cwt) express locomotive in Britain at the time[7]. Twelve were built up to 1865, numbered 76-87, and another four of modified, domeless design (Nos. 113-6), in 1875, all at St. Rollox. These engines burned coal: at this time the railways, having hitherto used coke, were increasingly switching to coal. This contravened an early Act of Parliament, but coal was much cheaper than coke, and by this time was also being burned by many other forms of industry. New firebox designs helped use coal more efficiently. Eight 2-4-0s with 6ft 2in driving wheels, the 189-class, formed Conner's first design for the CR, in 1858-59, followed by the slightly larger 197-class in 1860-61, numbering 25 engines. Mineral traffic was mainly served by sixty-three 0-4-2 engines of the 216-class, with 5ft 2in driving wheels, built by Dübs and Neilsons between 1861 and 1866. Conner's most notable innovation was his pioneering use of steam tenders, predating the patent of another Scottish engineer, Archibald Sturrock of the Great Northern, by four years. Four six-wheel tenders with auxiliary steam engines were attached first to 189-class 2-4-0s of 1859, then transferred to the first four 197-class 2-4-0 engines in 1860, but there were problems in providing enough steam, drivers wanted extra pay for operating 'two engines', and the cylinders and rods of the auxiliary equipment were

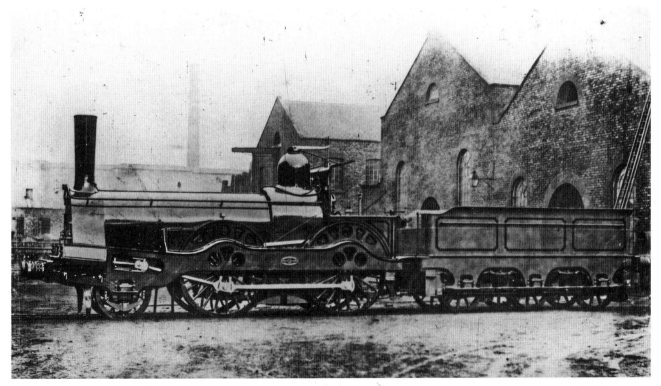

Conner 2-4-0 of 1861, one of six built by Beyer Peacock, Manchester. A further 19 were built by St. Rollox and Neilson. Originally intended to have steam tenders, the class was later rebuilt with flush-type boilers.

soon removed. Surviving records do not indicate whether Conner or Neilsons designed these tenders[8]. From the early 1860s new Caledonian locomotives were provided with modest shelter-cabs, an improvement over the early weatherboards which left the footplate completely open.

Absorption of the General Terminus & Glasgow Harbour company brought in two 0-4-0 and two 0-4-0ST engines in 1864 (CR Nos. 116, 117 and 93, 94), but following the amalgamations with the Scottish Central in 1865 and the Scottish North Eastern Railway in 1866, Conner became locomotive supremo of a much larger railway, with workshops at Perth, Arbroath and Dundee, and a locomotive stock spread from Aberdeen to Stranraer. Dundee and Arbroath were soon shut down and Arbroath's last two locomotives were completed at Perth in 1868. After that Perth too ceased to build locomotives, though it remained a repair centre. Most of the engines acquired in the amalgamations were very similar to the Caledonian types, and most survived in Caledonian livery for years to come, though reboilered or otherwise rebuilt. Of 92 engines taken over from the Scottish Central in 1865, only nine were withdrawn before 1870; and of the 83 Scottish North Eastern Railway locomotives acquired in 1866, 36 survived until at least 1880. Worst for wear seem to have been the former Aberdeen Railway engines, most of them dating back to 1848; only one survived into 1881. Two 0-4-0STs came with the acquisition of the Forth & Clyde Navigation Co. in 1867, becoming CR 116 and 117 (the ex-General Terminus & Glasgow Harbour 0-4-0s were scrapped that year); and seven locomotives of the Solway Junction Railway were incorporated into the stock in 1869, one 0-6-0T, No. 539, two 0-4-2s, Nos. 452-3; two 0-4-2WT, Nos. 540-1; and two 0-6-0s, Nos. 381-2[9].

From the later 1860s, Conner built mostly 2-4-0 types, for both goods and passenger work; his 98-class express design in 1867 had 7ft 2in driving wheels, the largest coupled wheels on any locomotive in Great Britain at the time, and sixteen were built between 1867-68. In all he built over 200 2-4-0s, some of which survived, with new boilers, until 1919. Neilson's (mostly) and Dübs's works were regularly used to supplement the products of St. Rollox. An 0-6-0 design appeared in 1874, the 631-class, with specially-designed linkage between locomotive and tender to help negotiate the tight curves of colliery and works lines; 39 of these were built, up to 1877. Unusually for this type of engine it had outside cylinders; but the Caley was still an outside-cylinder line[10]. Tank engines appear all to have been built by private works; mostly from standard designs, and mostly from Neilson's, though 0-4-0T and ST engines also came from Dübs and Andrew Barclay of Kilmarnock. The 14-strong 502-class 0-4-0ST of 1876-81, from Neilson's, was the most numerous. Fifty-two tank engines were added in Conner's time to Sinclair's 13, plus a handful from amalgamated lines, reflecting a steadily increasing need for shunting and dock locomotives.

CR 2-4-0 No. 30, built by Neilson's in 1872, takes on water at Larbert. Based at Stirling for many years, it was rebuilt in 1899 and ran until 1917. (Stephenson Locomotive Society)

In 1872 Barclays constructed a 7ft single "fitted with an apparatus for lifting the driving wheels off the rails when running without steam". It became CR No. 460 (renumbered 310 in 1877) but the apparatus was removed[11]. Conner also experimented with the Steel-McInnes continuous brake on one of his 30-class 2-4-0 engines, No. 33, built by Neilsons in 1872, and also tried out the Westinghouse brake system on several engines. He maintained a consistent programme of rebuilding older engines. But by the mid-1870s, although many locomotives dating from pre-1865 had been rebuilt, his main line engines were under-powered for the work required, and old-fashioned in appearance and, more importantly, in internal design.

Still in office, Conner died in February 1876 and was succeeded by George Brittain, who had been his chief assistant on the running side, and earlier locomotive superintendent of the Dundee & Perth & Aberdeen, then assistant to Alexander Allan on the SCR at Perth. Brittain appears to have altered the green of goods engines to black: the first batch of the 631-class 0-6-0s were green, but later deliveries from 1876 were painted black[12]. He introduced the Caledonian's first bogie locomotives, but the 125-class 4-4-0 of 1876, an adaptation of a Conner 2-4-0 design, was not a success. His 152-class of fifteen 2-4-2 tank engines, of 1880, intended for work on the Callander & Oban line, proved liable to derail and were put to use on Glasgow suburban trains (later fitted with steam condensing apparatus). Brittain's most successful design was the 179-class of ten 'Oban Bogie' 4-4-0s of 1882, built by Dübs & Co. in Glasgow, for £2,400 apiece, to work the C&O trains. But the board was becoming concerned about the condition of the locomotive department. By this time, despite Conner's rebuilding programme, most of the locomotive stock was run-down (some 31 of Sinclair's locomotives were still running in 1882) and generally not up to the more demanding loads and traffic requirements of the 1880s. There had been virtually no investment in the St. Rollox Works since 1856, and the board, under J.C. Bolton as chairman, accepted that drastic overhaul of the department was needed to bring things up to date. They did not have far to look. Having seen how Dugald Drummond had modernised the North British locomotive department since his appointment to Cowlairs in 1875, they made him such an offer as was unlikely to be refused. It is more than likely that certain guarantees were also given, about the company's willingness to support the new broom and invest in the long undernourished motive power side. Drummond also brought some of his own team from Cowlairs.

CR 0-4-2 No. 251, of the 670-class, built in 1881 by Dübs and originally numbered 703.
Originally a goods engine, after a rebuild in 1901 (and again in 1911) it was fitted for
Westinghouse brakes and ran on branch passenger services until 1928.

Drummond 'Jumbo' 0-6-0 No. 299, built by Neilson's in 1883 in the first batch of what would become the most numerous locomotive class in Scotland. It was withdrawn in July 1956. No. 2 steam crane is attached.

The New Broom

He arrived on 14 August 1882 and the new men got down to business energetically. Drummond, who according to one historian had dismissed Caledonian locomotives as "all legs and wings"[13], was a firm believer in inside-cylinder engines, and his first Caledonian designs were the inside-cylinder 0-6-0s of class 294, known as 'Jumbos', introduced in 1883 for goods and mineral trains, and a new 4-4-0 class of passenger engines. While St. Rollox was being enlarged and re-equipped, outside builders were used and Neilson's delivered fifteen 'Jumbos' between 13 November 1883 and 19 January 1884, at £2,900 apiece; and another twenty between July and December 1884. Ultimately there would be 244, with the last ones completed at St. Rollox in December 1897, making them the basic work-horse of main line goods services. Modifications of detail were made by Drummond's successors; some were fitted with Westinghouse brake pumps and five had condensing equipment for working on the Glasgow Central line[14]. The first ten 4-4-0s, also from Neilson's, were delivered in February-April 1884, numbered 66 to 75, and six more were built at St. Rollox between February and June 1885. In the Caledonian's idiosyncratic numbering system, they were given numbers 60-65. The 66-class gave first-rate service. St. Rollox put a programme of rebuilding the Conner goods 2-4-0s as passenger engines in hand, and by 1886 21 of them had been given Drummond boilers and bigger fireboxes. Less successful was his modification of the old 8ft 2in singles[15]. By then St. Rollox was building new engines, and from 1884 to 1914 most of the Caledonian's locomotives came from its own workshops. Drummond, in line with the trend of the time, developed Conner's "half-cab" into something more substantial with roofs and side-sheets. Locomotives for all purposes were needed, and within three years, the company had acquired 63 new main line locomotives and sixteen 4-4-0 tank engines. Also in 1886 two 15-ton steam-powered breakdown cranes were acquired from Cowans, Sheldon of Carlisle.

Curiously, neither of the gleaming new locomotives in Caledonian livery displayed at the Edinburgh International Exhibition of 1886 were built at St. Rollox. No. 123, a 4-2-2, was built by Neilson's, and No. 124, a 4-4-0, was from Dübs. Both were express engines, on Drummondesque lines[16]. These one-offs cost £2,600 each; the first 66-class engines had cost £2,900 each, so there may have been a discounted price. After all, the engines promoted their builders just as much as the railway company. Both went into regular express service in December 1886, and No. 123 – still, happily, preserved – would put in distinguished performances in the 1888 'races'. E.C. Poultney described the NBR and Caledonian 4-4-0 classes up to 1895 as "practically alike, differing only in detail"[17], with 28x16in inside cylinders and 6ft 6in driving wheels, due to Dugald Drummond's time as locomotive superintendent of both lines. But a 4-4-0 with 5ft 9in drivers was produced for the Greenock (and in anticipation of Gourock) trains in 1888, with the class of twelve complete by 1891 (the six built in the latter year had larger boilers). Known as the 80-class, or 'Coast bogies', they were effective in service and some lasted on the route for over thirty years. The year 1887 saw through locomotive working introduced over the full length of the system, from Carlisle to Aberdeen, and in the following year six new 4-4-0 express engines were built, based on the 66-class and with the same boiler dimensions, but with improved steam passages. Five out of six had the very high boiler pressure of 200 psi[18]. Numbered 76-79, 84 and 87, they were the first Caledonian locomotives to have steel rather than iron boilers. Four members of the class were employed in a set of tests arranged by Drummond in October 1889 to establish performance at varying boiler pressures between 150 and 200 psi, which indicated clearly that the higher pressure was more effective in generating steam and power, and therefore also more economical[19]. No. 79 was named *Carbrook* (J.C. Bolton's estate) and displayed at the Edinburgh Exhibition of 1890.

With the steady expansion of suburban services, the proliferation of mineral lines, and the expansion of dockyard railways, there was a constant call from the traffic department for more tank engines both for goods and passenger work. Under Drummond 82 were built, all of them at St. Rollox. Before his move to the Caledonian, he had favoured the 4-4-0T arrangement, but now switched to 0-4-4T, of which 24 were built between 1884 and 1891, as the 171-class. With 5ft coupled wheels, they were versatile engines and set a pattern for many successors. Tank locomotives, large or small, were "pugs", and in 1885 eight 0-4-0 saddle tanks were built for dockyard work, along with two 0-4-2ST, Nos 262 and 263, which were fitted with Westinghouse brake pumps, painted blue, and despatched into wildest Perthshire to work the new Killin Railway from 13 March 1886. Based on the 502-class Neilson off-the-peg design, these were the only CR locomotives produced under Drummond's reign with outside cylinders apart from the 272 class of 1888. The 0-4-0 saddle tanks had no rear coal bunkers (bunkers were added in some cases) and many trailed four-wheel wooden coal tenders. A more powerful 0-6-0 saddle tank, the 323-class, was introduced in 1887, nicknamed 'Jubilee pugs', as it was Queen Victoria's golden jubilee year. Ten were built that year, eight in 1888 and a final twelve in 1890. They had partial cabs (generally known as 'Stirling cabs'), whose roofs did not extend back to meet the bunker weatherboard. Six smaller 0-6-0STs, also for dock work, were completed in April-May 1888 as the 272 class (see below).

0-6-0ST No. 272, the first of six built at St Rollox in 1888, with Stirling cab.
(Stephenson Locomotive Society)

The Drummond Tradition

After eight years in command at St. Rollox, Dugald Drummond resigned in April 1890. He had added 287 locomotives to the company's stock, but his building programme also indicated clear lines of development, which were followed by the next three locomotive superintendents. Hugh Smellie as his successor had little time to make an impact, dying in April 1891, but left his mark on the 6ft 6in express class, of which twelve engines, Nos. 114-5 and 195-8, delivered between July and September 1891, and 13-18, delivered in April-May 1894, had a boiler designed by him[20]. John Lambie, who succeeded Smellie, had been the Caledonian's assistant locomotive superintendent, in charge of locomotive running, and his three years in charge were marked by improvements of practical detail rather than innovation. Additions to the locomotive stock were based on Drummond's still recent designs, though he parted from later Drummond practice with a 4-4-0 wheel arrangement for thirteen tank engines, completed in 1893-94 and fitted with condensing apparatus for the Glasgow Central line. From 1897 they worked through services between Maryhill and Airdrie. Originally painted blue, they quickly became black in the tunnels and were repainted in that colour by 1898[21]. This class was numbered from 1 to 12; previous holders of these numbers had all been scrapped or sold off long since. Lambie continued this sequence with his six 4-4-0s of 1894 being Nos. 13-18, and ten 0-4-4T of 1895 being Nos. 19-28. These 19-class were 'condensing' engines, with 5ft 9in wheels, intended for passenger work. No. 28 was not withdrawn from service until October 1961[22]. His final design, five 0-6-0ST, based on the Jubilee pugs but with an overall cab, were numbered 211-5. The six 13-class 4-4-0s of 1894, with 6ft 6in driving wheels, built at St. Rollox, were described as "Lambie's undoubted success"[23], and No. 17 was the Caledonian's prime racer against the East Coast in August 1895. By 1894, incidentally, the cost of a new express 4-4-0, built in the Company's works, was down to £1,832.

On Lambie's death in February 1895, John F. McIntosh was appointed locomotive superintendent. A practical engineer rather than a theoretician, his aim was to provide reliable locomotives that generated plenty of steam to do their work. Quoted as saying that he "saw greater virtue in locomotive reliability than fuel economy"[24], he attempted no refinements or experimental designs. At this time train loadings were from 160 to 200 tons, more than double the weight of a decade before. More powerful express locomotives were needed, and the Board approved an order for fifteen in July 1895. With no time to produce a wholly new design, McIntosh and his team rapidly modified the Drummond-Smellie-Lambie 13-class 4-4-0 of 1894, to produce the celebrated 'Dunalastair' class, beginning with No. 721, delivered in January 1896. All fifteen were ready by May, at an individual cost of

Dunalastair I: the CR's most celebrated locomotive class. No. 723, seen here at Perth,
carried the name *Victoria* between 1897 and the Queen's death in 1901.
No. 724 was *Jubilee* for the same period. (Stephenson Locomotive Society)

£2,104. The great but only significant difference to its predecessors was its bigger boiler, providing a total heating surface of 1,403.23sq ft, compared to 1184.12sq ft in the 13-class. Boiler pressure remained at 160psi, and the cylinders were 18.25x26in compared to the 18x26in of 1894. To contemporary eyes the locomotive seemed enormous. It has been suggested that at least some credit for the 'Dunalastair' design belongs to R.W. Urie, chief draughtsman, later works manager (from October 1896) at St. Rollox[25]. *Dunalastair* and its nameless fellows (Nos. 723 and 724 bore the names *Victoria* and *Jubilee* from 1897 to 1901) proved more than equal to the demands of the traffic managers, and reports of their exploits in newspapers and the new railway enthusiasts' magazines quickly made them famous. For the first time, the Caledonian had a locomotive class that seemed a world leader. In 1897 McIntosh developed the design substantially with what he called the 'Breadalbane' class, but which the world called 'Dunalastair II', and the leader, No. 766, bore this name (as *Dunalastair 2nd*) until 1917. It had slightly enlarged cylinders, 19x26in, a longer boiler, 11ft 4 1/2in between the tube-plates ('Dunalastair I' was 10ft 7in), and a boiler pressure of 175psi. They had what seemed vast tenders, of 4,125 gallon capacity, the first in Scotland to be mounted on double bogies[26]. Fifteen were built between December 1897 and April 1898, at £2,434 each, and numbered from 766 to 780. No. 779 carried the name *Breadalbane*. Again it was a resounding success. The Caley was running some of the fastest trains in the world, and its publicists made the most of the fact. Further prestige came from the Belgian State Railways' interest, which led to over 230 locomotives on the '766' model being built for their use. From 1897 McIntosh introduced a lighter shade of blue for Caledonian passenger locomotives (and for Westinghouse-brake fitted goods engines which frequently hauled passenger trains), and this became the standard colour[27].

At the other end of the locomotive spectrum, McIntosh was required to expand the tank engine fleet. Four 0-4-0 ST pugs were completed in October-November 1895 and nine larger 0-6-0Ts, with condensing equipment, came out between November 1895 and January 1896. Also adapted for the underground line were two sets of 0-4-4Ts, eleven completed in mid-1897, known as the 92-class, and another ten between January and March 1900, known as the 879-class (though two were numbered 437-8). The 0-4-4T with 5ft 9in coupled wheels had become a ubiquitous Caledonian type, working branch trains and workmen's trains, and often used as banking engines, and a further sixteen, non-condensing, were completed in the course of 1900. To work mineral branches and shunting yards, 43 0-6-0Ts, the 782-class, were built between August 1898 and January 1899; and followed in March-June 1899 by twelve 0-4-4Ts (104 class) with 4ft 6in coupled wheels to operate on the tight curves of the Balerno branch (one or two four-wheel tender 2-4-0s were also kept for this line) and the Cathcart Circle.

**0-4-0ST No. 612 at Perth. One of 14 built at St Rollox between 1895 and 1908,
a continuation of Drummond's 264-class of 1885. Coal bunkers were built into the
forward extensions of the cab side-sheets. This engine later became works pilot at Crewe,
as BR56027, and was not withdrawn until 1960. (Stephenson Locomotive Society)**

0-8-0 No. 604, built at St Rollox in 1903. This was the Caledonian's most powerful locomotive class, built to haul mineral trains of 30-ton bogie mineral wagons fully fitted with Westinghouse brakes. (Stephenson Locomotive Society)

McIntosh applied his big-boiler approach to the 0-6-0 tender type with the 812-class, built in two batches between May and December 1899. Though still to be the standard goods engine, this class, with 5ft driving wheels, was also intended for use on passenger trains and Nos. 812-828 were fitted with Westinghouse brake pumps and given the blue livery (the restored No. 828 is still running); they worked the Wemyss Bay line, also brake-fitted fish trains. But the prime need was for more goods engines. A further fifty 0-6-0s were required to keep up with the demand from commercial and industrial consignors, and the Company's expanding system. Apart from a boom in coal output, the Caledonian was now operating the Lanarkshire & Dumbartonshire line and the extension to Newton of the Glasgow Central Railway, and anticipating the need to work new lines in Renfrewshire and South Lanarkshire. St. Rollox, once almost in open country, was by the 1890s hemmed in by railway tracks, streets and factories, with little scope for expansion, and holding a running shed as well as the construction and repair shops. It could not cope with this surge in demand, and the massive order was placed with the three Glasgow builders, Neilson Reid (20), Sharp Stewart (15), and Dübs (15) for delivery in 1899-1900. The urgency can be gauged from the fact that these cost an average of £3,000[28] each whereas the second batch of St. Rollox engines were turned out at the same time for £2,189 – a premium of £40,000.

Continuing his line of passenger locomotive development, McIntosh produced sixteen express 4-4-0s of the 900-class, promptly named 'Dunalastair III' by the fans, completed between December 1899 and July 1900, and used to haul the heaviest expresses. Excellent engines, their performance had little novelty value: other designers had learned the lesson by now. An innovation came in July 1901 with a locomotive type not previously used in Scotland, the 0-8-0. Two were built initially, Nos. 600-601, with a further six between January and June 1903. Their introduction coincided with the company's interest in large mineral wagons and they were the most powerful engine built by any Scottish railway company, with a nominal tractive effort of 31,584lb[29]; on the Lesmahagow line between Merryton and Stonehouse they were allowed to haul 35 loaded four-wheel wagons, against 22 for the 812-class, and 20 for a pre-1899 'Jumbo'. Though they worked primarily on coal trains, they had Westinghouse brake pumps, enabling them to work the new mineral wagons, and on Glasgow Fair days they might, like all automatic brake-fitted engines, be called on to haul specials to the coast[30]. Expensive to maintain, with access to the slide valves particularly difficult, the class was not developed further, but in March 1903 an eight-coupled tank engine was ordered, the six-strong 492-class, for mineral train working, though No. 496 was used to bank goods trains on the Newtyle line[31]. The two eight-coupled classes both had 4ft 6in driving wheels, but were not mechanically identical; the tender engines having 21x26in cylinders compared to 19x26in on the tanks, and the boilers of the tender engines were larger[32].

0-8-0T No. 492, of 1903, the CR's most powerful tank engine, used to marshal heavy mineral trains (see caption to previous illustration). The second set of driving wheels have no flanges.

To improve service on the Callander & Oban line, the Caledonian's first 4-6-0 class was designed and built at St. Rollox, with five engines in 1902 and a further four in 1905. This was the 55-class, with 5ft driving wheels and inside cylinders, intended to work trains on the Oban line; and where it gave very satisfactory performance. In March and April 1903 a second inside-cylinder 4-6-0 class, of only two engines, appeared. Nos. 49 and 50 were so long, 65ft 6in, they had to be detached from their eight-wheel tenders to fit the turntable at Etterby Depot, Carlisle (in Glasgow they could run round the Cathcart Circle); they were the heaviest (73 tons) and claimed as the most powerful, express engines in Britain. With an original boiler pressure of 200 psi, they were designed to haul trains of around 400 tons. Though 49 was nameless, No. 50 was named *Sir James Thompson*, and they worked the heaviest trains over Beattock – the 'Corridor' and the overnight sleeper. Seen as prototypes for future development, their performance was carefully monitored. Progression of the 4-4-0 type also continued and the 140-class marked the peak of the 'Dunalastair' line: five were completed in May-June 1904, six between December 1905 and January 1906, five between December 1907 and February 1908, and a further three in June-July 1910. In every respect they were somewhat larger than the 900-class. No. 144 achieved what seems to have been the fastest speed recorded on the Caledonian Railway, 83 $\frac{1}{2}$ mph with the 'Grampian Corridor' between Forfar and Perth, when the 32$\frac{1}{2}$ miles were run in 31 min 1 sec, with a 260-ton train[33].

Edwardian Grandeur

Throughout the Caledonian's lifetime, rebuilding was an important feature of locomotive management. While the wiles of accountancy played a part at various times – 'rebuilds' being chargeable to repair and maintenance out of revenue rather than to capital – it was primarily a way of extending the running life of a locomotive or of improving a class that might badly need it, as with Brittain's five 4-4-0s of 1876, the 'Dundee Bogies' re-boilered by Drummond in the 1880s. Cannibalisation of parts from scrapped engines was also regular, as was tender-swapping. Like other railways, the Caledonian maintained a duplicate list (from around 1867), of locomotives still operational but whose capital cost had been written off in the accounts. Their original or previous running numbers were reallocated to new engines. Duplicate numbering policy altered from time to time; originally duplicates were numbered from 500, but some were also in the 600 and 700 series; then in 1883 the practice of adding an 'A' to the running number was introduced. In 1899 a new duplicate listing began, starting at 1200 and affecting 168 engines, up to No. 1368, but within a year this was changed again to the original or previous number prefixed by '1'[34].

**The steep descent to Oban, in 1914, with the ticket platform on left. 4-6-0 No. 53
takes on water. Note the gas-holder in right foreground.**

On 14 November 1905, the board approved the construction of 20 large engines at a cost of £55,000, on the capital account, additional to what was specified in the half-yearly programme. Ten were 4-6-0 express goods, five were 4-6-0 passenger express, and five were designated as 4-4-2 passenger express. But McIntosh did not pursue the 'Atlantic' format (the North British Locomotive Co. was building W.P. Reid's new locomotives of this wheel arrangement in 1906) and instead produced a modified version of the 49-class, five large 4-6-0s, completed between May and July 1906 at £3,500 each, and numbered 903-907. The class leader was named *Cardean*, after the estate of Edward Cox, the deputy-chairman. In the pre-superheating era (already past in Germany), the 903-class took the basic Drummond approach as far as it could go, at least within the British loading gauge. With 6ft 6in driving wheels, 20x26in cylinders, a boiler 17ft 7⁷/₈in long and 5ft 3¹/₂ in high, and a total heating surface of 2,265.8 sq ft, they "had an ample margin of power for most duties and were seldom unduly pressed"[35]. The sheer size and majestic appearance overshadowed the fact that it was essentially a 19th century design, and *Cardean*, with its regular working on the 'Corridor', became an iconic locomotive to the general public, helped from 1910 by its special 'Cunarder' siren provided by Colonel John Denny, a shipbuilding director of the Caledonian. In the end only five express goods 4-6-0 engines were built, very similar to the 55-class, with 5ft driving wheels, completed between July and September 1906 and numbered from 918 to 922; and ten rather than five passenger engines followed between October 1906 and January 1907. These formed the 908-class, with 5ft 9in driving wheels and dimensions slightly reduced from those of the 903s. Two were named, 909 as *Sir James King* and 911 as *Barochan* (estate of vice-chairman Renshaw), and the class worked both on Perth and Dundee and Clyde Coast services.

Between 1904 and 1907 a further 35 0-6-0 tanks of the 782-class were built, and distributed among major depots, with five going to Grangemouth where the new yards needed extra motive power; and another twenty-seven 0-4-4Ts of the 439-class appeared between 1906 and 1910. Around eight of these went to Forfar to work the new Brechin line. In 1907 two self-propelling steam breakdown cranes, capable of lifting 20 tons, were purchased from Craven Bros. of Manchester. The 812-class of 0-6-0s was extended by 17 slightly modified engines, usually known as the 652-class, completed between August 1908 and July 1909.

Considering that in the early years of the 20th century Glasgow was one of the world's great locomotive-building centres, rivalled in output only by Philadelphia, it is surprising how limited the effect of this was on home locomotive design. This was noted by James Reid of Neilsons, who referred to company locomotive superintendents as each "shut up very much in his own district"[36]. In 1903 the North British Locomotive Company had been formed by amalgamation to make a business which only Baldwins of Philadelphia could match for size. The North British Locomotive Company built locomotives very largely for export and many of its products incorporated the most up-to-date mechanical systems and accessories, often originated in the USA, as specified by the engineers who ordered them. But as far as the Scottish railway companies were concerned, the North British Locomotive Works might as well have been in Vladivostok. Design stayed firmly within a narrow, local tradition. This was not entirely unreasonable: the North British Works were often building engines to traverse mountains, deserts and vast plains far different to the relatively modest ups and downs, and short distances, of the Scottish landscape; and often to haul trains of far greater tonnage than the short colliery sidings of Scotland could allow. Many of the new accessories were patented and therefore expensive to use. As far as the Caledonian was concerned, the Board's anxiety to keep down expenditure, especially on the capital account, in the 1900s did not encourage innovation. But still there is a sense of opportunity bypassed; of failure to grasp new technical possibilities. While lines around London and in the north-east USA developed electric traction for their high-frequency services and underground lines, the Caledonian (and the North British) continued with their stygian fume-filled tunnels under Glasgow. But McIntosh was a steam man, concerned with practicalities, and knew that to the board, economies were of more interest than innovations. Since lineside fires cost the Company some £2,000 a year, McIntosh fitted his own patent spark-arrestor from 1908, combined with a redesigned blast-pipe exhaust[37]. And even if technical improvement at the level being achieved on the Great Western or the Prussian State Railways was not to be found at St. Rollox, he was quick to appreciate the possibilities of superheating, not least in cutting the coal bill. Further 4-4-0 locomotives of the 140-class were under construction in 1909-10, and No. 139, completed in July 1910, was fitted with a Schmidt superheater, the first in Scotland and one of the earliest in Britain. Tests showed a saving in coal consumption of 23.5% and in water of 25.5%[38], and the board approved the application of superheating to new tender locomotives. From 1911 a programme of applying superheating to existing engines was initiated, starting with Nos. 907 and 903-4. Orders for new superheated 4-4-0s were also placed, with ten built at St. Rollox between April 1911 and August 1912. Like No. 139, these had Schmidt superheaters. A further batch of eleven 4-4-0s, completed between April 1911 and May 1914, had larger cylinders, 20.5x26in compared to 19x26, and were fitted with Robinson superheaters[39]. Four superheated 0-6-0 engines, Nos. 30-33, were delivered in July-November 1912; they were painted blue and worked Wemyss Bay passenger trains. With a lengthened frame, the 0-6-0 design was adapted as a 2-6-0, Scotland's first 'Moguls', Nos. 34-38. The aim was to help bear the increased weight of a longer smokebox and the superheater, rather than to explore the potential of the 2-6-0 design as was being done elsewhere, at Doncaster for example. Delivered at the end of December 1912, they worked long distance goods trains from Carlisle. A larger express goods type

McIntosh 2-6-0 No. 38, built in 1912, on an Up goods near Rockcliffe, Cumberland.

0-6-0T No. 173 of the 782-class, built at St Rollox in 1912, at Carlisle. This was one of five engines fitted with Westinghouse brakes to handle passenger stock as station pilots, and which with the 600 and 492 Classes (see plates on pp 206 and 207) were exceptions to the rule that Westinghouse-fitted engines received the blue livery. It ran until 1960.

appeared as the 179-class 4-6-0, essentially a superheated version of the 908s, with the same cylinders, boiler and wheels. Eleven were completed between December 1913 and March 1915, in batches of five and six; minor differences in the second set included cylinders 19.5x26in rather than 19x26in. The 179-class also had cabs with two side-windows: the first Caledonian locomotives so provided, except for No. 917 which had a prototype cab fitted in 1907[40].

The 782-class of 0-6-0T was further enlarged with 41 new engines between January 1910 and October 1913, and a new outside-cylinder 0-6-0T, the 498-class, with 4-ft driving wheels, was introduced with two engines, Nos. 498-9, in 1912. A further 24 of the ubiquitous 0-4-4Ts were added between April 1910 and October 1914. By the latter date McIntosh had retired. At the end of his career, now in his late 60s, he was working on radically new designs, including an outside-cylinder 4-6-0 and a 4-cylinder Pacific. On his retiral in May 1914, William Pickersgill, appointed on 9 December 1913, took over at St. Rollox, and within three months the outbreak of war brought great constraints to his role, not only financial. Many of the skilled workers left to join the army and were impossible to replace.

The Pickersgill Years

McIntosh had been responsible for adding around 615 engines to the Caledonian stock (which meant that some 400 were more than 18 years old, though many had been rebuilt or re-boilered), but, as his final designs showed, he knew that the basic Drummond inside-cylinder design was now outmoded. A new approach was needed, and Pickersgill was expected to provide it. In normal conditions, he would have had time to plan his actions, but the outbreak of war changed that. The locomotive department was under immediate and heavy pressure. Pickersgill's first need was to boost the numbers of shunting engines, and 21 of McIntosh's 498-class 0-6-0T, with 4ft driving wheels, were built between April 1915 and 1921. In addition 18 0-6-0Ts of the 782-class, with 4ft 6in driving wheels, were built, seven in 1916 and the rest in 1921-22, by which time they were not really needed and were placed in store for several months[41]. Long delays in delivery dates made another problem for managers to contend with. Ten extra 0-4-4T engines of McIntosh's 439-class of 1900, with slight modifications, were also delivered, four in 1915 and six in 1922; a further four in 1922 were built as bankers for Beattock, with boiler pressure of 180psi, rather than 160; cylinders of half an inch greater diameter; and cast-iron front buffer beams[42].

60

**4-6-0 No. 60, built 1916, with a train of 12-wheeled coaches near Stirling.
The engine was withdrawn in 1953.**

At the end of 1915, the Caledonian traffic committee resolved to offer up to £5,500 each for the six new 'River' class 4-6-0s which had been rejected by the Highland Railway, and got them for £100 apiece less. Suddenly the company had six 'state of the art' main line mixed-traffic locomotives. Numbered from 938 to 943, four went to the new depot at Balornock, the others to Perth. Most of their work was on fast freight. Pickersgill set out to improve on the 'Dunalastair' theme with a superheated inside-cylinder 4-4-0, the 113-class. Six were delivered from St. Rollox in February-May 1916 and ten from the North British Locomotive Co. later in the same year. It weighed 61 1/4 tons compared with 59 tons for the 139-class, but had a slightly smaller boiler and less heating surface. The relatively massive construction helped to ensure its longevity as a class: they all lasted to 1959-62. The 4-4-0s were for secondary passenger services, and Pickersgill's first express 4-6-0 was the 60-class, with 6ft 1in coupled wheels. No. 60 was finished at St. Rollox in November 1916, with a further five between December 1916 and April 1917 – the Caledonian's first home produced outside-cylinder main line engines since Brittain's 'Oban Bogies' in 1882. As with the 4-4-0s, the build was more substantial than that of previous Caledonian 4-6-0 types. Despite the outside drive, the valve gear, Stephenson-type, was inside the frame. No. 61 replaced *Cardean* on the 'Corridor', but expert commentators reckoned that their performance never equalled that of their predecessors[43]. In defence it can be said that wartime and post-war operating conditions were very different to those prevailing in 1905. Pickersgill also designed a big superheated express tank engine in the course of 1915, the 944-class 4-6-2T with 5ft 9in coupled wheels, and twelve were built by the North British Locomotive Co., delivered in March-May 1917. Each cost £5,250, a large amount for a tank locomotive, but at 91 tons 13 cwt, these were not small engines. Numbered 944 to 955, they were mainly used on trains to Wemyss Bay, though some worked on the Beattock Bank; and four survived to 1952.

Pickersgill appears to have been something of a sceptic as far as superheating was concerned. His next project to come to fruition was an 0-6-0 class, a revised version of McIntosh's 30-class but without superheating. Commencing with No. 300, 35 were completed between February 1918 and September 1919. The first twelve had steel rather than copper fireboxes, but these were replaced by copper in 1920-22[44]. British builders were rarely successful with steel fireboxes. A further twelve were built between October 1919 and January 1920; their cost, unsuperheated, of £4,597, compared to the superheated 30-class's £2,312, was an indication of how labour and materials prices had risen since 1912[45]. By the end of 1918, of the handful of named engines, only *Breadalbane* still bore its name[46]. Most of the condensing engines (73 were fitted thus) had had the condensing apparatus removed

No. 671, the final version of the Caledonian 0-6-0. No. 671
was superheated in 1931 and remained in service until 1962.

Ex-ROD 2-8-0s with CR lettering on tender, Balornock Shed, around 1920.
It is not known how much work they did before being put in store at Gretna and
subsequently sold overseas. (Caledonian Railway Association)

by the end of 1917. From August 1919 until the end of the Railway Executive's control on 15 August 1921, the Caledonian acquired fifty 2-8-0 locomotives of Great Central Railway design, belonging to the War Office (Railway Operating Department), all built for military purposes but of which only 15 had seen service in Europe. Never given Caledonian numbers, most were eventually sold to Chinese railways[47]. Between 1920 and 1922, 32 further Pickersgill 4-4-0s of the 113-class of 1915-16 were built, ten at St. Rollox, ten by Armstrong, Whitworth of Newcastle, and twelve by the North British Locomotive Company at Hyde Park Works, Glasgow. Twenty-four were still in service in 1960.

In 1920 Pickersgill was President of the Institution of Locomotive Engineers, and his presidential address gave the members a brief account of the development of the Company's locomotives[48]. It gave away no secrets. He also arranged for members of the Institution of Locomotive Engineers to visit St. Rollox Works on a Saturday afternoon and inspect the various departments, "some quite recently rearranged and equipped with the most modern appliances" and others where modernisation was still in progress. But as Irvine Kempt Jr, assistant locomotive superintendent, remarked, the workshops as a whole had been designed 40 years before, and he implied that they had not been kept as up-to-date as might be: "I should say that the wish of the management to see their workshops shrinking in Scotland is not the wish of the works management"[49]. Already the prospect of grouping and rationalisation of facilities was casting a shadow ahead of itself. But the Caledonian designers were also looking to develop new heavy express engines, and drawings had been made for a 3-cylinder 4-6-0, of which four were completed at St. Rollox between June and August 1921, forming the 956-class. It was an ambitious project, which, had it worked well, might have been a model for the future LMS. Somewhat reminiscent of the 'Rivers' in appearance, weighing 81 tons, it was as imposing a locomotive as St. Rollox had ever built. The cylinders were $18\frac{1}{2}$ x 26 in, the boiler was 16ft 3in by 5ft 9in, heating surface was 2,640 sq ft (the superheater providing 270 sq ft), and the working pressure was 180 psi. But serious problems with the conjugated valve gear, designed in-house, working the inner cylinder from the external Walschaerts gear, overcame the merits of the overall design. Most of Pickersgill's designs for the Caledonian have been severely treated by later writers, but the 3-cylinder problem, in particular, was an intractable one, and he deserved credit for the attempt. At much the same time a new two-cylinder 4-6-0 intended for the Oban line was being developed – without a superheater. This was the 191-class, the final Caledonian locomotive class, built by the North British Locomotive Company at Queens Park. Eight were delivered in late 1922, and though they did not have the problems of the 956-class, they were not strong performers. In LMS days 'Clans' of the Highland Railway, built at the same time, were running on the Oban line after the 191s had been withdrawn (the last one went at the end of 1945). In 1923, Pickersgill became mechanical engineer of the LMS's Northern Division, retiring in 1925. A further twenty of his 60-class 4-6-0 were built under LMS auspices at St. Rollox in 1925-26, the last Caledonian locomotives to be constructed. The last four Caledonian locomotives in service were withdrawn at the end of 1963: all were 0-6-0s, the oldest, originally No. 830, was completed in December 1899. Three engines are preserved, No. 123 (1886), 0-6-0 No. 828 (1899), and 0-4-4T No. 419 (1907).

3-cylinder 4-6-0 No. 956, first of four engines, built in 1921. This was the CR's most powerful passenger engine, and marked a radical change from previous designs. All were withdrawn between 1931-35. (Stephenson Locomotive Society)

A CALEDONIAN RAILWAY TIMELINE

1820s

1824   Monkland & Kirkintilloch Railway Act, 17 May.
1826   Dundee & Newtyle, and Garnkirk & Glasgow Railway Acts, 26 May.
        Monkland & Kirkintilloch opens, October.
1828   Ballochney Railway opens, 8 August.
1829   Wishaw & Coltness Railway Act.

1830s

1830   Polloc & Govan Railway Act.
1831   Garnkirk & Glasgow Railway official opening 27 September (mineral traffic from May).
        Dundee & Newtyle Railway opens, 16 December.
1834   Wishaw & Coltness opens from Whifflet to Holytown, 23 January.
1835   Newtyle & Coupar Angus and Newtyle & Glammis Railways Acts.
1836   Locke reports on Preston-Glasgow route.
        Dundee & Arbroath Railway Act, Arbroath & Forfar Railway Act, 17 May.
        Provisional Committee for Carlisle-Glasgow line formed, 14 September.
1837   Glasgow, Paisley, Kilmarnock & Ayr Railway authorised, 15 July, also
        Glasgow, Paisley & Greenock Railway (to share a line between Glasgow and Paisley).
        Newtyle-Coupar Angus and Newtyle-Glamis Railways open.
1838   Edinburgh & Glasgow Railway authorised, 4 July.
        Dundee & Arbroath Railway opens, 6 October.
1839   Miller & Locke examine alternative routes between Glasgow and Carlisle.
        Arbroath & Forfar Railway opens, 3 January (parts open December 1838).

1840s

1840   Joint line between Glasgow and Paisley opens (see 1837), 13 July.
        Slamannan Railway opens 5 August to Union Canal at Causewayend.
        Temporary station at Bridge Street, Glasgow, from 12 August.
        Polloc & Govan Railway opens, 22 August.
1841   Report of Smith-Barlow inquiry into Anglo-Scottish route.
        Glasgow, Paisley & Greenock Railway opens to Greenock, 30 March.
        Drumpellier Railway Act (Monkland to Monkland Canal).
        Permanent station at Bridge Street from 4 April.
1842   Edinburgh & Glasgow Railway opens, 21 February.
1843   Garnkirk & Glasgow Railway opens a branch to Coatbridge from Gartsherrie.
1844   Lancaster & Carlisle Railway authorised.
        North British Railway authorised, 4 July, Edinburgh-Berwick.
        Caledonian Railway Preliminary Committee meets, 19 February.
        Garnkirk & Glasgow becomes Glasgow, Garnkirk & Coatbridge Railway, with retrospective Act for
        extension to Coatbridge.
1845   Caledonian Railway Act, 31 July. Acts passed also for Aberdeen Railway,
        Dundee & Perth Railway (31 July), Clydesdale Junction, Scottish Central, and Scottish Midland Junction
        Railways. Edinburgh-Hawick Railway Act also passed.
        Glasgow, Barrhead & Neilston Railway Act, 4 August.
        J.J. Hope Johnstone elected first CR chairman.
        Glasgow, Garnkirk & Coatbridge Railway opens line through to Whifflet, meeting the
        Wishaw & Coltness Railway, 14 July.
        Construction of CR begins, 11 October.
1846   James Butler Williams appointed CR secretary and general manager.
        CR absorbs Glasgow, Garnkirk & Coatbridge Railway.
        North British opens 19 June, Edinburgh-Berwick.
        Glasgow Southern Terminal Railway (joint) Act, 16 July.
        Glasgow, Airdrie & Monklands Junction Railway authorised.
        Caledonian & Dumbartonshire Junction Railway Act.

London & North Western Railway is formed.

Dundee & Perth Railway leases Dundee & Newtyle Railway (999 yrs) and Dundee & Arbroath (latter to 1850 only).

Stirlingshire Midland Junction Railway authorised between Polmont-Grahamston-Larbert, 16 July.

Glasgow, Dumfries & Carlisle Railway Act passed, 13 August.

CR absorbs Polloc & Govan and Clydesdale Junction Railways, 18 August.

General Terminus & Glasgow Harbour Railway Act.

Proposal for Scottish Central Railway to be worked by LNWR, Lancaster & Carlisle Railway and CR, for 25 years defeated in Parliament, 21 October.

1847   Williams dies; Joshua Coddington appointed secretary and general manager.

CR amalgamation with Glasgow Paisley & Greenock Railway is sanctioned (see 1851).

Dundee & Perth Railway opens 24 May, to Barnhill on east bank of Tay.

CR leases Wishaw & Coltness.

Monkland & Kirkintilloch, Ballochney and Slamannan Railways convert to standard gauge, 27 July.

Newcastle & Berwick Railway reaches Tweedmouth, 1 July.

CR's first public train, between Beattock and Carlisle, 10 September.

1848   Aberdeen Railway opens Guthrie-Bridge of Dun-Brechin and Dubton-Montrose, 1 February.

Arbroath & Forfar Railway leased "in perpetuity" to Aberdeen Railway, from 1 February.

CR Carlisle to Edinburgh and Glasgow routes open, 15 February.

SCR opens Greenhill-Stirling line 1st March, to Perth, 22 May.

Dundee & Perth starts new works at Seabraes.

Dundee & Perth Railway makes joint operating agreement with Dundee & Arbroath Railway; name changes to Dundee, Perth & Aberdeen Junction Railway, 31 August.

Parliament rejects CR-SCR amalgamation.

CR and SCR linked between Greenhill and Castlecary, 7 August.

Edinburgh & Northern Railway reaches Perth (Hilton Junction) from Ladybank, 18 July.

Scottish Midland Junction Railway opens from Perth to Forfar, 20 August.

Glasgow, Dumfries & Carlisle Railway opens Dumfries-Gretna line, 23 August.

Monkland & Kirkintilloch Railway, and Ballochney & Slamannan Railway merge as Monklands Railways, 14 August.

Glasgow, Barrhead & Neilston Direct Railway opened to Barrhead, 27 September.

1849   Agreement for CR/Lancaster & Carlisle Railway/LNWR to operate SCR and Scottish Midland Junction Railway, 3 January, lasts to 30 November.

General Terminus & Glasgow Harbour Railway opens, 3 March.

First (wooden) Tay Viaduct at Perth, 8 March.

Edinburgh & Northern Railway changes name to Edinburgh, Perth & Dundee Railway, April.

Clydesdale Junction Railway opens from Motherwell to Rutherglen, with services to Glasgow South Side, 1 June.

CR acquires Wishaw & Coltness Railway, 28 July.

CR acquires lease of Glasgow Barrhead & Neilston Direct Railway, 1 August.

Branch from Newton Junction to Hamilton opens, 17 September.

Buchanan Street Station, Glasgow, opens 1 November.

Mail traffic transferred from East Coast to LNWR/CR route.

CR Shareholders' Committee of Inquiry set up, September.

CR board asks first LNWR, then Thomas Brassey, to take over working the line.

1850s

1850   Board resigns; Capt. Edward Plunkett is second CR chairman, February-December; then John Duncan is elected.

Dundee & Arbroath Railway resumes independent operations, March.

Aberdeen Railway completed, first train London-Aberdeen, 1 April.

Scottish Central Railway opens branch Plean to Alloa South, 12 September.

GSWR formed by the Glasgow, Paisley, Kilmarnock & Ayr and Glasgow, Dumfries & Carlisle, 28 October.

1851   Caledonian Railway Arrangements Act passed, 7 August.

CR and Glasgow Paisley & Greenock Railway amalgamate, 7 August (see 1883).

SCR Perth Works completed.

SCR, Aberdeen Railway and Scottish Midland Junction Railway operate a locomotive pool (to 1855).

Act for Lesmahagow Railway, Motherwell-Bankend, 24 July.

1852   Coddington resigns, July; Robert Sinclair appointed General Manager.
Railway Steamboat Packet Company formed (sold 1854).
Duncan resigns; William Baird is 4th CR chairman.

1853   Crieff Junction Railway Act passed.
CR and E&G share management in anticipation of merger.

1854   CR and E&G Amalgamation Bill rejected. Joint management ends.
Baird resigns, September; William Johnston is 5th CR chairman.
Kirriemuir branch of Scottish Midland Junction Railway opens, November 15.

1855   Lanark branch opens for goods, 5 January.
Carmyllie line opened as mineral railway by Earl of Dalhousie.
Scottish Midland Junction Railway Blairgowrie branch opens.
Glasgow Barrhead & Neilston Direct extends to Crofthead (Neilston), 5 October.

1856   New 'English and Scotch Traffic Agreement'.
CR and E&G set up a 10-year joint purse arrangement, from January.
Crieff Junction Railway opens from Crieff Jct., 14 March, worked by SCR.
St Rollox Works opens, July.
Scottish Midland Junction Railway and Aberdeen Railways merge as Scottish North Eastern, which also takes over Dundee & Arbroath Railway, 29 July.
Dunblane, Doune & Callander Railway Act.
Perth, Almond Valley & Methven Railway Act.
Perth & Dunkeld Railway opens, worked by Scottish Midland Junction Railway.
Lesmahagow Railway opens to Coalburn, 1 December.
Christopher Johnstone succeeds Robert Sinclair as general manager.

1857   Benjamin Conner is appointed locomotive superintendent.
Hamilton & Strathaven Railway Act.
Portpatrick Railway Act.
Edinburgh-Granton branch authorised.
Motherwell Deviation opens between Wishaw & Coltness Railway and Clydesdale Jct lines, 8 October.
Dock Street Station (Dundee East) opens (Dundee &Arbroath Railway).

1858   Symington, Biggar & Broughton Railway Act.
Alyth Railway Act.
Perth, Almond Valley & Methven Railway opens, 1 January.
SCR opens Denny branch from Larbert West Junction, 1 April.
Dunblane Doune & Callander opens, worked by SCR, 1 July.
New through station opened in Arbroath, December 14.

1859   Thomas Salkeld is 6th CR chairman.
Border Union Railway (Hawick-Carlisle) Act, 21 July.
Act for Perth General Station Joint Commttee, 5 August.
Castle Douglas & Dumfries Railway opens, 7 November.
Conner tries out the steam tender.

1860s

1860   Dumfries Lochmaben & Lockerbie Railway Act.
CR-E&G-SCR Amalgamation Bill rejected, 15 May.
CR acquires the Lanark Railway, 23 July.
Hamilton & Strathaven line opens as far as Quarter, 6 August.
Wilsontown branch opens, 22 October.
Symington, Biggar & Broughton Railway opens, 5 November.

1861   Alyth and Kirriemuir branches open, worked by Scottish North Eastern Railway.
Portpatrick Railway opens from Castle Douglas to Stranraer, 12 March.
Dalmarnock branch opens, 24 June.
CR-E&G-SCR Amalgamation Bill again rejected.
CR absorbs Symington, Biggar & Broughton Railway, 1 August.
CR opens Slateford-Granton branch for goods and mineral traffic, 28 August.

1862   Tripartite agreement between CR, E&G, and SCR: joint purse, 28 January.
Greenock & Wemyss Bay Railway authorised.
Powers obtained to extend Granton line to Leith.
Scottish North Eastern Railway takes over the Dundee & Arbroath Railway.

Hamilton & Strathaven Railway fully open (goods only), 16 June.

NBR Hawick-Carlisle line opens, 1 July (goods service from 23 June).

NBR absorbs Edinburgh, Perth & Northern Railway, giving it full access to Perth, 29 July.

Portpatrick Railway reaches Portpatrick 28 August; Stranraer Harbour branch opens, 1 October.

1863 'Thirty Years Agreement' between CR, E&G and SCR intended to formalise tripartite arrangements after 1866.

Hamilton & Strathaven Railway opens to passengers, 2 February.

Scottish Central Railway absorbs Dundee & Perth & Aberdeen Junction Railway, 31 July.

Busby Railway Act.

Dumfries, Lochmaben & Lockerbie Railway opens, 1 September.

1864 Solway Junction Railway Act.

Perth, Almond Valley & Methven Railway absorbed by Scottish North Eastern Railway.

CR-E&G-SCR Amalgamation Bill rejected by Commons, February.

End of the CR-E&G-SCR tripartite agreement.

Broughton-Peebles line opens, 1 February.

Lanark-Douglas line opens, 1 April.

CR absorbs Hamilton & Strathaven Railway, 25 July.

CR Crewe Junction-Leith goods branch opens, 1 September.

Dalserf-Stonehouse-Cotcastle line completed, 1 September.

CR-Portpatrick Railway working agreement, 1 October.

Drumbowie mineral line opened.

1865 'Scotch Territorial Agreement' with North British Railway, 12 May.

Edinburgh & Glasgow and Monklands Railways amalgamate, 31 July, combine with North British, 1 August.

Crieff Junction Railway taken over by Scottish Central Railway, 29 June.

Dunblane Doune & Callander Railway absorbed by SCR, 31 July.

Dumfries, Lochmaben & Lockerbie Railway absorbed by CR, 5 July.

CR absorbs Scottish Central, 1 August (Act of 5 July).

CR also absorbs General Terminus & Glasgow Harbour Railway, 29 June.

Wemyss Bay Railway opens 13 May, worked by CR.

Callander & Oban Railway authorised, 8 July.

Montrose-Inverbervie Railway opens, worked by Scottish North Eastern Railway.

Rutherglen-Carmyle-Coatbridge line opens for goods, 20 September.

CR buys Gourock Pier: first Bill for a Gourock extension.

1866 Rutherglen-Coatbridge line passenger service, January.

Busby Railway opens 1 January, worked by CR.

Methven-Crieff line opens, 21 May.

CR absorbs the Scottish North Eastern Railway, 1 August.

Irvine Kempt joins CR from Scottish North Eastern Railway.

Lesmahagow Railway: Ferniegair-Brocketsbrae line opens, also Stonehouse and Blackwood branches, 1 December.

1867 Carstairs-Dolphinton line opens, 1 March.

CR makes working agreement with Solway Junction Railway, 22 March.

CR gains control of Forth & Clyde and Monkland Canals, and Grangemouth harbour. Forth & Clyde Navigation Act, 20 June.

Aberdeen Joint Station opens, 4 November.

Former Polloc & Govan Railway tracks lifted from West Street to Clyde.

James Smithells succeeds Christopher Johnston as general manager.

1868 Shareholders' committee of inquiry delivers critical report.

Thomas Hill is 7th CR chairman.

Ferniegair-Lesmahagow Junction line opens.

Hatton deviation on Dundee & Newtyle Railway; new station at Newtyle, 31 August.

Busby Railway extended to East Kilbride, 1 September.

Portpatrick-Donaghadee steamboat service begins.

Telegraph Act: CR receives £75,000.

1869 CR takes over Crieff & Methven Junction Railway, 26 July.

CR opens its Edinburgh-Glasgow via Midcalder line, 9 July (Cleland-Midcalder opened for goods 1 January).

Solway Junction Railway opens for goods, 13 September.

1870s

1870 CR extends to Princes Street, Edinburgh, 'temporary station', 2 May.
Callander & Oban Railway opens to Killin (Glenoglehead), 1 June.
Temporary abandonment of Callander & Oban line west of Tyndrum.
Solway Junction Railway opens for passengers, 8 August.
Balerno branch re-authorised.
Forfar-Broughty Ferry line opens for goods, 12 August, passengers 14 November.
CR carting department is set up.

1871 Caledonian-NBR amalgamation proposal fails.
NBR gets powers to build from Arbroath-Kinnaber Junction (North British Arbroath & Montrose Railway), 22 February.
Glasgow, Barrhead & Kilmarnock Joint Railway opens to Stewarton, 27 March
CR and GSWR agree joint purse operation between Greenock and Glasgow, March.

1872 Wigtownshire Railway Act (joint line).
Westinghouse brake trials on Wemyss Bay line, March.
Larne & Stranraer Steamboat Company begins operations.
Strawfrank curve opens at Carstairs, 10 October.

1873 CR buys parts of Solway Junction Railway and works the whole.
South Side Station, Glasgow, demolished.
CR gets powers to build across Clyde in Glasgow and erect a Central Station
Glasgow Barrhead & Kilmarnock Joint Railway completed 26 June, with Beith branch.
CR Lanark-Douglas-Muirkirk branch meets GSWR Auchinleck-Muirkirk branch, 1 January (goods only Douglas-Muirkirk until 1874).

1874 Douglas-Muirkirk passenger service from 1 June.
CR opens Balerno branch, 1 August.

1875 CR gets revised powers to build across Clyde to Gordon Street (Central Station)
Wigtownshire Railway opens April, to Millisle by August.
Polmadie Shed opens, September.

1876 Midland Railway opens to Carlisle, through trains from St. Pancras to Glasgow (St Enoch) via GSWR, 1 May.
CR opens Dalry link (Edinburgh), 3 July, and line between Haymarket West and Dalry Middle Junctions, for Stirling-Edinburgh trains to Princes Street.
Hamilton-Ferniegair link opens 18 September (goods), 2 October (passenger).
Benjamin Conner dies; George Brittain appointed locomotive superintendent.

1877 Bothwell branch opens, March.
London Road Goods Station, Glasgow, opens, 12 April.
Wigtownshire Railway opens to Whithorn, 9 July.

1878 Tay Bridge opens, 31 May.
CR reopens Glasterlaw Fork to facilitate NBR Arbroath-Aberdeen traffic.
Uddingston-Fullwood Junction line opens (goods only) 1 October.

1879 London Road, Glasgow, opens as a passenger terminus, 1 April.
Uddingston-Fullwood Junction line opens for passenger trains, 1 June.
Glasgow Central Station opens, 1 August.
CR opens Leith North branch for passenger service, 1 August.
South Side Station closed, 1 July; Bridge Street reconstruction complete, 12 July.
Tay Bridge falls, 28 December.

1880s

1880 JC Bolton is 8th CR chairman.
CR operates Alloa Railway Co.
Dundee & Arbroath line operated by CR-NB joint committee, from 1 February.
Callander & Oban line opened to Oban, 30 June.
Cathcart District Railway part authorised.
CR tries out tablet system, Dumfries-Lockerbie.
CR adopts the Westinghouse automatic brake.
Law Junction-Carfin (later Holytown) line via Wishaw Central opens, 1 June.
Dissolution of the 'Guaranteed Companies', August.

| 1881 | NBR opens Arbroath-Montrose-Kinnaber Junction for freight. |
NBR takes over Montrose & Bervie line.
Solway Viaduct put out of action, to 1884.
CR takes over Lesmahagow Railway, 8 December.
1882 Auchinraith-Blantyre cut-off opens, 1 May.
Carron Dock opens at Grangemouth, 3 June.
CR absorbs Busby & East Kilbride Railway.
James Thompson succeeds James Smithells as general manager.
Dugald Drummond appointed locomotive superintendent; Brittain retires;
St Rollox works enlarged.
1883 East Kilbride-Blantyre line opens for goods, 1 March (2 July for passengers).
Moffat branch opens, 2 April.
Alton Heights-Poniel link line opens, 2 April.
NBR Arbroath-Kinnaber fully open, 1 May.
Central Hotel, Glasgow, opens, 19 June.
CR promotes Barrmill & Kilwinning Railway, Act of 20 August.
Final settlement with 'Guaranteed Companies'.
1884 Barrmill & Kilwinning Railway reconstituted as Lanarkshire & Ayrshire Railway, through to Ardrossan. Act obtained 28 August.
CR leases Moffat Railway, 4 July.
CR takes over Alloa Railway from 1 September
1885 Portpatrick & Wigtownshire Railways become joint line owned by CR, GSWR, LNWR and Midland Railway.
London Road-Parkhead goods line (Glasgow) opens, 17 August.
Alloa Railway builds bridge across lower Forth; South Alloa harbour branch shuts to passengers, 1 October.
1886 Cathcart District Railway opens to Mount Florida, 1 March; to Cathcart, 25 May.
NBR opens Glasgow City & District Railway, 15 March.
Airdrie branch opened from Langloan, 19 April (goods), 1 June (passengers).
Greenhill-Bonnybridge branch opens, 2 August.
Parkhead-Blochairn Junction opens, 2 August, completing Rutherglen-Balornock line.
1887 Cairnhill Junction-Chapelhall opens, 1 September.
Cathcart District Railway fully authorised.
1888 Denny branch south fork opens, 1 February.
Kilsyth & Bonnybridge Railway opens, common line with NBR, 2 July.
Chapelhall-Newhouse line opens for Airdrie-Morningside trains, 2 July.
Glasgow Central Railway (underground) authorised, 10 August.
Lanarkshire & Ayrshire Railway, Barrmill-Ardrossan opens, 4 September, Ardeer, 3 November, Ardrossan harbour (via GSWR at first) 30 November.
Galawhistle extension of Coalburn line opens for coal traffic.
All timber bridges in Strathmore now replaced.
1889 Gourock extension completed, 1 June.
Caledonian Steam Packet Co established.
Lanarkshire & Ayrshire Railway Kilbirnie branch opens 1 November (goods), 2 December (passenger).
CR takes over Moffat Railway, 1 November.

1890s

1890 CR and NBR contest for takeover of GSWR.
Forth Bridge opens, 4 March.
Princes Street Station, Edinburgh, burns down, 16 June.
Lanarkshire & Ayrshire Railway opens to Ardrossan Montgomerie Pier, 30 May.
Lanarkshire & Ayrshire opens Irvine branch, 2 June.
CR takes over Glasgow Central Railway, 31 May.
Drummond resigns; Hugh Smellie is appointed locomotive superintendent.
Gibson dies; George Jackson (solicitor) takes over till 1891.
1891 Scottish Railway Strike, December 1890-January 1891.
Lanarkshire & Dunbartonshire Railway authorised (Stobcross-Dumbarton).
John Blackburn appointed secretary.
Smellie dies; John Lambie appointed locomotive superintendent.

1892	GSWR trains cease to use Bridge Street Station, 1 February.
1893	CR takes over Wemyss Bay Railway, 1 August.
	Crieff-Comrie Railway opens, 1 June.
1894	Edinburgh Princes Street rebuilt station opens.
	CR Craigleith-Davidson's Mains-Barnton branch opens, 1 March.
	Cathcart Circle completed 2 April.
	C&O and West Highland Railway link at Crianlarich completed 11 October, but not used.
1895	CR takes over whole Solway Junction Railway, 22 June.
	Forfar-Brechin line opens, 1 June (goods from 7 January).
	Broughton-Talla line opens (to 1905).
	'Races to the North' in August.
	Lambie dies; J.F. McIntosh appointed locomotive superintendent.
1896	Glasgow Central Railway completed, 10 August. Glasgow Central (Low Level) Station opens.
	Lanarkshire & Dumbartonshire Railway opened. Joint Committee formed by CR, NBR and Lanarkshire & Dumbartonshire Railway to operate services Dumbarton East Junction to Balloch Pier.
	Ballachulish branch authorised.
	Edzell branch from Forfar-Brechin line opens, March.
	Muirkirk-Glenbuck line completed, never used.
1897	J.C. Bunten is 9th CR chairman.
	Newton extension of Glasgow Central Railway opens, 1 February.
	Paisley & Barrhead District Railway authorised, 6 August (see 1902).
	Junction spur opens at Crianlarich, 20 December.
1898	CR absorbs Crieff & Comrie Railway, 2 August.
	First electric trams in Glasgow.
	Carmyllie branch operates as a light railway, 6 August.
1899	CR exercises running powers, Glasgow-Bo'ness, February-July.
	George Graham retires; Donald Matheson appointed chief engineer.

1900-1909

1900	William Patrick appointed general manager.
1901	Bunten dies; Sir James Thompson is 10th CR chairman.
	William Patrick dies; Robert Millar appointed general manager.
	Elvanfoot-Leadhills branch opens, 1 October.
	Comrie-St Fillans line opens.
	Wishaw-Newmains line opens, 1 October.
	Extension of Central Station, widening of Clyde Bridge (to 1905).
1902	Strathaven-Darvel line completed, 1 May.
	Leadhills branch extended to Wanlockhead (goods 19 September, passenger 12 October).
	CR takes over Paisley & Barrhead District Railway.
	CR absorbs Lochearnhead, St. Fillans & Comrie Railway, 21 July.
	Kempt retires; Guy Calthrop appointed as general superintendent.
1903	Caledonian Hotel opens in Edinburgh.
	Grampian Corridor Express introduced, 6 April.
	CR opens Newhaven-Seafield branch (goods only).
	Lanarkshire &Ayrshire Railway opens from Giffen to Cathcart, 1 April.
	Renfrew District Railway opens, 1 June.
	Prince's Dock Joint Railway opens, 17 August (CR, GSWR, NBR).
	Ballachulish branch opens, 21 August.
	Wemyss Bay new station opens, 7 December.
1904	Lanarkshire & Ayrshire Railway opens from Cathcart to Newton, 6 January.
1905	Comrie-Balquhidder line completed.
	Mid-Lanark lines open 1 June: Merryton Junction-Larkhall Central-Stonehouse; Strathaven Central-Stonehouse; Blackwood-Stonehouse.
	Strathaven (Central)-Darvel opened for passengers, 1May; goods 4 July.
	Paisley & Barrhead passenger service abandoned.
1906	Grange Dock opens at Grangemouth, 10 October.
	Thompson dies; Sir James King is 11th CR chairman.
	Bankfoot Railway opens, 1 May.
	Extension of Glasgow Central is completed.
	Elliot Junction collision, 28 December.
1907	Rothesay Dock opens on north bank of Clyde, 25 April.

1908 Sir C. Bine Renshaw is 12th chairman.
Final CR-NBR peace agreement.
Robert Millar dies; Guy Calthrop appointed General Manager.
East side of Friockheim Triangle closed.
Electro-pneumatic signalling installed at Glasgow Central.
1909 CR absorbs Lanarkshire & Dumbartonshire Railway, 1 August.
New goods sheds, Buchanan Street, 14 June.

1910-1923

1910 Calthrop resigns, Donald Matheson appointed General Manager.
Gleneagles Hotel Company formed.
1911 More rebuilding at Perth General Station.
New access loop to Grangemouth Docks completed.
1913 CR buys the Bankfoot Railway.
CR contracts for 17 Pullman cars.
1914 McIntosh retires; William Pickersgill appointed Locomotive Superintendent.
Railway Executive takes control of all lines.
1915 Disaster at Quintinshill, 22 May.
1917 Many stations and lines close as wartime economy measure.
1918 Henry Allan is 13th and last CR chairman.
1919 National railway strike, 27 September-5 October.
1920 Alloa Viaduct put out of action; repaired.
J.J. Haining appointed Secretary.
1921 Railways de-controlled, 15 August.
Railways Act passed, 19 August.
War service locomotives returned.
Solway Viaduct is closed permanently.
1923 CR acquires the Gleneagles Hotel company.
CR challenges terms of amalgamation.
CR absorbed into London, Midland & Scottish Railway, 1 July.

Note: The Caledonian Railway Association (www.crassoc.org.uk) maintains an archive of Caledonian documents, records, plans photographs and memorabilia (held by Glasgow University Archive Service). The CRA also publishes reprints of Company documents in addition to its own on-going programme of original publications.

Royal Naval Ambulance Train No. 2 on public display at Wishaw Central, in 1918.

APPENDIX 1
WHICH WAS BIGGER – CALEDONIAN OR NORTH BRITISH?

There are different ways in which the size of railway companies can be calculated and compared. Capitalisation, track and train miles, passenger numbers, goods tonnage, can all be brought into consideration. But the most basic ones are those of revenue and expenditure, and the following snapshots, using figures from the half-yearly reports, show how the North British, initially smaller, then neck and neck for some decades from the mid-1860s, eventually edged ahead of the Caledonian.

1869-70	Half-yearly revenue (Aug-Jan)	Total expenditure
	CR £978,652	£404,955
	NBR £762,399	£403,262
1878-79	Half-yearly revenue (Aug-Jan)	Total expenditure
	CR £1,447,936	£611,702
	NBR £1,162,960	£599,366
1903-04	Half-yearly revenue (Aug-Jan)	Total expenditure
	CR £1,707,273	£827,097
	NBR £1,715,038	£816,187
1907	Half-yearly revenue (Feb-July)	Total expenditure
	CR £2,191,245	£1,209,517
	NBR £2,440,108	£1,313,570
1913	Full year's revenue (Jan-Dec)	Total expenditure
	CR £5,129,155	£3,049,151
	NBR £5,254,607	£3,010,741

APPENDIX 2
THE CALEDONIAN IN 1913

The last 'normal' year for the Caledonian was 1913, which was also the first year in which the Scottish railways provided January-December accounts rather than February-January. Among the statistics it filed for the Board of Trade were these:

Authorised capital

1. Shares and stocks:	£46,194,317
2. Loans and debentures:	£12,687,533
	Total: £58,881,850

Total capital raised and ranking for dividend/interest (31/12/13): £70,910,471

Gross receipts:	£5,129,155
Gross expenditures:	£3,049,591
Net receipts:	£2,079,564
Expenditure on horses, capital account:	£38,659

Steamboats, receipts:	£5,172	Canals, receipts:	£41,807
Steamboats, expenditure:	£3,734	Canals, expenditure:	£34,653
Hotels, receipts:	£208,023	Docks & harbours, receipts:	£82,896
Hotels, expenditure:	£172,024	Docks & harbours, expenditure:	£33,121

Merchandise, gross receipts:	£1,663,496
Cartage:	£149,269
Net receipts:	£1,514,227

Mileage of lines open: 957

Tender locomotives: 609	Tank locomotives: 388	Rail-motors: 1

Passenger carriages: 2,242 (plus 730 'other'), with carrying capacity of 118,493 persons

Open wagons under 8 tons:	661	Covered wagons under 8 tons:	1,784
Open wagons over 8 tons:	13,709	Covered wagons over 8 tons:	693
Mineral wagons under 8 tons:	501	Mineral wagons over 8 tons:	28,103
Cattle trucks:	1,422	All other vehicles:	5,043

Train mileage, coaching:	10,561,177	Train mileage, goods:	7,678,876
Shunting mileage, coaching:	957,733	Shunting mileage, goods:	6,164,492

Passengers first class:	2,342,652	Passengers, third class:	34,442,595
Passengers, workmen:	10,720,225	Season tickets:	32,428

Tonnage, general merchandise:	6,108,313
Tonnage, coal:	15,708,040
Tonnage, minerals:	6,486,709
Livestock, numbers:	1,950,284

APPENDIX 3
THE CALEDONIAN IN 1922

The last full year of the Caledonian Railway's independent existence was 1922. These statistics provided for the Ministry of Transport give an anatomy of the company in its final form.

Authorised capital, shares & stocks:	£46,194,317
Authorised capital, loans & debentures:	£13,198,148
	Total: £59,392,465

Capital Account

1. Expenditure on Railway

(i) Lines open to traffic:	£38,807,704
(ii) Lines jointly owned:	£1,561,789
(iii) Rolling Stock:	£7,785,329
(iv) Land & buildings:	£262,916
(v) Plant & machinery:	£220,751

2. Other Expenditure

(i) Horses:	£38,659 *
(ii) Road vehicles:	£11,531
(iii) Steamboats:	£21,600
(iv) Canals:	£991,617
(v) Docks & harbours:	£1,868,752
(vi) Hotels:	£604,264
(vii) Electric power stations, etc.	£29,832
(viii) Land & property not part of railway stations, used in railway work:	£22,067
(ix) Land & property not part of railway stations, not used in railway work:	£1,471,311
(x) Subscriptions to other railway companies:	£1,419,900
(xi) Special items:	£1,187,656 **
	Total Capital Expenditure: £56,305,498

* The same figure was put in each year
** This was nine times greater than for any other Scottish railway company

Revenue Account

1. Expenditure

(i) Maintenance:	£1,174,578
(ii) Locomotives:	£499,549
(iii) Carriages:	£312,183
(iv) Wagons:	£493,423
(v) Locomotive running:	£1,615,813
(vi) Traffic:	£2,221,695
(vii) General charges:	£188,408
(viii) Law expenses:	£9,914
(ix) Parliamentary expenses:	£1,591
(x) Compensation (passengers):	£1,332
(xi) Compensation (workmen):	£15,623
(xii) Damages and loss:	£15,567
(xiii) Rates:	£254,719
(xiv) Government duty:	£16,485
(xv) National insurance:	£33,738
(xvi) Running powers (balance):	£37,000
(xvii) Mileage Demurrage and Wagon Hire (balance):	£13,149
(xviii) Joint lines, proportion of expenses:	£33,773
(xix) Miscellaneous:	£14,691
	Total: £6,954,176

2. Revenue Receipts

Gross:	£9,082,938

Passengers, first class:	£283,022
Passengers, third class:	£2,132,335
Season tickets:	£385,302
Workmen's tickets:	£85,672
	Total: £3,733,282

Goods (merchandise):	£2,919,641
Less cartage cost:	£255,359
Net merchandise revenue:	£2,664,382
Livestock:	£173,616
Coal:	£1,752,042
Minerals:	£609,060
Joint lines share:	£32,588
Miscellaneous:	£145,128

Non-railway receipts and expenditures

Steamboats:	revenue	£6,048	expenditure	£6,682	deficit	£634
Docks & harbours:	revenue	£177,342	expenditure	£72,395	balance	£104,947
Canals:	revenue	£20,036	expenditure	£59,809	deficit	£29,773
Hotels:	revenue	£336,392	expenditure	£291,674	balance	£74,718

Net income & appropriations (Interest, etc.):	£19,765
Savings bank funds:	£1,259,185
Compensation paid under Railways Act 1921:	£2,999,988
Liabilities and assets on balance sheet:	£9,318,898

Locomotives (tender): 655   (tank): 415   **Total** 1,070

		first class capacity	third class capacity
Carriages:	1,766	11,776	90,578
Composite carriages:	525	8,324	15,497
Restaurant cars:	12	128	215
Sleeping cars:	13	137	

Post Office vans:	15		
Parcel/brake vans:	247	Merchandise wagons (open):	14,060
Carriage trucks:	120	Merchandise wagons (covered):	3,296
Horse boxes:	171	Mineral wagons:	28,367
Miscellaneous vehicles:	171	of which 40 over 20 tons, one bogie-fitted	
		Locomotive coal wagons:	1,786
Horses (road):	718	Ballast wagons:	293
Horses (shunting):	16	Other vehicles:	206
Carts:	956	Departmental locomotives:	8
Motor delivery vehicles:	3		
Miscellaneous delivery vehicles:	6		

Running lines: 1,094 miles   Sidings: 980 miles

Engine miles (passenger):	9,301,997	shunting coaches:	909,830
Engine miles (goods):	6,178,954	shunting	4,551,662
	Total engine miles: 23,404,917		

Average train miles per hour

Passenger: 15.31   goods: 10.8

Average number of wagons per train

19.73 loaded   7.77 empty

Passenger numbers

first class: 1,691,387   third class: 24,780,635   workmen: 5,985,681   season: 48,580

Livestock numbers: 1,910,102

Goods tonnage

Merchandise: 4,573,174   coal: 13,117,141   minerals: 4,008,483

BIBLIOGRAPHY

1. ORIGINAL DOCUMENTS

Glasgow University Archive Service, Caledonian Railway Association Archive (GUAS.CRA)
Institution of Civil Engineers (ICE)
National Archives of Scotland (NAS)

National Library of Scotland (NLS)
National Railway Museum (NRM)
St Andrews University Library: Special Collections (ST.AND.)

2. OFFICIAL PUBLICATIONS

Edinburgh Gazette
Hansard
London Gazette

Parliamentary Papers (PP)
Parliamentary Papers, House of Lords (PPHL)

3. NEWSPAPERS, JOURNALS, SERIAL PUBLICATIONS, ETC.

Aberdeen Journal
Bradshaw's Guide, July 1922
Business History Review
Caledonian Mercury (*Cal. Merc.*)
Carlisle Patriot
Daily News
Dundee Courier & Argus (*Dund. Cour.*)
Economic History Review (*EHR*)
Engineer
Glasgow Herald (*Glas. Her.*)
Hamilton Advertiser
Herapath's Railway Journal (*Herapath*)
Highland Railway Journal
Journal of the Institution of Locomotive Engineers
Leeds Mercury

Mercantile Advertiser
Morning Post
North British Daily Mail
North British Shipping & Railway Journal
Railway Gazette (*RG*)
Railway Magazine
Railway News
Railway Times (*RT*)
The Scotsman
Scottish Railway Gazette (*SRG*)
The Times
Transport History (*TH*)
The True Line (*TL*)

4. PAMPHLETS

Notman, Robert Russell, *Railway Amalgamation: Addressed to the Shareholders of the Aberdeen, Scottish Midland, Dundee & Arbroath, Scottish Central, and Caledonian Railway Companies.* London, 1852

Porritt, Leslie, *The Scottish Central Railway, Perth General Station*
Railway & Canal Historical Society (RCHS), *Closed Passenger Lines of Great Britain, 1827-1947*

5. DOCUMENTS PRODUCED BY THE CALEDONIAN RAILWAY COMPANY

Caledonian Railway Christmas Annual, 1909
Matheson, Donald A., *Notes on the Engineering Features of American Railroads*, 1903

Caledonian Railway Rule Book, 1906
Caledonian Railway Timetable for Guards and others, 1856

6. DOCUMENTS ACCESSED ELECTRONICALLY AND WEBSITES REFERRED TO

ayrshirehistory.com
Curwen, 'The Later Records relating to North Westmorland: or the Barony of Appleby' (1932)
Groome, F.H., *Ordnance Gazetteer of Scotland*,

Public Services Programme Discussion Paper 0804, August 2008: Leunig, T., and Crafts, N., 'Did early utility regulation work?'
scottishmining.co.uk
stonehouseonline

7. BOOKS

Acworth, William, *The Railways of Scotland*. London, 1890

Alderman, Geoffrey, *The Railway Interest*. Leicester, 1973

Atkins, C.P., *The Scottish 4-6-0 Classes*. London, 1976

Bagwell, Philip S. *The Railway Clearing House in the British Economy, 1842-1922*. London, 1968

Baxter, David (ed.), *British Locomotive Catalogue 1825-1923, vol 5*. Ashbourne, 1984

Biddle, Gordon, *Historic Railway Buildings*. Oxford, 2003

Bremner, David, *The Industries of Scotland*. Edinburgh, 1869

Brown, J.L., and Lawson, I.C., *History of Peebles*. Edinburgh, 1990

Byrom, Bernard, *The Railways of Upper Strathearn*. Usk, 2004

Cairncross, A.K., *Home & Foreign Investment, 1870-1913*. Cambridge, 1953

Campbell, R.H., and Dow, J.B.A., *A Source Book of Scottish Economic & Social History*. Oxford, 1968

Checkland, S.G., *Scottish Banking: A History 1695-1973*. London, 1975

Clark, A.J.C., *Caley to the Coast*. Usk, 2001

Cobb, M.H., *The Railways of Great Britain: A Historical Atlas* (2nd ed.), Shepperton, 2006

Cornwell, H.J.Campbell, *Forty Years of Caledonian Locomotives*. Newton Abbot, 1974

Cummings, A.J.G, and Devine, T.M., *Industry, Business and Society in Scotland since 1700*. Edinburgh, 1994

Ellis, C. Hamilton, *The Trains We Loved*. London, 1947

Ellis, C. Hamilton, *Four Main Lines*. London, 1950

Ferguson, Niall, *The Dundee & Newtyle Railway*. Oxford, 1995

Ferguson, Niall, *The Arbroath & Forfar Railway*. Usk, 2000

Foxwell, E., and Farrer, T.C., *Express Trains, English & Foreign*. London, 1889

Fraser, W.H., and Maver, Irene, *Glasgow*, vol 2, 1830-1912. Manchester, 1996

Galt, William, *Railway Reform: Its Importance and Practicability*. London, 1865

Gillespie, John, *Humours of Scottish Life*. Edinburgh, 1904

Gourvish, T.R., *Mark Huish and the LNWR*. Leicester, 1972

Graham, George, *The Caledonian Railway: Its Origin*. Glasgow, 1888

Grinling, Charles H., *History of the Great Northern Railway*. London, 1903

Hawkins, C., and Reeve, G., *LMS Engine Sheds Vol. 5, The Caledonian Railway*. Didcot, 1987

Highet, Campbell, *The Portpatrick Railway*. Lingfield, 1964

Highet, Campbell, *The Glasgow & South Western Railway*. Lingfield, 1965

Highet, Campbell, *Scottish Locomotive History, 1831-1923*. London, 1970

Hull, Edward, *Our Coal Resources at the End of the Nineteenth Century*. London, 1897

Johnson, C., and Hume, J.R., *Glasgow Stations*. Newton Abbot, 1975

Johnston, Ronald, *Clydeside Capital, 1870-1920*. Phantassie, 2000

Kellett, J.R., *The Impact of Railways on Victorian Cities*. London, 1969

Kernahan, Jack, *The Cathcart Circle*. 2nd ed., Lydney, 2011

MacIntosh, Jim, *Caledonian Railway Livery*. Lydney, 2008

MacIntosh, Jim, *The Caledonian Railway's Wemyss Bay Station*. Lydney, 2009

Mackean, Charles, *Battle for the North*. London, 2006

MacLaren, Charles, *Selected Writings of Charles MacLaren*, vol. 2. Edinburgh, 1869

Marshall, Peter, *The Scottish Central Railway*. Usk, 1998

Martin, Don, *The Garnkirk & Glasgow Railway*. Kirkintilloch, 1981

Martin, Don, *The Monkland & Kirkintilloch and Associated Railways*. Kirkintilloch, 1995

Mavor, James, *The Scottish Railway Strike 1891: A History and Criticism*. Edinburgh, 1891

Measom, G..S., *Official Illustrated Guide to the Edinburgh & Glasgow and Caledonian Railways*. London, 1859

Middlemass, Thomas, *Mainly Scottish Steam*. Newton Abbot, 1973

Mitchell, Joseph, *Reminiscences of My Life in the Highlands*, vol 2. Newton Abbot (reprint) 1971

Neele, G.P. *Railway Reminiscences*. London, 1904

Nock, O.S., *The Caledonian Railway*. London, 1961

Nock, O.S., *Scottish Railways* (revised ed.). London, 1961

Oxford Dictionary of National Biography. Oxford, 2004

Paget-Tomlinson, E., *The Railway Carriers*. Lavenham, 1990

Paterson, A.J.S., *The Golden Age of the Clyde Steamers*. Newton Abbot, 1969

Pratt, Edwin A., *Railways and Nationalisation*. London, 1908

Pratt, Edwin A., *British Railways and the Great War*, 2 vols. London, 1921

Quick, Michael, *A Chronology of Railway Passenger Stations in Great Britain*. Oxford, 2009

Reed. M.C. (ed.), *Railways in the Victorian Economy*. Newton Abbot, 1969

Robertson, C.J.A., *The Origins of the Scottish Railway System, 1722-1844*. Edinburgh, 1983

Ross, David, *The Highland Railway* (2nd edition). Catrine, 2010

Scrivenor, Harry, *Railways of the United Kingdom*. London, 1849

Shaw, Donald, *The Balerno Branch, and the Caley in Edinburgh*. Oxford, 1989

Sherrington, C.E.R., *The Economics of Rail Transport in Great Britain*, 2 vols. London, 1928

Simnett, W.E., *Railway Amalgamation in Great Britain*. London, 1923

Slaven, A., and Checkland, S., *Dictionary of Scottish Business Biography*. Aberdeen, 1993

Steel, George Maclennan, *Dundee's Iron Horses*. Edinburgh, 1974

Stephenson Locomotive Society, *Caledonian Railway Centenary*, London, 1947

Sullivan, Dick, *Navvyman*. Eye, 1983

Thomas, John, *The North British Railway*, 2 vols. Newton Abbot, 1969

Thomas, John, *Gretna: Britain's Worst Railway Disaster*. Newton Abbot, 1969

Thomas, John, *A Regional History of the Railways of Great Britain, Vol 6* (revised Alan J.S. Paterson). Newton Abbot, 1971, 1984

Thomas, John, and Turnock, David, *A Regional History of the Railways of Great Britain, Vol 15*. Newton Abbot, 1989

Thomas, John, *The Callander & Oban Railway* (2nd edition). Newton Abbot, 1990

Thorne, H.D., *Rails to Portpatrick*. Prescot, 1976

Webster, N.W., *Joseph Locke: Railway Revolutionary*. London, 1970

Williamson, James, *The Clyde Passenger Steamer*. Glasgow, 1904

NOTES AND REFERENCES
CHAPTER 1

1. They are reprinted in MacLaren, *Selected Writings*, vol. 2, 1ff.
2. Robertson, *Origins of the Scottish Railway System*, 268.
3. Robertson, *op. cit.*, 59.
4. Robertson, *op. cit.*, 124.
5. Martin, *Monkland & Kirkintilloch*, 24.
6. Robertson, *op. cit.*, 62.
7. Quick, *Chronology*, Slamannan. From August 1847 re-gauging of the Slamannan Railway enabled trains to run between Airdrie and Linlithgow.
8. Acworth, *Railways of Scotland*, 105.
9. Ferguson, *Dundee & Newtyle*, 2.
10. Ross, *George & Robert Stephenson*, 61.
11. Graham, *The Caledonian Railway: Its Origin*, 16.
12. Highet, *Glasgow & South Western*, 14.
13. Locke's Report, quoted in Graham *op. cit.*, 10.
14. *Cal. Merc.*, 25 January 1836.
15. NLS.GB233. Ms 6354.17.
16. NLS.GB233. Ms 6354.4.
17. NLS.GB233. Ms 6354.5.
18. Fourth Report of the Commissioners, 15 March 1841, quoted in Graham, *op. cit.*, 42.
19. NLS.GB233. Ms 6354.41.
20. Patrick Maxwell Stewart, M.P. for Renfrewshire and a director of the Grand Junction, had been instrumental in the appointment of Locke to the Greenock line. See Robertson, *op. cit.*, 197.
21. Graham, *op. cit.*, 51.
22. Robertson, *op. cit.*, 288ff.
23. J.F. Curwen, 'The Later Records relating to North Westmorland: or the Barony of Appleby'.
24. *Liverpool Mercury*, 4 November 1842.
25. Quoted in Robertson, *op. cit.*, 290.
26. NLS.GB233. Ms 6354.46.
27. Robertson, *op. cit.*, 317.
28. NLS. MS6355.1.
29. NLS.GB233. Ms 6354.62.
30. Letter in *RT*, 15 April 1854, p. 400. Just possibly, he meant the 'Caley' by-name, which was current from an early stage.
31. NLS.GB233. Ms 6354.64.
32. GUAS.CRA1/2/1
33. NLS.GB233. Ms 6354.64.
34. Robertson, *op. cit.*, 298.
35. *ODNB*, David Brooke, 'Thomas Brassey'.
36. Webster, *Joseph Locke*, 175.
37. ST.AND. Robertson Coll., 38291, SCR Prospectus and map; Marshall, *Scottish Central*, 11.
38. NAS.BR/CAL/1/7 Caledonian Committee minutes of 23 March 1844.
39. Thomas & Turnock, *Regional History*, xv, 147ff.
40. *SRG*, 20 October 1849, document of 18 March 1844, quoted by Hope Johnstone.
41. Ferguson, *Arbroath & Forfar*, 50.
42. NLS.MS6355.5.
43. Marshall, *Scottish Central*, 14.
44. *Reminiscences of My Life in the Highlands*, ii, 151-7.
45. ICE. TBV77. 'Correspondence as to the Appointment of Principal and Consulting Engineer to the Scottish Central Railway'.

CHAPTER 1 CONTINUED

46. See also Locke's letters to Charles Stewart, in NLS.MS6355.
47. *Bremner, The Industries of Scotland*, 33. Neilson's brother William was founder of the Glasgow works which built many Caledonian locomotives.
48. NLS.GB233.MSS 6355. 11,25.
49. See for example an advertisement in the *Carlisle Patriot*, 25 October 1844.
50. *TH*, vol 3, No. 3, 1970, Butt & Ward, 'The Promotion of the Caledonian Railway'.
51. *Glas. Her.*, 17 May 1847.

52. *TH*, Butt & Ward, *op. cit.*, 226ff.
53. NLS.GB233.MSS 6355. 31.
54. NLS. *Ibid.*
55. NLS. *Ibid.*
56. Robertson, *Early Scottish Railways*, 294.
57. Robertson, *op. cit.*, 299.
58. Robertson, *op. cit.*, 295.
59. *Times*, May 20, 1845.
60. *Times*, June 4, May 20, 1845.
61. *Times*, June 5, 1845, 8.

CHAPTER 2

1. Graham, *Caledonian Railway*, 85.
2. *TH*, vol 3, no. 3, 1970. Butt & Ward, 'The Promotion of the `Caledonian Railway Company', 243.
3. At an early stage the name 'Float Junction' was intended, the station being some way from Carstairs village. See *Glas. Her.*, 18 February 1848.
4. *TH*, vol 3, no. 3, Butt & Ward, *op. cit.*, 228.
5. *Glas. Her.*, 5 September 1845. The same issue noted that "Mr Hope Johnstone has contracted for supplying the Company with railway sleepers, to the tune of £10,000."
6. NLS.GB233.MSS6355.60.
7. Acworth, *The Railways of Scotland*, 37.
8. Thomas & Turnock, *Regional History*, xv, 150f.
9. NLS. GB233.MSS 6355. 60.
10. NAS.BR/CAL/1/7. Board minutes, 2 October 1845; see also Marshall, *Scottish Central*, 36.
11. *Times*, January 26, 1846.
12. NAS.BR/CAL/1/7. Board minutes, 12 August 1845.
13. *TH*, Butt & Ward, *op. cit.*, 232. Originally the GP&G company had been going to work the Barrhead line, see *Glas. Her.* 19 September 1845, reporting the Glasgow, Paisley & Greenock half-yearly meeting.
14. NAS.BR/CAL/17. Board minutes, 5 December 1845, 8 January 1846.

15. NLS.GB233.MSS 6355. 68.
16. *TH*, Butt & Ward, *op. cit.*, 231.
17. NAS.BR/CAL/1/7. Board minutes, 20 November 1846; Scrivenor, *Railways of the U.K.*, 567.
18. NAS.BR/CAL/1/8/99. Report of Committee of Inquiry, 2.
19. Ferguson, *Dundee & Newtyle*, 86f.
20. *RT*, 14 March 1846.
21. Gillespie, *Humours of Scottish Life*, 132.
22. Highet, *Glasgow & South Western*, 17.
23. Marshall, *Scottish Central*, 68.
24. Marshall, *op. cit.*, 67.
25. NAS.BR/CAL/1/7. Board Minutes, 2 November 1846.
26. *EHR*, vol. 17, 1964. Kellett, J.R., 'Glasgow's Railways', 363.
27. NAS.BR/CAL/1/7. Board minutes, 15 October 1846.
28. *Times*, 2 September 1847. Johnson & Hume, *Glasgow Stations*, 94.
29. NAS.BR/CAL/1/7. Board minutes, 26 November 1846.
30. NLS.GB233.MSS 6355. 80.
31. NAS.BR/CAL/1/7.Board minutes, 19 February 1847.
32. *Glas. Her.*, 21 September 1846, 11, 12 and 29 March 1847.

CHAPTER 3

1. *Glas. Her.*, 2 October 1849.
2. *Times*, July 31, 1847, 5.
3. *Glas. Her.*, 10 September 1847.
4. *Glas. Her.*, 2 January 1846.
5. *Times*, July 9, 1847, 6.
6. Quoted in Sullivan, *Navvyman*, 51.
7. NAS.BR/CAL/1/7. Board minutes, 27 May 1847. *Glas. Her.*, 12 July 1847.
8. *TH*, Butt & Ward, *op. cit.*, 241.
9. *Scotsman*, 1 September 1847, reporting the CR half-yearly shareholders' meeting.
9. *Scotsman*, 1 September 1847
10. NAS/BR/CAL/1/8. Board minutes, 22 October 1847, item 3.
11. *Cal. Merc.*, 22 July and 9 August 1847.
12. NAS.BR/CAL/1/8. CR board, 28 July 1847; see also *Times*, 24 July, 1847, 6.

13. Marshall, *Scottish Central*, 76.
14. *Times*, 25 January 1848, 3.
15. *Cal. Merc.*, 28 February 1848.
16. Gillespie, *Humours of Scottish Life*, 132. He also claimed that the Greenock line in early days had some 'standing-only' carriages: a minister found using one said, 'Where else would you find me, but in the congregation of the upright?'
17. NAS.BR/CAL/1/8/99. Report of Committee of Inquiry, 2.
18. NAS.BR/CAL/1/8. CR board, 15 February 1848.
19. *Times*, 29 February 1848.
20. *Cal. Merc.*, 17 and 22 July 1848.
21. NAS.BR/CAL/1/8. Board minutes, 23 December 1847. See also *Scottish History Review*, No. 164, October 1978, C.J.A. Robertson, 'Early Scottish Railways and Observance of the Sabbath.'

22. Noted in SMJ half-yearly report, March 1849. See *SRG*, 17 March 1849.
23. NAS.BR/CAL/1/8. Board minutes, 5 May 1848, items 1, 12.
24. NAS.BR/CAL/1/8. Board minutes, 13 May 1848. The N&C was eventually bought by George Hudson.
25. *Times*, 6, 15, 18 July; 10, 23 August; 2 September, 1848.
26. *Cal. Merc.*, 10 August 1848.
27. Ellis, *Four Main Lines*, 38.
28. *Times*, 2 December 1848; 10 January 1849.
29. Scrivenor, *Railways of the U.K.*, 587.
30. *TH*, vol. 3 No. 3, 1970. Butt & Ward, 'The Promotion of the Caledonian Railway', 231.
31. NAS.BR/CAL/1/8. Board minutes, 2 October 1848.
32. NAS.BR/CAL/1/8. CR board, 20 October 1848, item 5.
33. Scrivenor, *op. cit.*, 607.
34. Quoted in Scrivenor, *op. cit.*, 690.
35. *North British Shipping & Railway Journal*, 17 February 1849.
36. Quoted in Scrivenor, *op. cit.*, 685.
37. *Cal. Merc.*, 12 February 1849. Another vehicle was an ex-London & Birmingham first, converted to second class; it is not clear whether it belonged to the Caledonian or the Lancaster and Carlisle.
38. PP1850 (1249) Appendix to Report of Railway Commissioners.
39. *SRG*, 3 March 1849, 654.
40. *Times*, 28 February 1849.
41. *Cal. Merc.*, 9 April 1849.
42. *Times*, 6 March 1849.
43. *North British Railway & Shipping Journal*, 22 February 1849.
44. *Times*, 1 June 1849.
45. *SRG*, 11 August 1849; *Glas. Her.*, Report of G,B&N extraordinary meeting, 21 September 1849.
46. *SRG*, 11 August 1849.
47. *Cal. Merc.*, 20 September 1849.
48. *Times*, 19 June, 1849.
49. *SRG*, 29 September 1849.
50. Marshall, *Scottish Central*, 104.
51. Acworth, *The Railways of Scotland*, 105.
52. *Times*, 19 October 1849.
53. *Glas. Her*. 19 October 1849.
54. *SRG*, 20 October 1849.
55. *Times*, 7 November 1849.
56. NAS.BR/CAL/1/8/99. Report of the Committee, 7.
57. NAS.BR/CAL/1/8/99. Report of the Committee.
58. NAS.BR/CAL/1/8/99. Report of the Committee, 13,14.
59. *Times*, 31 December, 1849, 6.
60. Quick, *Chronology*, Glasgow, says this station was briefly called Gushetfaulds by the CR. This is unlikely as it was already named as South Side by the Barrhead Company. See also O.S. Glasgow town plan, 1857.
61. Quick, *op. cit.*, Motherwell.
62. *Glas. Her.*, 29 May 1848, advertisement offering "capitalists" the chance to acquire properties "almost bounding the proposed terminus of the Caledonian Railway … and therefore may be expected to increase in value daily."
63. *Glas. Her.*, 2 October 1849.
64. *Glas. Her.*, 2 November 1849.
65. Grinling, *Great Northern*, 75.
66. GUAS.CRA2/2/1/1/1.

CHAPTER 4

1. *Glas. Her.*, 12 June 1876.
2. NAS.BR/CAL/1/8/99. 'Brassey's Proposal'. Incidentally, Brassey worked the Lancaster & Carlisle Railway on a similar basis, at first.
3. Nock, *Caledonian Railway*, 37.
4. Lord Eglinton's statement, quoted in SRG, 21 April 1849.
5. *Glas. Her.*, 9 September 1847, 6 April and 17 November 1849, 1 April 1850. *Edinburgh Gazette*, 18 July 1848, 353; 21 November 1851, 1071. PPHL 1849 (145) xvi.
6. *Railway Magazine* 104, 1958. C.E. Lee, 'The Dundee & Arbroath Railway'.
7. *Hansard*, HoC debates, 18 March 1850.
8. Grinling, *Great Northern*, 96.
9. NAS.BR/CAL/1/9. Board minutes, 8 March 1850
10. NAS.BR/CAL/1/9. Board minutes, April 1850.
11. *Railway Magazine*, September 1907, 216.
12. *Glas. Her.*, 13 September 1850.
13. NAS.BR/CAL/1/9. Board minutes, 17 May 1850.
14. *Glas. Her.*, 12 and 14 June, 1850.
15. *Dund. Cour.*, 14 August 1850.
16. NAS.BR/CAL/1/9, Board minutes 2, 14, 15, 26 November 1850.
17. NAS.BR/CAL/1/9.
18. *RT*, 11 January 1851, 31.
19. *Cal. Merc.*, 3 February 1851.
20. *SRG*, 18 September 1852, 298.
21. NAS.BR/CAL/1/8. Board minutes, 15 February 1851.
22. NAS.BR/CAL/1/9. Board minutes, 10 January 1851.
23. Quoted in *RT*, 22 February 1851, 184.
24. ST.AND. Robertson coll., 238291. SCR timetable for December 1850.
25. Notman, *Railway Amalgamation*, 4.
26. *EHR*, Kellett, 'Glasgow's Railways', 365.
27. *Herapath*, 11 January, 1851.
28. *RT*, 29 March 1851, 321.
29. *Hansard*, HoC, Debates, 14 March 1851. Maule was eldest son of Lord Panmure, and from 1860 to his death in 1874 was Earl of Dalhousie.
30. NAS.BR/CAL/1/8, Board minutes, 26 March 1851.

CHAPTER 4 CONTINUED

31. Quoted in Bagwell, *The Railway Clearing House*, 251.
32. Gourvish, *Mark Huish & the LNWR*, 203, 293ff.
33. NAS.BR/CAL/1/8. Board minutes, 9 and 25 April 1851.
34. *Glas. Her.*, 13 September 1850.
35. NAS.BR/CAL/1/8. Board minutes, 7 March 1851.
36. NAS.BR/CAL/1/8. Board minutes, 20, 21, 23 May 1851.
37. *RT*, 19 July 1851, 722.
38. NAS.BR/CAL/1/8. Board minutes, 5 June, 3 September 1851.
39. Thomas, *Regional History*, vi, 161.
40. NAS.BR/CAL/1/8. Board minutes, 27 November 1851.
41. *SRG*, 3 January 1852.
42. NAS.BR/CAL/1/8. Board minutes, 26 February, 25 March 1852.
43. *Glas. Her.*, 15 March 1852.
44. *SRG*, 27 March 1852.
45. NAS.BR/CAL/1/8. Board minutes, 26 February, 10 April, 28 October 1852.
46. *Times*, 10 June 1852.
47. Notman, *op. cit.*, 6,7, 15.
48. NAS.BR/CAL/1/8. Board minutes, 29 July 1852.
49. *SRG*, 10 July 1852.
50. *SRG*, 16 October 1852.
51. Williamson, *The Clyde Passenger Steamer*, 158.
52. *Times*, 11 September 1852.
53. *Times*, 14 March 1853.
54. *Times*, 3 March 1853.
55. *Times*, 21 March 1853.
56. NAS.BR/CAL/1/8.
57. *Times*, 14 September 1853, note on half-yearly report.
58. *EHR*, Kellett, 'Glasgow's Railways', 365.
59. *EHR*. Kellett, *op. cit.*, 365.
60. GUAS.CRA2/3/1/9.
61. *RT*, Report of Special Meeting on 21 March, 25 March 1854, 327.
62. *Glas. Her.*, 14 May 1849, advertises a sale of railway contractor's equipment on a site "behind the Caledonian Railway Company's engine sheds, St. Rollox".
63. *RT*, 1 July, 707; *Times*, 15 July 1854.
64. *Glas. Her.*, 26 September 1855. The chairman's speech at the CR half-yearly meeting (25 September) gives a résumé of past events.

CHAPTER 5

1. BR/CAL/1/8. The minute refers to the "Electric Telegraph Co." but the CR's dealings were with the 'Magnetic'.
2. NAS.BR/CAL/1/8. Report to the Board, 22 August 1854.
3. Times, 21 July 1854.
4. RT, 12 August 1854, 872.
5. RT, ibid.
6. RT, 30 September 1854, 1079.
7. Times, 22 September; 23 September 1854.
8. NAS.BR/CAL/1/8. Board minutes, 26 September 1854.
9. Cal. Merc., 15 September 1853, 14 March 1854.
10. Letter in Cal. Merc., 18 January 1855.
11. *Glas. Her.*, 16 January 1855, report of special general meeting; also NAS. 1.D.RHP21154, Act of 1853. Some accounts state that the 'Hayhill fork' was built in 1860 or later, but it appears on the O.S. six-inch map, ist edition, surveyed in 1859 or before. In 1856, the Aberdeen-Glasgow goods train was still going via Gartsherrie Junction in both directions, but this would have been for shunting purposes. See NLS.ABS.3.84.48, 'CR Timetable for the Guidance of Guards', 1856.
12. Thomas & Paterson, *Regional History*, 125; Quick, *Chronology*, Neilston.
13. *Glas. Her.*, 23 March 1855.
14. *Glas. Her.*, 26 September 1855, report of CR half-yearly meeting, 25 September.
15. Bagwell, *The Railway Clearing House*, 251; NAS. BR/CAL/1/ Board minutes 8, 16, 24 January 1856; *Cal. Merc.*, 29 August 1856.
16. *Glas. Her.*, 17 March 1856, CR half-yearly report.
17. *Glas. Her.*, 21 March 1856.
18. NAS.BR/CAL/1/ 8. Board minutes, 22 April, 15 May, 16 September 1856.
19. NAS.BR/CAL/1/8. Board minutes, 16 September, 12 November, 1856
20. NAS.BR/CAL/1/8. Board minutes, 25 July 1856; PP 1857 (469) lxii.
21. Ferguson, *Arbroath & Forfar*, 83.
22. Letter of 31 July 1856, quoted in *Glas. Her.*, 10 September 1856. The Greenock Works were pulled down to make a coal depot (*Cal. Merc.*, 16 September 1857); CR half-yearly report, *ibid*.
23. NAS.BR/CAL/1/8. Board minutes, 16 September 1856.
24. NLS.ABS.2.75.11. CR Timetables for the Guidance of Guards and Others, 1856.
25. NAS.BR/CAL/1/8. Board minutes, 28 October 1857.
26. NAS.BR/CAL/1/8. Report of Thomas Mackay. Board minutes book, 31 December 1856.
27. NAS.BR/CAL/1/8. Board minutes, 3 January 1860.
28. *Cal. Merc.*, 20 February 1857.
29. NAS.BR/CAL/1/8. Board minutes 26 May 1857.
30. *Glas. Her.*, 9 September 1857.
31. NAS.BR/CAL/1/8. Board minutes, 23 September, 14 October 1857.
32. PP 1857 (469) lxii.
33. NAS.BR/CAL/1/8. Board minutes, 11 November 1857.
34. Checkland, *Scottish Banking*, 467f.
35. NAS.BR/CAL/1/8. Board minutes, 2 June, 1 September 1858.
36. NAS.BR/CAL/1/8. Board minutes, 27 July 1858.

CHAPTER 5 CONTINUED

37. GUAS.CRA2/1/2/6; Thomas, *North British*, i, 88.
38. Letters published in *Daily News*, 21 October 1859.
39. NAS.BR/CAL/1/ Board minutes, 27 September 1859.
40. NAS.BR/CAL/1/ Board minutes, 15 November 1859.
41. *RT*, 19 November 1859, 1271.
42. MacIntosh, *Caledonian Railway Livery*, 243f.
43. Measom, *Official Illustrated Guide*, 284.
44. NAS.BR/CAL/1/ Board minutes, 1 November 1859.
45. *Glas. Her.*, 12 September 1860.
46. NAS.BR/CAL/1 Stores Committee, 11 December 1860.
47. *RT*, April 13, April 27, 1861. 473, 555.
48. *Cal. Merc.*, 22 May 1861.
49. Vamplew, 'The Railways and the Iron Industry', in Reed, *Railways in the Victorian Economy*, 36.
50. *RT*, 20 September 1862, 1386.
51. *Glas. Her.*, November 26 1880.
52. Thomas, *North British*, i, 116f.; *Glas. Her.*, 28 February 1862.
53. Neele, *Railway Reminiscences*, 105ff.
54. Quick, *Chronology*, Perth.
55. Johnson & Hume, *Glasgow Stations*, 101.
56. *RT*, 21 March 1863, 380.
57. *RT*, 28 March 1863, 428.
58. *RT*, 19 September 1863, 1259.
59. Ferguson, *Arbroath & Forfar*, 94.
60. Thomas, *Regional History*, vi, 146.

CHAPTER 6

1. O.S. Glasgow town plan, 1857. See also *EHR*, vol. 17, December 1964. Kellett, J.R., 'Glasgow's Railways', 363ff.
2. *EHR*, Kellett, J.R., *op. cit.*, 366, quoting Commons Select Committee on Union Railway Bill, 12 May 1864, pp 243-253.
3. *RT*, 12 March 1864, 701.
4. Thomas, *North British*, i, 116f.
5. *Scotsman*, 4 May 1864.
6. Thomas, *North British*, i, 116f.
7. *RT*, 24 September 1864, 1074. *RT*, 6 August 1864, 1055.
8. *RT*, 24 September 1864, 1074; 1 October, 1308f.
9. NAS.BR/CAL/1/ Board minutes, 12 November 1856.
10. Acworth, *Railways of Scotland*, 169.
11. See Thorne, *Rails to Portpatrick*, 41f, for a fuller account.
12. Thomas & Paterson, *Regional History*, vi, 151.
13. *RT*, 18 March 1865, 331; *Glas. Her.*, 16 March 1865. The price emerged some years later, see *Glas. Her.*, 6 May 1869.
14. *RT*, 20 May 1865, 640.
15. Ross, *Highland Railway*, 34.
16. Grinling, *Great Northern*, 222.
17. Paterson, *Golden Years of the Clyde Steamers*, 20.
18. *Dund. Cour.*, 7 September 1865; *Cal. Merc.*, 18 November 1865.
19. NAS.BR/CAL/1/8/120. Minutes of the Joint Committee.
20. Paget-Tomlinson, *The Railway Carriers*, 24, but an earlier relationship with the CR is suggested by an advertisement in *Glas. Her.*, 22 June 1849, from Wordie, McArthur & Co., claiming to act as Agents for the CR, Scottish Central, Scottish Midland, and Dundee, Perth & Aberdeen Railways.
21. Byrom, *Railways of Upper Strathearn*, 13, 16.
22. PP 1865 (155) xlix.
23. NAS.BR/CAL/1 Board minutes, 22 August 1865.
24. *Times*, 18 September 1865.
25. *RT*, 9 September 1865, 1198.
26. Galt, *Railway Reform*, 373.
27. *RT*, 7 October 1865, 1312.
28. *RT*, 4 November 1865, 1417.
29. Quoted in *RT*, 23 December 1865, 1637; see also *Glas. Her.*, 22 December 1865.
30. *Glas. Her.*, 1 February 1866.
31. Thomas, *North British*, i, 81, 127.
32. *RT*, 27 January 1866, 100.
33. *Glas. Her.*, 4 September 1862.
34. *Cal. Merc.*, 17 May 1865.
35. Brown & Lawson, *History of Peebles*, 329.
36. *Times*, 24 March 1866.
37. Acworth, *Railways of Scotland*, 86.
38. *RT*, 16 June 1866, 732.
39. PP 1865 (155) xlix, and 1867 (516) lxii.
40. *TL*, 71, December 2000. David Hamilton, 'The Financial Crisis of 1867-68'.
41. Ross, *Highland Railway*, 37.
42. *Times*, 8 September 1866, 7; 13 September, 5.
43. Quoted in *RT*, 10 November 1866, 1309.
44. A protest meeting said that travellers were worse off than in stagecoach times, see *Glas. Her.*, 2 February 1866
45. PP 1866 (483) lxii; and PP 1867 (616) lxii.
46. See *TL* 10, August 1985, J.F. McEwan, note on Lampits Fork; and 26, August 1989, T.B. McGhie, 'Lampits Fork'. O.S. 6in maps, Lanarkshire 1864 and 1898
47. *Times*, 28 March 1867, 10.
48. *Glas. Her.*, 17 April 1867.
49. Thomas & Paterson, *Regional History*, vi, 78.
50. PP 1857 (469) lxii; PP 1867 (3844-11) xxxviii pt 2.

CHAPTER 7

1. Ross, *Highland Railway*, 42.
2. *Glas. Her.*, 26 September 1867.
3. *Morning Post*, 13 November 1867.
4. *RT*, 11 January 1868, 37.
5. NAS.BR/CAL/1/8/99. Report to the Shareholders, 1868.
6. *RT*, 4 January 1868, 11.
7. *Glas. Her.*, 29 January 1868.
8. *RT*, 15 February, 1868, 193.
9. *Glas. Her.*, 14 February 1868.
10. *Glas. Her.*, 6 and 11 March 1868.
11. *North British Daily Mail*, 24 March 1868.
12. *North British Daily Mail*, 1 April 1868.
13. *RT*, 4 April, 1868, 382.
14. *Glas. Her.*, 15 April 1868.
15. *RT*, October 31, 1868, 1115.
16. Quick, *Chronology*, Motherwell.
17. Thomas & Paterson, *Regional History*, vi, 158.
18. See Ferguson, *Dundee & Newtyle*, 131ff.
19. *RT*, 19 September 1868, 969.
20. *Times*, 23 September 1869.
21. *Times*, 17 February and 23 March, 1869.
22. *Times*, 12, 13, 22 April 1869.
23. *Times*, 7 May 1869.
24. *Times*, 21 and 23 September 1869.
25. Caledonian half-yearly meeting of 30 March 1870, quoted in *Times*, 31 March 1870.
26. NB half-yearly report, 20 September 1869.
27. Grinling, *Great Northern*, 244.
28. *Glas. Her.*, 14 July 1869.
29. *RT*, 28 November 1868, 1216.
30. *Glas. Her.*, 10 September 1880.
31. *Glas. Her.*, April 23, 6 May 1869.
32. *Glas. Her.*, 11 May 1869.
33. *Glas. Her.*, 6 May 1869.

CHAPTER 8

1. Andrew Park, 'The Greenock Railway' (1843), quoted in Williamson, *The Clyde Passenger Steamer*, 108.
2. Thomas & Paterson, *Regional History*, vi, 177.
3. *Mercantile Advertiser*, 14 January 1870.
4. Johnson & Hume, *Glasgow Stations*, 101.
5. *Times*, 9 February 1870.
6. NAS. GB234/BR/LSS.
7. *Glas. Her.*, 4 February 1870.
8. *Dund. Cour.*, 29 March 1870.
9. *Times*, 16 July 1870.
10. PP 1870 (169) xli.
11. *RT*, 29 July 1871, 732, quoting *North British Daily Mail*.
12. *RT*, 30 September 1871, 941.
13. Thomas, *North British*, i, 159.
14. *Scotsman*, 2 December 1871.
15. Letter in *RT*, 2 December 1871, 1187.
16. *RT*, 30 December 1871, 1255.
17. *RT*, 23 December 1871, 1247.
18. *RT*, 2 December 1871, 1187.
19. Cobb's *Atlas* states it was closed in 1860 but see ch.6, note 46
20. Johnson & Hume, *Glasgow Stations*, 35f.
21. Thomas & Paterson, *Regional History*, 153.
22. *EHR*, vol. 24, February 1971. Vamplew, W., 'Railways and the Transformation of the Scottish Economy', 48.
23. Full details in Shaw, *The Balerno Branch*.
24. *Glas. Her.*, report of NBR special meeting, 11 February 1870; report of Commons committee, 23March 1870.
25. Letter in *Scotsman*, 3 September 1874.
26. Advertisement in *Scotsman*, 17 September 1872.
27. *Dund. Cour.*, 23 September 1874; *Glas. Her.*, 25 June 1874. In fact the purchase was only nine years before, but the price, for a fraction of the 6-acre site, reflects the surge in property values in the new city centre. Some of the poor-house land was re-sold for use as a monumental masonry works (see O.S. Glasgow town plan, 1894).
28. Groome, *Ordnance Gazetteer*, 'Caledonian Railway'.
29. *EHR*, vol. 22, August 1969, Hawke, G.R. and Reed, M.C., 'Railway Capital in the UK in the 19th Century'.
30. *Leeds Mercury*, 6 February 1875, apparently an eye-witness report.
31. *Engineer*, 25 June 1875 and 29 December 1876; also MacIntosh, *Caledonian Railway Livery*, 319. *RT*, 21 September 1878, 793.
32. *TH*, vol 4, 197. Highet, 'Continuous Brakes', 52, 54, 61.
33. Johnson & Hume, *Glasgow Stations*, 35f.
34. Quick, *Chronology*, Ferniegair, Hamilton. The horse-bus was operated by the Caledonian.
35. *RT*, 23 September 1876, 867.
36. *RT*, 21 September 1878.
37. Ferguson, *Dundee & Newtyle*, 148.
38. NAS.BR/CAL/1/28. Traffic committee, 27 December 1883.
39. Thomas, *North British*, i, 234.
40. *RT*, 21 September 1878, 793.
41. Checkland, *Scottish Banking*, 469.
42. *Glas. Her.*, 27 June 1879.
43. *Glas. Her.*, 1 August 1879.
44. James Schmiechen, 'Architecture, Townscape and Society' in Fraser & Maver, *Glasgow*, vol 2, 507.

CHAPTER 8 CONTINUED

45. *North British Daily Mail*, 1 August, 1879.
46. *Glas. Her.*, 8 July 1882.
47. Cobb's *Atlas* gives 1878 but the depot is not shown on the O.S. 1-inch map of Glasgow published in 1890. It is shown in the 1898 edition, from revisions made 1885-90.
48. O.S. 1-inch map, first ed., Sheet 31. A rare error in Cobb's *Atlas* places the new station west of the junction.

49. Quick, *Chronology*, Granton, Leith.
50. NAS.BR/CAL/1/25. Stores committee, 26 November 1879.
51. NAS.BR/CAL/1/25. Traffic committee, 30 September 1879.
52. Ferguson, *Arbroath & Forfar*, 100ff.

CHAPTER 9

1. *Glas. Her.*, 31 May 1880.
2. *Glas. Her.*, 14 February 1880.
3. NAS.BR/CAL/1/25. Board minutes, 20 January 1880.
4. NAS.BR/CAL/1/26. Board minutes, 12 April 1881.
5. *Dund. Cour.*, 9 February 1880.
6. *Glas. Her.*, 26 February 1880.
7. *Glas. Her.*, 18 February 1881.
8. *Glas. Her.*, 8 and 9 April 1881.
9. *Glas. Her.*, 12 July 1882.
10. NAS.BR/CAL/1/26. Stores committee, 18 November 1881.
11. NAS.BR/CAL/1/27. Stores committee, 10 October 1882.
12. NAS.BR/CAL/1/27. Locomotive committee, 14 February 1882.
13. NAS.BR/CAL/1/28. Board minutes, 16 October 1883.
14. NAS.BR/CAL/1/27. Board minutes 20 December 1881, 20 March 1882; Finance committee, 25 April 1882.
15. *Glas. Her.*, 30 May 1882.
16. *Glas. Her.*, 5 June 1882.
17. NAS.BR/CAL/1/27. Traffic committee, 30 May 1882.
18. NAS.BR/CAL/1/27. Stores committee, 19 September; Board minutes, 1 November 1882.
19. NAS.BR/CAL/1/28. Stores committee, 12 June 1883.
20. PP1867 (516) lxii.
21. NAS.BR/CAL/1/27. Board minutes, 5 July, 1882.
22. Mavor, *The Scottish Railway Strike, 1890-91*, 7.
23. NAS.BR/CAL/1/152
24. *Glas. Her.*, 5 May 1881.
25. Advertisement in *Glas. Her.*, 3 May 1886.
26. *Scotsman*, 15 August 1882.
27. *RT*, 8 April 1876, 328.
28. NAS.BR/CAL/1/30. Board minutes, 19 January 1886.
29. Neele, *Reminiscences*, 245. See illustration p.44
30. NAS.BR/CAL/1/28. Traffic committee, 11 December 1883.
31. NAS.BR/CAL/1/27. Board minutes, 31 October 1882; Hotel committee, 26 May 1884; Board, 7 October 1884.
32. Marshall, *Scottish Central*, 191.

33. GUAS.CRA2/2/1/2/9, 'Foreign Junction Arrangements'.
34. NAS.BR/CAL/1/29. Stores committee, 18 November 1884.
35. NAS. *Ibid.*
36. NAS.BR/CAL/1/32. Board minutes, 29 September, 6 November 1888.
37. BR/CAL/1/29. Traffic committee, 18 November 1884.
38. NAS.BR/CAL/1/29. Board minutes, 3 March 1885.
39. NAS.BR/CAL/1/31. Traffic committee, 11 June 1887.
40. See Highet, *The Portpatrick Railway*, 28; Thorne, *Rails to Portpatrick*, 111f, 122.
41. Smith, History of Greenock website.
42. Acworth, *Railways of Scotland*, 100f.
43. NAS.BR/CAL/1/32. Traffic committee, 2 September 1884; Hawkins & Reeve, *LMS Engine Sheds*, 5, 59.
44. GUAS.CRA2/1/2/8.
45. NAS.BR/CAL/1/28. Traffic committee, 23 September 1882. It was quite usual to transport prisoners by train, in reserved compartments. On 24 June 1874 two prisoners jumped from the Glasgow-Edinburgh train near Bellshill after overpowering their two guards (*Glas. Her.*, 25 June 1874).
46. NAS.BR/CAL/1/29. Stores committee, 16 April 1885.
47. Ellis, *The Trains We Loved*, 138.
48. NAS.BR/CAL/1/30. Stores committee, 29 September 1885; 1/34. Stores committee, 4 September 1991. The second batch cost 15*s*. 3*d*. each.
49. Cairncross, *Home and Foreign Investment*, 58.
50. *Dund. Cour.*, 13 December 1888.
51. NAS.BR/CAL/1/30. Board minutes, 2 February 1886.
52. *Glas. Her.*, 15 March 1866.
53. Kernahan, *Cathcart Circle*, 9ff.
54. Kernahan, *op. cit.*, 27.
55. *Glas. Her.*, 17 December 1880.
56. See Clark, *Caley to the Coast*, 137f.
57. NAS.BR/CAL/1/30. Board minutes, 8 April, 11 May, 1886; Finance committee, 8 June 1886.
58. NAS.BR/CAL/1/30. Traffic committee, 14 September 1886.

CHAPTER 9 CONTINUED

59. Thomas & Turnock, *Regional History*, xv, 132.
60. NAS.BR/CAL/4/149. Memorandum regarding the Relations Between the Caledonian Railway Co. and the Highland Railway Co.
61. *Bradshaw*, August 1887.
62. NAS.BR/CAL/1/31. Board minutes 31 August 1886; Traffic committee, 13 December 1887.
63. *Morning Post*, 10 May 1888.
64. *Scotsman*, 31 January 1887.

65. NAS.BR/CAL/1/30. Board minutes, 10 August 1886.
66. NAS.BR/CAL/1/30. Traffic committee, 17 April 1888.
67. NAS.BR/CAL/1/32. Board minutes, 26 June, 14 September, 1888.
68. *Glas. Her.*, 30 October 1895.
69. Neele, *Reminiscences*, 245ff.
70. Neele, *op. cit.*, 329.

CHAPTER 10

1. Paterson, *The Golden Years of the Clyde Steamers*, 42.
2. Paterson, *op. cit.*, 46.
3. NAS.BR/CAL/1/33. Board minutes 27 August 1889; Traffic committee, 29 April 1890.
4. Paterson, *op. cit.*, 62.
5. Williamson, *The Clyde Passenger Steamer*, 221.
6. Williamson, *op. cit.*, 237.
7. Nock, *Caledonian Railway*, 77.
8. Acworth, *Railways of Scotland*, 75
9. Acworth, *op. cit.*,77.
10. GUAS.CRA2/1/2/9, 'The Proposed Transfer of the GSWR'.
11. GUAS.CRA2, *Ibid*.
12. Quoted in *Railway Times*, 15 March 1890, 346.
13. NAS.BR/CAL/1/33. Traffic committee, 15 April 1890.
14. NAS.BR/CAL/1/33. Traffic committee, 18 March 1890.
15. Thomas, *North British*, ii, 45.
16. Foxwell & Farrer, *Express Trains*, 58, 60.
17. Acworth, *Railways of Scotland*, 58
18. Acworth, *op. cit.*, 65.
19. Acworth, *op. cit.*, 195.
20. Acworth, *op. cit.*, 179.
21. Acworth, *op. cit.*, 185.
22. Acworth, *op. cit.*, 102, 87, 89, 97.
23. Acworth, *op. cit.*, 172.
24. *RT*, 8 February 1890, 182.
25. *RT*, 17 May 1890, 629.
26. Half-yearly report, quoted in *RT*, 27 September 1890, 367.
27. *RT*, 9 August 1890, 176.
28. NAS.BR/CAL/1/30. Board minutes, 27 July 1886.
29. *RT*, 4 October 1890.
30. *Glas. Her.*, 19 January 1892.
31. *Scotsman*, 21 November 1893.
32. Mavor, *The Scottish Railway Strike*, 32.
33. Mavor, *op. cit.*, 10.
34. Mavor, *op. cit.*, 20; *TL* 107, January 2010, Fred Landery, 'The Motherwell Riots of 1891', 13f.; NAS.BR/CAL/1/34. Traffic committee 3 March 1891.
35. *TL* 84, April 2004. David Hamilton, 'The Railway Strike of 1890-91 and Its Effect on Greenock'.
36. *Economic Journal*, 1891. Mavor, 'The Scottish Railway Strike', 204.
37. *Glas. Her.*, 8 January 1891.

38. *Glasgow Evening Times*, 14 January 1891.
39. *TL* 107, Landery, *op. cit.*, 14
40. Mavor, *The Scottish Railway Strike*, 20.
41. NAS.BR/CAL/1/34. Board minutes, 3 February 1891.
42. Mavor, *op. cit.*, 20.
43. Quoted in *Recent Findings of Research in Economic & Social History*, Autumn 1991, Chris Wrigley, 'Labour and Trade Unions in Great Britain, 1880-1939'.
44. See Thomas & Paterson, *Regional History*, vi, 217.
45. *Glas. Her.*, 21 September 1892.
46. *Aberdeen Weekly Journal*, 3 November 1891.
47. *Hansard*, 13 April 1893, vol II c302-7.
48. *Glas. Her.*, 21 January 1893.
49. NAS.BR/CAL/1/152. Minutes of Caledonian/ North British meeting, 28 December 1888.
50. Neele, *Reminiscences*, 410ff.
51. *Strathearn Herald*, 17 August 1889, quoted in Byrom, *Railways of Upper Strathearn*, 22.
52. *Glas. Her.*, 21 February 1894.
53. O.S., one-inch, Glasgow, 2nd ed., 1906.
54. Half-yearly report, *Times*, 16 March 1895.
55. *Glas. Her.*, 22 February 1894.
56. *Dund. Cour.*, 11 September 1895.
57. *Glas. Her.*, 22 August 1895.
58. Thomas & Turnock, *Regional History*, xv, 161.
59. *Times*, 29 June 1895.
60. *Glas. Her.*, 14 May, 17 June 1895.
61. Ellis, *Four Main Lines*, 50.
62. *RT*, 12 and 19 January, 1895.
63. Efforts were still being made to have it reopened in 1909, but the CR's demand for a £2,000 annual guarantee was impossible to meet locally (*Scotsman*, 11 June 1909).
64. *Dund. Cour.*, 18 March 1896.
65. GUAS.CRA2/2/1/1/5; *Scotsman*, 13 October 1900.
66. *Glas. Her.*, 30 April 1896.
67. *Edinburgh Gazette*, 26 November 1895, 1572.
68. *Muirkirk Advertiser*, summer 1918, quoted in 'Cairntable Echoes', 46, on ayrshirehistory.com
69. *Glas. Her.*, 30 April 1896.
70. Quick, *Chronology*, Maryhill, Possil.

CHAPTER 10 CONTINUED

71. Quick, *Chronology*, Dawsholm. Rail access to the gasworks was under two arches of the Forth & Clyde Canal aqueduct, with two bridges over the Kelvin, one to the north, one to the west. See O.S. Glasgow town plan, 1894. This map shows the entire Lanarkshire & Dumbartonshire Railway system on the ground.

72. Ellis, *The Trains We Loved*, 71.

73. See Thomas, *Regional History*, vi, 280f for more details.

74. *Aberdeen Journal*, 6 September, 1897.

75. *Dund. Cour.*, 3 December 1897.

76. NAS. RHP34916/1-2; RHP34960/1-3, etc.

77. *Dund. Cour.*, 17 November 1897.

78. *Glas. Her.*, 29 June 1897.

79. *Dund. Cour.*, 10 February 1898.

80. *Glas. Her.*, 16 March 1898, report of half-yearly and extraordinary general meetings of 15 March.

81. *Glas. Her.*, 27 June 1898.

82. *Dund. Cour.*, 5 October 1898.

83. *Aberdeen Journal*, 3 March, 28 April, 2 May 1899. These companies, with the North British, had running powers over the CR line but this did not include access to the station. Following a legal battle in 1893, the NBR paid a rent for its use of Aberdeen Station.

84. Johnson & Hume, *Glasgow Stations*, 37, 102.

85. Kellet, *The Impact of Railways*, 93.

CHAPTER 11

1. Vamplew, 'The Railways and the Iron Industry' in Reed, *Railways in the Victorian Economy*, 33ff.

2. Hull, *Our Coal Resources*, 82.

3. *Ibid*.

4. Vamplew, *op. cit.*, 62f.

5. *Glas. Her.*, 30 April 1896.

6. Proceedings of the Engineering Congress, 1901', 182, 185.

7. *Glas. Her.*, 5 February 1899.

8. Cornwell, *Forty Years*, 115.

9. Ellis, *British Railway History*, ii, 301.

10. RCHS, *Closed Passenger Lines*.

11. Thomas & Paterson, *Regional History*, vi, 234.

12. *Glas. Her.*, 26 May 1897; 16 March 1898.

13. *Glas. Her.*, 19 September 1900, report of half-yearly meeting, 18 September.

14. *Scotsman*, 6 May 1905. At the shareholders' meeting of 19 March 1907, Sir James King admitted that "The Paisley & Barrhead had been a great disappointment"; see *Scotsman*, 20 March 1907.

15. Quick, *Chronology*, Renfrew.

16. See Ordnance Survey map of 1894; also *Railway Magazine*, September 1907, 'A Glasgow Suburban Station with 12 Platforms', 1475.

17. NAS.BR/CAL/1/30. Board minutes, 21 August 1886.

18. *Glas. Her.*, 8 March 1897.

19. *TL*, 37, May 1992. George Robin, 'Lanarkshire & Ayrshire'.

20. *Glas. Her.*, 19 September 1900.

21. NLS.X.229c. 'Notes on the Engineering Features of American Railroads', v.

22. NLS.X.229c. *op. cit.*, 241ff.

23. NLS.X.229c. *op. cit.*, 287.

24. NLS.X.229c. *op. cit.*, 158f, 68, 53, 277.

25. NAS.BR/CAL/1/106. Report of shareholders' meeting, February 1923.

26. See Clark, *Caley to the Coast*, and MacIntosh, *The Caledonian Railway's Wemyss Bay Station*. Wemyss Bay Station was sympathetically restored in 1993-94.

27. Clark, *op. cit.*, 248.

28. Occasional specials used the line, for example to military reviews at Pilrig in 1905 and 1908. See Quick, *Chronology*, Leith. The *Scotsman*, 8 December 1900, describes the line.

29. Hawkins & Reeve, *LMS Engine Sheds*, 5, 130.

30. *Glas. Her.*, 19 September 1900.

31. MacKean, *Battle for the North*, 323.

32. Quick, *Chronology*, 486

33. *TL* 100. F. Landery, 'The Mid-Lanark Lines in Retrospect', 21.

34. *TL* 101. D. Stirling, 'The Mid-Lanark Lines: the Debate Continues', 18f.

35. O.S. 1-inch, 3rd ed., Sheet 22, Hamilton, 1905; 'Popular ed.' Sheet 73, Falkirk & Motherwell, 1926.

36. NLS.S1.76.28. CR Rule Book, 1906.

37. *Railway Times*, 25 September 1909, 323.

38. Atkins, *The Scottish 4-6-0 Classes*, 39.

39. *Scotsman*, 11 May 1905. One correspondent put it down not to public demand for luxury but "inner cussedness of the Caledonian Railway Company" (*Scotsman*, 14 March 1907).

40. Ellis, *The Trains We Loved*, 154.

41. *Glas. Her.*, 17 May 1905; Millar added that "schoolboys were just as bad" (*Scotsman*, 17 May 1905).

42. Biddle, *Historic Railway Buildings*, 641; Nock, *Scottish Railways*, 112.

43. Quoted in Clark, *Caley to the Coast*, 139.

44. Clark, *op. cit.*, 168.

45. *Scotsman*, 30 June 1909.

46. *Railway Magazine*, September 1907, 239.

47. Quick, *Chronology*, Grangemouth. There were no scheduled services into the docks.

48. *Scotsman*, 29 December 1906 and *passim* January 1907.

49. Checkland, S.G., in *Dictionary of Scottish Business Biography*, i.

50. *RG*, 27 March 1907, 286a; *Scotsman*, 20 March 1907.

51. *Scotsman*, 10 September 1907.

CHAPTER 11 CONTINUED

52. *Railway Magazine*, June 1907, 165. Such inter-company borrowings of rolling stock were common at peak periods.
53. *Scotsman*, 24 September 1907.
54. *RT*, 28 November 1908, 586.
55. Caledonian 'Christmas Annual', 1909, 3.
56. Thomas, *Callander & Oban*, 131; see also *TL*, No. 10, August 1985. J.F. McEwan, 'A Caledonian Bus Story'.

57. *Railway News*, 15 August 1903; NAS.BR/CAL/5/4.
58. *Times*, 12 March 1908.
59. *Scotsman*, 9 March 1908.
60. NAS.BR/CAL/1/117.
61. *RT*, 22 August 1908, 229.
62. *Times*, 6 March 1909.
63. NAS.BR/CAL/1/167, 168.
64. *Times*, 5 June 1909.

CHAPTER 12

1. NAS.BR/CAL/1/25. Traffic committee, 25 November 1879.
2. Quick, *Chronology*, Carsebreck; The *Scotsman*, 10 February 1900, refers to "a special siding beyond Blackford"; See also Caledonian 'Christmas Annual' 1909, 18; and a Scottish Screen Archive clip, ref. 6030, of curlers dismounting from a train here in 1935.
3. *Times*, 20 February 1909.
4. *Times*, 17 March 1909.
5. Hawkins & Reeve, *LMS Engine Sheds*, 5, 7ff.
6. Quoted in Campbell & Dow, *Source Book*, 276f.

7. Johnson & Hume, *Glasgow Stations*, 148.
8. Pratt, *Railways & Nationalisation*, 389.
9. *Hansard*, 21 October 1909; *Hamilton Advertiser*, 23 October 1909.
10. *Times*, 7 August, 1909.
11. *Glas. Her.*, 21 August 1909.
12. *Times* 27 November 1909.
13. *RT*, 28 January & 1 April 1911.
14. *RT*, 25 March 1911. Half-yearly meeting of 21 March.
15. GUAS.CRA2/2/1/4, Pullman correspondence; *TL*, 28, March 1990. N. Ferguson, 'Pullman Cars'.
16. *RT*, 6 September 1913.

CHAPTER 13

1. Regulation of the Forces Act, 1871, Section 16.
2. Pratt, *British Railways and the Great War*, ii, 844-5. Niall Ferguson notes that the Highland Brigade was on manoeuvres near Blairgowrie, *Dundee & Newtyle*, 202f.
3. Pratt, *op. cit.*, 859.
4. NAS.BR/CAL/1/71. Board minutes, 20 August 1918, and supplementary details courtesy of Jim MacIntosh.
5. GUAS.CRA3/6/9, 'Accident Reports'.
6. Hawkins & Reeve, *LMS Engine Sheds*, 5, 20.
7. *Glas. Her.*, 3 February, 1917.
8. Pratt, *op. cit.*, 539f.
9. NAS.BR/CAL/1/70. Traffic committee, 27 December 1917.
10. McIntosh, *Caledonian Railway Livery*, 279; Pratt, *op. cit.*, ii, 855.
11. Quick, *Chronology*, Carmyllie.
12. NAS.BR/CAL/1/70. Traffic committee, 2 October 1917.

13. NAS.BR/CAL/1/71. Board minutes, 16 April 1918; Finance committee, 9 July 1918. *Muirkirk Advertiser*, summer 1918, quoted in 'Cairntable Echoes', 46, on ayrshirehistory.com
14. Quick, *Chronology*, Inchture. *TL* No. 7 says 1/4/16.
15. Pratt, *op. cit.*, 526f.
16. Pratt, *op. cit.*, 852, 845.
17. Pratt, *op. cit.*, 856.
18. NAS.BR/CAL/1/71. Traffic committee, 3 September 1918.
19. NAS.BR/CAL/1/71. Traffic committee, 23 July 1918.
20. NAS.BR/CAL/1/23 July, 3 September 1918.
21. NAS.BR/CAL/1/71. Traffic committee, 16 April 1918.
22. NAS.BR/CAL/1/71. Board minutes, 29 October 1918. The proposal included a coaling tower, though this was not provided until after the LMS was formed.

CHAPTER 14

1. Johnston, *Clydeside Capital*, 56f.
2. NAS.BR/CAL/1/72. Board minutes, 4 February 1919.
3. *Scotsman*, 4 October 1919.
4. NAS.BR/CAL/1/72. Board minutes, 27 May; Traffic committee, 29 April 1919.
5. NAS.BR/CAL/1/72. Traffic committee, 27 May 1919.
6. NAS.BR/CAL/1/72. Finance committee, 7 January 1919.
7. GUAS.CRA2/2/1/4, Pullman correspondence; *TL* 28, March 1990. N. Ferguson, 'Pullman Cars'.
8. *Scotsman*, 27 June 1921.
9. *Scotsman*, 15 December 1920.
10. NAS.BR/CAL/1/76. Board minutes, 8 February 1921.
11 *Scotsman*, 31 January 1921.
12. *Scotsman*, 19 November 1920.
13. *Scotsman*, 23 February 1921.
14. NAS.BR/CAL/1/76. Traffic committee, 22 February 1921.
15. NAS.BR/CAL/1/71. Traffic committee, 23 July 1918.
16. Ellis, *Midland Railway*, 172.
17. *Scotsman*, 4 June 1921.
18. NAS.BR/CAL/1/77. Board minutes, 6 September 1921.
19. Simnett, *Railway Amalgamation*, 264.
20. *Scotsman*, 10 February 1923.
21. *Glas. Her.*, 31 January 1922.
22. NAS.BR/CAL/1/78. Board minutes, 15 November 1921, 28 March 1922.
23. NAS.BR/CAL/1/78. Board minutes, 30 May, 13 June, 11 July 1922.
24. *Scotsman*, 12 January 1922.
25. *Scotsman*, 7 September, 6 November, 1922.
26. *Hansard*, HoC, vol 163, 1 May 1923.
27. Thomas, *Callander & Oban*, 119.
28. Simnett, *Railway Amalgamation*, 68, 254.
29. *Scotsman*, 26 June 1923.

CHAPTER 15

1. *Scotsman*, 19 January 1922.
2. NAS.BR/CAL/1/8, Board minutes, 29 January 1852
3. *Dund. Cour.*, 22 June 1898; Caledonian 'Christmas Annual', 1909, 14.
4. GUAS.CRA3/6/7, 'Accident Reports'.
5. NAS.BR/CAL/1/28. Board minutes, 1 May 1883.
6. NAS.BR/CAL/1/8, 26 April 1853.
7. NAS.CR board minutes, 24 December 1861.
8. NAS.BR/CAL/1/ Board minutes, 2 December 1857.
9. NAS.BR/CAL/1/27. Board minutes, 28 November 1882.
10. NAS.BR/CAL/1/30. Board minutes, 19 January 1886.
11. NAS.BR/CAL/1/25. Traffic committee, 17 February 1880.
12. NAS.BR/CAL/1/77. Finance committee, 12 December 1922.
13. *Glas. Her.*, 20 February 1879.
14. *Glas. Her.*, 11 September 1899; *Dund. Cour.*, 17 August 1899.
15. Caledonian 'Christmas Annual', 2.
16. NAS.BR/CAL/1/76. Traffic committee, 22 February 1921.
17. Middlemass, *Mainly Scottish Steam*, 24.
18. *Scotsman*, 6 March 1903.
19. NAS.BR/CAL/1/8, 28 February 1851.
20. NAS.BR/CAL/1/8, 13 March 1851.
21. 'Blantyre 1877' on scottishmining.co.uk
22. Quoted in *ODNB*, S.P. Parissien, 'Sir William Tite'.
23. Caledonian 'Christmas Annual,' 17.
24. Ellis, *The Trains we Loved*, 74.
25. Brown, *The House with the Green Shutters*, 110.
26. T.S. Denholm, signalman, from Caledonian 'Christmas Annual', 1909.
27. Caledonian 'Christmas Annual', 1909.
28. *Glas. Her.*, 6 November 1897.
29. Scottish M.P. in *Hansard*, vol 163, 1 May 1923.
30. *Dund. Cour.*, 2 February 1895.

The *Duchess of Hamilton* one of the later steamers, with full -length upper deck.

CHAPTER 16

1. Baxter, *British Locomotive Catalogue*, 4, 39-45.
2. Baxter, *op. cit.*, 45.
3. Highet, Scottish Locomotive History, 44ff.
4. Ellis, *Some Classic Locomotives*, 243.
5. Baxter, *op. cit.*, 11.
6. Baxter, *op. cit.*, 14-19. The CR also acquired 16 or 17 traders' engines, "at the time of the competition with the Edinburgh & Glasgow Railway", paid for over a 5-year period (*Cal. Merc.*, 16 September 1857); these do not appear to be listed in Baxter.
7. Ellis, *op. cit.*, 26.
8. Baxter, *op. cit.*, 52-3. See also *International Journal for the History of Engineering & Technology*, Vol. 80, No. 1 (January 2010), Tony Vernon, 'Archibald Sturrock and the Steam Tender Experiment', 133-52.
9. Figures from Baxter, *op. cit.*, 19-38.
10. Highet, *op. cit.*, 87; MacIntosh, *Caledonian Railway Livery*, 233.
11. *Locomotive Engineers' & Firemen's Journal*, May 1896. D.H. Littlejohn, 'The Caledonian Railway', 285ff. Baxter notes (*op. cit.*, 47) that the CR agreed to buy it if there was no other taker.
12. MacIntosh, *Caledonian Railway Livery*, 233. This book gives the fullest possible account of CR livery, and much else besides.
13. Ellis, *The Trains We Loved*, 23.
14. Highet, *op. cit.*, 131. As this book went to press, H.J.C. Cornwell's *The Caledonian Railway 'Jumbos'* was published
15. Cornwell, *Forty Years*, 27.
16. Jim MacIntosh has pointed out to the author that the Bryce-Douglas valve-gear originally fitted on No. 124 "was partly a St. Rollox idea."
17. Poultney, *British Express Locomotive Development*, 22.
18. Cornwell, *op. cit.*, 45.
19. Drummond's subsequent paper, 'Investigation into the Use of Progressive High Pressure in Non-compound Locomotive Engines' (Proc. I.C.E., Section ii, 1896-7) won him a Telford Medal.
20. Cornwell, *op. cit.*, 55.
21. Cornwell, *op. cit.*, 62.
22. Baxter, *op. cit.*, 84.
23. Highet, *op. cit.*, 185. As noted, the boilers were designed by Smellie.
24. Atkins, *The Scottish 4-6-0 Classes*, 10, quoting from *Cassier's Magazine*, 1910.
25. Ellis, *Some Classic Locomotives*, 104.
26. Baxter, *op. cit.*, 85.
27. MacIntosh, *op. cit.*, 37.
28. Cornwell, *op. cit.*, 85.
29. Highet, *op. cit.*, 197.
30. Cornwell, *op. cit.*, 97.
31. Cornwell, *op. cit.*, 112.
32. Baxter, *op. cit.*, 100f. Boiler dimensions of the 0-8-0 were 10ft 11^7/$_8$in x 4ft 9^1/$_4$in; of the 0-8-0T 10ft 3^1/$_2$in x 4ft 6^1/$_4$in.
33. Cornwell, *op. cit.*, 114.
34. See MacIntosh, *op. cit.*, 105. A paper by A.G. Dunbar on CR locomotive numbering, while primarily concerned with the duplicate list, states that "after the list reached about 500 engines added to stock built to Revenue Account replaced engines in the list, while additions to stock built on Capital Account took unallocated numbers". It is not clear that this distinction was always observed, and Dunbar accepts that there was some blurring of this distinction in 1899-1901 and 1921-22 (NAS. GD344/1/63/1).
35. Cornwell, *op. cit.*, 122.
36. Quoted in *Business History Review*, vol. 46, no. 3. Vamplew, W., 'Scottish Railways and the Development of Scottish Locomotive Building', 336.
37. Cornwell, *op. cit.*, 132ff. See also MacIntosh, *Caledonian Railway Livery*, who notes that J.F. McIntosh was initially reluctant to fit any device that restricted free steaming.
38. Cornwell, *op. cit.*, 140; Baxter, *op. cit.*, 87.
39. Cornwell, *op. cit.*, 143. No. 134, built in 1911, can be seen in action on Beattock Bank on a preserved film sequence from around 1912: Scottish Screen Archive ref. 0044
40. Cornwell, *op. cit.*, 146.
41. Cornwell, *op. cit.*, 176.
42. Baxter, *op. cit.*, 102.
43. Highet, *op. cit.*, 225, suggests that their by-name of 'Greyback' (i.e. louse) indicated a low opinion on the crews' part. Cornwell, *op. cit.*, 169, notes that "In skilled hands, the class was capable of good work."
44. Baxter, *op. cit.*, 104.
45. Cornwell, *op. cit.*, 172.
46. Cornwell, *op. cit.*, 176.
47. Baxter, *op. cit.*, 106f. The basis on which these engines were acquired is not clear. Baxter says that crews named them 'Froggies', and disliked their right-hand drive. He notes that the tenders were lettered CR, but the paint colour is not recorded.
48. I.L.E. *Journal*, vol x, 1920, 568.
49. I.L.E. *Journal*, vol x, 1920, 335ff.

INDEX

Towns and villages are in the general index, but for references to particular stations, see under 'Stations'.
Locomotive references are grouped under 'Locomotives'. References to illustrations are in bold type.

Stations and Goods Depots:

No

250

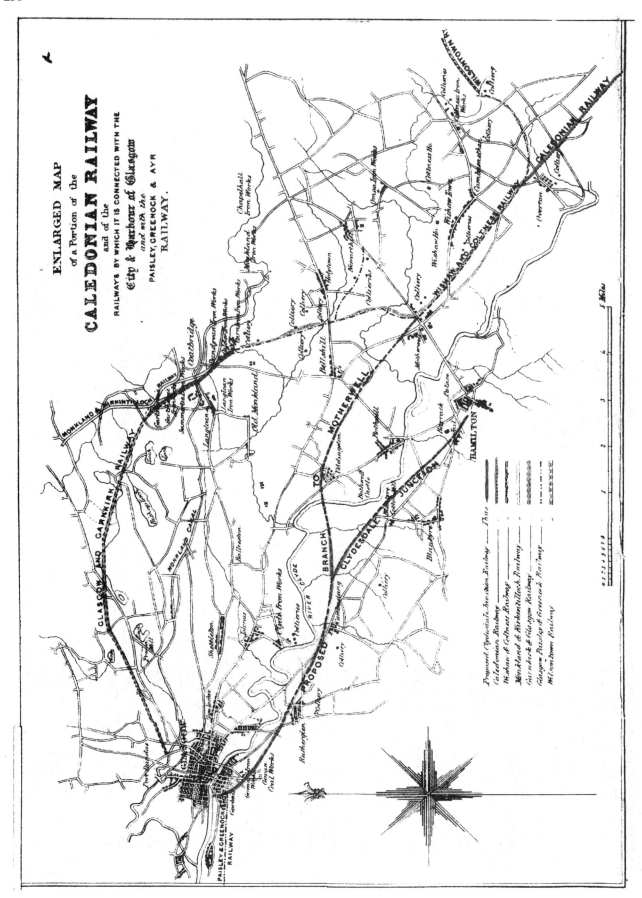

A CR promotional map of 1844.

A train from the south approaches Carstairs, just north of Float Junction, around 1900.

Barry opened in 1843 or earlier, and was renamed Barry Links on 1 April 1919.
Many military specials called to serve the adjacent training camp.

A somewhat doctored picture of the Clydeside scene at Bowling, between Old Kilpatrick and Dumbarton, where the Lanarkshire & Dumbartonshire Railway crossed the Forth & Clyde Canal. The sidings were laid in the early 20th century.

The publishers wish to thank John Alsop for his contribution to this book. His pictures from his extensive collection of railway photographs and postcards are used on pages 2, 21, 30, 36, 46, 51, 54, 57, 62, 69, 74, 75, 78, 79, 82, 86, 98, 111, 117, 118, 119, 122, 123 (lower), 125, 129, 142, 144, 145, 146, 154, 157, 159, 162, 173, 177, 192, 194, 198, 199, 201, 202, 207, 208, 209, 210, 211 and 212.